The New World of Commercial Banking

The New World of Commercial Banking

Eric N. Compton
Chase Manhattan Bank

Lexington Books
D.C. Heath and Company/Lexington, Massachusetts/Toronto

Library of Congress Cataloging-in-Publication Data

Compton, Eric N., 1925–
The new world of commercial banking.

Includes index.
1. Banks and banking—United States. 2. Bank management—United States. I. Title.
HG2491.C646 1986 332.1'2'068 86–45602
ISBN 0–669–14017–1 (alk. paper)

Published simultaneously in Canada
Printed in the United States of America
Casebound International Standard Book Number: 0–669–14017–1
Library of Congress Catalog Card Number 86–45602

The paper used in this publication meets the minimum requirements of American National Standard for Information Sciences—Permanence of Paper for Printed Library Materials, ANSI Z39.48–1984. ∞™

87 88 89 90 91 8 7 6 5 4 3 2 1

To my wife, Maire, who made it possible.

Contents

Figures and Tables

Figures

Tables

Introduction

During the Golden Age of Greek philosophy, Heraclitus became known as the leader of a school of thought that focused on *change* as the principal element in all reality. He and his followers held that no human being ever remains unchanged from day to day and that everything in our universe is in a constant state of flux.

Were Heraclitus and those who shared his thinking with us today, they might well point to the commercial banking industry in the United States as a prime example to support their thesis. It is true that in medicine, new drugs and new treatments are identified with great regularity; in science and technology, new developments are commonplace and significant advances steadily recorded; and in law, new precedents are set and new questions adjudicated. We can argue, however, that today's bankers are confronted with changes even more numerous, more dramatic, and more permanent than those that face other professionals.

The fundamental nature of the commercial banking business has changed. Along with it, the regulatory environment is far different—more challenging and more to be challenged; the problems to be resolved are unprecedented; and the competition has grown, quantitatively and qualitatively, to such an extent that the commercial banks have lost what was once their exclusivity in providing financial services. In 1950, they held 50.6 percent of all the financial assets in the United States; by 1980, that market share had declined to 35.4 percent, and further decreases seem inevitable.[1]

The bankers of today who for one reason or another remain unaware of the plethora of developments that affect them, and who cannot or do not react appropriately, may find that their institutions have followed in the footsteps of the dinosaurs and the railroads. Many of them must cope with a host of problems on a daily basis that their predecessors never faced.

Consider, for example, a cross-section of the issues and topics that management in a large, money-center bank might have to address during a typical business day. How will federal and state regulators and the courts resolve the thorny questions of interstate banking and the banks' desire to enter into new lines of business? What techniques are necessary to provide for the type of asset/liability management that will adequately fund the organization while generating profits? Do existing management information systems provide the bank with all the necessary information on country risk? What will be the impact of the new Sears, Roebuck financial centers, which offer consumers a broad spectrum of services? How can the various, and often conflicting, demands of all the bank's constituencies best be satisfied? With what segments of its total marketplace can the institution most profitably and effectively deal?

Perhaps most important, bankers must try to determine how to counter the fears and concerns of the public regarding the soundness of their banks and of the entire system. Nineteen eighty-four has been described as one of the most tumultuous years in the entire history of U.S. banking; one consequence of that tumult has been a very significantly downgraded perception of the industry by major institutional investors and by the public in general.[2] One survey indicated that the percentage of Americans professing a high degree of faith in the system had fallen from sixty in 1979 to fifty-one in 1984.[3] Similarly, a study of 1,004 American households, conducted by Reichman Research, Inc. in conjunction with *American Banker* in July 1985, disclosed that only 22 percent of respondents classified bankers as "very honest,"[4] while 37 percent expressed concern about the extent of federal insurance coverage on deposits.[5] In the fourth quarter of 1984, the FDIC (Federal Deposit Insurance Corporation) stated that over 750 banks were on its problem list, requiring close scrutiny because of potentially serious situations.[6] And although the nation's insured commercial banks reported an impressive total net income of $14.9 billion for 1983, their returns on assets and equity fell to 0.67 and 11.2 percent respectively, largely due to the need for increased loan-loss provisions.[7] This downward trend in the two most significant ratios of bank performance continued in 1984; the fifty largest banks averaged a return of 0.42 on assets and 9.33 on equity.[8]

Bank failures traditionally serve as a yardstick by which the public measures the soundness of the system. In 1981 there were ten; in 1983, forty-eight; in 1984, seventy-nine; and in the first nine months of 1985, ninety-five.[9] When these sheer statistics are compounded by widely circulated accounts of the global debt crisis, reports of the problems of farm banks, and news of discussions about whether institutions as large as Continental Illinois should simply be allowed to fail without government intervention, the most basic concern of every depositor surfaces: How safe are my funds?

Samuel Armacost, BankAmerica Corporation's President, has said that "there is nothing more important to us than to restore the public's faith." John McGillicuddy, Chairman of Manufacturers Hanover, concurs, noting that "the confidence factor is the most serious issue we face."[10] It is clearly incumbent on the banks to address this topic, which in itself manifests change in the public perception of the industry.

However, anxieties over the integrity of individual bankers, the financial strength of their institutions, or the extent of their insurance coverage are but one characteristic of the new breed of customers. Consumers and the financial officers of government agencies and corporations have this in common today: they are far more knowledgeable than their forebears, more aware of the value of their deposits and the yield opportunities that are available, and more willing to move funds from one account or financial intermediary to another. Their sophistication has changed the fundamental nature of commercial banking and has posed another vital question that bankers must address: how to cope with the increasing costs of money that must be acquired to fund ongoing operations.

One of the most meaningful, dramatic, and permanent changes in the history of U.S. banking has occurred since 1961. It is the transformation of the basic deposit structure from an interest-free, demand-deposit orientation toward a time-deposit, interest-bearing foundation. Major readjustments in the techniques of bank management have been required as a result of this change.

The structural change is graphically reflected in the figures for the ten largest commercial banks for 1984 (table I–1). Although these ten are the giants of the industry, they also serve as prototypes; for the entire commercial banking system in 1984, demand (that is, non-interest-bearing) deposits represented only 23 percent of total deposits. The era when bankers enjoyed large interest-free checking account balances from their customers is clearly a thing of the past.

Table I–1
Deposit Structure of the Ten Largest Commercial Banks, 1984

Bank	*Deposits ($ Millions)*	*Interest-Bearing Accounts (Percent)*	*Non-Interest-Bearing Accounts (Percent)*
Citicorp	90,349	88	12
BankAmerica	94,048	81	19
Chase Manhattan	59,680	79	21
Manufacturers Hanover	44,206	80	20
Morgan Guaranty	38,760	78	22
Chemical New York	33,698	75	25
Security Pacific	31,006	78	22
First Interstate (Los Angeles)	31,006	70	30
Bankers Trust	25,559	81	19
First Chicago	28,592	82	18

Source: "Bank Scoreboard," *Business Week,* April 8, 1985, p. 107.
Note: Banks are ranked by size of total assets.

When the term *disintermediation* was coined, it described the flow of money away from thrift institutions (savings banks and savings and loan associations) into higher-yielding forms of investment. Today, the same term can be more broadly used to reflect the overall mobility of money, whether from demand deposits to those that yield interest or from one type of financial institution to another.

The so-called Money-Market Deposit Accounts (MMDAs), first authorized in December 1982, offer a classic example of this movement of money. Within one year, these accounts totaled $226 billion, and by May 1984 the total had risen to $395 billion.[11] MMDAs, together with NOW (negotiable order for withdrawal) and Super-NOW accounts, provided customers with interest-bearing relationships against which checks could be written, and funds moved rapidly into them from former demand deposits.

This type of disintermediation epitomizes one of the basic customer attitudes prevalent in the new world of banking: there is no longer any justification for leaving funds in a non-interest-bearing checking account when other, far more attractive vehicles are available. Businesses large and small, consumers, institutions, and units of government today tend to keep their levels of demand deposits at a minimum, and when higher yields are available outside the banking system, assuming the same basic services are obtainable, they are not reluctant to desert their institutions entirely.

A paradox in this change in the deposit structure is that it was the banks that educated their customers to recognize the newer types of interest-bearing relationships that had become available and encouraged them to seize the new opportunity. This education of the public took place out of sheer necessity; without it, the banks could never have gained access to the funds they needed.

By the same token, an educational process is needed equally today if bankers are to convince the marketplace that the industry remains fundamentally strong and viable. In an era when news stories of laundered money at banks, global and agricultural debt crises, the Drysdale and Penn Square cases, and numerous bank failures have lowered public confidence in the banking system, a concerted effort to present a positive image is vitally necessary.

The need for education and explanation is especially great in the huge consumer population. Few consumers understand why they must begin paying for services that were formerly free or why so many service charges have been increased. Similarly, bankers must cope with consumer activists who hold that banks represent a type of quasi-public utility through which so-called lifeline services (checking and savings accounts, card-driven systems, and credit) must be made available to all consumers, possibly without regard to price and profit.[12]

Within the industry, the need for continuing education is at least as great.

The difficulty for bankers in trying to keep abreast of all the developments and issues in their industry grows steadily. Pressures to understand all the implications of regional banking agreements, explicit pricing by the Federal Reserve Bank, point-of-sale terminals, and new forms of global and electronic cash management are unremitting. If in any way this text contributes to a better understanding of this new world of banking and provokes some thoughts about the means through which bankers can adjust to the many and dramatic changes that affect them, it will have fulfilled one of its primary objectives.

The word *survival* is heard perhaps more frequently among bankers today than ever before. Walter Wriston, among others, has used it in pointing out that bankers who cannot adjust to change will fall by the wayside:

> The survivors will be those who listen and respond to what the customer wants. Even the finest technology will not save those who fail to understand and meet the customer's needs at a price he or she will pay in a manner and place of the customer's choosing.[13]

Numerous and dramatic changes have occurred in recent years. Others appear imminent, and still others are being considered for the future. During 1985, the courts debated the constitutionality of interstate banking agreements; Congress contemplated curbs on the activities of the so-called nonbank banks; revamping of the existing systems of federal deposit insurance were considered; new developments took place in the evolution and acceptance of point-of-sale technology; thrift institutions took increasing advantage of their expanded powers; and bankers and legislators discussed possible expansion of banks into the insurance, securities, and real estate fields. *Innovation* and *change* continue to be the watchwords, and developments follow one another with unprecedented speed and impact.

It is admittedly far easier to compile a listing of the major problems facing banks today than to devise solutions for each. However, the first step in problem solving always takes the form of identifying the problems; only then can some form of constructive response be devised. This text focuses on that process of identification in an effort to provide broader understanding of the topics, issues, and developments that affect commercial banking today.

Although every effort has been made to ensure the timeliness of the text material, the time lag between composition of manuscript and publication of the finished product inevitably outdates some of that material. I appreciate the reader's indulgence in recognizing and understanding this process.

The text makes extensive references to those newspaper and magazine articles that highlight matters affecting the commercial banks. It is only through these media that current topics and events can be cited and evaluated as an important part of the total framework of change.

The ideas, examples, and guidance of many individuals in the field of financial services and banking-oriented education have contributed to the preparation of this text. I cannot acknowledge them all individually here. However, I send special thanks to Francis A. McMullen, who served the American Institute of Banking in New York with distinction for almost twenty years as its Executive Director. His unfailing support and encouragement have earned my ongoing gratitude.

Notes

1. "The Evolving Financial Services Industry: Competition and Technology for the '80s," *HBS Case Services* (Harvard Business School No. 183-007, 1983), p. 4.
2. John P. Forde, "For the Big Banks, a Tumultuous Year," *American Banker,* January 2, 1985, p. 1.
3. Stephen Koepp, "Banking Takes a Beating," *Time,* December 3, 1984, p. 48.
4. David LaGesse, "Bankers' Integrity Suffers a Setback," *American Banker,* October 20, 1985, p. 1.
5. Ibid.; "Public Worries About Adequacy of Federal Insurance," *American Banker,* October 19, 1985, p. 2.
6. "The Mounting Casualties in Banking," *Business Week,* October 29, 1984, p. 101.
7. Deborah J. Danker and Mary M. McLaughlin, "Profitability of Insured Commercial Banks," *Federal Reserve Bulletin,* November 1984, p. 802.
8. "How the Top 50 Banks Performed," *Business Week,* March 22, 1985, p. 100.
9. Bartlett Naylor, "5 More Banks Closed by Regulators," *American Banker,* October 21, 1985, p. 49.
10. In Koepp, op. cit., pp. 48–49.
11. Danker and McLaughlin, op. cit., p. 804.
12. Raoul D. Edwards, "The Public Perception of Banking," *United States Banker,* March 1985, p. 7.
13. In "Insights, Consequences and Competition," *The Sears Sounding Board* (undated).

The New World of Commercial Banking

1
The Evolution of U.S. Banking

It is perhaps paradoxical that the early 1980s were marked by increasingly numerous and strong demands by the commercial banks for greater freedom: freedom to enter additional areas of financial services, freedom to expand geographically, and freedom from what they considered anachronistic, excessive, and duplicative regulation. The paradox lies in the history of banking in the United States: in its earliest days the embryonic industry enjoyed a degree of freedom that would be considered unthinkable today.

The current regulatory pattern in banking is a form of layered mosaic in which one restrictive control has been superimposed on another. Some of these controls were reactions on the part of governments to financial panics and widespread bank failures; others appear to have reflected fears that banks, if left unchecked, would embark on extremely speculative and/or monopolistic courses. In the words of William Isaac, then Chairman of the Federal Deposit Insurance Corporation,

> We've had periods when banking was relatively free of regulation. Those periods were characterized by one crisis after another. It's not realistic to think that government will ignore banking.[1]

The spectrum from virtually complete freedom to rigid restriction describes the evolution of U.S. banking from colonial times to the present day. To understand the contemporary scene it is necessary to trace that evolution, with particular reference to the legislative landmarks that have had an impact on the system.

Colonial Banking

The basic posture of the colonists in the seventeenth and eighteenth centuries toward banking was entirely in keeping with their overall philosophy and way of life. Because many of them had left Europe to seek freedom of worship and speech, freedom of opportunity, and freedom from government oppression and intervention in their private lives, they extended the concept of freedom to all forms of entrepreneurship and operated in their new environment on a laissez faire basis. Therefore, individuals were as free to open and operate a bank as they were to establish any other type of business venture.

Because rigid British regulations had prevented the colonists from bringing substantial supplies of specie (i.e., gold and silver) with them, they used the barter system widely in trading.[2] Tobacco and furs were among the most commonly used media of exchange. The shortage of specie was exacerbated by a highly unfavorable balance of trade, with imports to the colonies continually exceeding exports. The colonists' need for banks was minimal since merchants often provided safekeeping and extended credit. The first paper money in the New World did not appear until 1690, when the colonial treasury of Massachusetts, in order to pay its soldiers, issued one-year notes that were to be redeemed through collection of taxes.[3] Other colonies soon followed this pattern of note issuance. In addition, despite opposition from colonial legislatures, several land banks, which issued notes secured by the value of real estate, were established[4]; however, in 1741 the British Parliament placed the colonies under the restraints of a 1720 Act designed to prohibit speculative organizations, and this ruling effectively terminated the land banks' activities.[5]

With the passage of time, it became evident that commercial banks were necessary to meet the needs of a burgeoning economy and a growing population. In 1780 the Pennsylvania Bank opened in Philadelphia, followed by the Bank of North America (organized by Robert Morris, Superintendent of Finance for the new colonial government) in 1782 and the Massachusetts Bank and the Bank of New York in 1784.

In 1790 Alexander Hamilton, the nation's first Secretary of the Treasury, began efforts to persuade Congress that a central bank, not affected by local partisanship or the actions of state authorities, was necessary to meet the needs of both the economy and the government. Opposition to his proposal came from those who, like the colonists, disliked the notion of a national institution and specifically from the followers of Thomas Jefferson. In addition to his antipathy toward banks in general, which he once described as being "more dangerous than standing armies," Jefferson argued that the Constitution did not give Congress the power to establish such an institution. This question of constitutionality persisted for many years. Hamilton's efforts succeeded, however, and the First Bank of the United States began operations in 1791.

Banks of the United States

The provisions of the charter granted to the First Bank of the United States constitute a significant effort to develop public confidence. One-fifth of the institution's initial capital was supplied directly by the federal government. Its ability to incur liabilities and to charge interest exceeding 6 percent on loans was restricted, and its authority to function was to extend for twenty years, subject to renewal by Congress.

During its lifetime opposition to the First Bank persisted, both on constitutional grounds and because it could regulate the amount of money in circulation. That opposition resulted in a refusal by Congress in 1811 to renew the charter.

Throughout the ensuing five years, the need for banks grew. Local institutions, often undercapitalized, proliferated. The concept of "free banking" allowed state legislatures to charter new banks with minimal regulation or supervision. Because the system of crediting loan proceeds to customers' accounts had not been established, each institution issued its own notes, often with no regard for the security that supposedly lay behind them. As note issues multiplied, counterfeiting became widespread. In addition, merchants were often reluctant to accept this paper because they feared that the issuing bank might have already been liquidated. Banks opened and closed with great regularity. To conserve their precious supplies of specie, many institutions implemented a system known as "wildcat banking," requiring the holders of notes to present them at remote locations where predatory beasts presumably roamed.

In 1816, again responding to the identified need for a strong central bank, Congress authorized the opening of the Second Bank of the United States, under conditions resembling those of the charter issued to the First Bank. In this case, the financial situation created by the War of 1812 and the renewed need for public confidence, both in a nationalized bank and in a stable currency, provided the impetus.

The election to the presidency of Andrew Jackson in 1828 became the primary reason for the refusal of Congress to renew the Second Bank's charter. Jackson had won the election through the public perception of him as not only a frontier hero but also a prototype of the common man and an opponent of strong central government. His view of the Second Bank as a dangerous and monopolistic institution and his personal dislike for its managers and supporters were evidenced by his vehement attacks on it—attacks which, in retrospect, were quite unjustified. The Second Bank was, in fact, well managed; it served as a depository for federal funds and as a collection agent for notes issued by state banks. In 1819 a landmark decision of the Supreme Court (*McCulloch* v. *Maryland*) paved the way for an increased involvement by the federal government in banks. Nevertheless, Jackson's reelection in 1832, after a campaign in which his opposition to the Second Bank had become a key issue, sealed its fate. He ordered the withdrawal of all federal funds from it and was the individual most responsible for the failure of Congress to renew the charter when it expired in 1836.

State Banks

The demise of the Second Bank eliminated the single agency that could provide the growing nation with a uniform, dependable form of currency. It also depleted the already scarce supply of specie, since about $7 million in that form had to be repaid to foreign stockholders.[6] More important, the demise provided state legislatures with a rationale for transforming free banking from a mere philosophical concept into specific laws. New York passed a Free Banking Act in 1838; other states soon followed, thus opening up the banking business to everyone. In 1837 there were 788 state banks with aggregate capital of $300 million, as compared with their loan-and-discount portfolios of $500 million.[7]

Every increase in the number of state banks brought with it a corresponding increase in counterfeiting and a decrease in public confidence in the system. Forged, depreciated, or otherwise spurious note issues became so prevalent that merchants were forced to refer to periodic publications in which as many as 5,500 types of worthless paper were described, and public resentment against banks became so strong that by 1852 nine states had enacted legislation prohibiting banking.[8] Despite that fact, by 1860 the number of state banks had increased to 1,562; they showed capital of $422 million, deposits of $254 million, and outstanding loans of $692 million.[9]

The National Bank Act

A severe money crisis in 1857 led to the closing of many banks; 1861 witnessed the outbreak of the Civil War; and by 1862 there were only 253 banks whose notes had not been counterfeited.[10] The combination of these factors forced Salmon P. Chase, Secretary of the Treasury under Abraham Lincoln, to begin efforts to reform and strengthen the banking system while at the same time raising the funds the federal government desperately needed. His proposal for a uniform national currency, backed by government bonds, took the form of an Act, which was signed into law by Lincoln in 1863; that legislation was rewritten and expanded in 1864 and became the National Bank Act—one of the most important milestones in U.S. banking history.

The National Bank Act contained three major provisions that form the basis for much of the banking system, and its regulation, that exists today:

1. The Act authorized formation of a new type of financial institution, the *national bank*. Each such bank, to obtain its charter from the federal government, had to meet certain capital requirements and buy a quantity of U.S. bonds proportionate to that capital. These bonds were then to be deposited with the Treasury Department.

2. A new office was created within the Treasury Department, and its head, who was to be known as the *Comptroller of the Currency,* was to be responsible for chartering, examining, and supervising all operations of the national banks.
3. All national banks were authorized to issue a uniform type of currency, the *national bank note,* in amounts proportionate to the quantity of U.S bonds they had purchased.

The Act also required all national banks to maintain reserves against deposits as an additional protection for depositors. Those national banks in designated "reserve cities" had to keep a 25 percent reserve in their vaults; those in other cities could maintain half the required reserve in New York City.

Although the National Bank Act significantly mitigated the chaotic banking conditions that preceded its passage, it did not provide all the solutions for which Secretary Chase had hoped. State banks proved reluctant to convert to national charters and preferred to operate under the less rigorous conditions set by their respective authorities, and they continued to issue their own bank notes. In recognition of this reluctance, in 1865 Congress imposed a 10 percent tax on all state bank notes and thus exerted further pressure for charter conversions.

It is questionable whether any single piece of legislation can prove to be a panacea for all problems, and the National Bank Act, while it was of tremendous benefit in reforming the system and generating increased public confidence, displayed subsequent weaknesses. These, in turn, created a need for further efforts to correct the post-1865 problems.

One such weakness was identified in the direct relationship between the quantity of national bank notes in circulation and the amount of government bonds held by those banks. In times of prosperity, the federal authorities naturally used increasing revenues to retire some of the outstanding bonds and thus reduced the supply of currency. Logically, the opposite effect would have been desirable.

A second problem arose as a result of the designation of the reserve cities as depositories for required reserve funds. In the case of New York City, in particular, postwar experience indicated that these reserves were put to profitable use by the depository banks in the form of short-term loans and investments. When the New York City depositories were called on to release some of those funds, they could respond only by calling in loans, to the detriment of their customer relationships and with a negative effect on the local economy.

The National Bank Act had also failed to provide any system for the rapid nationwide collection of checks. Similarly, it had not included any form of centralized control over the flow of credit from banks to borrowers—possibly because opposition to any type of nationalized central bank, comparable to the Bank of England, still existed. By 1908 it had become clear that the national bank system that Secretary Chase had envisioned was not fulfilling the objectives for which he had held such high hopes: state banks had not been displaced,[11] and the money supply remained inelastic and unresponsive to the country's economic needs. The National Monetary Commission was created in 1908 to determine what changes needed to be made in the overall system. Its deliberations and recommendations were supplemented by input from various banking associations, spokespersons for diverse factions, and President Woodrow Wilson.

Federal Reserve Act

The end result was the Federal Reserve Act of 1913, which was intended to provide for "the establishment of Federal Reserve banks, . . . an elastic currency, . . . a more effective supervision of banking, and . . . other purposes."[12]

The Act represented a compromise that was designed to satisfy the demands of several discrete groups.[13] National banks were required to become members of the Federal Reserve System; state-chartered banks could join if they wished. Ownership of the Federal Reserve Banks, created by the Act, was to rest with the member commercial banks who became their stockholders. The Federal Reserve was given autonomy, so that it could act to control the flow of money and credit independent of the Congress and the President.

The problems and weaknesses that had existed in the post-1863 period were directly addressed in the Federal Reserve Act. To prevent concentration of reserve funds in certain cities, a system of twelve Federal Reserve Districts, each with its own Federal Reserve Bank, was created, and members were directed to maintain their reserves with the district facility. The Act provided for creation of a check collection system so that checks could be cleared at par (i.e., at face value, without cost to the payee or payor) throughout the country.

In its newly created role as the agency responsible for control of the flow of money and credit, the Fed was given three tools or techniques, which today are still the basic instruments that determine monetary growth. While *fiscal* policy—that is, the budgeting of government revenues and expenses—remains within the province of Congress, the Fed is entrusted with *monetary* policy, a term describing the actions that may be deemed necessary to achieve desired goals.

Control over monetary growth can be approached in two ways by the Federal Reserve. Its three policy instruments can be used in a discretionary fashion in response to excessively weak or strong money growth; alternatively, the Fed may assume a more active role and use those instruments to reduce the likelihood of excessive growth.[14]

First, the Fed has authority to establish the specific *reserves* that banks must maintain against demand and time and savings deposits. By raising or lowering the reserve requirements, the Fed can decrease or add to the availability of credit and money supply.

The Fed also operates a so-called discount window through which it can extend credit to financial institutions, the second tool. Whenever it does so, it charges the *discount rate*. Changes in this rate directly affect other interest rates charged by lenders.

Third, and most important, the *Federal Open Market Committee* (FOMC) was formed to be responsible for determining the amount of sales and purchases of all U.S. government obligations (Treasury bills, notes, and bonds). The FOMC consists of the seven members of the Fed's Board of Governors, plus five of the twelve Reserve Bank presidents, and determines the quantity and types of government obligations to be issued, refinanced, or redeemed. Its actions have an immediate and direct effect on bank reserves and the overall economy.[15]

Federal Reserve Services

The Federal Reserve Act required member banks to keep reserves with their local Federal Reserve Banks without interest. In exchange for these, the Fed was established as the source of various services that, with the single exception of loans, were to be extended without specific charges.[16] The range of services includes supplying member banks with coin and currency, operating a nationwide check collection system, providing safekeeping facilities for securities, and operating a nationwide wire transfer system for the movement of funds. More recently, as electronic funds transfer systems (EFTS) have become more widely accepted, the Fed has assumed an active role in the Automated Clearing Houses (ACHs) that process such transfers.

The Fed, in addition to its services to banks, also serves the federal government by operating the basic checking account through which all receipts for and payments by the government flow. It conducts periodic examinations of banks to ensure their compliance with all laws and regulations and prudent operations. It compiles and makes available a great many detailed financial, economic, and statistical reports.

Federal Reserve Organization

The overall operations of the Fed are directed by a seven-member Board of Governors named by the President and confirmed by the Senate and who serve fourteen-year terms. Each of the twelve district Federal Reserve Banks has a Board of Directors, consisting of nine members; six of these members

Table 1–1
Federal Regulations by Subject Matter

Area of Coverage	*Letter Identification*
Bank Holding Companies	Regulation Y
Federal Reserve Banks	Regulations A, BB, I, J, N, and V
Foreign Banking Business	Regulations K, M, and N
Interlocking Directorates	Regulations L and R
Consumer Protection	Regulations B, C, E, M, Z, and AA
Monetary Policy	Regulations A, D, and Q
Securities Credit	Regulations G, T, U, and X
Financial Privacy	Regulation S
Fed Membership Requirements	Regulation H
Member-Bank Loans to Executive Officers	Regulation O
Community Reinvestment	Regulation BB

Source: Board of Governors, Federal Reserve System, *A Guide to Federal Reserve Regulations* (Washington, D.C., September 1981), p. iv.

are elected by the district's member-bank stockholders and three of whom are named by the Board of Governors.

As the agency responsible for controlling the flow of money and credit, the Fed uses various Federal Reserve Regulations, each of which is identified by letters of the alphabet. These regulations are subject to revision at any time. Table 1–1 shows the extent to which they affect banks and the economy.

In summary, note that the Fed is sometimes called the nation's central bank, a term which may imply that it is analogous to the central banks in other countries. It differs from all such counterparts, however, in two important respects. First, the decisions of the Board of Governors are made on an independent basis rather than at the direction of the U.S. Congress or the president. The Chairman of the Board of Governors is in frequent contact with both and reports to them regularly, but the board remains autonomous. Second, the ownership of the twelve district Federal Reserve Banks rests with the member banks who are its stockholders; the Fed is not an agency of the Treasury Department or other entity of the federal government.

The 1913–1933 Period

In retrospect, the Federal Reserve Act was essential to the needs of the nation in the period preceding World War I. On the one hand, it addressed and corrected previous weaknesses by providing a quick, efficient, and inexpensive method of check collection; by eliminating the pyramiding of reserves in money-center cities; and by giving the nation a new form of currency in the

Table 1–2
Bank Statistics, Selected Years from 1920 to 1933

Year	*Number of National Banks*	*Number of State Members*	*Total Number of Members*	*Number of Nonmembers*	*Total Number of Banks*
1920	8,024	1,374	9,398	20,893	30,291
1925	8,066	1,472	9,538	19,904	29,442
1930	7,247	1,068	8,315	15,364	23,679
1931	6,800	982	7,782	14,319	22,101
1932	6,145	835	6,980	11,754	18,734
1933	4,897	709	5,606	8,601	14,207

Source: Helen M. Burns, *The American Banking Community and New Deal Financial Reforms 1933–1935* (Westport, Conn.: Greenwood Press, 1974), p. 4.

Federal Reserve note. Through the discount window it became a lender of last resort to banks, and its examining function assisted both the government and the institutions.

On the other hand, in the interests of compromise the authors of the Act had made System membership optional for all state-chartered banks. As is shown in table 1–2, most of the banks in that category declined to join. The costs of the stock purchase necessary for membership and the need for submitting to Fed regulations and examinations made them unwilling to participate. Therefore, the Fed could not control these banks' operations, examine them for signs of weaknesses, or supply them with credit. It remains true today that less than one-half of all commercial banks are Fed members.

Those responsible for the Federal Reserve Act could not have foreseen the total collapse of the economic system that took place in the late 1920s and early 1930s, when the Roaring Twenties—an era of unrestrained optimism and widespread belief that nothing but further growth and prosperity would occur—gave way to the Great Depression. During the 1920s virtually every type of loan and investment was considered prudent. For competitive reasons, many banks offered to pay interest on demand deposits, but the resulting interest expense forced them to expand their loan portfolios to gain offsetting income. Because commercial and investment banking were commingled, banks could and did act as both underwriters of and investors in common stock and revenue bonds.

The McFadden Bank Branching Act

During this hectic period, Congress took action to address the controversial question of allowing national banks to expand by opening branches. The National Bank Act of 1863 had severely limited their ability to do so, while state banks could open branches if their state legislatures gave permission. The McFadden Act, passed in 1927, amended the provisions of the National Bank Act by placing national and state banks on the same basis regarding branching but with the important caveat that national banks were subject to the regulations of the individual states on the matter. Since twenty-two states at that time had laws prohibiting branch banking, the act had little real impact. In addition to its section on branch banking, the Act enlarged the powers of national banks to make loans on real estate, allowed them to buy securities for investment purposes, and increased their latitude regarding maximum loan amounts to individual borrowers.

The aforementioned section of the McFadden Act is best remembered today since it effectively prevents expansion of banks across state lines. This point is discussed in more detail in chapter 12.

The Financial Crisis

The first signs of trouble appeared during the agricultural crisis of the 1920s, when farm prices collapsed and large-scale migrations of individuals away from rural areas took place. From 1925 through 1929, 3,420 banks failed, 2,840 of which were nonmembers, often in farm areas and small towns.[17] The stock market collapsed in October 1929; England renounced the gold standard; and unemployment in the United States steadily increased, from 3.5 million in 1930 to 15 million in 1933. In a single month (October 1931), 1,200 banks closed their doors.[18]

Franklin D. Roosevelt, Democratic nominee for President in 1932, included in his acceptance speech an advocacy of banking reforms designed to discourage and prevent speculation, to divorce investment banking from commercial banking, and to provide "vastly more rigid supervision of the banking system." Herbert Hoover, the outgoing President, agreed, stating that "widespread banking reforms are a national necessity and are the first requisites for national recovery."[19] In the first quarter of 1933, panic among bank depositors became commonplace. In major cities, long lines of depositors, hoping to withdraw their funds before the institution collapsed, were a frequent sight. During the week that ended March 1, 1933, over $200 million in gold was withdrawn from Federal Reserve Banks; by March 2 twenty-one states had declared moratoriums on banking activities, and by March 4, the date of Roosevelt's inauguration, all forty-eight states had declared bank holidays. Roosevelt followed suit and suspended all banking operations from March 6 through March 9.

Long and bitter debates took place in Congress over the forms of legislation to address this financial crisis, and from today's perspective it is difficult to understand why one of the major points of contention involved the question of providing some type of insurance on bank deposits. Agreement on other reforms was reached in the hearings of the House Banking and Currency Committee, but resistance to any form of federal guarantees on deposits came from individual banks and banking associations in every part of the country.[20] Nevertheless, their objections were overcome, and the Banking Act that has become commonly known as Glass-Steagall was signed into law on June 16, 1933.

The Glass-Steagall Act

To a nation that had lost about $7 billion in deposits through the failures of over 9,000 commercial banks during a five-year period,[21] the feature of the Glass-Steagall Act that provided for federal deposit insurance may have been the most noteworthy. However, other sections of Glass-Steagall were of great importance in reforming the banking system at that time and remain so today:

1. Glass-Steagall prohibited payment of interest on demand deposits.
2. It gave the Fed authority to control bank loans made in connection with securities transactions.
3. The Act required the separation of all securities affiliates from commercial banks, thus effectively taking the banks out of the securities business.[22]

The Glass-Steagall legislation also expanded on the provisions of the McFadden Act by giving national banks permission for statewide branching wherever state laws permitted this. Until that time, the McFadden Act had confined the operations of national banks to their immediate localities.

Section 20 of the Glass-Steagall Act stated specifically that

> [N]o member bank shall be affiliated in any manner . . . with any corporation, association, business trust, or other similar organization engaged principally in the issue, flotation, underwriting, public sale, or distribution at wholesale or retail . . . of stocks, bonds, debentures, notes, or other securities.[23]

This section of the Act led to controversy in 1985 as the banks sought relief from its provisions. When the Act was drawn up, Congress recognized the public opinion that banks had strayed beyond the proper boundaries of their business by entering investment banking and that they had been guilty of speculative abuses. Senator Carter Glass, co-author of the Act, held that the only proper activities of commercial banks lay in the area of self-liquidating, short-term loans made to finance business trade. Spokespersons for the securities industry maintained that bank affiliations in that field "were a major cause of the stock market crash of 1929."[24] A greater concentration of economic power in the hands of the banks was another widely held fear at the time the Act was formulated.

In 1986, as the competitive climate intensified in the financial services industry, many banks attempted to engage in securities activities, including the underwriting of corporate debt issues. In some cases they achieved at least partial success. BankAmerica Corporation was allowed to acquire a discount brokerage firm, Charles Schwab & Co., and the acquisition was subsequently approved by the U.S. Supreme Court. Thereafter, the Chase Manhattan Corporation acquired Rose and Company, also a discount broker. The Federal Deposit Insurance Corporation ruled that banks that are not Fed members are not restricted by Section 20 of Glass-Steagall and therefore are free to have affiliates engaged in securities-related activities.[25] During 1985, two major New York institutions, Citicorp and Bankers Trust, applied to the Federal Reserve board for permission to enter some phases of securities-related business through affiliates.[26] Further controversy over the appropriateness and possible legality of ties between the banking and securities fields appears likely.

Federal Deposit Insurance Corporation

Despite the opposition of the groups mentioned earlier, among which was the American Bankers Association (whose President described deposit insurance as "unsound, unscientific, and dangerous"[27]), the Glass-Steagall Act contained an amendment to Section 12-B of the Federal Reserve Act and thus created the Federal Deposit Insurance Corporation (FDIC). The FDIC began operations under a temporary plan on January 1, 1934, with the chief purpose of providing protection for depositors at insured banks and acting as a regulator so that the safety of those banks would not be impaired. The Federal Deposit Insurance Act of 1935 contained the permanent plan under which the FDIC has functioned ever since.[28]

All national banks and all state-chartered member banks are required to join the FDIC; nonmembers and mutual savings banks may join if they wish and if they meet FDIC standards. As of year-end 1983, 14,469 banks (96.2 percent of the total number in the United States) were insured.[29] Depositors at savings and loan associations (S&Ls) have comparable protection through the Federal Savings and Loan Insurance Corporation (FSLIC).

Operations of the FDIC are managed by a three-member Board of Directors in Washington, D.C. The Comptroller of the Currency, ex officio, is one member, while the other two are presidential appointees. The Corporation has the authority to set standards for its members, to examine them, to take any one of several actions designed to prevent their failure, and to pay their depositors up to a maximum of $100,000 per insured account if failure should occur. In addition, the FDIC has the right to establish maximum interest rates on time and savings deposits at those banks whose rates are not otherwise regulated.

Insured banks pay an annual premium, known as the FDIC Assessment, of 1/12 of 1 percent of average annual deposits for the coverage. Part of this may be rebated to them if operating results are favorable. The FDIC also has the privilege, at any time, of borrowing up to $3 billion directly from the U.S. Treasury. At year-end 1983 the FDIC fund, available to meet possible emergencies, amounted to $15.4 billion, of which $14 billion was invested in U.S. Treasury obligations.[30]

By comparison with the staggering numbers of bank failures that took place in the years immediately preceding the creation of the FDIC, the records achieved since 1934 have been excellent. From 1934 through 1942 there were 393 insured and 97 noninsured bank failures, for a nine-year total of 490; from 1943 through 1978 the thirty-six-year total was 199, of which 162 were insured banks.[31] Total outright losses to the Corporation for the years 1934 through 1982 in the 620 cases of bank failures that required FDIC disbursements were less than $2 billion.[32]

In addition to its functions as an insurer, the FDIC has assumed a much more visible role in the 1980s as an activist organization in dealing with troubled banks and S&Ls. Its counterpart agency, the FSLIC, has adopted a similar posture. The rationale for this action is the viewpoint that it is less expensive for them to pump resources into such institutions to keep them functioning than to allow them to fail and thus to incur the costs of paying depositors. The FDIC and FSLIC have acted as intermediaries, arranging for the mergers of banks and S&Ls that are in financial difficulty with stronger institutions, designated and approved by the two agencies or simply meeting their standards.

The need for the FDIC and FSLIC to become more strongly proactive in preventing failures was identified in 1980, 1981, and 1982, when thrift institutions in increasing numbers began reporting severe financial difficulties. As money-market rates rose to record levels during those years, S&Ls and savings banks found it necessary to pay far more for deposits than they could recover through interest income on their portfolios of long-term, fixed-rate home mortgages. Nine of the ten largest savings banks in New York City reported net operating losses for 1980 totaling $264 million,[33] and by 1982 the financial condition of thirty-four New York State savings banks had deteriorated so severely that they required special approval from the State Banking Department before being allowed to pay interest to depositors.[34] During the first four months of 1982, the FDIC found it necessary to spend $983 million in the process of assisting in six thrift institution mergers.[35] The nation's S&Ls experienced similar difficulties; their 1981 operating results showed losses aggregating over $6 billion.[36]

To preserve the traditional lines of demarcation, the actions of the two federal insurers generally took the form of arranging mergers within the same industry; that is, a thrift institution was merged with or acquired by another of the same type, often with direct FDIC or FSLIC financial aid. When this solution was impossible, however, the agencies breached the long-standing barriers and allowed the takeover of troubled savings banks or S&Ls by major commercial banks. The first instance of this type of cross-industry merger occurred in Minnesota in 1982.[37] Later in that same year Citicorp gained approval to acquire the $3 billion Fidelity Savings & Loan Association of San Francisco, and this marked the first time the FDIC had consented to the acquisition of a thrift by a commercial banking institution in another state.[38] In 1984, the Federal Reserve and the Federal Home Loan Bank Board (the thrift institutions' regulatory agency) jointly approved Citicorp's acquisitions of two additional thrifts, First Federal Savings & Loan Association (Chicago) and New Biscayne Federal Savings and Loan Association (Miami).[39] As a result, Citicorp Savings, a subsidiary of Citicorp, now has a strong presence in three states outside New York. The Fed, in approving these acquisitions, noted that in its judgment the public benefits resulting from the preservation of these two thrift institutions outweighed any disadvantages.[40]

In terms of both size and importance to the banking community and the nation as a whole, no single action previously taken by the FDIC compared with its rescue of the Continental Illinois National Bank (Chicago) in 1984. This rescue was described in the media as "the biggest bailout of a private company in U.S. history."[41] To prevent the failure of the bank (the nation's seventh largest at year-end 1983, with total assets of $40.7 billion), the FDIC bought its loan portfolio for $3.5 billion and agreed to provide an additional $1 billion in direct funding; it also ousted the two senior members of Continental's management and ten members of the board.[42]

In this case, the FDIC appears to have acted not solely to avoid having to pay the depositors but also out of concern over the repercussions throughout the banking industry had Continental been allowed to fail. The rescue was not accomplished without criticism from those who feared that a precedent might have been set for the salvaging of any bank of comparable size, and the question was posed whether Continental, or any other major bank that is found to be in serious distress, should simply be allowed to fail, without the intervention of any agency. To forestall any future questions about the costs to U.S. taxpayers of rescues of this type, the FDIC has suggested that its annual assessments should be variable rather than fixed, with additional premiums to be paid into the fund by institutions with weak loan portfolios.[43]

The Monetary Control Act

During the 1970s, money-market rates began to show regular and steep increases so investment yields became far more attractive and banks were forced to pay escalating interest to attract or keep various forms of time and savings deposits. The increasing value of money prompted many banks to rethink the question of Fed membership on the grounds that the funds they were required to keep as non-interest-bearing reserves with the Fed could, if withdrawn, be put to highly profitable use. In 1978, for example, Walter Wriston, then Chairman of Citicorp, stated that Citibank's pretax income could be increased by $80 million–$90 million if its reserves could be utilized for loans and investments[44]; had he made the same calculations in 1981, by which time the prime rate had reached 21.5 percent, the potential yield would have been significantly higher.

During 1978, ninety-nine commercial banks determined that the opportunity cost of their Fed membership made it impractical and withdrew from the system.[45] In some cases, these were national banks, which therefore found it necessary to convert to state charters to resign their membership. The attrition continued in 1979: the percentage of commercial bank deposits subject to reserve requirements at the Fed, which had been 86 percent in 1945 and 80 percent in 1970, fell to 69 percent.[46] Given that each decline in Fed membership lessens the ability of the Board of Governors to control the flow of money and credit, Chairman Paul Volcker appealed for Congressional aid through new legislation. His testimony before Congress in 1980 indicated that sixty-nine additional banks, with aggregate deposits of about $7 billion, had announced their intention of withdrawing from the system.[47]

At the same time, the nation's thrift institutions, as noted earlier, were experiencing severe financial losses, again as a result of the negative spread between their portfolio income and their interest costs. In 1980 the average yield on prime six-month commercial paper was 12.29 percent; in the same year thrift institutions reported that their average rate of return on home mortgages (which at that time were 79.8 percent of total S&L assets and 59 percent of mutual savings bank assets) was only 9.31 percent.[48] The Comptroller of the Currency, spokespersons for commercial banks and thrifts, and the Treasury Secretary joined in the appeal to Congress for legislative relief.

The Depository Institutions Deregulation and Monetary Control Act, known more familiarly by the latter half of the title, was signed into law by President Carter in March 1980. It had two stated objectives:

1. to improve the effectiveness of monetary policy by making the fulcrum on which that policy operates stabler;
2. to provide competitive equity among financial institutions, which given uniform reserve requirements, will be placed on a more equal footing and, given new authorities, will be able to offer more equivalent services to their customers.[49]

The following significant provisions were included in the act[50]:

Transaction accounts: This new term was coined to include all checking and NOW (Negotiable Order for Withdrawal) accounts, all share draft accounts,[51] all savings accounts that allow automatic transfers or payments, and all accounts that permit more than three preauthorized or telephone payments per month.

Reserve requirements: All financial institutions offering transaction accounts were required to maintain non-interest-bearing reserves directly with the Fed or through a member; new percentage ranges for required reserves were established, to be phased in on a gradual basis through 1987 (table 1–3).

DIDC: A Depository Institutions Deregulation Committee (DIDC) was established to determine the timing of the gradual phaseout of interest-rate ceilings on savings and time deposits, with the stipulation that all controls over such rates would be eliminated by March 31, 1986. The DIDC consists of the Secretary of the Treasury and the Chairmen of the Federal Reserve Board of Governors, the Federal Home Loan Bank Board, the FDIC, and the National Credit Union Administration.

Discount window: All institutions offering transaction accounts were given the right to apply to the Fed for credit.[52]

FDIC: Insurance coverage was increased to $100,000 per insured account.

Fed services: The Federal Reserve was directed to implement a system of explicit pricing for all its services to financial institutions.

NOW accounts: All depository institutions were authorized to offer these interest-bearing relationships, against which checks can be written.

S&Ls: The lending powers of S&Ls were enhanced, allowing them to invest up to 20 percent of their assets in commercial paper, consumer loans, and corporate debt issues. Federally chartered associations were authorized to grant mortgage loans in unlimited amounts without geographic restrictions and to offer credit cards and exercise trust powers.

Savings banks: Federally chartered savings banks were given the right to offer consumer loans, commercial loans, and trust services.

The Monetary Control Act, in retrospect, has drastically changed the nature of the banking industry and has validated the opinion of Senator William Proxmire, then Chairman of the Senate Banking Committee, who called it "the most significant banking legislation since 1913."[53] By making all federally insured institutions subject to reserve requirements, it solved the problem of attrition from the Federal Reserve System and simultaneously enhanced the ability of the Fed to control M_1—the principal measure of the

Table 1–3
Reserve Requirements for Depository Institutions as a Percentage of Deposits

Before the Monetary Control Act		*After the Monetary Control Act*	
Type of Deposit and Deposit Interval	*Percentage of Reserves Required (Members)*	*Type of Deposit and Deposit Interval*	*Percentage of Reserves Required (All Institutions)*
Net Demand			
$0–2 million	7	*Net Transaction Accounts*	
$2–10 million	9.5		
$10–100 million	11.75 } as of 12/30/76	$0–28.9 million	3 } as of 12/29/83
$100–400 million	12.75	Over $28.9 million	12
Over $400 million	16.25		
Savings	3 as of 3/16/67	*Nonpersonal Time Deposits*	
		Less than 1½ years	3 } as of 10/16/83
		1½ years or more	0
Time			
$0–5 million			
30–179 days	3 as of 3/16/67	*Eurocurrency Liabilities*	
180 days–4 years	2.5 as of 1/8/76		
4 years or more	1 as of 10/30/75	All types	3 as of 11/13/80
Over $5 million			
30–179 days	6 as of 12/12/74		
180 days–4 years	2.5 as of 1/8/76		
4 years or more	1 as of 10/30/75		

Source: *Federal Reserve Bulletin,* January 1984, p. A7.

nation's money supply, consisting of currency, demand deposits, and other transactions accounts.[54]

By expanding the range of services permitted for S&Ls and savings banks, the Monetary Control Act gave them opportunities to diversify into potential areas of profit previously denied them and made them more competitive with commercial banks. For example, by 1982, 54 percent of all mutual savings banks were involved in commercial lending.[55] That diversification was intended to relieve the pressures created on thrift institutions by the traditional basic nature of their business, resulting in negative profit margins.

In requiring the Fed to implement a system of explicit pricing for all its services, Congress included in the Monetary Control Act a stipulation that a charge be levied by the Fed for its *float,* which in 1979 had reached an all-time average daily peak of $6.7 billion. This stipulation was based on the belief that the money represented by Fed float could have generated some $1 billion in annual earnings for the Fed if it had been available to the latter for investment purposes.[56]

At the same time, implementation of Fed procedures for the explicit pricing of services increased the need for commercial banks—the largest users of those services—to improve their systems of cost accounting and account analysis and, ultimately, to change the nature of their relationships with customers by passing along the costs incurred in basic transactions such as check collection. Because of those costs, it can be anticipated that the use of paperless payments through EFTS will increase substantially.[57]

By making NOW accounts available at all federally insured institutions, the Monetary Control Act gave consumers additional opportunities to move their funds into interest-bearing bank relationships. This form of disintermediation will make the problem of liability management in banking even more important, forcing each institution to know its cost of funds and to ensure that those costs can be recovered on a profitable basis. At year-end 1983 the nation's ten largest commercial banks (ranked according to deposit size) alone had $2.3 billion in the form of NOW account deposits, despite the fact that one of these banks, Morgan Guaranty, does not offer them.[58] As of December 31, 1983, NOW accounts represented 3.8 percent of the total assets of domestic offices of all insured commercial banks.[59] These figures again indicate the increased degree of customer sophistication in banking, particularly among consumers who no longer see any logical reason for leaving funds in a non-interest-bearing account.

The Garn–St Germain Act

The change from a demand-deposit to an interest-bearing-deposit base in U.S. commercial banking received its major impetus from the introduction of the large-denomination negotiable certificate of deposit (CD) in 1961 by the then First National City Bank of New York (now Citibank, N.A., the major component of Citicorp). Since CDs issued for amounts of $100,000 or more were exempt from the interest-rate restrictions of Federal Reserve Regulation Q and could be sold easily in the secondary market, they became the favorite interest-earning vehicle for corporate, institutional, and affluent individual investors. Within twenty years, large-denomination CDs had come to represent 18 percent of the total deposit liabilities of all commercial banks[60]; at year-end 1983 they accounted for 15.5 percent of total assets among insured commercial banks.[61]

Maximum interest rates, however, were available only to those who could meet the $100,000 criterion; thus, less affluent depositors were at a constant disadvantage. To meet their needs, a type of mutual fund that became known as the money-market fund was introduced by brokerage firms in 1971 and quickly achieved tremendous popularity. In December 1982 these funds reached their peak at $230 billion, with Merrill Lynch alone responsible for $50 billion.[62] With each increase in money-market rates during the 1970s, an increasing amount of disintermediation took place. C. Todd Conover, then Comptroller of the Currency, encapsulated the problem: "The public wants financial services, but it couldn't care less whether it gets them from banks."[63]

When financial institutions, restricted by interest-rate ceilings, were paying 5 or 5¼ percent on savings accounts, the money-market funds were offering 8 percent or more. During a Congressional hearing in 1981, Walter Wriston commented on the growth of the funds, noting that in twenty-four months Merrill Lynch had built up fund balances exceeding Citibank's total domestic deposits, which had been acquired over the course of 160 years.[64]

In response to persistent pressures from commercial banks and thrift institutions, which had been forced to stand by in relative helplessness while money-market funds grew at their expense, Congress enacted the Garn-St Germain Act in October 1982. It is another landmark in the history of deregulation in banking. The major provision of the Act directed the DIDC to authorize a new type of account, to be offered by commercial banks and thrifts as a vehicle to compete with the funds by providing smaller investors with a higher-yielding, insured relationship. Criteria for the MMDAs included a minimum deposit of $2,500, insurance coverage by the FDIC or FSLIC, certain restrictions on withdrawals, and most important, fully and freely competitive interest rates. The MMDAs achieved virtually instant popularity with the public. Unfortunately, some banks, in their overzealousness to attract new accounts, took full advantage of deregulation and offered interest rates of 20 percent or more when they first made the accounts available in December 1982.[65]

MMDAs have been of tremendous help to commercial banks and thrifts in recapturing funds. By year-end 1983, commercial banks held $226 billion in MMDAs,[66] and in May 1984 the total nationwide volume for all financial institutions was estimated at $394 billion.[67]

One month after the introduction of MMDAs, the DIDC took further action to arrest disintermediation by authorizing financial institutions to offer the so-called Super-NOW accounts. These provided broader check-writing privileges than MMDAs but were not made available to corporations; because they were made subject to reserve requirements, they were typically offered at rates about 100 basis points below those on MMDAs. As of December 1983, insured commercial banks held $29 billion in Super-NOW accounts.[68]

As of January 1985, the minimum denomination for MMDAs and Super-NOW accounts was reduced to $1,000, and as of January 1986 the minimum was eliminated completely. Thus, all small savers, without exception, will be able to earn a market rate of interest on their savings while enjoying the benefits of federal deposit insurance through the FDIC or FSLIC.[69]

To help thrift institutions diversify and thereby improve both liquidity and earnings, the Garn–St Germain Act also

gave federal S&Ls and federal savings banks authority to make general business and agricultural loans, limited to 10 percent of their assets (as of January 1, 1984),

authorized them to engage in nonresidential secured lending, inventory financing, and equipment leasing, again with limitations based on asset size.[70]

Summary

The U.S. banking system, in contrast to those that exist in other parts of the world, is entirely unique, both in terms of fragmentation among banks and in diversity. In Canada, for example, five banks hold some 90 percent of the total banking assets; six clearing banks in Great Britain control about 70 percent; the three largest French banks have about 55 percent; and in West Germany, three banks hold 45 percent of that nation's total bank assets.[71] In the United States, the ten largest banks, seven of which are headquartered in New York City, command only 31.4 percent of total bank assets,[72] and the one hundred largest hold only 53.9 percent.[73]

This diversification is closely related to the second unique feature of the U.S. system—namely, the limitations that prevent commercial banks from opening full-scale branches across state lines. Elsewhere in the world, the customer of a particular bank may deal with it through its nationwide network of branches. Although loan production offices, increased facilities for electronic transfers of funds, and operations of subsidiaries such as Edge Act offices and trust units are growing and enable bank holding companies to disregard state boundaries, it remains true that the barriers to actual nationwide branching exist, placing commercial banks at a severe disadvantage vis-à-vis competitors. (The operations of Edge Act facilities are outlined in chapter 4.)

By providing an overview of the history of U.S. banking, this chapter has tried to explain how that uniqueness came about. Many of the regulations and restrictions that affect commercial banks today are the results of a series of federal legislative actions, often in response to problems and weaknesses in the system, that represent the opposite end of a spectrum that began in colonial times.

The early history of U.S. banking is one in which *free banking* became a watchword. The basic concepts of free enterprise and states' rights combined to create a climate that allowed banks to open, operate, and close with relative ease. The National Bank Act, the Federal Reserve Act, the Glass-Steagall Act, the Monetary Control Act, and the Garn–St Germain Act are the milestones in a chronicle of regulatory constraints. Whether these milestones are in fact, as some observers have described them, anachronisms that should be revised to meet the needs of today's highly competitive marketplace is one of the major topics of controversy and discussion that Congress and the courts must eventually face.

Within the limitations imposed by these regulations, commercial banks traditionally operated with a high degree of exclusivity in providing financial services. Demand deposits, not offered by other financial intermediaries, were their basic stock in trade, and therefore they became the controlling force in the processing of payments and the extending of credit.

At the same time, the banks, particularly in the largest cities, lived up completely to the term *commercial* by concentrating on the needs of businesses, units of government, and correspondents and allowing other institutions to serve the consumer. Savings banks, credit unions, and S&Ls filled this vacuum by providing the accounts and home mortgage loans that commercial banks did not offer. The lines of demarcation between thrifts and commercial banks were easily identified.

Today, homogenization has taken place to a large extent in the New World of the financial services industry, to the extent that commercial bankers now hear increasing numbers of their former customers question the real need for doing business with them. As is discussed in detail later in this text, those bankers who see thrift institutions, insurance companies, financial conglomerates, brokerage firms, and retailers capitalizing on a relative freedom from regulation and providing many service products that formerly were within the purview only of the commercial banks feel strongly disadvantaged and seek relief.

Deregulation of the airlines and the trucking industry took place in the early 1980s, both as part of an overall effort by the federal government to make competition more equitable and as an attempt to provide consumers with a freedom of choice that was not available in prior years. For the commercial banks and thrifts, the term may have different connotations, depending on the viewpoint of its user. To the former group, *deregulation,* as seen in the Monetary Control and Garn–St Germain Acts, means that they can offer new types of accounts and operate without many of the interest-rate restrictions that inhibited their operations in the past; to the thrift institutions, however, the word means even more. Federally chartered thrift institutions, for example,

> [C]an make nearly every type of home loan imaginable. They may act as fiduciaries, issue credit cards, act as fiscal agents for the United States, and act as escrow agents. All federal associations may merge or branch intrastate without restriction . . . [and] interstate under certain conditions; . . . and indirectly diversify into any other business without application to or approval by the Federal Home Loan Bank Board.[74]

Deregulation, then, in the New World of the banking industry, while it has improved the ability of the commercial banks to operate with fewer restrictions, does not appear to have been as meaningful for them as for some other intermediaries. In 1970 a member of the Federal Reserve Board of Governors expressed the opinion that "Banking, with its three federal and fifty state supervisory authorities and bodies of law to match, is the most overregulated industry in the country."[75] One may speculate on the extent to which his words remain true today.

One final point may be made on the question of possible further deregulation of commercial banks: it appears likely that an overriding consideration among legislators will involve the risks that banks may take, assuming they are given more freedom. In addition to asking whether banks should be allowed to expand across state lines, underwrite corporate debt issues or municipal revenue bonds, or offer insurance and other services that are not pure banking functions, lawgivers will undoubtedly ask whether banks should be allowed to fail. If a perception exists in Congress or the courts that increased interest expenses and the costs inherent in entering into new areas of activity may lead banks to assume greater risks (e.g., lowering of credit criteria), deregulation will be limited and the question will again be raised of the role of federal agencies as lenders of last resort. If institutions encounter financial difficulty as a result of their own actions, does government have an obligation, regardless of costs, to keep them from failing?[76]

Notes

1. In Robert A. Bennett, "A Banking Puzzle: Mixing Freedom and Protection," *The New York Times,* February 19, 1984, p. B1.

2. Elvira Clain-Stefanelli and Vladimir Clain-Stefanelli, *Chartered for Progress: Two Centuries Of American Banking* (Washington, D.C.: Acropolis Books, Ltd., 1975), p. 13.

3. Paul Studenski and Herman E. Krooss, *Financial History of the United States,* 2nd ed. (New York: McGraw-Hill Book Company, Inc., 1963), pp. 14–15.

4. Edward W. Reed; Richard V. Cotter; Edward K. Gill; and Richard K. Smith, *Commercial Banking,* 3rd ed. (Englewood Cliffs, N.J.: Prentice-Hall, Inc., 1984), p. 24.

5. Clain-Stefanelli and Clain-Stefanelli, op. cit., p. 22.

6. Studenski and Krooss, op. cit., p. 73.

7. Ibid., p. 107.

8. Clain-Stefanelli and Clain-Stefanelli, op. cit., pp. 68–69.

9. Studenski and Krooss, op. cit., p. 121.

10. Paul B. Trescott, *Financing American Enterprise: The Story of Commercial Banking* (New York: Harper & Row, 1963), p. 47.

11. The proportions have fluctuated from time to time; however, state-chartered banks have typically accounted for some two-thirds of all commercial banking institutions. The side-by-side competitive existence of state and national banks gives rise to the term *dual banking system.*

12. Studenski and Krooss, op. cit., p. 258.

13. For a detailed discussion of the events leading to the Act, see Roger T. Johnson, *Historical Beginnings: The Federal Reserve* (Boston: Federal Reserve Bank of Boston), 1977.

14. Gordon H. Sellon, Jr., "The Instruments of Monetary Policy," *Economic Review* (Federal Reserve Bank of Kansas City), May 1984, pp. 5–6. Information on Fed policy decisions is published monthly by the Fed Board of Governors in the *Federal Reserve Bulletin.*

15. A detailed discussion of Fed operations can be found in William F. Staats, *Money and Banking* (Washington, D.C.: American Bankers Association, 1982), pp. 147–159.

16. Rules on reserve requirements, access to the Fed for credit, and pricing of Fed services were revised in 1980 by the Monetary Control Act, to be discussed subsequently.

17. Studenski and Krooss, op. cit., p. 335.

18. Clain-Stefanelli and Clain-Stefanelli, op. cit., p. 130.

19. Burns, op. cit., pp. 23–24.

20. Burns, op. cit., pp. 67–68, 87–88.

21. Reed et al., op. cit., p. 205.

22. Studenski and Krooss, op. cit., pp. 395–396.

23. In Bart Fraust, "Bank Subsidiaries Underwriting Securities," *American Banker,* January 4, 1985, p. 1.

24. Ibid. See also Carter H. Golembe, "The Organization of Modern Banking,"

in Herbert V. Prochnow and Herbert V. Prochnow, Jr., eds., *The Changing World of Banking* (New York: Harper & Row, 1974), p. 17.

25. Richard C. Keller, "Glass-Steagall: Fact vs. Folklore," *The Bankers Magazine,* September–October 1984, pp. 81–85.

26. Fraust, op. cit.

27. Federal Deposit Insurance Corporation, *1983 Annual Report,* p. 46.

28. 12 U.S.C. 264 and 1811–1831.

29. "Changes Among Operating Banks and Branches," Federal Deposit Insurance Corporation, Washington, D.C. 1984, p. 3.

30. Federal Deposit Insurance Corporation, *1983 Annual Report,* pp. 18–19.

31. Joseph F. Sinkey, Jr., *Problems and Failed Institutions in the Commercial Banking Industry* (Greenwich, Conn.: JAI Press, Inc., 1979), p. 15.

32. Harry D. Hutchinson, *Money, Banking, and the United States Economy,* 5th ed. (Englewood Cliffs, N.J.: Prentice-Hall, Inc., 1984), p. 93.

33. Karen Slater, "Nine Big NYC Mutuals Lost $264 Million in 1980," *American Banker,* February 10, 1981, p. 1.

34. Paul J. Browne, "Bank News Is Bad News," *Empire State Report,* June 7, 1982, p. 227.

35. Karen Slater, "FDIC Thrift Aid Nears $1 Billion," *American Banker,* April 6, 1982, p. 1.

36. William D. Marbach, "The Fidelity Takeover," *Newsweek,* April 26, 1982, p. 68.

37. Karen Slater, "First Government-Assisted Merger of Mutual, Commercial Bank Completed in Minneapolis," *American Banker,* February 23, 1982, p. 1.

38. Linda W. McCormick and Robert E. Norton, "Fed Lets Citicorp Acquire Fidelity Savings & Loan," *American Banker,* September 29, 1982, p. 1.

39. "Fed Approves Citicorp Bids for 2 Thrifts," *American Banker,* January 23, 1984, p. 1.

40. Ibid.

41. Stephen Koepp, "Betting Billions on a Bank," *Time,* August 6, 1984, p. 48.

42. "Continental Illinois: Salvaged But Not Really Saved," *Business Week,* August 6, 1984, p. 20; and Ruth Simon, "Looking for Red Flags," *Forbes,* February 11, 1985, p. 43.

43. Stephen Koepp, "Banking Takes a Beating," *Time,* December 3, 1984, p. 58.

44. In "Banking in Transition," *The Bankers Magazine,* September–October 1978, p. 35.

45. Peter D. Schellie, *Manager's Guide to the 1980 Monetary Control Act* (Washington, D.C.: American Bankers Association, 1981), p. 23.

46. Ibid.

47. Elbert V. Bowden, *Revolution in Banking* (Richmond, Va.: Robert F. Dame, Inc., 1980), p. 120.

48. Andrew S. Carron, *The Plight of the Thrift Institutions* (Washington, D.C.: The Brookings Institution, 1982), p. 15.

49. Board of Governors of the Federal Reserve System, *The Monetary Control Act of 1980* (Washington, D.C., 1981), p. 1.

50. Excerpted from *Federal Reserve Bulletin,* June 1980, pp. 444–453.

51. A *share draft* is a negotiable, checklike instrument, drawn by a member of a credit union and used as a payment vehicle.

52. Prior to passage of this Act, *only* member banks had that borrowing privilege.

53. In *Federal Reserve Bulletin,* June 1980, p. 444.

54. J.A. Cacy and Scott Winningham, "Reserve Requirements Under the Depository Institutions Deregulation and Monetary Control Act of 1980," *Economic Review* (Federal Reserve Bank of Kansas City), September–October 1980, pp. 3–16.

55. Harvey Rosenblum, "Banks and Nonbanks: Who's in Control?," *The Bankers Magazine,* September–October 1984, p. 16.

56. Fed float results from the fact that the Fed gives sending banks availability of funds on deposited checks before each of those checks has been presented to drawees and collected. See Daniel M. Ferguson and Steven F. Maier, "Reducing the Risk in Corporate Disbursement Systems," *Bank Administration,* June 1984, p. 29.

57. Richard Gilgan, "Deregulation's Impact on Check Processing," *ABA Banking Journal,* June 1982, p. 35.

58. Chart, *American Banker,* April 9, 1984, p. 19.

59. Deborah J. Danker and Mary M. McLaughlin, "Profitability of Insured Commercial Banks in 1983," *Federal Reserve Bulletin,* November 1984, p. 804.

60. *Federal Reserve Bulletin,* September 1982, p. A13.

61. Danker and McLaughlin, op. cit.

62. Rosenblum, op. cit.

63. In Koepp, "Banking Takes a Beating," p. 50.

64. In Carol J. Loomis, "The Fight for Financial Turf," *Fortune,* December 28, 1981, p. 62.

65. Charles P. Alexander, "A Big Brawl in Banking," *Time,* January 17, 1983, pp. 34–35.

66. Danker and McLaughlin, op. cit.

67. Rosenblum, op. cit., p. 17.

68. Danker and McLaughlin, op. cit.

69. Depository Institutions Deregulation Committee, Press Release, Washington, D.C., October 3, 1983.

70. Thomas P. Vartanian, "If You're Thinking of Acquiring a Thrift," *ABA Banking Journal,* November 1983, pp. 70–74.

71. Thomas E. Boland; Dan W. Mitchell; and John E. Porta, "Banking 3Ds in the 1980s: Deregulation, Disclosure, and Dependency," *Journal of Commercial Bank Lending,* June 1984, p. 6.

72. L. Michael Cacace, "Citibank Tops B of A as Largest Bank in Yearend Asset Size," *American Banker,* March 2, 1984, p. 1.

73. Martha R. Seger, "Given Effective Legislative Controls, Interstate Access Will Help Banking," *American Banker,* January 4, 1985, p. 1.

74. Vartanian, op. cit., p. 72.

75. Henry C. Wallich, "Banks Need More Freedom to Compete," *Fortune,* March 1970, p. 114.

76. For additional discussions of this subject, see Charles S. Sanford, "Tradeoff for Banking System: Playing It Safe or Competitive?," *American Banker,* November 7, 1984, p. 12; and Bennett, op. cit., p. B1.

2
The New World of Funds Management

One fundamental reason for the chaotic conditions that existed in colonial banking lay in the degree of freedom given to banks by the early settlers. By treating banking on the same basis as other industries, they failed to recognize the essential differences that exist—for example, the element of public trust without which banking cannot operate and the vital role played by banks in the overall economy. It was not until 1863 that the first real systems of chartering and supervision were introduced.

Commercial banks today control by far the largest portion of the U.S. money supply, handle the bulk of the total payments function, serve as the custodians of public funds, create new demand deposits through their credit function, and accommodate businesses, governments, and consumers with every type of loan under virtually every set of conditions. The soundness of the system is critical to national well-being, and governments feel an obligation to preserve it. Every bank failure has a drastic and immediate effect on public confidence and the economy. For these reasons, regulation of banks by both federal and state authorities, while some observers may view it as excessive in a highly competitive and increasingly fragmented financial environment, is unquestionably needed.

If no external constraints of any kind were imposed on banks, however, an internal need would still exist for management to meet certain objectives through the effective use of the funds that have been made available to each institution. In essence, banking is a risk-taking business. Management has an unavoidable obligation to assess risks quantitatively and qualitatively and, through proper approaches to the problem of the bank's sources and uses of funds, to protect the institution's assets and the money entrusted to it by customers. Failure to do so can only result in the eventual liquidation of the bank, to the detriment of stockholders, depositors, and the economy.

The need for adequate programs of funds management is not new; the specifics have changed, in reaction to all the factors that affect each institution's daily operations. There are three basic objectives in these programs, and the contemporary measures taken to achieve them constitute a most important element in the New World of banking.

Goals of Funds Management

Liquidity

Individuals, governments, and businesses have in common the fact that they require available funds with which to meet their current obligations. The ability to do so with cash or with those assets readily convertible into cash is described as *liquidity*. The family budget, the cash flow projections of a corporation, and the fiscal and monetary policies of governments all reflect attempts to determine whether funds are or will be at hand to cover payments that must be made.

For commercial banks, liquidity assumes different proportions. A business may be able to defer making payments to creditors; a government may delay issuing tax refunds; an individual may postpone some obligations and selectively concentrate on those that are most urgent. No bank has this degree of latitude. The need for liquidity in banks reflects a realization that every deposit, regardless of size or type, must be repaid in one form or another at some time.

Demand deposits can be immediately converted into currency or drawn down at any time, without prior notice to the bank, through the issuing of checks. In the case of saving accounts, banks technically have the right to insist on advance notification of a depositor's intent to withdraw; however, that requirement is almost universally waived, and funds are made available to the customer on request. Time deposits must be repaid, with interest, as they mature. No bank can ever place itself in a position of being unable to honor any type of order for payment against deposits. Any refusal to honor depositors' demands for withdrawal will trigger a run on the bank and precipitate the institution's collapse.

At the same time, it is unrealistic and illogical for any bank to act on the premise that all demand, savings, and time deposits will be depleted at the same time. If a bank were to strive for absolute liquidity based on such an assumption, it would have to maintain excessive amounts of currency in its vaults, reserves at the Fed above the requirements, and large balances with its correspondents. Such a course of action would indeed provide maximum liquidity but would also lead to serious questions about the prudence of a policy that ignores the other objectives of funds management.

In addition to the need for liquidity as a means of meeting demands for payment against deposits, each commercial bank must approach the subject with another concern in mind—that is, its role as the primary supplier of credit to its customers. Many of these customers have dealt with the bank for years, have favored it with balances, have established their creditworthiness, and feel that they have a claim on it for loans when the need arises. Economic conditions and seasonal factors may dictate their patterns of borrowing, and the bank should be in a position to meet their legitimate credit needs. In addition, each bank has extended commitments and lines of credit to many of its customers that may be activated at any time, and the bank would place itself in a highly unfavorable position were it to renege on them. The need for liquidity, then, must address both the deposit and credit functions.

To determine their liquidity needs—that is, the amount of funds required to provide for deposit reductions and loan increases—banks attempt to forecast a potential deposit floor and a loan ceiling. The first of these involves a prediction, usually for a one-year period, of the low point to which total deposits will drop. The projection will consider maturities of time deposits, seasonal patterns of inflow and outflow of funds, possible disintermediation if nonbank vehicles offer more attractive yields, and any specifics peculiar to the community and the clientele served.

Similarly, calculating the loan ceiling requires that the bank use all available historical data, seasonal factors, and knowledge gained from customer contacts. The objective is to estimate the high point of portfolio exposure for the forthcoming period. The geographic area in which the bank functions and the types of customers with whom it deals are again important elements in the process. For example, a bank with a network of branches serving the jewelry and toy industries will display borrowing needs closely tied to the Christmas season, when inventories must be built up in anticipation of sales. A bank whose customers are primarily in farm areas will have an entirely different set of month-by-month projections.

Despite the ability of a bank's computer systems to create various scenarios and the variety of data that may be fed into those systems, the process of estimating total liquidity needs cannot be an exact science. Too many unforeseen events can take place in the national or local economy or in new forms of competition from other sources of financial services, thereby invalidating the forecasts. A sudden frost or drought can drastically affect the finances of farmers. A bank that serves a community in which a single major corporation operates is closely tied to the operations of that business. If the firm obtains an unexpected large order for its product, its need for credit and its bank balances will change; conversely, should a recession, new competition, or management problems force it to close its plant, the bank's projected liquidity needs must be completely revised. Unfortunately, there is no logical alternative to the best estimate process.

As is true with the other objectives of funds management, a bank must be conscious of the fact that there can easily be too much of a good thing. Liquidity is of paramount importance to a bank, but when it is overemphasized and the other objectives are neglected, problems result as both income and safety suffer. Money that is not put to profitable use is sterile. Coin and currency in vaults, excess balances left with the Fed, or large amounts maintained with correspondents produce no income, and the oversupply of currency raises the additional question of security.

To meet their liquidity needs, commercial banks have both *primary* and *secondary reserves* that can be called on whenever necessary. The first category consists of the three elements mentioned previously: cash on hand, accounts with other banks, and reserves at the Fed. These elements provide direct liquidity but do not generate income. Secondary reserves consist principally of short-term U.S. government obligations such as Treasury bills and, to a lesser extent, bankers' acceptances or other highest quality instruments that can be converted into cash almost immediately.

Safety

Safety, the second objective of funds management, is, like liquidity, essential in the prudent operations of banks. It resembles liquidity also in that it can be stressed at the expense of the other objectives, with highly detrimental results.

With very few exceptions, the loans and investments made by banks carry certain types and degrees of risks. Each risk must be analyzed so that both the institution and the funds entrusted to it by depositors will be protected. However, an overly conservative approach will ratify only those loans and investments that are as nearly free of risk as possible, and such a policy severely limits a bank's ability to generate profits. If maximum safety were to be sought, the bank would lose many of its customers who depend on it as their source of credit. In addition, a bank that adopted this policy would probably be in violation of the Community Reinvestment Act, the federal statute that requires that every financial institution try to satisfy the legitimate credit needs of its community by reinvesting funds in the geographic area from which they are drawn.

Income

Unlike their counterparts in other countries, banks in the United States are not nationalized; they are individual profit-making businesses, and income is as important to them as it is to any other industry. Stockholders expect a reasonable rate of return on their equity in a bank, and profits provide the only means of meeting their expectations. Retained earnings, built up over a period of time, form an important part of the bank's total capital base as a cushion against unforeseen events.

For reasons discussed in more detail later in this chapter, the words *profit margin* have assumed increased importance in today's banking and are critical not merely to the success but also to the actual survival of many institutions. Annual operating costs including labor, equipment, and occupancy increase each year, as do interest payouts to depositors. Management must devise and implement strategies so that they know the costs of doing business and how to cope with these escalating expenses.

As a further illustration of the interdependence of the three objectives in the management of bank funds, it must be noted that income from loans has always been the major source of profits. Table 2–1 shows the extent to which this single factor contributes to total income for all insured commercial banks.

If considerations of liquidity and safety were neglected and a bank concentrated solely on income, it could simply lower its credit criteria and open its doors to applications who would not otherwise qualify. There is never a shortage of potential borrowers. Any bank that wishes to display increased earnings and portfolio growth can make its relaxed credit standards known and attract new customers as a result. However, this course of action, while it may produce short-term benefits in the income statement, eventually leads to large amounts of charge-offs when the weak loans prove uncollectible. In addition, an examination of the bank's portfolio by federal or state agencies would reveal that substandard credits were being approved, thus causing the institution to be placed on the problem list.

As mentioned earlier, historical evidence illustrates the results of this overemphasis on income. Prior to passage of the Glass-Steagall Act, commercial banks often vied with one another in offering interest on demand deposits. To offset the interest expense, they liberalized their credit standards and accepted questionable loans. The prohibition on demand-deposit interest was a reaction to this problem. In retrospect, that same prohibition eventually became the reason for the disintermediation out of non-interest-bearing accounts that has become a prominent characteristic of the contemporary banking scene.

In sum, funds management requires a high degree of skill in the daily bal-

Table 2–1
Analysis of Income Factors, All Insured Commercial Banks, 1979–1983

Factor	*1979*	*1980*	*1981*	*1982*	*1983*
Total operating income ($ billions)	$150	$190.1	$247.9	$257.2	$239.3
Total interest income ($ billions)	137.4	174.4	228.7	235.1	214.1
Total loan interest ($ billions)	101.9	126.7	163.2	166.6	151.4
Loan interest as a percentage of total operating income	67.9%	66.6%	65.8%	64.8%	63.3%
Loans as a percentage of average total assets	N.A.	55.4	55.2	56.1	55.7

Source: Deborah J. Danker and Mary M. McLaughlin, "Profitability of Insured Commercial Banks in 1983," *Federal Reserve Bulletin,* November 1984, p. 812.

ancing of all three objectives and in the resolving of the conflicts that often arise among them. A bank's stockholders make no secret of their desire for higher earnings leading to increased dividends; yet at the same time they logically expect that everything possible will be done to protect their investment. By the same token, bank investments in long-term U.S. government obligations fully meet the need for safety since there is no *credit risk*. The full faith and credit of the federal government are pledged toward repayment. These bonds, however, do create a degree of *market risk* and affect both liquidity and income. The bank cannot predict with certainty the price the bonds might bring if sold, nor can it be sure that other investment media, offering higher yields, will not be available at the time of the sale, so that marketability is diminished.

If conflicts exist between the need for safety and the desire for profitability, prudence would clearly suggest that any errors be made on the side of the former.[1] This fundamental principle apparently was ignored in most of the classic cases of bank failures in recent years.

Sources of Bank Funds

Capital

When a bank is in the process of incorporation, the initial group of stockholders makes an investment, equal to or greater than the legal requirement, in the first shares of stock. The funds are used to meet start-up expenses. Subsequently, retained earnings, issues of additional stock, and various reserves are added to the original amount. These components, in total, comprise what is now classified as *primary capital.*

Further increases in a bank's capital base may take place through the issuing of various types of fixed- or floating-rate notes and debentures, which are interest-bearing obligations of the bank, with a fixed claim on earnings and assets.[2] These form the basic elements in *secondary capital.*

Total capital—equity and debt—in banks can be compared to a corporation's net worth because it represents the excess of total assets over total liabilities and is the ultimate protection against insolvency. Again, however, there is a very significant difference between banks and other forms of business. On a nationwide basis, bank capital normally ranges between 5 percent and 9 percent of total assets, which means that 91–95 percent of assets are financed through liabilities. For this reason, banking is often referred to as a highly *leveraged* industry. By contrast, a typical manufacturing company might have a ratio of net worth to assets some three times higher, so that one-third or less of its assets would be financed through borrowings.[3]

The amount of a bank's capital is important to stockholders as a measure of the institution's financial strength, to depositors as evidence of the protection of their funds, and to management as a source that can be utilized. The amount of capital has recently assumed increased importance in the eyes of regulatory authorities. Reports of mounting loan losses, which eat into capital, and of huge global loans that may become losses have brought the question of capital adequacy to the forefront in Washington, D.C. The guidelines of the Comptroller of the Currency, the FDIC, and the Federal Reserve suggested, in early 1985, that a ratio of 5.5 percent primary capital plus 0.5 percent secondary capital was desirable for all commercial banks.[4] Severe loan losses at two of the nation's largest banks prompted even more stringent requirements in 1984; the Comptroller directed those banks to establish ratios of 6 percent in primary capital alone.[5] In February 1985, the Comptroller, the FDIC, and the Fed jointly ruled that all commercial banks must maintain a capital ratio of 6 percent.[6]

A bank's maximum loan to any one borrower is a direct function of the amount of its capital. For national banks, U.S. Revised Statutes, Section 5200, limited unsecured loans to a maximum of 10 percent of capital and surplus. Most states had comparable restrictions. In 1982, however, the Garn–St Germain Act revised this restriction so that unsecured loans to a single borrower can be made up to 15 percent of capital and surplus, with larger amounts allowable if the borrower can provide collateral.

Capital increases enhance the financial soundness of banks, but achieving them poses further problems. Using continued retention of profits and/or issues of additional common stock as the sources of such increases creates immediate difficulties. If, for example, the focus is placed on retained earnings, pressure for higher profits results, and the interrelationship of safety and income again comes into play, simply because the highest profits invariably result from assumption of higher degrees of risk.

Additional issuing of common stock as a means of increasing a bank's capital carries with it certain risks that must be considered. First, any such issue would provoke objections from existing stockholders on the grounds that their investments were being diluted. Furthermore, the possibility exists that the new issue would not be favorably received by the investment community, in which case the bank's image would immediately suffer.

If price/earnings ratios in the marketplace are a criterion, bank stocks as a group trade on a basis significantly lower than the securities of other issuers, and stockholders might greet a new issue with limited enthusiasm. This situation is particularly true in the 1980s, when the public perception of bank stocks as prudent investments has weakened considerably. This perception reflects a growing uneasiness with the soundness of the banking system and a concern over the ability of banks to cope with contemporary problems. The introduction to this text alluded to a lessening of public confidence, and the results of a survey conducted among 1,219 affluent individuals by the

Gallup Organization, Inc., in August 1984 reinforce the point. In that survey, 58 percent of the respondents stated that they had lost confidence in the stability and safety of banks in recent years; 64 percent attributed considerable risk or some risk to investing in the stocks of large banks, as opposed to 53 percent for utility stocks, 48 percent for municipal bonds, and 42 percent for local real estate.[7]

Alternatively, if common stock, rather than preferred stock, were to be issued as the means of increasing capital, the bank would be faced with a need to meet additional stockholders' expectations of annual dividends, thus creating further pressures on earnings to offset that expense.

Increases in loan-loss reserves, within the limits allowed by law, may be used to broaden the capital base. All such increases generate corresponding reductions in net income, however.

One final possibility involves a bank's reduction of its total asset size to reach the desired ratio. This may be done through the sale of loans or other assets or simply through the adoption of a more selective policy in extending all types of credit to customers. The latter course of action could prove harmful to the economic base served by the bank by diminishing the role it serves in meeting the needs of borrowers.

Deposits

Chronologically, the second source of bank funds is the base consisting of all types of deposits; after capital requirements for the establishment of the bank have been met and all necessary approvals obtained from regulatory authorities, the institution immediately embarks on a program of business development aimed at attracting the deposits it needs. In terms of importance, however, this deposit base outranks all other sources of funds. As previously noted, this is the aspect of the overall operations of U.S. banks in which the most dramatic single change has occurred in recent years. The inexorable movement of funds from the basic non-interest-bearing demand deposits to various types of interest-yielding relationships has brought about a massive and permanent readjustment in the banker's approach to the problem of funding the institution. The introduction of the negotiable CD in large denominations, and the subsequent availability to the public of NOW and Super-NOW accounts and MMDAs have all played a part, so bankers can no longer rely on the historic inflow of relatively free deposits—relatively free because they were left with banks in exchange for certain basic services.

In a hypothetical case, a product manufacturer might be seen in the fortunate position of being able to obtain the raw materials necessary for the conduct of the business without direct costs; thus, the manufacturer would achieve maximum profitability. If the situation were to change and the raw material became subject to direct costs, the manufacturer would immediately find it necessary to revise the entire structure of his or her product prices to purchasers. There is an exact parallel in this case to the recent history of commercial banking. The banker must now buy the raw material in a competitive market, and the so-called new breed of bank customer—whether corporate, governmental, institutional, or consumer—knows the value of funds to the bank and uses deposits to obtain value, usually in the form of direct interest payouts.

For the U.S. banking system as a whole, demand deposits, as a percentage of the total base, stood at 26.9 percent at the beginning of 1983 and at 25.02 percent at the end of that year.[8] Therefore, three-quarters of all deposits at commercial banks now consist of purchased money, and only one-quarter comes from the interest-free source that traditionally formed the core of funds management.

In addition to the internal disintermediation occurring in a bank through transfers of funds from checking accounts to any of the various types of interest-bearing relationships, external reasons contribute to the fundamental change in deposit structure. For example, the corporate treasurer now uses many of the techniques of cash management, which ironically, the banks marketed to him or her, as a means of keeping demand-deposit balances to a minimum.[9] Furthermore, bank loans to major corporate borrowers traditionally required compensating balances in proportion to the size of the line of credit or actual loan—for example, 10 percent of a line or 20 percent of borrowings. Today, the corporate treasurer negotiates with banks on an all-in-the-rate basis, possibly paying a higher rate of direct interest but simultaneously freeing up balances that can be put to profitable use.

For consumers, the former requirement that checks be drawn only against demand deposits has disappeared, and they can now enjoy the best of both worlds: competitive interest rates on funds that can be drawn down at any time. Similarly, the use of ATS (Automatic Transfer Service) relationships has enabled consumers to benefit; arrangements can be made with banks for automatic transfers of funds from savings to checking accounts whenever the latter need replenishing.

The change in the deposit structure has necessarily brought about a corollary transformation in the profit-and-loss figures for commercial banks. In 1946, interest payments represented 15 percent of the total expenses of all insured commercial banks; in 1962, when the effects of the introduction of jumbo (large-denomination) CDs were first noted, the percentage rose to 34; and by 1971 it had reached 45.[10] Since then, as noted in table 2–2, the ratio has become far more significant.

Interest paid to depositors is not only the largest single component of bank expense but also the least controllable. All signals point to a continuation of the relative shrinkage of demand deposits as every category of bank customer takes advantage of yield opportunities. The rates banks must pay to

Table 2–2
Expenses, Insured Commercial Banks, 1979–1983

Factor	*1979*	*1980*	*1981*	*1982*	*1983*
Total operating expenses ($ billions)	$132	$170.7	$227.7	$238	$220.2
Interest paid on deposits ($ billions)	71.7	98.1	139	141.1	119.8
Interest paid as a percentage of total operating expenses	54.3	57.5	61	59.3	54.4

Source: Deborah J. Danker and Mary M. McLaughlin, "Profitability of Insured Commercial Banks in 1983," *Federal Reserve Bulletin,* November 1984, p. 812.

attract or maintain deposits are a function of external money-market conditions over which the banks have no control.

As purchasers of deposits, which always represent their largest liability, commercial banks and thrift institutions must now place major emphasis on knowing the effective costs of the funds required on a daily basis and on determining the most effective means of recovering those costs with a profit margin. Liability management has therefore become a key element in today's banking environment, and traditional ways of doing business no longer suffice.

Borrowings

In addition to capital and deposits as sources of funds, banks may resort to various types of direct *borrowings.* One commonly used method involves applications to the Federal Reserve for short-term credit.

Regulation A of the Fed establishes the conditions for all such borrowings. The Monetary Control Act of 1980 supplemented that Regulation by imposing additional constraints to prevent any abuses of the borrowing privilege. The word *privilege* is used here advisedly; approval by the Fed of any loan request from a financial institution is not automatic, and banks that apply too frequently can be denied further credit. All loans from the Fed must be secured by specified types of eligible collateral and are subject to the prevailing discount rate.

Financial institutions may also borrow directly from one another or through the Fed Funds market. In the latter case, a bank that finds itself short of the level of required reserves or that draws down its reserves to meet immediate needs borrows from another institution that happens to have excess reserves. These Fed Funds transactions are almost invariably overnight dealings. In 1963 James J. Saxon, then Comptroller of the Currency, ruled that all national banks could consider Fed Funds transactions as purchases by the borrowing bank and sales by the lender; therefore, there was no longer a need to show them on the balance sheet. This ruling gave strong impetus to the Fed Funds market.

Asset/Liability Management

The management of bank funds traditionally focused largely on the asset side of the balance sheet, simply because liquidity could always be achieved through conversion of investments and loans into cash through sales, collection, or assignments as collateral. Demand deposits, the basic source of funds, typically displayed enough growth, on a year-to-year basis, to provide the needed operating wherewithal.

Until 1951, the Federal Reserve was required by law to redeem all government obligations at par value, at any time, without regard for market prices. Therefore, banks concentrated on these investments without fear of losses due to market prices. The Accord of 1951 between the Treasury Department and the Fed abrogated this requirement by eliminating the system of fixed-price support so that all government obligations traded openly in a free market. This Accord immediately brought about a change in the composition of the typical bank balance sheet.

For comparison, table 2–3 shows the total deposits, loans, and investments in government obligations of U.S. commercial banks in selected years, beginning with the start of World War II. It is noteworthy that at the end of that war, the amount of government obligations held by banks represented over one-third of the national debt.[11]

As long as the inflow of demand deposits provided the banks with an adequate reservoir of usable funds, and as long as government obligations could be sold quickly at guaranteed prices, banks achieved liquidity with relative ease. However, the Accord of 1951 eliminated the latter facility, and the era that began in 1961 with the introduction of the large-denomination CD was also the era during which disintermediation from commercial banks began to manifest itself in the face of steadily growing competition from other financial intermediaries. It was also the period of increasing demands for bank credit, so the ratio of loans to deposits changed dramatically.

Examples of the competition that banks encountered during the post–World War II period are plentiful and are illustrative of the minimal attention they gave to an expanding consumer population. Thrift institutions and credit unions were quick to capitalize on this perceived neglect. From 1946 to 1971 total deposits at commercial banks increased only 3.76 times, while those at the nation's S&Ls increased 21.8 times.[12] From 1950 to 1970, total deposits at credit unions grew from $1 billion to $15 billion.[13]

Table 2–3
Selected Statistics, All Commercial Banks, 1941–1961

Year	*Total Deposits ($ billions)*	*Total Loans ($ billions)*	*Loan/Deposit Ratio*	*Total U.S. Governments ($ billions)*	*U.S. Governments/ Deposits Ratio*
1941	$71.2	$21.7	30.5%	$21.8	30.6%
1942	72.3	20.3	28.1	26.4	36.5
1943	96.1	17.7	18.4	52.5	54.6
1944	116.1	21.0	18.1	68.4	58.9
1945	136.6	23.7	17.3	84.1	61.6
1946	142.9	27.1	19.0	84.5	59.1
1953	160.8	67.6	42.0	63.4	39.4
1955	175.6	82.6	47.0	61.6	35.1
1957	184.3	93.9	50.9	58.2	31.6
1959	202.8	110.8	54.6	58.9	29.0
1961	230.3	124.9	54.2	66.6	28.9

Source: Paul Studenski and Herman E. Krooss, *Financial History of the United States,* 2nd ed. (New York: McGraw-Hill Book Company, Inc., 1963); 1941–1946 data from p. 456; 1953–1961 data from p. 553.

As table 2–3 illustrates, commercial banks in the years prior to 1961 could easily use the investment portfolio as a type of liquidity valve, selling securities as necessary to meet growing demands for credit. Thereafter, the emphasis on funding gradually shifted to various types of borrowings as a source of funds. For many years, corporations of unquestioned credit standing had used commercial paper (i.e., short-term unsecured promissory notes) as a means of borrowing, thereby dealing directly with one another and bypassing the banking system. It may be noted parenthetically that in late 1984 the total volume of outstanding commercial paper stood at $228 billion.[14] During the 1960s, the bank holding company (BHC) became the preferred type of organizational structure, and BHCs began to issue their own commercial paper as a means of raising funds for the banks, which were their major components. In that same era, the Eurodollar, discussed in detail in chapter 4, began its rise to prominence, and U.S. banks began to borrow Eurodollars from their foreign sources.

The 1970s witnessed credit crunches of dramatic proportions, intensifying the pressures on banks to raise funds while simultaneously achieving the appropriate profit margins in putting those funds to use. The emphasis on an integrated approach to asset and liability management increased steadily, and the concept of *matched funding*—the use of short-term assets against short-term liabilities and long-term assets against long-term liabilities and stockholders' equity—spread rapidly. Prior to the basic change in deposit structure, the liabilities of commercial banks had not been particularly sensitive to rates; with the gradual but steady shift away from a demand-deposit core, the matter of rate sensitivity received far more attention. The chronic problem of the thrift institutions—that is, borrowing short (paying competitive prices for deposits) to lend long (funding fixed-rate, long-term home mortgages paying lower rates)—reached its peak in the early 1980s, and commercial bankers were forced to implement policies designed to prevent any similar situation in their institutions. For example, long-term, fixed-rate loans were far less acceptable to banks, and they introduced various forms of variable- or floating-rate loans.

The fundamental concept of asset/liability management can best be explained through a simple example. Assume that a bank has a single interest-sensitive liability in the form of a 90-day CD for $100,000, paying 10 percent, and a single loan for the same amount, maturing in 180 days and yielding 12 percent. In the first 90-day period, the bank earns net interest income of $500 (loan interest, $3,000; interest payout, $2,500). If interest rates rise during that period, the holder of the CD can be expected to roll it over at the new competitive rate of 14 percent; however, the loan interest rate remains constant at 12 percent. At the end of the second 90-day period, the bank shows negative net interest income of $500 and its former profit is wiped out.

This example may illustrate the problem of interest-rate sensitivity, but it ignores the fundamental reality of banking, which must deal with a multitude of liabilities and assets at the same time rather than with only one on each side of the balance sheet.

Deposits are always fungible. The depositors cannot expect to receive at withdrawal the exact same currency he or she originally left with the bank, and a single asset cannot be directly matched against a single liability in virtually all cases. The problem is exacerbated by the facts that equity and non-interest-bearing deposits also provide funds and that interest on both assets and liabilities may be received or paid before the stated maturity.

One suggested solution to the problem takes the form of a division or grouping of balance sheet items, first according to maturity and then according to sensitivity to rate changes. For example, one category on the asset side would include all short-term loans and highly liquid investments. This grouping could then be subdivided to distinguish fixed-rate from floating-rate loans. A similar breakdown could be made of long-term credits and less liquid investments. On the liability side, the same process would categorize the various types of deposits and segregate all equity items. In this way, an attempt is made to balance interest-sensitive assets with comparable liabilities so that wide changes in rates will not have a negative effect on earnings.[15] A perfect matching of specified assets with specified liabilities may be unattainable; however, the approach outlined here can result in a major step forward toward what has become known as *gap management*. The so-called gaps represent the spreads between interest-sensitive assets and liabilities.[16]

To assist financial institutions in addressing the problem of liquidity and determining risks, computer-based systems can be of tremendous value. They can create a wide variety of what-if? scenarios, using input on possible rate changes and buildups of asset and liability components to display the effects of gaps and suggest methods of managing them. These systems can quickly identify mismatches among the components so that banks can take appropriate steps toward adjustment.

Effects of Implementation

Bankers today must recognize that the liability side of the balance sheet will undoubtedly become even more rate-sensitive as both deregulation and competition have their impacts on the industry. As rate ceilings are lifted, with the possibility that there may be a return to the former practice of paying interest on demand deposits, and as other types of financial service institutions proliferate and compete aggressively for deposits, commercial banks will find they need even more sophisticated techniques of funds management.

Although the implementation of these techniques directly affects every phase of daily bank operations, the two largest balance sheet items—deposits and loans—are those on which the results are greatest and most obvious. Daily decisions about what types of deposits to seek and what prices to pay for them can be made by using the answers gained through the funds management process. Similarly, the composition of the loan portfolio and the bank's pricing structure on all types of loans can be adjusted wherever necessary. The knowledge of funding costs is an integral part of the lending process.[17] If banks are to achieve profits, then the spread between earnings on loans and interest payouts (commonly referred to as Net Interest Margin, or NIM) is critical.

During the first four years of the 1980s, loans accounted for an average of 55.6 percent of the consolidated assets of all U.S. commercial banks,[18] and in 1982 and 1983 the loan-to-deposit ratios for those banks were 73.5 percent and 73.9 percent respectively.[19] Given this degree of importance, banks must make the right strategic decisions on every aspect of their lending activities. The effects of funds management on the overall planning process in banking, and specifically on the credit function, are referred to again in chapter 7.

Summary

In essence, banking is nothing more than a funds-gathering and funds-using business. Money is acquired through capital, deposits, and borrowings, and the task is to use it to the best advantage. In putting available funds to work, a systematic program of funds management, in which liquidity, safety, and income are carefully interrelated, is essential.

If any one of the three objectives of funds management becomes overemphasized at the expense of the others, the bank inevitably suffers. The program of funds mangement takes into account all the changes in the institution's own deposit structure, because interest expense has assumed steadily increasing importance, and conditions in the money markets, over which the bank has no control.

Thrift institutions, in particular, experienced serious problems during the early 1980s because of the negative profit margin that resulted from the spread between the income on their loan portfolios and their costs of acquiring or retaining deposits. Commercial banks, in their efforts to avoid similar problems, now devote a great deal of attention to the problem of profit margins. They must consistently analyze their need for funds, the costs of those funds, and the yield to be derived from the use of available funds.

Because of the failures of many banks during the 1980s, federal and state regulators began to place increased emphasis on the capital adequacy as reported by each institution. Each bank must consider various ways of increasing its capital base and evaluate the advantages or disadvantages of each method.

Traditionally, banking concentrated on asset management. There was a steady inflow of the deposits the banks needed, and the principal task consisted of putting those deposits selectively to work. Today, the emphasis has shifted. Bankers must combine asset management and liability management, and make every effort to use a combination of term data and yield data so that matched funding of assets with liabilities takes place.

Each bank's statement of income and expenses clearly shows that interest income (from loans) and interest expense (paid to all categories of depositors) are the two most important elements. Therefore, the program of funds management concentrates on the lending and investment strategies that will best enable the institution to meet its profit goals. The cost of raw material (principally deposits) and the profits resulting from its use (principally through loans) must be evaluated on a continuing basis.

Notes

1. Roland I. Robinson, *The Management of Bank Funds,* 2nd ed. (New York, McGraw-Hill Book Company, Inc., 1962), p. 13.

2. These debt instruments have priority over both common and preferred stock in a bank liquidation but are subordinated to the claims of depositors. See Howard D. Crosse and George H. Hempel, *Management Policies for Commercial Banks,* 2nd ed. (Englewood Cliffs, N.J.: Prentice-Hall, Inc., 1973), p. 301.

3. Jay M. McDonald and John E. McKinley, *Corporate Banking: A Practical Approach to Lending* (Washington, D.C., American Bankers Association, 1981), p. 8.

4. Maggie McComas, "More Capital Won't Cure What Ails Banks," *Fortune,* January 7, 1985, p. 80.

5. Ibid.

6. "New Rule for Banks," *The New York Times,* February 11, 1985, p. D17.

7. In William E. Blundell, "As Basic Institutions . . . and Banks Change, Public Chafes," *Wall Street Journal,* February 5, 1985, p. 1. See also G. David Wallace, "More Capital for Banks: The Cure May Be Worse than the Disease," *Business Week,* January 28, 1985, p. 54.

8. *Federal Reserve Bulletin,* December 1984, p. A18.

9. The range of cash management services in banks is discussed in detail in chapter 8.

10. Federal Deposit Insurance Corporation, *Annual Report* (selected years from 1946 to 1971).

11. Martin Mayer, *The Bankers* (New York: David McKay & Co., 1974), p. 187.

12. Carter H. Golembe, "The Organization of Modern Banking," in Herbert V. Prochnow and Herbert V. Prochnow, Jr., eds., *The Changing World of Banking* (New York, Harper & Row, 1974), p. 14.

13. Paul H. Nadler, *Commercial Banking in the Economy* (New York, Random House, 1968), p. 153. See also Edward W. Reed; Richard V. Cotter; Edward K. Gill; and Richard K. Smith, *Commercial Banking* (Englewood Cliffs, N.J.: Prentice-Hall, Inc., 1976), p. 84.

14. *Federal Reserve Bulletin,* January 1985, p. A24.

15. George W. McKinney; William J. Brown; and Paul M. Horvitz, *Management of Commercial Bank Funds,* 2nd ed. (Washington, D.C.: American Bankers Association, 1980), pp. 301–307.

16. Robert P. Prince, "A Portfolio Approach to Asset/Liability Management," *Mid-Continent Banker,* January 1985, pp. 45–49.

17. Thomas F. Brady, "Changes in Loan Pricing and Business Lending at Commercial Banks," *Federal Reserve Bulletin,* January 1985, pp. 1–13.

18. Danker and McLaughlin, op. cit.

19. *Federal Reserve Bulletin,* December 1984, p. A25.

3
The New World of Strategic Planning

The evidences of change in commercial banking since 1960 are overwhelming. The basic deposit structure has changed, once and for all, largely due to the introduction of the large-scale negotiable CD; EFTS applications have been implemented in many cases; bank debit and credit cards have proliferated; Eurodollars have become a major source of funds; global debt problems have surfaced in huge proportions; major developments have occurred in the banks' efforts to gain parity with their competitors in interstate operations, while the latter have grown in numbers and importance; and deregulation has taken place, at least in part.

There is equally incontrovertible evidence of an area in which the banks, generally speaking, have persisted in a type of management by crisis and have ignored the lessons that could have been learned from major corporations. This area of neglect involves the concept and implementation of strategic planning.

One of the classic ironies in U.S. banking history is that borrowing customers traditionally have been expected to provide documentation of their ability to generate future earnings by anticipating and coping with change, while the bankers who looked for such documentation could not point to similar planning efforts in their institutions. Borrowers, in essence, were expected to plan ahead even though that same discipline was usually lacking among the lenders.[1]

A study conducted from 1976 to 1978 among ninety-seven large commercial banks disclosed that 60 percent either had not implemented any strategic planning system or had done so only within the previous three years.[2] In a similar survey of 302 banks having assets of $10 million or more in 1980, two-thirds of the respondents reported no effort at planning beyond a two-year time frame; among the banks with assets of over $500 million, 40 percent fell into the same category.[3] In a third study by a bank consultant, only 3 of the 107 respondents had developed clear and specific objectives for the ensuing three years, and only 13 percent had drawn up definite statements of their purposes or missions. This study took place in 1982, by which time every one of the major developments mentioned earlier had contributed to the revolution in the financial services industry and the banks had lost much of their previous exclusivity and market share.[4]

During the hectic 1970s, the then Chairman of the FDIC identified that decade as being as productive of change in banking as the previous fourteen[5]; yet in an unfortunately large number of cases the banks continued to operate on what appears to have been a bland assumption that the future would somehow take care of itself. Efforts to anticipate it, prepare for it, and devise techniques to react to it were strangely lacking.[6] Among banks with assets of $200 million or less, in particular, that same assumption may still have existed in 1984; an accounting firm study of 270 such banks disclosed that almost one-third of them devoted no attention to asset/liability management beyond following a general policy of keeping maturities short.[7]

The underlying rationale for a widespread failure to systematize strategic planning among banks, as seen in the responses in a 1981 study, lies in the belief that too many external factors (e.g., changing economic conditions and wide fluctuations in money markets) beyond the bankers' control can negate the benefits of any plans that might be drawn up.[8] In other cases, banks have explained their failure to plan by citing a lack of trained personnel and an already excessive burden of work required to meet the demands of all the federal and state regulatory authorities.[9] Again, these excuses reflect banking's failure to learn from other industries, where the planning function has been found to be indispensable. A survey of 280 chief executives in 1972 revealed that two-thirds identified planning as their most important single activity, requiring 44 percent of their time.[10]

In the face of all the empirical data regarding the dynamics of change in the financial services industry, it is disheartening to note that many banks still pay little attention to planning, while their competitors, in particular in areas such as insurance, retailing, and brokerage, not only are developing long-range plans but also are implementing them in ways that can result only in further shrinkage in banking's share of the financial marketplace.

No system of strategic planning will ever be foolproof. No guarantees can be given that the plans that are prepared are infallible. The most carefully constructed forecasts, on which the strategies and tactics of the organization are based, can be negated by unforeseen events. Conversely, to neglect the planning function and thereby perpetuate the syndrome of management by crisis is to invite further, and even severer, problems for commercial banks in an era of new, intense competition, deregulation, changing deposit mix, and interest-rate volatility. As expressed by one observer,

> A storm of change is overtaking the banking industry. . . . Managers cannot simply ride this one out in the hope that its turbulence will end and business will return to normal.[11]

The remarks of Stephen C. Fuller, formerly of Harvard's Graduate School of Business Administration and subsequently Vice-President in charge of all personnel for General Motors Corporation, apply to banks at least as well as to other industries:

> One of the most significant responsibilities of any management is to make sure that the strategies and tactics of the organization are not only perceiving changes, but anticipating them.[12]

Corporate Culture

In recent years, many bankers have introduced *corporate culture* into their lexicons. These words have been used to designate the total set of beliefs, values, and assumptions that determine how a business operates. For U.S. commercial banks, this culture was relatively stable, reflecting the stability of the environment of which they were part. Asset management was relatively simple, demand deposits flowed in steadily, customer loyalties were strong and enduring, competition was minimal, technology (compared with that found in the 1980s) was evolving with relative slowness, and bank employees tended to stay with their employers for long periods of time. Adaptability and orientation toward change were not normally required of managers.[13]

For these reasons, the lack of attention to strategic planning may perhaps be more easily understood, if not entirely condoned. If the previously expressed comments regarding that neglect seem unduly critical, the views of Vice-Chairman James Weisler of Bank of America may be of interest. He has described the traditional culture of many banking institutions as being that of a paternalistic type of organization

> [W]here mediocrity is condoned, . . . where there is a big emphasis on short-term profits at the expense of long-term investment, where there is limited understanding of . . . marketing, and where the emphasis is on tactical rather than strategic thinking.[14]

Wherever this type of corporate culture exists, the need for modification is clear and urgent. The most unaffordable luxury in today's banking environment is traditionalist thinking. A corporate culture that remains rooted in the business-as-usual philosophy must be revised to adjust to the new world of the financial services industry. Numerous predictions point to a substantial reduction in the number of commercial banks in the 1990s,[15] and these forecasts reflect a belief that the institutions most likely to fall by the wayside are those whose managers have been unwilling or unable to anticipate and cope with change. Indeed, those bankers who press for further deregulation must realize that their demands presuppose an ability to manage not only today's challenges but also the added challenges that would result from greater freedom to operate.[16]

Defining Strategic Planning

In 1976 the Corporate Planning Executive Committee of the American Bankers Association drew up the following comprehensive definition of strategic planning:

> [It is] the process of determining the overall mission and major objectives of an organization, as well as the policies that will determine the acquisition, use, and disposition of resources to achieve those objectives. . . . Because the purpose of strategic planning is to provide direction for more specialized types of planning, its scope is broad, its time frame is long, and its nature may be characterized as conceptual.[17]

Strategic planning, therefore, provides a systematic approach to decision making so that an organization can establish its future direction. Such planning unifies the discrete components of a bank or company into a functioning whole and outlines the means for attaining management's desired objectives.[18]

These definitions and explanations may serve to correct some of the misunderstandings about strategic planning that have been identified in the past. It is not budgeting, although budgeting is closely related to it and may flow from it. It is not forecasting, although forecasting is one of its necessary components. It is not necessarily the cure-all for a bank or corporation that is experiencing difficulties, although it can lead to solutions for problems. It is rather a management technique designed to commit resources to action to arrive at certain clearly defined objectives.[19]

If the strategic planning process is to work, there must be a thorough commitment to it from the highest level of corporate or bank management. Managing and planning are inseparable. The word *strategies* identifies the courses of action the organization is to follow, and the Chief Executive Officer (CEO) must be the principal strategist who sets the pace and who clearly and effectively communicates to the entire staff his or her total commitment.[20] If this identified and understood involvement on the part of the CEO is lacking in the process, then the CEO can expect little more than lip service from subordinate levels.

This is not to suggest that the CEO should assume responsibility for every phase of the function, however. Indeed, the concept of participatory management should be directly applied to planning. Individuals whose careers and lives are directly affected by the outcomes of the process should have opportunities to contribute to it. Depending on the size of the institution, planning committees, consisting of officers at several levels, may be appointed, and their input should be given full consideration.

Benefits of Strategic Planning

Does concrete evidence exist to show the tangible benefits of a well-designed, effectively communicated, properly implemented, and carefully monitored strategic plan? According to analysis of the data regarding thirty-five banks whose deposits ranged from $400 million to $4 billion in the 1976–1980 period, the answer is affirmative. The benefits appear to have been in direct proportion to the attention devoted to planning; the four banks that had concentrated most heavily on planning displayed significant growth in Return on Equity (ROE) and were able to reward their stockholders with increased dividends.[21] Unlike their counterparts who neglected the process, these banks focused on it and reaped the rewards.

If the planning process is to prove fruitful, however, the CEO must make it clear that growth statistics alone are not viewed as its purpose. Instead, his or her communication with the planning committee and the staff should also identify the many intangibles: the sense of definite mission, direction, and purpose that can flow from it and the fact that the discipline in thinking that the process requires is, in itself, a contribution to the institution's success.[22]

Steps in the Process

Before a bank makes any direct attempts at introducing strategic planning, the responsible individuals should re-examine some of the fundamental assumptions on which the industry has traditionally operated and reject those that are no longer valid. For example, the banker who felt that his or her only competitors were the other commercial banks in the community must recognize that other, possibly more formidable, entities are vying for a share of the financial activity. Those bankers who have staked the ongoing growth and profitability of their institutions on continued customer loyalty must revise their thinking, giving weight instead to the degree of sophistication that now exists in the marketplace. Those who believed that the planning process was little more than an exercise in asset/liability management and/or a series of programs aimed at cutting costs must come to a realization that much more can be done and needs to be done. Those who may have felt that fee income would never contribute significantly to earnings or that it was unnecessary for them to merchandise the bank's range of services must develop a different viewpoint, more in keeping with the realities of the industry today.[23]

The changing nature of the financial services environment presents new opportunities, not merely new problems. This situation creates a need for willingness among the bankers to depart from traditional beliefs and approaches and to meet change with creative, innovative responses.[24] With that statement as background, the strategic planning process can move to a thorough self-evaluation, through which the bank tries to answer the basic question, Where are we now?[25] The range of additional questions that flow from this one is almost limitless.

What is the real nature of the bank's business today? What are the organization's strengths and weaknesses? What resources does it have and how effectively is it utilizing them? How is the bank perceived by its customers, by other banks, by financial industry analysts, and by its staff? Is the balance sheet properly structured, according to the need for adequate systems of asset/liability management?[26] Which market segments is the bank trying to serve? How successful has it been in serving them? Is the present organizational structure producing the desired results for the institution?

This evaluative process should employ all possible internal and external sources of information. The bank's management information systems should supply data on the profits or losses of each department and branch and the results of providing each service product. Key changes in the composition of the bank's profit-and-loss statement can be identified and the causes determined. Trends in key ratios and profit margins for the preceding five years should be reviewed.

To supplement the internal data, Federal Reserve and FDIC statistical reports can be used to measure the bank's performance against institutions of a similar size in the same geographic area and in the nation. Outside consultants may assist materially by conducting market research to determine the existing degree of satisfaction among the bank's customers, the likelihood that they would turn to it for additional services, and its image as customers perceive it: overly stodgy and conservative or highly innovative, strongly customer-oriented or autocratic and aloof, prompt and efficient or slow and negligent in handling inquiries and adjustments, a leader or a follower. Superimposed on the Where are we now? scenario is the candid assessment by the bank's managers of any existing conditions that inhibit growth and profits, the application of regulatory and statutory constraints on operations, and a statement of likely changes in the regulatory climate.

Planners must also consider a wide range of economic and demographic projections. What changes appear probable in the demand for credit, in interest rates, in the competitive environment, and in the local, national, or global economy? What rate of inflation is predicted? What population shifts are taking place in the community? Will businesses, especially the large ones, remain in the bank's geographic area or move? What major technological developments loom on the horizon to affect the bank's spectrum of services and internal operations? With what degree of acceptance have customers greeted existing pricing structures and technological innovations?

In increasing numbers, banks have selected off-premises sites in which to conduct the self-assessment and strategic planning processes so that discussions can take place without interruptions and distractions. Meetings of the group(s) involved in the process should be conducted on a brainstorming basis, with managers free to express their suggestions, ideas, and evaluation of the present condition of the bank with complete candor. When this comprehensive evaluation of the bank's current status is completed, the planning process can move ahead to the next step: the formulation of desired objectives. Here, the basic question to be answered is Where would we like to be?

A distinction may be made here between *objectives* and *goals*. Objectives are considered to be long-term, broad, and qualitative rather than specifically quantitative, whereas goals usually establish quantitative standards on a near-term basis. Objectives frequently apply to the entire organization; goals may target the specific areas in which the organization seeks measurable results. The following statement by Walter Wriston during his tenure as chairman of Citicorp exemplifies an objective: "to deliver a financial service in every market in the world in every segment where we are legally permitted to do so at a profit."[27] This comment meets the definition: it expresses no time frame, and the terminology is broad, general, and not specifically quantitative. By contrast, a bank's statement of goals might include the following:

1. Within the course of the next three years, we will achieve bottom-line net earnings of $X.
2. During the coming year, we will achieve cost reductions of *X* percent in specific areas.
3. We will expand our overseas network of branch locations by establishing a presence in *X* (countries).

Goals contribute to attaining the objectives and must be realistic and attainable within the stated time frames. At the same time, they must have some degree of flexibility so that they can be revised, added to, or deleted as a result of all the external and internal factors that have an impact on operations. Goals also require a commitment from senior management to provide the necessary funding.

The process of developing a list of objectives and goals for the bank is clearly completely meaningless unless accompanied by a statement of the means that will be developed to achieve them. A goal that states a specific percentage increase in income is meaningless unless its authors identify how they will reach it. Therefore, the third step in strategic planning is an attempt to answer the question How will we get there? This phase of the process leads to an enumeration of specific *policies* to be implemented, and these, in turn, form the basis for *practices.*

Policies

The policies of any organization provide the guidelines under which the staff is to conduct its business. In commercial banking, which is subject to so much regulation and examination by federal and state governments and to increasing scrutiny by a public that may concentrate on weaknesses and problems rather than on strengths and accomplishments, policies may be shaped by external forces and requirements. In other cases, policies result from management's best assessment of the steps needed to achieve the desired objectives. The following examples may highlight the manner in which a bank establishes various types of policies:

1. All laws and regulations will be scrupulously followed throughout the institution. A Compliance Committee will be established to monitor this.
2. The bank will make no financial contributions to agencies or organizations of a purely sectarian or fraternal nature.
3. Staff members will neither solicit nor accept any type of personal commissions or fees resulting from their conduct of the bank's business, and they will not accept or solicit any lavish gifts or forms of entertainment that might influence their decision making.
4. The bank will maintain complete equality of opportunity in every instance, both in all phases of employment and advancement and in all dealings with borrowers.
5. The bank will not consider loans that are designed to provide venture capital for new business enterprises.
6. The bank will establish incentive-compensation plans in the retail banking sector, providing non-official staff members with financial rewards based on their success in introducing new consumer nonloan business.

In each of these examples, policies have been deemed appropriate for particular reasons. The first is an addition to the organizational structure, made necessary by the plethora of federal, state, and local regulations affecting all phases of bank operations. The second is designed to ensure that any funds allocated by the bank to philanthropic or community activities will go only to specific types of recipients. The third example establishes ethical standards by which personnel are to be guided, while the fourth conforms both to the demands of various laws and to principles of enlightened management of human resources. In the fifth instance, the policy is aimed at eliminating a certain type of risk from the loan portfolio. The sixth example gives recognition to the increased importance of the selling function and motivates clerical personnel to participate in the effort to attract desirable new business along with those officers specifically charged with marketing.

The time and effort involved in the strategic planning process are such that meetings of the involved personnel cannot be held on other than an annual or semiannual basis. Between those meetings, changes in policy are frequently necessary. Senior management must make it clear throughout the organization that the stated policies are not irrevocable; exceptions are possible, and new or revised policies can be developed to meet specific needs.

Every exception to policy, however, must be thoroughly justified and documented, and the responsible parties must be aware that each approval of an exception usually leads to requests for more of the same. Examples of this truism may be found both within and outside the organization. If the bank's personnel policies call for a certain course of action and an exception is made for one employee, others will expect the same latitude. If one customer is given some type of treatment that goes against stated policy, others will cite it as a precedent. Conversely, flexibility in policy setting is an absolute necessity in banking—again, both internally and externally. Changes in the global, national, or local economy; the money markets; the competition; or the community served by the bank may mandate adjustments. By the same token, personnel policies frequently have to be revised as employee lifestyles, dress codes, and expectations change. In all instances, the senior members of management must assume the initiative and provide a response to the changing conditions affecting the entire bank.

Practices

After policies have been clearly enunciated, well communicated, properly explained, and accepted and understood, they translate into the actual daily approaches to work of individuals at all levels of the organization. For example, a bank's policy at a given point in time may state that commercial loans will be considered only to those customers who have maintained longstanding relationships; therefore, an individual entrusted with business development will not use credit as a tool to attract new accounts. Personnel policies, often detailed in a manual or handbook, prescribe certain procedures, standards, and conditions that are implemented in everyday practices by the entire staff. Policy may require that any officer of the bank who is invited to serve as a director or trustee of any outside organization must obtain the prior approval of senior management; therefore, he or she implements the policy through a simple practice.

Strategies

Readers should not confuse the terms *strategies* and *tactics*. The strategies of an organization are the broadly delineated courses of action that implement policies and lead to attainment of objectives and goals; the tactics represent the specific steps taken to fulfill the strategies. There is an analogy to military operations in this context. The word *tactics* is derived from the Greek word that refers to the placing of troops in battle formation. Military strategy may call for attacking a certain town or city to cut the enemy's supply lines; tactics, the means to accomplish the desired end, must then be developed. Strategic planning focuses on broader issues; tactical planning addresses the operational systems and modes of procedure in detail so that strategies will be carried out.[28]

In a large bank, each major department or division should devise its own set of goals, conforming to and supportive of those of the overall organization. For example, if the bank's stated goal is an increase of 15 percent in earnings per share for the coming year, units within the bank translate that goal into their particular areas of operations and then devise the strategies that will make the appropriate contribution to profits.

Assume that a major bank expects its Consumer Banking Department to make an increased dollar contribution to earnings. The strategies to be employed may include reduction in expenses through consolidation or elimination of some branch offices, accompanied by an increased emphasis on Automated Teller Machines, or through a concerted effort to attract new retail business, such as NOW accounts, Individual Retirement Accounts (IRAs), or MMDAs. The strategies for the Consumer Banking Department lead, in turn, to a game plan in which tactics will be drawn up, accompanied, of course, by an analysis of all the resources needed. Like objectives, strategies are long-term; tactics are immediate.

Tactics and practices are intimately related. If a bank has stated an objective of improving its share of the market in the field of correspondent banking, a quantified goal—for example, the opening of a certain number of new correspondent accounts, with a specified dollar volume of additional balances, and a stated percentage increase in the balances carried by existing correspondents—will follow from the objective. The goal forms the basis for the strategies necessary to attain it, such as the establishment of an officer call program so that business-development personnel will personally make a certain number of calls each month on customers and prospects. As part of the strategy, a marketing training unit may be formed to enhance the calling officers' selling skills. The entire process results in those officers' systematically soliciting new accounts and endeavoring to improve relationships with existing clients. The success of the marketing effort will then create a ripple effect in the operations areas, the back office of the bank, where the daily work of the staff will increase and new procedures may have to be implemented to respond to the needs of the correspondent banks.

For any particular strategy, a varying amount of tactical moves can be designed to bring about the desired results. If a bank seeks increased penetration of the petroleum industry, the strategy might be to acquire whatever additional expertise is called for in that specialized field. The tactics might then involve hiring petroleum engineers or geologists as technical specialists or market analysts who are already familiar with the particular nature of oil companies. The bank might introduce orientation programs aimed at familiarizing bank officers with the requirements and problems of the industry.

The tactical approach to business development may be based in part on what was learned during the self-assessment stage that preceded the formulation of strategies. For example, banks should be able to identify their individual strengths and weaknesses in the marketplace. If competitors have been able to achieve success in penetrating certain markets while Bank X has been unable to do so, the bank must discover why. It can research the strategies used by those competitors, perhaps with input from line officers whose customers and prospects deal with other banks. Specific market research may provide further assistance. The task here requires a great deal of creative thinking to develop tactics that will differentiate a bank from its competitors.[29] In banking, as in all other industries, buyers purchase products and services not because of what they are, but because of the benefits the buyer perceives in them. The tactics used in business development in banking should stress this notion of user benefits, and this is nothing more than a response to the consumer's commonly heard vernacular question, "What's in it for me?"

Monitoring

Whenever business plans have been formulated, they quickly become useless unless there is a consistent effort to follow up by measuring their progress and effectiveness. If changes in external and/or internal conditions or unsatisfactory results create a need for new strategies or tactics, these must be developed and implemented rapidly so that problems are resolved, losses reduced or eliminated, and competitive advantages gained.

Here again, the management information systems developed in many banks are invaluable. Division executives, department heads, managers, and line officers can be provided with detailed data identifying income and expenses for each unit, key changes in balances, increases in loan activity, and the profitability of each service product.

Because the concept of management by objectives calls for quantitative and qualitative measures of the contributions of various components to the goals of the entire organization, the performance of individual personnel in those components becomes an integral part of the monitoring process. Not only should the bank's degree of success in reaching certain targets be identified, but also emphasis should be placed on what individual officers have done or failed to do. Therefore, performance reviews become part of the overall monitoring process because they compare the results achieved by individuals with the specific goals that were established for them. This assumes that the goal setting was not a purely arbitrary situation in which autocratic managers simply told subordinates what the targets (in loans, balances, profits, controllable expenses) were but a form of participatory management in which managers mutually agreed on the targets. Effective communication in the goal-setting process can take place in both directions, and this motivates the subordinate to perform in such a way that the targets will be reached or exceeded.

In implementing its system of monitoring progress toward goals, bank management must accept the possibility that the goals for a department, branch, or individual may have to be revised as the year progresses. In today's changing environment, this need is virtually constant. Unexpected developments may occur, making the goals unrealistic and no longer attainable. This situation in no way negates the value of and need for goal setting and planning, but gives weight to the principle that no one should be unjustly penalized because of conditions beyond his or her control.

Some banks have found themselves in a prototype of this situation in recent years. They are located in communities whose economic well-being depends almost entirely on a single major company. If an economic downturn in the industry, aggressive new competition, or other adverse circumstance forces the corporation to close its local operations and terminate the employees, there will be an immediate effect on the bank's balances, loans, and profits, and the agreed-on goals must be restated. The same logic applies to banks that are heavily engaged in lending to agriculture and therefore are extremely sensitive to the effects of drought, changes in farm price supports, and overall economic conditions. Among the 269 U.S. bank failures that took place during the 1982–1985 period, almost 40 percent occurred in only five states (Texas, 27; Oklahoma, 20; Kansas, 19; Illinois, 18; Iowa, 16).[30]

The monitoring process can be tied to a bank's system of individual profit centers, with components such as branches treated on an accounting basis as though they were separate banks. Since they are both sources (through deposits) and users (through loans) of funds, branches at any point may be contributing excess funds to an overall bank pool or drawing from that same consolidated reservoir. Monthly operating data for each branch reflect this, and the branch is then credited or debited at prevailing interest rates.[31] A development in a community such as those mentioned earlier will show up at once in the branch's summary performance report, and the bank should identify the underlying causes.

As seen in the goal-setting process, management by objectives takes the form of an agreement between the bank and its line managers and staff: a form of performance contract with a specific time frame. By assuring that managers know what is to be done to meet standards and attain goals, it represents a major step toward reconciling the goals of the organization with those of individuals.[32] At the same time, it assigns definite *accountability* to certain key members of the team for the end results of their efforts.

Accountability

The parallel between banking and organized sports has led many banks to introduce the concept of "teams" into their organizations. The objective of a sports team is to win; its goals may be quantified to show that a certain number of annual victories are sought, and its strategies for the season and its tactics in individual games are designed to contribute to the desired goals. In the same way, the organized, cohesive, directed actions of a group of bankers handling a number of accounts, loans, trust relationships, or processing functions are designed to relate directly to organizational objectives.

The parallel goes a step farther by making individuals in a bank accountable for the successes or failures of their teams. Just as managers and coaches in professional sports are rewarded or relieved of their duties, department heads, branch managers, or other leaders in a bank must expect to be judged on the basis of the results achieved under their guidance and direction. They cannot try to rationalize a failure by pointing to the incompetence of subordinates or to other weaknesses on the team that they could and should have recognized and corrected. The end results constitute the yardstick for the evaluation of performance.

The concept of accountability in banking is by no means confined to the middle and lower levels of management; it affects the entire hierarchy, including the Chairman and the President. In other industries, corporate boards of directors have no hesitation in bringing about the departures of senior officers when a succession of financial losses surfaces. In the same way, those who occupy the key positions in the pyramid of bank management must accept the risks along with the rewards. They are stewards in whom stockholders and depositors have placed a high degree of trust and from whom a high level of performance is expected. If these key members of the hierarchy find that the loan portfolio is in poor condition, that the operating departments cannot process work with accuracy and timeliness, or that subordinates have acted imprudently or in violation of regulations, they must take the necessary action to correct the situation or face the consequences. Ignorance of internal weaknesses or problems cannot be used as an alibi, nor can ineptness on the part of subordinates be accepted as an excuse.

Organizational Structuring

Accountability also requires that the senior officers of the bank ensure that the various components are organized for maximum effectiveness and that responsibilities for each are clearly assigned. The American Bankers Association's program of advertising is designed to create the image of commercial banks as full-service institutions; this image connotes an ability to serve a wide range of markets with a wide variety of service products, and the organization chart under which each bank, large or small, operates should separate the various functions and designate the responsible officer in each case.

In banks of modest size, separate units for Loans, Trusts, Investments, and Operations, reporting to the President, and Auditing, reporting to the board of directors, might suffice, with additional units handling International business and Bank Marketing if necessary. By contrast, the organization chart for the Chase Manhattan Bank, N.A. in 1985 is shown in figure 3–1. This chart, as shown in the bank's Annual Report, displays a combination of functional and geographic structures as well as a division of components according to the segments of the marketplace being served. This is not to suggest a complete fragmentation; extensive interface necessarily takes place among many of the components (e.g., Corporate Systems and Operations interlocks with more than one unit), and the officers responsible for bank-wide credit policy, funding, human resources management, legal matters, and financial planning cross all departmental lines.

The process of strategic planning often leads to reorganization of the bank's structure. If, as part of its answer to the basic question "Where do we want to be?", a bank determines that it is no longer feasible or profitable to try to be all things to all people, it will adopt a strategy of market segmentation, directing resources to those specific areas that present the best opportunities for profits.

The concept that strategic planning in a bank can lead to major structural change is exemplified by the decision made during the 1970s by Bankers Trust Company (New York). At that time, the bank had combined all elements of wholesale (i.e., corporate, government, institutional, and correspondent bank) and retail (i.e., consumer) business and operated a network of some 120 branches in the New York metropolitan area.

After a comprehensive evaluative process, senior management determined that future profitable growth could not result from a continuation of that course of action and that a complete revision of the bank's mission and structure was in order. The decision directed the bank to capitalize on its internal strengths in certain areas while eliminating one entire component. The new policy called for the outright sale of the assets and liabilities of virtually all the retail branches, divestiture of a great deal of the consumer business handled by those branches, and a full-scale concentration on the other market segments.[33] The cumulative results of this decision are as follows. From 1978, when the reorganization and restructuring occurred, through 1983, the bank's ROE increased from 9.7 percent to 15.7 percent, and Bankers Trust is now perceived by corporate treasurers as being among their most highly rated institutions.[34]

Product Development and Management

The turbulent state of the financial services industry has occasioned many predictions about the inability of many of the existing 14,500 commercial banks to survive. In addition to their inherent problems in managing assets and liabilities in a radically changed deposit-seeking environment,

> [M]any banks and thrifts will simply not be able to compete with Merrill Lynch, American Express, Sears, and other financial institutions which are already putting more banking and banking-related products through the vast coast-to-coast infrastructures they already have in place.[35]

In that competitive climate, banks must incorporate into the overall planning process a technique that was introduced in the corporate sector several years ago. The concept of making individuals specifically responsible for the development and total management of products can be applied in banking to create new opportunities, within regulatory constraints, for differentiated, profitable services that can be effectively marketed.

The objective here is to ensure that the bank provides the *right* service products to the *right* market segments in the *right* way in the *right* places at the *right* time and the *right* price. Product managers are fully responsible for *managing* their products.

The methodology used by those corporations that introduced the concept of product management can readily be applied to banking. Units can be formed to take charge of all phases of the development, marketing, pricing, support, and delivery of letters of credit, NOW accounts, or lock box. Internally or with the help of outside firms, they can conduct research to identify the wants and needs of the marketplace and the quantity and quality of competition. They calculate the profit potential and startup costs for new services

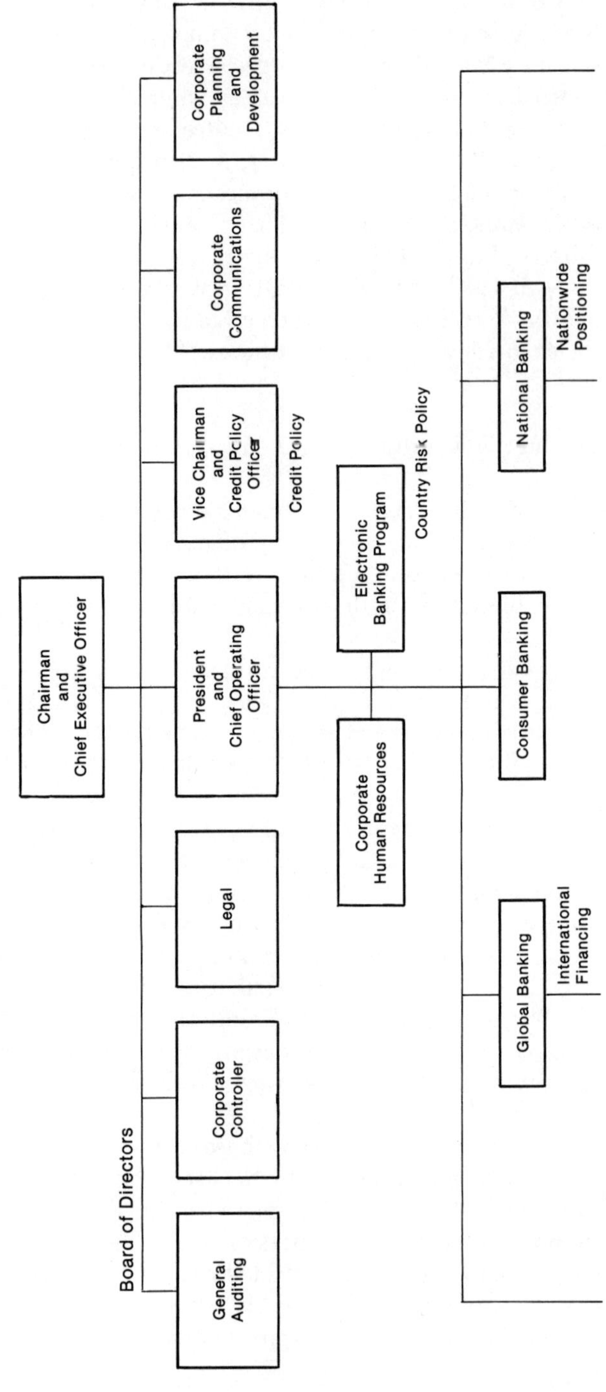
Board of Directors
General Auditing
Corporate Controller
Legal
Chairman and Chief Executive Officer
President and Chief Operating Officer
Vice Chairman and Credit Policy Officer
Credit Policy
Corporate Communications
Corporate Planning and Development
Corporate Human Resources
Electronic Banking Program
Country Risk Policy
Global Banking
International Financing
Consumer Banking
National Banking
Nationwide Positioning

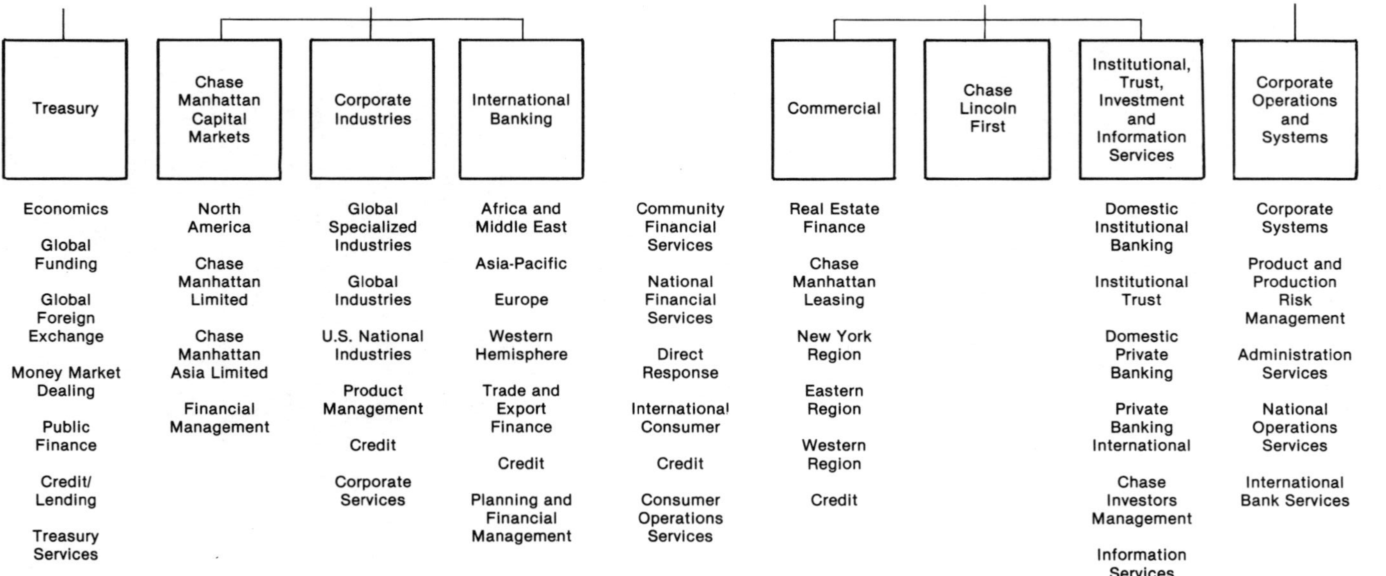

Source: The Chase Manhattan Corporation, Annual Report, 1984, p. 52.

Figure 3–1. Organizational Chart of the Chase Manhattan Corporation, March 1985

and document the synergies that may exist with current ones. They relate their work to the bank's operating units and capacities so that human resources and equipment needs are known. After a service product has been introduced, the product managers are fully responsible for its modification, delivery, and profitability.[36]

Whether or not a formal unit, entrusted with development of new products, exists within a bank, senior management must always be concerned with the risks that entry into new areas of service entails and not merely with profit potential. Strategic planning must address both sides of the equation. Management must resist any temptation to plunge into such new areas simply because another financial intermediary is doing so or because innovation per se seems desirable. In 1984, Anthony M. Solomon, President of the Federal Reserve Bank of New York, expressed this thought:

> The fact is the blurring of distinctions among commercial banks, thrifts, securities firms, and insurance companies is unleashing waves of new competition. . . . As a result, . . . our financial landscape is becoming cluttered with products and institutions that have been contrived to exploit regulatory loopholes.[37]

A survey conducted in 1984 among 252 commercial banks in eighteen states disclosed that 78 percent of the respondents were planning to introduce one or more new products or services in 1985, with the greatest emphasis being placed on financial counseling and attention to the needs of affluent individuals.[38] It is to be hoped that each such introduction will take place only after the banks have given sufficient thought to any hazards or pitfalls that actually or potentially exist.

Although the emphasis on planning has been increasing among banks, there is also evidence that due consideration has not always been given to this question of risk. For example, when MMDAs were legally authorized in December 1982, certain banks, especially those in the southeastern United States, ignored the fundamentals of profit planning and made a decision to attract new deposits by offering interest rates of 20 percent or more, despite the fact that Treasury Bill rates were falling at the time. In one instance, a bank quadrupled its new-business goal by paying 25 percent on new MMDAs. Its shortsightedness in this policy led to severe earnings problems.[39] Similarly, a bank consultant noted that

> Several small commercial banks jumped into the brokerage area without research beforehand. Today, many are reconsidering their position as costs continue to outweigh income with little, if any, value added.[40]

Learning from history is an important element in strategic planning. As deregulation brings about the elimination of interest-rate ceilings, bankers must take heed of the lessons learned during the 1920s, when interest was paid on demand deposits and rate wars created intolerable pressures on income. Any overemphasis on introducing new services, or a policy of competing aggressively without regard to the costs involved, can only exacerbate the problems banks already face. Escalating labor costs and interest expenses are inherent in banking in the 1980s, but no institution needs additional relationships that are loss leaders. Anthony Solomon suggested that banks use three criteria in their planning for new products:

> New activities should represent natural extensions of the types of financial services banks now provide . . . ; they must be acceptable from the standpoint of prudential and conflict-of-interest concerns; and they should contribute to . . . earnings capacity.[41]

Marketing

The objectives and goals developed in the planning process can never come to fruition unless they are accompanied by an effective marketing program that ties together a number of key elements. The fact that so many banks are now focusing on this concept is another example of the dynamics of change in the industry; a change that has required another basic readjustment in the thinking of many bankers and another rejection of a philosophy formerly held by many members of senior management—in particular, those who occupied key roles in banks located in some of the nation's largest cities.

In bygone days, the very word *selling* was anathema to many of these individuals. They saw themselves occupying highly prestigious positions, and the word *salesperson* appears to have had strongly pejorative connotations to them. Because they believed they would automatically be consulted whenever financial needs arose in their marketplace, they saw no need to bring their service products—of which relatively few were offered—to the attention of potential users. Their banks enjoyed a great deal of exclusivity in providing financial services. They controlled virtually all commercial loans and demand deposits, and they could rely on a steady inflow of the latter to fund operations. Thus, they were able to focus on asset management and to concentrate on dealings with the corporations, institutions, correspondent banks, and units of government that they saw as their market segments. Innovation was something to be avoided, and Paul Nadler has characterized these traditionalists in the old school of banking as practitioners of the motto, "Never do something for the first time."[42]

In 1950 commercial banks in the United States spent less than $50 million on all forms of advertising.[43] By 1971 that sum had increased tenfold as banks learned the need for and value of publicizing their services through all forms of media and overcame their former opposition to consumer banking.[44]

This evolutionary process resulted from a growing perception of certain basic truths that had not formerly been recognized:

1. No vacuum is ever allowed to exist for a period of time in the financial marketplace. If commercial banks fail to identify and respond to customer needs, other types of financial institutions will quickly seize the opportunity and attract new business.
2. Customers will not automatically seek out commercial banks. They will do so only if they are convinced of the benefits to be gained. Bankers must be salespersons. Marketing programs, in which financial services are properly researched, designed, costed and priced, sold in various ways, and monitored thereafter, are essential to growth and profitability. Money is a commodity that can be marketed.
3. In consequence of the foregoing, the parochialism of those bankers who felt that they alone were equipped to solve all the problems of their industry is no longer valid. Bank staff members whose skills were acquired and used in a highly regulated industry, which enjoyed a high degree of exclusivity and in which selling was not emphasized, need to have their efforts supplemented by others who have gained expertise in nonbank companies.[45]

The truth of the first of these perceptions is demonstrated by, among other evidence, the manner in which the thrift institutions, the S&Ls, in particular, capitalized on the commercial banks' neglect of the consumer market and assumed an increasingly important role in the financial marketplace. Between 1955 and 1974, while the commercial banks were still generally concentrating on what they considered their core business, S&Ls opened a total of 8,174 offices.[46] By 1984 these institutions had taken advantage of their relative freedom from the restrictions on commercial banking and had attained total assets of $876 billion.[47] Home mortgages are high on the list of consumer priorities, and the reluctance of commercial banks to make such loans created opportunities for S&Ls to expand their portfolios by serving the market; by 1984 they had total outstanding residential mortgage loans of $425 billion.[48] As is detailed in chapter 6 on consumer banking, the thrift institutions were granted additional competitive powers under the terms of the Monetary Control and Garn–St Germain Acts.[49]

The second perception, involving the need for selling and for relating directly to customers' wants and needs, has given rise to the creation in many banks of integrated marketing departments. These may interface with and support all sectors of the organization or be subdivided to concentrate on individual components such as trust and consumer. Complete marketing units typically include teams engaged in research among existing and prospective customers, the performance of demographic studies, the development of new service products, the determination of appropriate advertising techniques, and the conduct of in-house seminars in all aspects of marketing training.

This last function is especially important as a means of enhancing the selling skills of individuals specifically charged with new business development. However, additional programs can be designed to motivate all staff members to become part of the bank's overall sales team. There is no logical reason why tellers, whose customer contacts are more frequent than those of any other group of bank personnel, cannot be trained to take advantage of their daily opportunities and motivated to sell installment loans, safe deposit services, and IRA relationships. There is no reason why other members of the clerical staff cannot be encouraged to capitalize on their interfaces with friends, family members, and neighbors by recommending their bank's services and displaying its desire to attract new clients. Some banks use direct incentive compensation as part of this effort[50]; others make specific mention of employees' cross-selling accomplishments in their annual performance reviews.

As competition intensifies and commercial banking's spectrum of services becomes even more diversified, the need increases for personnel to understand what a service product actually is, which service products should be sold to which likely prospects, what benefits the user can gain, how to take advantage of existing relationships to cross-sell, which selling techniques are most effective, how to overcome any objections that may be encountered, and why their individual efforts are important in attaining the objectives and goals of the organization.[51]

The third of the relatively recent perceptions by bankers flows from the second. Banks in the past years typically lacked the in-house capability to design and manage marketing departments, to train individuals in the techniques of effective marketing, and to communicate product knowledge to the staff. Once they realized this weakness, they had no alternative other than to recruit professionals from those industries in which this expertise already existed.

Major banks today frequently draw from the pool of talent represented by market research firms, advertising agencies, corporate marketing units, and sales consultants. If prior generations of bankers expressed disdain for advertising, their successors must recognize the need for it; if selling was considered demeaning for bankers, they must remove that stigma permanently; and if bankers felt that the skills and experiences of professionals in other industries had no application to commercial banking, they must discard that insular attitude. The talents of nonbankers are making a significant contribution to the successes of many banks in the new world of financial services.

Summary

The environment in which commercial banks must function today is one in which changes occur rapidly, have drastic impact, are virtually continuous, and create questions about the ability of many institutions not merely to grow and prosper but also to continue in existence. Therefore, the need for strategic planning—a process which bankers often expected their corporate customers to implement and document, but to which most of them paid little attention until the late 1970s—has never been greater.[52]

Hamlet spoke of being besieged by a sea of troubles; banks today similarly find themselves beset with "new dimensions of financial service competition, financial disintermediation, and decreased customer loyalty based on long-term banking relationships."[53] Regardless of size, they must contend with volatile interest rates, technological change, new competitors whose numbers are increasing, heightened public concerns about the soundness of the banking system, a radically changed deposit mix, deregulation and the removal of interest-rate ceilings, new capital needs, and perhaps most important, an internal resistance to anything that contradicts past assumptions or represents innovation. In increasing numbers, especially among large banks, this environment has led to a recognition that effective planning is not a luxury but an absolute necessity. The fact that only 3 percent of the 711 major banks responding to a survey conducted in 1984 reported no formal planning procedures gives some indication of a new, widespread acceptance of the need.[54]

Although predictions regarding the future of commercial banking vary, there is one on which many authorities and analysts agree: it will be significantly different from the old world of the industry. Institutions that persist in a philosophy of management by crisis will be most likely to disappear from the scene, and those that lack the desire or ability to anticipate and manage change must suffer the consequences.

Without a systematic planning process, management may never perceive the necessity for a detailed analysis of the bank's present status: its strengths and weaknesses, the quantity and quality of its resources, its image, and the actual nature of its business. Without such a process, it is extremely difficult, if not impossible to establish and communicate, both internally and externally, a clear sense of direction. Without planning, management becomes merely reactive rather than proactive and allows things to happen to the bank instead of making them happen.

Conversely, the planning process forms the basis for decisions and establishes the action plans leading to the achievement of desired objectives. When such plans have been correctly prepared, effectively communicated, understood and accepted, implemented, and properly monitored, the bank is displaying an understanding of tomorrow's probable financial services industry environment, a willingness to accept its challenges, and a professionalism in designing and carrying out strategies that will provide quicker reactions to problems, reduce risks, and lead to improved earnings.

What should next year's budget look like? What segments of the market can the bank serve most effectively and profitably? What scenarios appear most likely on interest rates, demand for credit, and the national and local economy? Should new emphasis be placed on automated facilities for consumer use? What will be the impact of Sears, Roebuck's plans to open a network of integrated financial centers or Merrill Lynch's entry into commercial lending? Are banks prepared for the possibility of further deregulation, federal or local, that permits intrastate or interstate expansion? What problems of asset/liability management and capital constraints must the banks address? Should banks' existing organizations be revised? Should they recruit more nonbankers who are oriented to marketing and can train others to sell effectively?[55]

As mentioned earlier, large-scale revision of a bank's structure and organization may be one outcome of the strategic planning process. In 1985 the nation's eighth-largest bank holding company, First Interstate Bancorp, decided that its largest component, First Interstate Bank of California, should be split into two wholly distinct units so that one could handle all wholesale business while the other focused on the retail market.[56]

The final question in the foregoing lengthy list, pertaining to marketing, again brings the word *culture* to the forefront. This generic term embraces the external and internal image a bank may present and describes its willingness to recognize and adjust to the environment in which it operates. The Senior Officer of Bank of America, whose critical comments on the culture of banks were cited earlier, is by no means alone in his thinking; a Senior Vice-President of a major bank holding company in Baltimore has been equally outspoken in identifying the failure of many banks to understand and respond to customer needs and wants:

> Most bankers have a set of values that are totally contradictory to survival in a deregulated environment. . . . Banks, by and large, are not sales oriented, not promotion oriented, and not team oriented. And today you have to be all those things in order to survive.[57]

The editor of *United States Banker* has the same perception of the industry:

> The culture which the commercial bank . . . has lived under for the past 50 years is the wrong culture for the next 50 . . . because the world . . . [and] the market have changed. The financial services provider also must change and adopt a new, more appropriate culture if it is to succeed, to survive, and to prosper. . . . Salesmanship is a key element in shaping a new banking culture. . . . [It] is the tool our new competitors use best.[58]

The Chief Financial Officer of one of California's largest banks has suggested that his colleagues in other institutions stop thinking of their business as being entirely unique, and that they recognize instead the similarities that exist between banking and other industries.[59]

The corporations in the United States that are not merely survivors but also winners in every sense of the word are those in which management has anticipated, prepared for, adjusted to, and managed change. These corporations have designed and implemented strategic planning for many years. They know their objectives, their strengths and weaknesses, their costs, the quantity and quality of their competitors, and their markets. Regardless of the terminology they may have employed in doing so, they have developed answers to the fundamental questions Where do we want to be? and How will we get there? Can commercial banks afford to ignore the experience of these successful corporations and do any less?

Notes

1. In Cass Bettinger, "Strategic Planning for the Commercial Lender," *Journal of Commercial Bank Lending,* November 1983, p. 26.
2. In Jonathan Hakim, "A New Awakening," *The Economist,* March 24, 1984, p. 12.
3. Richard W. Sapp, "Banks Look Ahead: A Survey of Bank Planning," *Bank Administration,* July 1980, p. 12.
4. Philip L. Zweig, "Banks Called in Need of Strategic Planning," *American Banker,* June 24, 1982, p. 2.
5. Kenneth A. Randall, in Herbert V. Prochnow and Herbert V. Prochnow, Jr., eds., *The Changing World of Banking* (New York, Harper & Row, 1974), p. 322.
6. John M. Mason, *Financial Management of Commercial Banks* (Boston: Warren, Gorham & Lamont, 1979), p. 110.
7. John Morris, "Asset-Liability Management Minimal at Many Small Banks," *American Banker,* January 3, 1985, p. 3.
8. Eric N. Compton, "Bank Planning: A Status Report," *The Bankers Magazine,* May–June 1981, p. 75.
9. Robert O. Metzger, "Barriers to Bank Productivity Improvement," *The Bankers Magazine,* January–February 1982, p. 58.
10. John W. Humble, *How to Manage by Objectives* (New York, AMACOM, Division of American Management Associations, 1972), p. 45.
11. George G.C. Parker, "Now Management Will Make or Break the Bank," *Harvard Business Review,* November–December 1981, p. 140.
12. In "GM Zeroes in on Employee Discontent," *Business Week,* May 12, 1973, p. 28.
13. George G. Gordon and Monroe J. Haegele, "'Corporate Culture' in Financial Services," *Bankers Monthly Magazine,* December 15, 1984, p. 16.
14. In Hakim, op. cit., p. 10.
15. Paul S. Nadler, "Staying Alive in '85," *Bankers Monthly Magazine,* December 15, 1984, pp. 5–7.

16. George J. Vojta, "New Competition and Its Implications for Banking," *Bank Administration,* July 1983, pp. 34–44.

17. In Bettinger, op. cit., p. 27.

18. Herbert E. Johnson, "Comprehensive Corporate Planning for Commercial Banks," *Bank Administration,* January 1978, p. 21.

19. Thomas W. Thompson; Leonard L. Berry; and Philip H. Davidson, *Banking Tomorrow: Managing Markets Through Planning* (Richmond, Va.: Robert F. Dame, Inc., 1981), pp. 34–36.

20. N. Berne Hart, "Strategic Planning: Responsibility of the CEO," *Bank Administration,* March 1984, pp. 74–78.

21. S. Benjamin Prasad, "The Paradox of Planning in Banks," *The Bankers Magazine,* May–June 1984, pp. 79–80.

22. Dimitris N. Chorafas, *Money: The Banks of the '80s* (New York: Petrocelli Books, Inc., 1982), p. 38.

23. Robert O. Metzger; Ian I. Mitroff; and Susan E. Rau, "Challenging the Strategic Assumptions of the Banking Industry," *The Bankers Magazine,* July–August 1984, p. 29.

24. Robert C. Isban, "New Levels of Opportunity for the Financial Industry," *Bank Administration,* July 1984, p. 21. See also Frederick W. Gluck, "Taking the Mystique Out of Planning," *Across the Board,* July/August 1985, pp. 56–61.

25. Eric N. Compton, *Inside Commercial Banking,* 2nd ed. (New York: John Wiley & Sons, Inc., 1983), p. 48.

26. Raymond R. Reilly and Alan Beauchaine, "Managing a Bank's Investment Portfolio," *Bankers Monthly Magazine,* December 15, 1984, p. 10.

27. In Hakim, op. cit., p. 10.

28. Anat Yalif, "Strategic Planning Techniques," *Bank Administration,* April 1982, pp. 22–26.

29. Laura Gross, "Creativity Called Key to Effective Planning," *American Banker,* July 1, 1983, p. 3.

30. "Bank Failures 1982–85," *American Banker,* November 12, 1985, p. 40.

31. John W. Ennest and Gerald E. Patera, "Planning and Control Systems for Commercial Banks," in Prochnow and Prochnow, Jr., op. cit., p. 259.

32. Chorafas, op. cit., p. 84.

33. Bankers Trust New York Corporation, *Annual Report: 1978,* p. 3.

34. Hakim, op. cit., p. 12.

35. Robert R. Douglass, "The Outlook for Nationwide Expansion," *The Bankers Magazine,* November–December 1984, p. 10.

36. Robert A. Mocella and Lawrence C. Rhyne, "Developing and Implementing an Effective Corporate Development Program," *Managerial Planning,* November–December 1984, pp. 23–27.

37. Anthony M. Solomon, "Banking Deregulation—Where Do We Go from Here?," *Federal Reserve Bank of New York Quarterly Review,* Autumn 1984, p. 2.

38. Ralph B. Cox, "In 1985 Banks will Be More Sales-Oriented," *Mid-Continent Banker,* January 1985, p. 7.

39. Jerry Adams, "Rate War Abates in Southeast," *American Banker,* January 4, 1983, p. 1.

40. Robert A. Nascenzi, "How to Develop a Strategic Marketing Plan," *Bank Marketing,* October 1984, pp. 26–27.

41. In Federal Reserve Bank of New York, op. cit., p. 3.

42. In Prochnow and Prochnow, Jr., op. cit., p. 381.

43. Howard D. Crosse and George H. Hempel, *Management Policies for Commercial Banks,* 2nd ed. (Englewood Cliffs, N.J.: Prentice-Hall, Inc., 1973), p. 281.

44. "Now Banks Are Turning to the Hard Sell," *Business Week,* June 24, 1972, p. 78.

45. Michael T. Higgins, "Planning for Banking's Future," *Bank News,* December 15, 1984, p. 10.

46. United States League of Savings Associations, *Savings and Loan Fact Book* (Chicago: 1976), p. 4.

47. *Federal Reserve Bulletin,* January 1985, p. A28.

48. Ibid., p. A40.

49. A complete list of the increased powers given to S&Ls may be found in Donald T. Savage, "Depository Financial Institutions," in Richard C. Aspinwall and Robert A. Eisenbeis, eds., *Handbook for Banking Strategy* (New York: John Wiley & Sons, Inc., 1985), pp. 194–195.

50. "A Banker's Advice: Try Incentive Pay," *ABA Banking Journal,* February 1985, p. 20.

51. Thompson et al., op. cit., pp. 239–241.

52. Gary A. Giroux and Peter S. Rose, "An Update of Bank Planning Systems: Results of a Nationwide Survey of Large U.S. Banks," *Journal of Bank Research,* Autumn 1984, p. 147.

53. Frederick C. Militello, Jr., "Marketing the Corporate Treasurer: A Financial Approach," *Bank Marketing,* October 1984, p. 31.

54. Giroux and Rose, op. cit., p. 139.

55. Jack Retterer, "Changing to a Business Development Culture," *Bank Administration,* May 1984, p. 66.

56. Teresa Carson, "First Interstate Puts All Its Eggs into Two Baskets," *Business Week,* February 18, 1985, p. 72.

57. In Dr. Thomas W. Thompson, "It's a Selling Business," *United States Banker,* December 1983, p. 6.

58. Raoul D. Edwards, in ibid.

59. In Hakim, op. cit., p. 10.

4
The New World of Global Banking

The era in U.S. banking that began in 1961 with the introduction of the large-denomination negotiable CD has been characterized repeatedly in this text as a period of major change. On the domestic scene, the changes have been both numerous and drastic; regulatory, economic, competitive, technological, and structural developments have significantly transformed the banking institutions, and there is no indication that the future will bring fewer, or less dramatic, changes.

However, the revolution that has taken place since the end of World War II, and more particularly since the 1960s, in international banking is of at least equal importance. The politicians who, prior to that war, preached the doctrine of isolationism and stated that the problems and actions of other nations did not affect and need not concern Americans and the bankers who mirrored that thinking by doing little to position their institutions on an international basis now seem to have been completely misguided.

The concept of a unified world, rather than one in which nations operate unilaterally or in a vacuum, is now accepted. Countries are increasingly interdependent. Developments in one affect many others, and geographic distances have lost their former importance as the age of electronic money, in which funds move from one corner of the globe to another with the speed of light, has evolved. Major banks, tending increasingly to look on the entire world as their marketplace, have become elements in an industry that is truly global in nature.

To contemporary observers or students of banking, it may be difficult to accept the premise that the steadily growing penetration of the U.S. financial industry by foreign banks and the worldwide expansion of so many American banks are relatively recent developments; yet such is the history in both cases. This chapter explores the events and trends that represent the milestones in that history and that brought terms such as *country risk, Eurocurrencies, global cash management, loan syndications, interest-rate swaps,* and *trade finance* into the lexicon.

Historical Developments

Prior to 1913, national banks were not permitted to establish overseas branches or to finance foreign trade through bankers' acceptances or bills of exchange.[1] Although state-chartered banks were free to engage in global banking, they chose to do so only on a limited scale, preferring instead to call on their overseas correspondents for various services. Even when the Federal Reserve Act of 1913 allowed national banks with capital of $1 million or more to open branches abroad and otherwise operate on an international basis, growth was extremely slow, and only a handful of U.S. banks took advantage of this latitude.

World War II provided the impetus for the revolution referred to earlier; however, the United States' industrial giants were first to act, and the banks were the followers rather than the leaders in becoming global. Major corporations such as General Electric, IBM, DuPont, Westinghouse, General Foods, Dow Chemical, United States Steel, and National Cash Register were among those who identified the needs for their products in war-ravaged countries and became the suppliers to nations that lacked productive capacity. U.S. factories supplied the chemicals, fertilizers, and farm machinery; the raw materials needed to rebuild factories, railroads, and bridges; and the office equipment needed for accounting and internal control. The balance of payments—that is, the excess of U.S. exports over imports—was consistently favorable.

Every business transaction, however, creates the need for some type of payment, whether self-generated or externally financed, and the U.S. commercial banks were ideally positioned to assist customers with every aspect of the phenomenal growth in foreign trade. The banks' steady purchases of U.S. government obligations had built up a reservoir they could use to fund expansion, and they possessed or could acquire all the necessary resources in expertise and technology.

As major corporations, in increasing numbers, established their foreign factories, refineries, distribution facilities, sales offices, and market shares, U.S. banks—whose clients they already were—began following them to provide on-the-scene services. In 1947 only seven U.S. commercial banks had foreign branches.[2] By 1970 that number had grown to sixty-one, and by 1981, 152 Federal Reserve member banks had established 787 overseas locations.[3] In addition to serving the local needs of corporate customers, these facilities proved to be a source of other benefits to the banks.

The capital strength of the major U.S. banks allowed them to become increasingly active in direct lending to the public and private sectors in many countries so that portfolio expansion, with a consequent increase in interest income, could take place. More important, however, their overseas locations became a major source of funds for them at a time when they were experiencing disintermediation at home, and the term *Eurodollars* was added to the bankers' lexicon. By 1982 total assets of foreign branches of U.S. banks had grown to $459 billion,[4] and one year later the 924 overseas locations reported total assets of $466 billion.[5]

Eurodollars

The opening of foreign branches of U.S. banks, backed by the capital strength of their home offices and building on the relationships that had already been established with globally expanding corporations, provided depositories for the funds resulting from those firms' local operations. The Cold War gave further impetus to the placing of deposits in those banks. As countries in Eastern Europe began to fear that any deposits they might have in the United States could be impounded because of deteriorating relations between the two superpowers, they embarked on the practice of using bank branches in London, which accepted their deposits and maintained them in dollars. Thus the word *Eurodollars,* which are simply dollars deposited outside the United States, was introduced into the language. They differ from domestically deposited dollars only in location and can readily be brought back to the U.S. by the banks' home offices.

Federal Reserve Regulation Q played an important part in the growth of the Eurodollar market. For member banks, it placed a ceiling on the interest they could pay on all savings and time deposits *in the United States.* It did not apply to deposits that the banks might attract in Europe, Nassau, or other offshore locations; therefore, in the late 1960s major U.S. banks, through their overseas facilities, often bid as much as 13 percent for short-term funds and found large numbers of willing depositors. In 1966, London banks and branches began to offer negotiable CDs at highly competitive rates; U.S. banks, in increasing numbers, used these as a prime source of funds largely because, more than exemption from the restrictions of Regulation Q, Eurodollars enjoyed the major advantage at that time of freedom from reserve requirements.[6]

The growth of the Eurodollar market continues today, due to three aspects of the operations of U.S. banks. As I shall discuss subsequently, the global lending activities of U.S. institutions can lead to additional deposits in foreign branches. In addition, dollars in huge amounts can be bought in the foreign exchange market for delivery abroad. Finally, the status of the United States as a net importer, and the resulting deficit in the balance of payments, leads to payments in dollars that are deposited overseas. During the first six months of 1984, for example, the United States' international trade created a negative balance of $51.6 billion.[7]

Global Deposits and Earnings

The importance of foreign deposits to the major U.S. banks is indicated graphically by their published figures for 1984. Of the ten largest commercial banks, Bankers Trust reported that 65 percent of its total deposits were offshore, while Morgan Guaranty showed 62 percent, Citibank 53, Chase Manhattan 52, First Chicago 49, Manufacturers Hanover 47, Chemical 34, and Bank of America 31.[8]

For the same ten banks, the contributions of their international activities and services to overall earnings are shown in table 4–1. This growth in earnings took place at a time when the banks were experiencing relatively smaller increases in their total income. From 1973 through 1975, actual dollar earnings of the ten largest commercial banks rose approximately 20 percent, but during the period covered by table 4–1, that rate of growth had slackened to 13 percent. This slowdown is attributable to aggressive competition from other smaller banks (resulting in lower lending rates) and a conscious effort by many of the largest institutions to lower their total risk exposure.[9] That policy was reversed in the ensuing five-year period, as U.S. banks' foreign loan portfolios grew from $105 billion at year-end 1975 to some $400 billion in 1981.[10]

The Call Report of Citibank, N.A., submitted to the Office of the Comptroller of the Currency as of June 30, 1985, showed total deposits of $85.1 billion, of which 63 percent ($53.7 billion) was in foreign offices and similar facilities. Of that $53.7 billion of overseas deposits, 94 percent ($50.7 billion) was in interest-bearing deposits. (For Citibank's deposits, the figures were 72 percent [$22.6 billion] interest-bearing and 28 percent [$8.8 billion] non-interest-bearing.)

The Scope of International Activities

Today, major U.S. banks consider the entire world to be their marketplace for a wide range of financial services. Aside from their direct lending to foreign governments, these institutions provide trade finance, play a significant role in loan syndications along with local participants, conduct retail banking to serve consumers in various countries, trade in foreign exchange and Eurobonds, supply direct services to their local correspondent banks, service multinational firms through various fee-based services such as cash management, and lend to companies for the latter firms' overseas use.

Under their structure as holding companies, which are governed entirely by local laws and thus can operate in ways that would be prohibited in the United States, banks can form subsidiaries to act as securities underwriters. They may also become involved in leasing, act as merchant banks to provide venture capital or financial and investment advice, and offer trust services, especially in countries with highly favorable tax structures and secrecy laws.[11]

Table 4–1
International Earnings as a Percent of Total Earnings for the Ten Largest U.S. Banks, 1975–1980

Bank	*1975*	*1976*	*1977*	*1978*	*1979*	*1980*
Citibank	71	72	82	72	65	62
Bank of America	55	47	42	35	38	45
Chase Manhattan	64	78	65	53	47	49
Manufacturers Hanover	47	59	60	51	49	49
Morgan Guaranty	60	46	48	51	52	58
Chemical New York	41	41	39	42	35	38
Bankers Trust	59	61	83	68	51	58
Continental Illinois	14	23	17	18	18	33
First National (Chicago)	33	15	20	16	4	0
Security Pacific	12	7	12	15	10	13

Source: Arturo C. Porzecanski, "Profitability of International Banking," in Emanuel N. Roussakis, *International Banking: Principles and Practices* (New York: Praeger, 1983), p. 135.

The global activities of Citicorp provide a classic example of the manner in which a major bank can capitalize on a variety of opportunities in every part of the world and enhance its image as an innovator. In Great Britain, Citicorp's activities have led to its being called a "financial supermarket." Its thirty-eight branches in that country offer consumer credit and credit card insurance through a subsidiary. It is also working with the so-called middle market companies—that is, those that rank below the industrial giants—on foreign exchange, loans, and trade finance and has a substantial interest in a London brokerage firm that also operates in Tokyo and Hong Kong. In 1984 Citicorp sought permission to become a full-scale member of the British national check-clearing system so that it might be viewed as a fully indigenous British bank rather than as an intruder from abroad. Through its London headquarters in 1983, it was the lead manager for about $450 million of Eurobonds, which are offshore long-term debt issues.[12]

The commercial banks that have diversified and expanded into some or all of the global activities mentioned earlier found a new competitor in 1985, when Merrill Lynch announced the formation of a specialized group to handle all international investment banking, bonds, and preferred securities. Floating-rate corporate issues, investment services, and redemption of commercial paper were also scheduled on the Merrill Lynch agenda.[13]

Edge Act Facilities

Although they did not take advantage of it at the time, the Edge Act, enacted by Congress in 1919 as an amendment to the Federal Reserve Act, gave commercial banks added opportunities to broaden the scope of their international services. The Act allows banks to form Edge Act corporations for the specific purpose of assisting customers with transactions involving foreign trade.

Edge Act corporations compete today with foreign-owned banking institutions. As exceptions to the broad restrictions in the United States on interstate banking, they can establish facilities across state lines. They can also open offices abroad for investment and mortgage banking, consumer financing, leasing, and factoring.

The Edge Act offices of banks in the United States are limited by law to activities incidental to foreign business. The Federal Reserve Board has broad discretionary power to interpret the word *incidental,* and in 1985 it amended Regulation K, which pertains to all international banking operations, so that the banks would have authority to provide full banking services to a limited category of companies, such as foreign airlines and shipping firms, that are restricted by their charters to international business.[14]

Because so much of the foreign trade in which U.S. companies are engaged originates in cities such as Miami, Houston, San Francisco, and Chicago, many Edge Act offices of banks are located there. New York, however, remains the most favored location; at year-end 1984, 40 of the 200 Edge Act facilities in the United States were located there. Miami, which has thirty-seven such facilities, is the leading city in terms of the total assets of Edge Act offices, with 41 percent of the nationwide total of $19.5 billion.[15] Foreign banks have also been empowered to establish Edge Act corporations in the United States; these, too, provide a wide range of services directly related to international transactions, usually arising out of foreign trade.

Foreign Banks in the United States

While the expansion of U.S. commercial banks into overseas marketplaces has been remarkable in the post–World War II era, it has been paralleled by a growth in the operations of foreign banks in the United States. Although some of these had formed U.S. banking subsidiaries in the late nineteenth century, only since the mid-1970s have they become such a noteworthy competitive force in the financial services industry.

As noted earlier, major U.S. corporations led the way in becoming international in scope during the postwar years, and the commercial banks followed their lead by establishing their networks of overseas facilities. An identical pattern exists in reverse. Industries from the largest foreign countries acquired U.S. corporations, established subsidiaries here or, more simply, became the major exporters in the course of their postwar economic reconstruction. Japan, West Germany, Italy, and other nations became important suppliers of the electronic goods, automobiles, steel, and apparel that could be sold in the United States at significantly lower prices. The commercial banks from those same countries, recognizing the need to have a dollar base in the United States and to capitalize on the strength of the dollar as a world currency, followed their customers across the oceans and became major forces in the overall industry.

The facilities established in the United States by foreign banks allowed them to provide services to their own corporate customers and to gain access to the capital and money markets. Due to time-zone differences, they could extend their periods of operations in the area of foreign exchange. The United States, given the size of the market, its growth potential, and its economic stability, proved to be extremely fertile ground for those banks. Perhaps most important, they found that they could capitalize on certain advantages in competing with their U.S. counterparts.

While U.S. commercial banks, under the Douglas Amendment to the Bank Holding Company Act and the McFadden Act, were not permitted to offer full-scale branch banking and deposit taking across state lines, foreign banks were allowed to do so. U.S. commercial banks that were Fed members were subject to deposit insurance and reserve requirements; foreign banks in the United States in the 1970s were free from these. While U.S. commercial banks were prohibited from diversifying into areas such as securities underwriting, foreign banks were unrestricted. And while antitrust legislation and the rulings of federal and state regulators would undoubtedly have barred any U.S. commercial banks from making such acquisitions, between 1979 and 1981 the twelfth, thirteenth, thirtieth, and thirty-second largest banks in the United States were all acquired by foreign interests. The combination of these factors and advantages provides a rationale for the entry and remarkable growth of foreign banks in the United States in recent years.

At year-end 1973, sixty-one banks, representing twenty-two foreign nations had established a presence in the United States. Ten years later, the number of foreign banks had increased to 230, representing fifty-three countries.[16] During that ten-year period the total assets of foreign banks in the United States grew from $32.3 billion to $332 billion, and their share of total commercial banks assets grew from 3.8 percent to 14.7 percent.[17] By year-end 1983, foreign banks owned 9 of the 100 largest U.S. commercial banks and accounted for over 18 percent of all commercial and industrial loans booked here.

Foreign banks in the United States may operate in any of four different ways. The simplest of these is the *representative office,* which cannot accept deposits, make loans, or perform other banking functions; it serves only as a liaison between its home office and customers in a geographic area. *Agencies* of foreign banks obtain either a federal or state license; they can accept credit balances incidental to the exercise of their powers (e.g., receipts from transactions in international trade or undisbursed portions of loans), but they are not allowed to accept conventional demand or time deposits or to perform fiduciary functions. Agencies of foreign banks normally concentrate on money-market operations and trade finance. In lending, they are not bound by the regulatory restrictions that affect U.S. commercial banks regarding maximum loans to a single borrower.

Branches are organizations licensed by either individual states or the federal government. In lending, they are restricted as to legal limit, based on the size of their parent bank's capital and surplus and the regulations of their home countries. The branches of foreign banks in the United States may accept any and all deposits and have full banking powers. *Subsidiaries,* the fourth type of representation, are legally incorporated entities in the United States and have their own capital base, although the outstanding stock is often wholly owned by the parent. They operate along the same lines as domestic banks, again with full banking powers.[18] Figure 4–1 shows the growth in the percentage of total banking assets in the United States held by foreign banks from 1973 to 1983.

Foreign banks operating in New York State have a fifth option. They may establish *New York Investment Companies,* which can maintain credit balances for clients and can deal in corporate securities. These entities cannot accept deposits.

Through their subsidiaries, branches, agencies, Edge Act facilities, and New York Investment Companies, the 230 foreign banks mentioned earlier operated a total of 548 banking offices in the United States at year-end 1983. In addition, they used over 300 representative offices as a means of referring business and maintaining liaisons with corporate customers.[19]

Most foreign banks have selected financial centers in New York and California as the bases for their U.S. operations, and at year-end 1983 almost 75 percent of all their offices were in those two states. New York City, in particular, because of its status as the hub of international trade activity and its role in the domestic and international money markets, was the site of 46 percent of all foreign bank offices at that time. In addition to New York State and the District of Columbia, foreign banks operate in eleven states. As mentioned in connection with the discussion of Edge Act offices, Florida shows an increasing concentration of foreign bank facilities, resulting from its proximity to the Caribbean and Latin America.

The International Banking Act

In 1979 the Standard Chartered Bank (Great Britain) acquired the thirtieth largest U.S. commercial bank, Union Bank (Los Angeles), and the National Westminster Bank (also Great Britain) acquired the thirty-second largest, New York's National Bank of North America.[20] The LaSalle National Bank (Chicago) was subsequently acquired by Algemene Bank Nederland, head-

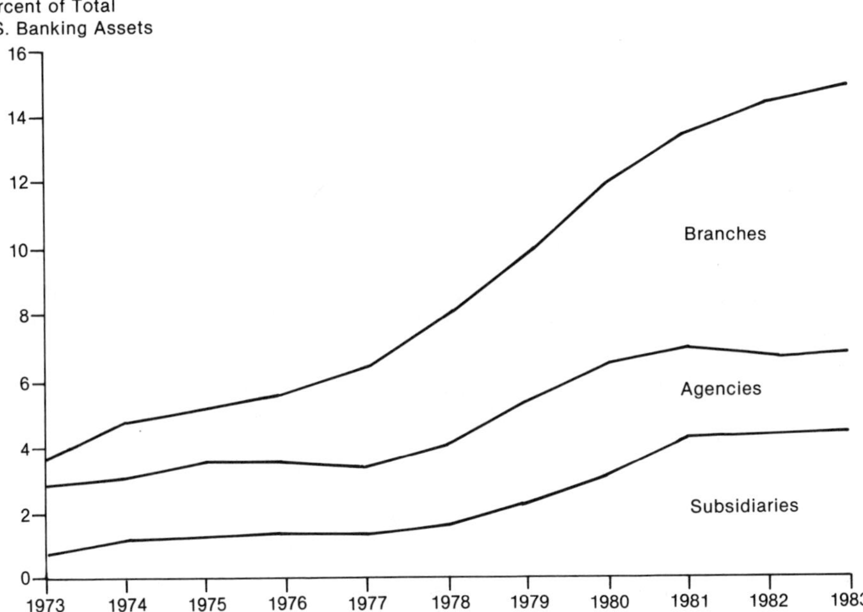

Source: "Foreign Banking Organizations in the United States," Office of the Comptroller of the Currency, *Quarterly Journal,* September 1984, p. 7.

Note: Includes domestically chartered commercial banks, branches and agencies of foreign banks, Edge Act and Agreement Corporations, and New York Investment Companies.

Figure 4–1. Growth in Foreign Bank Share of U.S. Market

quartered in Amsterdam, and in the largest acquisition, the Hong Kong and Shanghai Banking Corporation bought New York's Marine Midland Bank, which at that time (1980) ranked twelfth among all U.S. commercial banks, with assets of $14.3 billion. In 1981 Midland Bank (Great Britain) acquired Crocker National Bank (San Francisco); a group of investors from OPEC (Organization of Petroleum Exporting Countries) purchased Financial General Bankshares, a bank holding company with twelve banks located in four states and the District of Columbia; and Banca Commerciale Italiana acquired the holding company that owned the $1.1 billion Long Island Trust Company (New York).[21]

These acquisitions, as indicated earlier, would undoubtedly have been prevented if any domestic commercial bank had proposed them. The significant point, however, is that they took place even after federal legislation, in the form of the International Banking Act of 1978, had been passed to create greater parity between U.S. commercial banks and those entering the domestic marketplace from foreign countries. American bankers who had protected the competitive advantages enjoyed by foreign banks were given some measure of relief through the International Banking Act; but the legislation was not designed to exclude foreign banks or to curb their right to function; it was intended to "promote competitive equality between domestic and foreign bank institutions in the United States."[22]

The International Banking Act, with its 1980 amendments, called for every foreign bank to designate a home state in the United States and to limit its deposit-taking activities to that one state; however, those foreign banks that had conducted interstate banking in the United States as of July 27, 1978,were "grandfathered" and permitted to continue those activities across state lines.[23] Under the terms of the Act, any foreign bank with consolidated worldwide assets of $1 billion or more became subject to the Fed's reserve requirements, and all U.S. offices of foreign banks that accepted deposits of less than $100,000 were required to become members of the FDIC.

Despite any restrictions the International Banking Act may have imposed on the operations of foreign banks in the United States, several more acquisitions have taken place since its passage. In recent years the Bank of Montreal (Canada) has taken over the thirty-fifth largest U.S. commercial bank, Harris Trust and Savings Bank (Chicago)[24]; Mistubishi Bank (Japan) has acquired the seventy-seventh largest, the Bank of California; and Allied Irish Banks, Ltd. (Dublin), which had already opened branches in New York City and Chicago that were grandfathered under the Act, acquired the $3.4 billion First Maryland Bankcorp (Baltimore), which operates First National Bank of Maryland, the eighty-fourth largest in the United States and the largest in that state.[25]

International Banking Facilities

The ability of domestic commercial banks to compete more effectively with their foreign counterparts through various international activities was enhanced in 1981, when the Fed authorized the establishment of International Banking Facilities (IBFs) and ten states granted favorable tax treatment on income derived from operations conducted through those facilities.

IBFs can transact loan and deposit business with foreign banks and foreign residents without being subject to either Federal Reserve Regulation D (reserve requirements) or Regulation Q (interest-rate ceilings on time and savings deposits). They can neither accept deposits from or lend to U.S. companies nor issue negotiable CDs; however, they have the ability to provide other authorized services in a regulatory environment that makes the use of offshore facilities unnecessary.[26]

A statistical survey prepared by the Federal Reserve Board as of August 31, 1983 indicated that IBFs held aggregate total assets of $197 billion, of which $144 billion was concentrated in New York.[27] Foreign banks were active in establishing IBFs, and at year-end 1983 there were 320 foreign bank IBFs, with total assets of $100 billion.[28]

The Growth of Global Lending

At the conclusion of the joint annual meeting of the World Bank and International Monetary Fund (IMF) in Toronto in September 1982, a veritable bombshell burst on the financial community as the scope of the global debt crisis—in particular, as it involved bank loans in Latin America—was publicized for the first time. Numerous dire predictions of the collapse of the entire world banking system began to be heard. Public confidence in the soundness of many of the largest commercial banks in the United States was significantly weakened by a succession of newspaper and magazine articles, televised interviews and commentaries, and books forecasting an imminent financial catastrophe.

> As recently as . . . 1983, it was widely feared that billions of dollars in debt run up by less-developed countries would be repudiated through a simple inability to repay, if not through a debtors' cartel. This would torpedo the big lending banks, . . . destroy the international financial network, and plunge the world into economic depression.[29]

By the mid-1980s there was some evidence that these nightmarish prophecies of calamity had been overstated.[30] This evidence was more than offset, however, by continuing expressions of serious concern and, in the opinions of some observers, questions about whether the debt problem could ever be totally resolved.[31]

In addition to questioning when and how the magnitude of the debt problem can be mitigated, many observers have asked how major commercial banks in the United States ever allowed it to reach such proportions. There can be little doubt that many lending banks—possibly relying on a basic assumption that all loans made to sovereign governments would always be repaid and could never become workouts or charge-offs,[32] possibly acting because both the Federal Reserve and the Treasury Department had created the impression that increased global lending was a means of strengthening economic conditions in other countries, and possibly sacrificing prudence for potential profits[33]—very seriously overextended themselves.

One lengthy study of the global debt situation characterizes these banks as being guilty of "disaster myopia"[34]; that is, they acted as if the probability of a major shock affecting their portfolios were zero. The authors of that study point to the banks' willingness to lend amounts equal to a substantial portion of their capital to any one country at preferential interest rates offering minimum spreads above their costs of funds and to their having ignored all the storm signals that surfaced during the 1970s.

Much of the increase in international lending occurred as a consequence of the 350 percent rise in oil prices in 1973 and 1974. U.S. banks benefited from a sudden influx of large deposits placed with them by the oil-producing countries and, within a six-year period, increased their foreign loan portfolios from $105 billion (1975) to $400 billion (1981),[35] thereby recycling these so-called petrodollars. Much of the expansion took the form of loans to the public and private sectors in Latin American countries.

Although the magnitude of the debt crisis was not completely disclosed until the Toronto meetings in September 1982, there were earlier indications of serious problems, including evidence that the growth in foreign lending was starting to create disproportionate losses. Table 4–2 shows the net international loan losses for 1980, as a percentage of total net loan losses, incurred by the ten largest commercial banks.

Despite these losses, the banks continued to expand their global loan portfolios. Mexico's foreign debt grew by $16.4 billion and Brazil's by $11.2 billion in a single year (1980),[36] and by 1984 statistics indicated that the total foreign debt of the four largest Latin American borrowers (Argentina, Brazil, Mexico, and Venezuela) amounted to $271 billion, with Brazil having the largest portion ($98 billion).[37] The sixteen largest Third World debtors reportedly had total foreign debt of $520 billion in 1984, with interest on it

Table 4–2
Net International Loan Losses, Ten Largest Banks, 1980

Bank	*Loan Losses as a Percent of Total Net Loan Losses*
Citibank	20
Bank of America	19
Chase Manhattan	15
Manufacturers Hanover	6
Morgan Guaranty	8
Chemical New York	10
Bankers Trust	5
Continental Illinois	[a]
First National (Chicago)	21
Security Pacific	19

Source: Arturo C. Porzecanski, "Profitability of International Banking," in Emmanuel N. Roussakis, *International Banking: Principles and Practices* (New York: Praeger, 1983), p. 138.

[a]Not meaningful due to recoveries.

accruing at an annual rate of $55 billion.[38] Loans made by the nine largest U.S. commercial banks to Caribbean and Latin American nations were said to represent 157 percent of the total capital of those banks—hence, the fear that defaults could literally wipe out the entire capital structures of these major lenders.[39] The same nine banks reportedly represented three-fifths of the total exposure of U.S. banks to Argentina, Mexico, and Brazil.[40]

Had the loans made to foreign governments in each case been used exclusively to meet their real economic needs—steel mills, port facilities, new factories and refineries, and airports—the 1982 forecasts of financial disaster might have been unjustified. It is unfortunately true, however, that a significant portion of those loans, extended by U.S. banks in Latin American countries, was channeled into the hands of individuals who immediately reinvested it outside their borders.

For example, a study prepared by the Federal Reserve regarding 1980 debt extensions indicated that the foreign assets held by Argentine residents increased by $6.7 billion during a year when that country's debt grew by $9 billion; when Mexico's foreign debt, mentioned earlier, increased by $16.4 billion, its citizens' assets in other countries rose by $7.1 billion.[41] When a government defaults on its debt, its assets in U.S. banks can be seized by lenders under the inherent right of set-off against deposits. This was done when Iran repudiated its debts in 1979.[42] However, the private assets of citizens of the debtor nation are not subject to this seizure. This principle may have been ignored by the lending banks as they increased their loan exposure.

If bankers and economists in 1985 appeared more optimistic regarding the global debt situation, their feelings may have reflected the draconian austerity measures imposed by some foreign debtors to strengthen their economies and reduce the staggering inflation rates many of them had experienced. Rimmer de Vries, chief international economist for Morgan Guaranty, stated in the early part of that year that "progress in the debt crisis is coming about three times as fast as we thought possible."[43] In addition, the cautious optimism of some bankers may have been based on the specific agreements that lenders were able to negotiate with the largest debtors.

These agreements took the form of restructuring the existing debt and lengthening the loan maturities. For example, the Mexican government agreed to a multiyear debt restructuring in September 1984 so that the amount of maturities from 1985 through 1990 would be reduced and a "more manageable schedule of amortization" would extend from 1986 through 1998. Adjustments in interest-rates were included in this agreement.[44] Further restructuring, covering $20.1 billion of Mexican debt maturing through the year 1990, was agreed to in September 1985.[45]

Brazil, which achieved a record trade surplus in 1984, was similarly able to meet all its interest payments on a timely basis, and the 1984 maturities of its medium-term loans were refinanced on a nine-year basis.[46] In 1984 the

IMF agreed to act as a negotiator between the lending banks and the Brazilian government regarding that country's economic goals and reduction or extension of its debt.[47]

Nevertheless, any optimism engendered by these developments was necessarily tempered by indications of ongoing problems in other countries. For example, in mid-1985 the installation of a new government in Peru led to renewed fears that that nation might face a downgrading of its creditworthiness since its incoming President publicly announced his intention of withholding interest payments on $14 billion of foreign debt. At the time, Peru was already $250 million in arrears.[48]

In April 1985 the Argentine government implemented changes in the financial system, making it impossible for the nation's banks to avoid central bank reserve requirements. As a result, Banco de Italia y Rio de la Plata, Argentina's third largest bank, closed its doors, and seven lesser bank liquidations took place. Banco de Italia had been obligated for $250 million in loans. These liquidations, coupled with Argentina's annual inflation rate of over 900 percent, prompted new concerns about possible nationalization of the entire banking system in that country and renewed questions about the eventual repayment of Argentina's total foreign debt of $45 billion.[49]

The 1982 annual meeting of the IMF and World Bank led to a disclosure of the severity of the global debt problem; similarly, the 1985 annual meeting, held in Seoul, Korea, led to a proposal by James Baker III, Secretary of the Treasury, for a new infusion of funds to help ease the crisis. His proposal would call for the major U.S. commercial banks to lend an additional $20 billion to the fifteen largest debtor nations. Concurrently, the World Bank would be expected to make $9 billion available by the end of 1988. The World Bank would also act as a monitor of the borrowers' economic policies and repayment schedules.[50] Assuming acceptance by all parties of this proposal, the United States would help provide for a multi-billion-dollar increase in the World Bank's capital, and the possibility arose that the U.S. Treasury and the Fed would use their regulatory powers to reward those banks that increased their global lending and to downgrade the creditworthiness of major banks that did not do so.[51]

Negotiating and Monitoring

Because it is obviously impractical for the debtor countries to negotiate rescheduling and/or restructuring of their obligations individually with each lender, a group known as the Bank Advisory Committee (BAC), consisting of the commercial banks in the United States that are most heavily involved in lending to Latin America, has been formed. The BAC has played a major role in the foreign-loan scenario by providing financial guidance to the borrowers, working on the details of new financing, and monitoring the outstandings of the major borrowers.[52]

The Office of the Comptroller of the Currency is another active participant in the effort to gather timely information on the extent of global debt and to resolve the problems it creates. In 1983 the Comptroller's Office implemented the International Lending Supervision Act, requiring all national banks to submit quarterly reports on the composition and amount of international assets. The Act also establishes uniform accounting standards for national banks regarding fee income restructurings and requires them to establish special reserves out of current income against certain classified foreign loans. The concerns and requirements of the Comptroller are based on the degree of involvement of national banks in global lending; as of June 30, 1984, those banks showed international outstandings of $76 billion and therefore are now required to disclose much more detailed information on their activities and progress.[53]

During February 1984 the Office of the Comptroller, the Federal Reserve, and the FDIC, as the three federal banking agencies, acted jointly to implement a provision of the International Lending Supervision Act that requires banks to establish an Allocated Transfer Risk Reserve (ATRR) against certain categories of international assets. A bank whose asset quality has been impaired by the inability or unwillingness of foreign debtors to make scheduled payments must create an ATRR, entirely separate and distinct from its normal allowance for possible loan losses. The ATRR is charged against current income. The three federal agencies are empowered to require an ATRR of 10 percent of the principal amount of each specified international asset and may increase that requirement to 15 percent if necessary.[54]

Prior to their action in implementing the creation of ATRRs, the three federal agencies had established a new classification system for international loans. Under this system, loans may be classified as substandard, value-impaired, or outright losses, according to the debtors' progress in meeting obligations.

Coping with Crises

Agreements that call for restructuring and rescheduling of debt have been the most commonly used methods of attempting to resolve the crises faced by less-developed countries. Some economists and investment bankers, however, have suggested other innovative approaches that could serve to reduce the lenders' exposure while giving the debtor countries a means of minimizing their burdens.

The first of these approaches, proposed by an economics professor at Carnegie-Mellon University, contemplates the same type of equity-for-debt trade-off that has sometimes been used in domestic finance. Under this plan, a foreign government would transfer its ownership of a major national asset, such as a petrochemical plant or hydroelectric utility, to lending banks in exchange for a reduction in its outstanding loans. Lenders, in turn, would have the ability to market their equity interest to third-party investors. Whether this proposal would be both palatable to the borrowers and acceptable to the lenders is, of course, questionable; however, it has been advanced as a novel approach to the global debt problem.[55]

An alternative proposal suggests the purchase of outstanding loans of the less-developed countries from the lending banks by an entity such as the World Bank, which would issue bonds to obtain the necessary funding for the purchase. The creditworthiness of the World Bank as an issuer would reflect the capital commitments of its member nations. If, for any reason, the World Bank rejected this idea, the author of the proposal envisions the establishment of a new fund, capitalized by the governments of countries whose global debt does not constitute a burden or problem. In either case, the bonds that served to replace outstanding loans would carry interest rates that related to the debtors' payment capacity.[56]

Two other possible approaches to the global debt crisis have been suggested by André de Lattre, Managing Director of the Institute of International Finance.[57] He has pointed out that a large portion of the debt of Latin American borrowers was originally denominated in dollars, so the strength of the dollar as an international currency has decreased the debtors' ability to repay. Therefore, diversification of a country's outstanding loans into other currencies would be helpful. De Lattre's second proposal calls for the issuing of some type of insurance guarantee covering loans made by those nations that maintained their creditworthiness, but he concedes that the cost of such insurance might be extremely high.

International Consumer Banking

As is discussed in detail in chapter 6, one of the dramatic changes in commercial banking in the post-World War II period involved placing new emphasis on the retail sector. Many of the largest banks, which had previously concentrated on the corporate, institutional, and government markets, came to recognize the size and potential profitability of services to consumers. In the face of aggressive competition from the thrift institutions and credit unions, they embarked on large-scale promotions to attract retail business. Automobile loans, home mortgages, checking accounts with no minimum balance, and credit cards became important components of their operations.

What those banks accomplished on the domestic scene has more recently been paralleled in the international area. In the transition from wholesale to retail banking, a bank is able to diversify its risks, and the problems that have surfaced in large cross-border loans have helped in large measure to convince several banks that mass-market business is desirable. Instead of a single credit to a foreign government, corporation, or government-sponsored project, a lending bank can spread the same funds among numerous individual borrowers and thus avoid the possible severe impact of a default.

The attraction of overseas consumer markets is enhanced by the fact that in many countries a significant percentage of total banking assets is controlled by a small number of banks. The perception is that this high degree of concentration may have made those banks competitively slow in marketing services to individuals. Similarly, the innovativeness of major U.S. banks in expanding their range of services, coupled with the technological advances they have made, can prove attractive wherever the local banks have proved to be less sophisticated.

Numerous examples of new efforts to capitalize on global opportunities for doing business with consumers have become evident in the mid-1980s. For example, Citibank now offers checking, savings, and loan-related services (including those provided through finance company subsidiaries) to some 5 million households in thirty-one countries outside the United States and thereby generates consumer deposits of over $7 billion; Bank of America has established the Global Consumer Division to provide insurance, trust, private banking, and discount brokerage services to affluent individuals through its network of foreign branches; and Security Pacific likewise focuses on the upscale segment of the consumer market, offering a range of financial services tailored to specific needs.[58] Citicorp (the holding company of Citibank, N.A.) has acquired banks in Spain, Belgium, and France; bought an insurance broker and two stock brokers in London; made substantial investments in branch networks in Great Britain and West Germany; and opened investment banking offices in fourteen European cities.[59] Chase Manhattan has announced the formation of a Global Electronic Banking unit, has plans for expansion of consumer services in several countries, and has implemented automated teller facilities in Singapore and Hong Kong.[60] Chase Direktbank in the Netherlands opens new accounts and markets new products directly by mail and serves some 300,000 consumers.[61]

The same forces—competitive, technological, and regulatory—that induces many large U.S. banks to become retail in nature now drive them to follow the example of multinational businesses by mobilizing marketing resources to meet the wants and needs of foreign populations. However, the banks are not alone in their recognition of the profit potential in global consumer services. Merrill Lynch has formed a specialized unit for international retail marketing, and American Express is developing strategies for marketing its services to consumers throughout the world.[62]

Twenty percent of bank customers have traditionally supplied 80 percent of deposits. By offering services such as insurance, financial planning, trust, private banking, and brokerage, banks hope to change that ratio and simultaneously generate fee income. Comprehensive packages of financial services for affluent individuals create the likelihood of lasting loyalty.[63] Financial transactions are no longer constrained by time zones or national boundaries, and the consumer in a foreign country can be a source of funds and profits for a U.S. bank for the same reasons as his or her domestic counterpart.[64]

Legislative Developments

The globalization of banking has been furthered significantly by specific legislation. In 1981 congressional approval for IBFs, mentioned earlier, gave U.S. banks the right to conduct international business without being subject to interest-rate ceilings and reserve requirements. Formation of the DIDC, mandated by the Monetary Control Act of 1980, has already resulted in relaxation of those ceilings, and by 1987 all such restrictions on interest rates will have been phased out. The International Banking Act, implemented in 1979 and amended in 1980, placed the operations of U.S. and foreign banks on a more comparable footing and, by eliminating some of the advantages enjoyed by the latter group, enhanced the ability of domestic institutions to compete.[65]

In an attempt to increase the number of U.S. manufacturers who export their goods, Congress passed the Export Trading Company Act in 1982. This legislation defines Export Trading Companies (ETCs) as businesses engaged exclusively in activities related to international trade and deriving over 50 percent of their revenues from the export of goods or services. Smaller companies are encouraged to pool resources in the formation of an ETC and may obtain a Certificate of Review from the U.S. Department of Commerce, protecting themselves against antitrust legislation. Bank holding companies can lend to ETCs or acquire partial or total ownership of them through equity investment; Edge Act subsidiaries of those holding companies may also do so.

Joint ventures, consisting of partnerships between a bank and an exporter, are also possible. An example is the agreement between First Chicago Corporation (parent holding company for First National Bank of Chicago) and Sears World Trade, Inc. (wholly owned subsidiary of Sears, Roebuck and Company). The ETC they have formed provides the synergy of the bank's business ties to manufacturers and the Sears commitment to global trading.[66]

Within two years after passage of the 1982 Act, 24 bank holding companies obtained the necessary approval from the Federal Reserve and established ETC subsidiaries.[67] These companies are intended to help alleviate the

U.S. balance-of-payments deficit by facilitating export trade; in addition, they serve to increase a bank's visibility and reputation internationally without significantly increasing risk and can generate fee income for the bank by providing letters of credit and bankers' acceptances for customers.[68]

Technological Advances

With the growth of the Eurodollar market, the expansion of international trade, and the emergence of increasingly important financial centers in various parts of the world, the volume of interbank transactions rose steadily and the need for speed, cost efficiency, and accuracy in daily settlements among banks became more evident. Technological change became a necessity; traditional paper- and labor-intensive methods of transferring funds would no longer suffice.

The twelve major banks in New York City that comprise the membership of the New York Clearing House jointly arrived at a solution with the formation of the first fully automated funds transfer network: the Clearing House Interbank Payments System (CHIPS). Since its inception in 1970, CHIPS has displayed steady and remarkable growth and has become one of the most important mechanisms in the internationalization of money. Approximately 25 million fully automated transactions per year are now processed for the 138 participating CHIPS banks.[69] The daily dollar volume averages $300 billion, and settlements among the banks now take place on a same-day basis through electronic debits and credits to accounts at the Federal Reserve Bank of New York.[70]

A second major development in the area of international money transfers occurred in 1972 with the formation of the Society for Worldwide Interbank Financial Telecommunications (SWIFT). The objectives of speed, accuracy, and cost effectiveness in this system parallel those of CHIPS; SWIFT, however, does not actually handle settlements among banks. It provides instead a universally accepted standard format for message transfers, so speed and accuracy improve while costs decrease. The system was designed jointly by U.S. and European banks and was implemented in 1977.

The Foreign Exchange Market

The explosive growth of foreign trade in the post–World War II era has had a major impact on many functions and services of banks in the United States. High on the list of these is the global foreign exchange market, which in 1985 handled an average daily volume of $150 billion. There are several reasons for the dramatic increase seen in this market:

1. Many bank customers are required to settle their transactions in a specific foreign currency; for example, the terms of payment under a letter of credit may call for this type of settlement. Banks accommodate their customers by making such currencies available.
2. As a matter of policy, some banks regularly "take a position"; that is, they make and maintain a market in the most actively traded currencies, and their traders may, on any given day, buy, sell, or swap specific currencies.
3. Many major U.S. banks have substantial deposits on the books of foreign banks, and these are maintained in the local currencies.
4. Purchases and sales of various assets that are denominated in local currencies (e.g., securities) may deplete or add to a bank's inventory position.
5. Major banks, in addition to handling *spot* transactions in foreign exchange (i.e., those that call for immediate delivery of a certain currency), often enter into *forward* contracts. In effect, these guarantee delivery of a specified quantity of pounds, yen, francs, and so forth at a stated future date based on that currency's value against the dollar at the time the contract is executed.
6. Companies that are involved in bidding on international contracts frequently enter into currency *options,* arranged through their banks. These are purchased rights to buy or sell specific currencies at specific prices at future dates; the purchaser of an option pays an up-front premium for the protection that is gained.

The Federal Reserve is a major holder of foreign currencies such as German marks, Swiss francs, and Japanese yen, chiefly as a result of intervention transactions by central banks in other countries in their efforts to achieve greater monetary stability. At year-end 1984 the Fed inventory, consisting chiefly of these three foreign currencies, stood at $3.6 billion. The appreciation of the dollar against this inventory during the year resulted in valuation losses of $1.3 billion for the Fed.[72]

The volatility of the foreign exchange market—the sudden and meaningful changes that regularly take place in quoted values against the dollar—makes it an area of high risk for banks. A high degree of sophisticated, alert management is essential if that risk is to be mitigated.[73] The collapses in 1974 of the Franklin National Bank in New York and the Bankhaus Herstatt in West Germany were attributed to the losses both had experienced in trading in that market.[74] Conversely, substantial profits can be made in foreign exchange; for three consecutive years (1982, 1983, 1984) the Chase Manhattan Bank reported income of $131 million, $117 million, and $119 million (pretax) from such transactions, and these profits represented 40.6, 16.7, and 18.9 percent respectively of the bank's total pretax income for those years.[75]

Interest-Rate Swaps

As capital markets have become increasingly international in nature, as banks have sought to keep pace with the new demands and needs of their global customers, and as the velocity of funds movements among the world's financial centers has been maximized electronically, sophisticated corporations have joined with the banks in developing new mechanisms that enable them to cross national boundaries while investing, borrowing, or changing their stream of cash flow. For the banks, one of these new mechanisms, the swap, has proved to be an important source of fee income. For businesses, the same swap affords a means of managing liabilities and mitigating exposure to changes in interest rates.

Within a three-year time frame following its introduction in 1982, the interest-rate swap became a driving force in the Eurobond market and a favored technique among many corporate treasurers. In terms of dollar volume the market, estimated at $3 billion in 1982, is now believed to be in the $70 billion–$100 billion range; Citibank, usually regarded as the most active single entity in the market, alone handled $17.5 billion in swaps during 1984.[76] In 1983 an estimated 40 percent of all bond issues in capital markets were said to be swaps-related, and Deutsche Bank uses swap techniques in connection with some 40 percent of all its Eurodollar lending.[77] Swaps are often made in huge dollar amounts, with an average transaction estimated at $25 million–$50 million; therefore, the banks—although their profit margins on swaps have narrowed considerably—reap handsome profits in acting as intermediaries.[78]

The origins of interest-rate swaps are found in the currency swaps that came into vogue during the 1970s and provided an exchange of, for example, U.S. dollars for Canadian. These swaps were frequently used as institutions raised non-dollar-denominated funds overseas and exchanged them for dollar-based funds held by organizations in need of foreign currencies.

Through a natural evolution, the concept of swapping interest rates within a single currency arose. Banks recognized it as a fee-producing tool; at the same time, money managers saw its value in taking a longer-term view of rates without tying up funds and in hedging against rate swings. Since 1982 the transactions have frequently become more complicated, involving both interest rates and currencies at the same time.

In an interest-rate swap, a company, in effect, exchanges fixed-rate debt for floating-rate debt or vice versa or one floating-rate-indexed obligation for another. Both rates are calculated on an agreed amount in the same currency, with the dollar currently serving as the most frequently used. A major commercial bank may act as the intermediary between two parties or may take a position, as Citibank does, by purchasing or selling before it has found a contra party.[79]

Assume that Company A borrows at the floating three-month LIBOR (London Interbank Offered Rate) plus 0.5 percent, while Company B, with a different credit standing, borrows at LIBOR plus 1 percent.[80] In the bond market, the longer-term risk widens that differential so that Company A would pay 12 percent and Company B, 14 percent (all figures are purely hypothetical). Company A enters into an agreement to issue bonds at 12 percent and receives a flow of funds at that rate, covering its coupons, from an intermediary bank. The latter is paid 12.5 percent by Company B. Company A pays the intermediary at the LIBOR rate; the bank, in turn, passes those payments along to Company B, which has arranged short-term borrowing at LIBOR plus 1 percent.

From the viewpoints of all three parties, this is an ideal situation, since each one benefits. The intermediary receives 0.5 percent (= 50 basis points); Company A obtains short-term money at LIBOR rather than at LIBOR plus 0.5 percent; and Company B is effectively raising money at a total cost of 13.5 percent, thereby reducing its interest expense by 0.5 percent.[81]

Although profit margins like those in this simplistic example have dwindled in 1985, the point must again be made that even at a lower spread a swap can be highly profitable for a bank to arrange. If the transaction is for $25 million, a spread of 12.5 basis points (1/8 of 1 percent) yields a fee of $31,250. And even if profit margins are reduced, the basic advantages of the swap technique remain:

1. The swap is entirely off the balance sheet. Since swaps cannot be quantified as contingent liabilities, they need not be footnoted in financial statements.
2. Swaps are entirely private and anonymous and do not require reporting in the United States to the Securities and Exchange Commission.
3. Unlike any other forms of barter, a swap consists only of an agreement to exchange interest flows; principal amounts are not exchanged.
4. The documentation is relatively simple and brief.
5. Companies can convert one type of debt or a portion of total debt from one rate to another without renegotiating terms with a lender or restructuring an entire facility.[82]

Since the first interest-rate swaps were consummated, options and innovations have been introduced in many cases. The Federal Home Loan Bank Board, as the regulatory body for U.S. S&Ls, has authorized their use by its members as a means of hedging against the risk in mortgage loan portfolios. Interest-rate swaps have also been arranged in the commercial paper market. The potential for even further growth seems enormous, as corporations in increasing numbers seek the benefits of flexibility, hedging, and less expensive financing that these swaps can provide.

International Cash Management

The discussion of strategic planning in chapter 3 suggested three vital questions that management would have to address. A knowledge of the bank's present condition, a statement of its key objectives, and an agenda for the steps required to reach those objectives are the essential building blocks upon which the planning process rests.

Similarly, as corporations have grown in size, the individuals who are responsible for tracking and expediting the inflow of remittances, managing disbursements, and obtaining information from banks for decision-making purposes must pose a series of questions if the funds position of the business is to be most efficiently controlled. Those individuals need to know, on a daily basis,

how much "money" they have,

where that "money" is domiciled,

where it should be concentrated,

how much of it is needed over various time frames,

how and where any excess funds can be put to profitable use.[83]

The generic term *cash management* can be used to desribe the range of services that answers these questions for a company. Its value to domestic corporations, its use of state-of-the-art technology, and its role in the new world of bank relationships with customers are discussed in chapter 8.

Corporations that have become international in nature by engaging in various types of foreign operations increasingly look to their banks to provide services that will

accelerate worldwide collections of funds;

control the outflow of payments;

provide information on the status of all bank accounts, regardless of where those accounts are located;

monitor the status of outstanding obligations such as letters of credit;

enhance decision making on investments.

The need for a company to utilize one or more of these highly customized services increases geometrically as the scope of its global operations expands. If it sells its products in ten countries, receives payments and makes disbursements in each of them, and makes all investments through its headquarters in the United States, its profit objectives can best be met if it has access to those deposit, payment, and information products that are grouped under the umbrella of cash management.

In a 1985 survey of *Fortune* 1000 corporations, 85 percent of the 200 respondents felt that global cash management was indeed an important topic for them. While usage of classic banking services such as letters of credit, international money transfers, and bank drafts was commonplace, many respondents were also using newer and more sophisticated techniques to obtain worldwide information and to concentrate funds from overseas locations. Forty-seven percent stated that their earnings had improved as a result.[84]

Today the corporate cash manager, through a simple terminal in his or her office, can obtain timely data on the status of bank accounts in various parts of the world. Through a personal computer, he or she can submit complete applications for, amend, or cancel letters of credit and can initiate funds transfers so that the corporation's funds are always in the right locations at the right time, with surplus funds being invested on a daily basis. Through the international cash management consultants at major banks, the cash manager can become familiar with the availability of specialized services in other countries, business practices and culture in any of them, and any regulatory constraints that inhibit movements of funds.[85] Through priority services such as the air courier facilities offered by some U.S. banks, he or she can substantially reduce the time frame required to convert checks drawn on foreign banks into usable cash.[86]

Regulatory Constraints

The internationalization of banking has raised questions about where ultimate supervisory control should rest. For example, a national bank in the United States is chartered, examined, and regulated by the Comptroller of the Currency, must belong to the Federal Reserve, and must be a member of the FDIC; which of those agencies, or the British government, should supervise its branch in London? Conversely, which government should supervise the operations of a branch of a Swiss bank in New York City?

Representatives of twelve nations met in Basle, Switzerland, in 1983 to discuss these questions and ultimately drew up a Concordat, providing guidelines on supervisory responsibilities. This agreement provides that authorities in the parent country—that is, the country in which the bank's parent is located—would assume responsibility for the liquidity of all its operations, while a host country was authorized to supervise liquidity in branches and subsidiaries within its borders. Overseas branches of U.S. national banks are supervised by the Office of the Comptroller; those operated by state-chartered member banks are supervised by the Federal Reserve; and overseas branches of state nonmembers by the FDIC and the appropriate state agencies. Regulation K of the Federal Reserve requires all U.S. banks to submit sufficient data on their overseas subsidiaries to allow for examination from their home offices. Banks in the United States that are controlled by foreign interests are subject to the same reporting requirements as other, purely domestic banks.[87]

Summary

One of the oldest clichés in commercial banking held that the international department of a large money-center institution could be called a bank within a bank; that is, it consisted of a unit that duplicated many of the components on the domestic side. Through these specialized units, a customer could obtain all the services he or she needed to handle imports and/or exports, finance ongoing needs in foreign trade, and cope with the language, business-culture, and monetary-policy differences that exist among nations.

If an observer had visited one of these major banks twenty years ago, he or she would indeed have found teller, bookkeeping, credit, collection, and money transfer facilities paralleling those serving domestic customers. This observer no doubt would have learned that bills of exchange, letters of credit, collections, and bankers' acceptances were the essentials of international banking. A return visit to the same major bank today would provide ample evidence of the impact that change—whether in terms of policy, range of services, organization, philosophy, or technology—has made.

Instead of relying on its foreign correspondent banks to provide services for its customers, the bank probably has established branches in key locations around the world. Instead of acting alone in extending credit, it probably has become a participant with foreign banks in large loans to governments or businesses outside the United States. Instead of conducting its activities in only one U.S. city, it may have taken advantage of the provisions of the Edge Act and opened offices in Houston, Miami, New York, or San Francisco to assist customers with various types of transactions involving foreign trade.

The bank has undoubtedly revised its thinking so that money is now recognized as nothing more than a mere debit or credit that can be moved electronically to or from any corner of the globe in practically no time. It may have become an institution that relies heavily on Eurodollars, unknown to former generations of bankers, for much of its funding. Perhaps it has become one of the banks that are active in the burgeoning interest-rate or foreign currency swaps, like those entered into by Sears, Roebuck and Company in 1984 on $2 billion of debt to establish long-term fixed rates on variable-rate short-term credits.[88]

The bank's operations units undoubtedly now handle a vastly increased volume of letters of credit, bankers' acceptances, and foreign collections and do so with automated facilities that may be replicated in customers' offices through microcomputers or other terminals. Its extensions of credit to foreign banks, governments, and corporations have become so important that it may have established new units, dedicated to recording and analyzing country risks.

Perhaps most important, the observer today would probably find that the international department has become a far more important contributor to the institution's total income so, more than ever before, it earns the title of a bank within a bank.

Notes

1. A *bill of exchange* is a written order (also known as a draft), directing that a payment be made and commonly used as a payment medium in international transactions. A *bankers' acceptance* is a draft, drawn on a bank and officially signed and stamped by that bank as a guarantee of payment at maturity.
2. Martin Mayer, *The Bankers* (New York: David McKay Co., 1974), p. 437.
3. Emmanual N. Roussakis (Ed.), *International Banking: Principles and Practices* (New York: Praeger, 1983), p. 19.
4. *Federal Reserve Bulletin,* September 1982, p. A56.
5. Sydney J. Key, "The Internationalization of U.S. Banking," in Richard C. Aspinwall and Robert A. Eisenbeis, eds., *Handbook for Banking Strategy* (New York: John Wiley & Sons, 1985), p. 271.
6. Paul S. Nadler, *Commercial Banking in the Economy,* 3rd ed. (New York: Random House, 1979), pp. 153–154.
7. *Federal Reserve Bulletin,* January 1985, p. A53.
8. "Bank Scoreboard," *Business Week,* April 8, 1985, p. 107.
9. Arturo C. Porzecanski, "Profitability of International Banking," in Roussakis, op. cit., p. 135.
10. Ibid., p. 138.
11. Key, op. cit., pp. 273–275.
12. Lynne Curry, "Citicorp Growth Spreads Fear Among Competitors," *International Herald Tribune,* June 11, 1984, p. 8.
13. Andrew Albert, "Merrill Lynch Creates Global Coordinating Unit," *American Banker,* March 7, 1985, p. 3.
14. Federal Reserve Bank of New York, "Activities of Edge Act Corporations," Circular 9929, October 8, 1985.
15. "Edge Banks USA," *American Banker,* October 23, 1985, p. 1A.
16. Office of the Comptroller of the Currency, "Foreign Banking Organizations in the United States," *Quarterly Journal,* September 1984, p. 5.
17. Ibid.

18. *Banking in the United States: A Guide for Foreign Bankers* (New York: Peat, Marwick, Mitchell & Co., 1980), pp. 21–23.

19. "Foreign Banking Organizations in the United States," p. 8.

20. This bank now operates in the United States under the name of National Westminster Bank USA.

21. These acquisitions were cited by Henry C. Wallich, member of the Federal Reserve Board of Governors, in a speech to Congress (*Federal Reserve Bulletin,* October 1982, pp. 621–624).

22. Sydney J. Key and James M. Brundy, "Implementation of the International Banking Act," *Federal Reserve Bulletin,* October 1979, p. 787.

23. Federal Reserve Bank of New York, "Interstate Banking Activities of Foreign Banks," Circular 8930, October 9, 1980.

24. Jinny St. Goar, "Who's Next?," *Forbes,* December 19, 1983, p. 220.

25. Andrew Albert, "Fed Approves Allied Irish Takeover of First Maryland Bankcorp," *American Banker,* November 29, 1983, p. 3.

26. Sydney J. Key, "International Banking Facilities," *Federal Reserve Bulletin,* October 1982, p. 566. See also Bowman Brown and Emmanuel N. Roussakis, "Offshore Banking Centers," in Roussakis, op. cit., pp. 84–85.

27. In Charles W. Hultman and L. Randolph McGee, "International Banking Facilities: The Early Response," *The Bankers Magazine,* May–June 1984, p. 84.

28. "Foreign Banking Organizations in the United States," p. 6.

29. Charles N. Stabler, "Defusing the Debt Bomb," *Wall Street Journal,* April 1, 1985, p. 1.

30. For example, Nicholas D. Kristof, "Debt Crisis Called All But Over," *The New York Times,* February 4, 1985, p. D1; and Gary Hector, "Third World Debt: The Bomb Is Defused," *Fortune,* February 18, 1985, p. 36.

31. Lenny Glynn, "Is the Latin Debt Crisis Over?," *Institutional Investor,* May 1985, pp. 86–90.

32. "The view . . . was widely held in the past that a country cannot go bankrupt and will always meet its obligations." Hugo Colje, "Provisioning for Country Risk," *The Banker,* January 1985, p. 31.

33. Charles P. Alexander, "Jumbo Loans, Jumbo Risks," *Time,* December 3, 1984, p. 59.

34. Jack M. Guttentag and Richard J. Herring, "The Current Crisis in International Lending," in *Studies in International Economics* (Washington, D.C.: The Brookings Institution, 1985), p. 2.

35. Porzecanski, op. cit., p. 139.

36. Larry A. Sjaastad, "Where the Latin American Loans Went," *Fortune,* November 26, 1984, p. 5; and Norman Gall, "Games Bankers Play," *Forbes,* December 5, 1983, p. 172.

37. Kristof, op. cit.

38. Hector, op. cit.

39. Alexander, op. cit.

40. Guttentag and Herring, op. cit., p. 5.

41. Sjaastad, op. cit.

42. "The Banks Squabble over Iran's Assets," *Business Week,* December 3, 1979, p. 110.

43. In Hector, op. cit.

44. Cited in The Chase Manhattan Corporation Form 10-Q for the period ending September 30, 1984, and filed with the Securities and Exchange Commission.

45. Donald Shoultz, "2 Latin Debtors Sign Accords," *American Banker,* September 3, 1985, p. 8.

46. The Bank Of New York Company, *1984 Annual Report,* p. 52.

47. "IMF Pact with Brazil on Additional Financing," *The New York Times,* May 13, 1985, p. D10.

48. Sarah Bartlett, "Latin American Debtors Are Spoiling for a Fight," *Business Week,* May 27, 1985, p. 52.

49. George Hatch, "Argentina's Banking Woes," *The Wall Street Journal,* May 24, 1985, p. 29.

50. Jonathan Friedland, "Baker Urges $20 Billion Boost in Bank Lending to 3d World," *American Banker,* October 9, 1985, p. 2.

51. Blanca Riemer; Sarah Bartlett; and James B. Treece, "Facing Reality on Latin Debt," *Business Week,* October 21, 1985, pp. 36–37.

52. Office of the Comptroller of the Currency, *1984 Annual Report,* p. 3.

53. Office of the Comptroller of the Currency, *1984 Annual Report,* pp. 22–23.

54. Guttentag and Herring, op. cit., p. 23.

55. Allan H. Meltzer, in Charles N. Stabler, "Defusing the Debt Bomb the Less Painful Way," *The Wall Street Journal,* April 1, 1985, p. 1.

56. Richard S. Weinert, "Coping with LDC Debt," *The World of Banking,* Bank Administration Institute, March–April 1984, pp. 20–21.

57. "Innovative Approaches to the Debt Crisis," *The Bankers Magazine,* May–June 1985, pp. 34–36.

58. Ellen S. Perelman, "The Ultimate Frontier: Globalization of Consumer Banking," *American Banker,* May 23, 1985, p. 1.

59. Andrew B. Wilson, "Citicorp's Gutsy Campaign to Conquer Europe," *Business Week,* July 15, 1985, p. 46.

60. The Chase Manhattan Corporation, *1984 Annual Report,* pp. 16–18.

61. James H. O'Connor, "New Approach to Consumer Is Focus of Chase in Europe," *American Banker,* November 14, 1985, p. 2.

62. Perelman, op. cit.

63. Philip T. Sudo, "Survey Pinpoints a Growing, Upscale Bank Market," *American Banker,* May 28, 1985, p. 8.

64. David W. Wise, "The Mending Wall: The Rise of the Universal Financial Market," *The World of Banking,* Bank Administration Institute, March–April 1984, p. 16.

65. Key and Brundy, op. cit.

66. Robert E. Norton, "First Chicago Sees Trade Venture as Big Cog," *American Banker,* December 12, 1983, p. 8.

67. Ann Watson, "Export Trading Is Not Just a Big-Bank Game," *ABA Banking Journal,* November 1984, p. 18.

68. W. Michael Latimer and Laura G. Moses, "Banks and the U.S. Export Trading Companies Act of 1982," *The World of Banking,* Bank Administration Institute, March–April 1983, pp. 30–33.

69. Tom Ferris, "You've Never Heard of CHIPS?," *American Banker,* June 4, 1985, p. 20.

70. David M. Mace, "The Role of Correspondent Banking in the 80's," Speech delivered to the Bankers Association for Foreign Trade, New York, April 10, 1984, p. 5.

71. Gordon Matthews, "Foreign Exchange Flourishes," *American Banker,* November 25, 1985, p. 2.

72. Board of Governors of the Federal Reserve System, *71st Annual Report: 1984,* pp. 24–25.

73. Edward W. Reed; Richard V. Cotter; Edward K. Gill; and Richard K. Smith, *Commercial Banking,* 3rd ed. (Englewood Cliffs, N.J.: Prentice-Hall, Inc., 1984), pp. 478–480.

74. Mayer, op. cit., pp. 476–477.

75. The Chase Manhattan Corporation, *1984 Annual Report,* p. 50.

76. Lisabeth Weiner, "Citibank Sits on Top of Swap Heap," *American Banker,* June 12, 1985, p. 1.

77. Jonathan Hakim, "A New Awakening," *The Economist,* March 24, 1984, p. 14.

78. Sanford Rose, "Random Thoughts," *American Banker,* November 6, 1984, p. 1.

79. Hakim, op. cit.

80. LIBOR and the U.S. Treasury bill rate are the commonly used indexes.

81. For examples of other types of interest-rate swaps and detailed explanations, see Tanya S. Arnold, "How to Do Interest Rate Swaps," *Harvard Business Review,* September–October 1984, pp. 96–101; and Charles Grant, "Why Treasurers Are Swapping Swaps," *Euromoney,* April 1985, pp. 19–30.

82. Trevor S. Ricards, "Interest Rate Swaps . . . ," *Cashflow,* December 1984, pp. 37–39.

83. Claire Makin, "Cash Managers Come of Age," *Institutional Investor,* December 1984, pp. 273–278.

84. J. Markham Collins and Alan W. Frankle, "International Cash Management Practices of Large U.S. Firms," *Journal of Cash Management,* July–August 1985, pp. 42–47.

85. William N. Oosthoek, "International Cash Management Consulting: A Conceptual Framework for Analyzing Corporations," *Bank Administration,* February 1985, p. 71.

86. Marcia Berss, "Free Ride," *Forbes,* December 5, 1983, p. 54.

87. Charles W. Hultman, "U.S. International Bank Supervision & the Revised Basle Concordat," *Bank Administration,* pp. 76–80.

88. Keith Wishon and Lorin S. Chevalier, "Interest Rate Swaps: Your Rate or Mine?," *Journal of Accountancy,* September 1985, p. 64.

5
The New World of Electronic Banking

A staff member at the Federal Reserve Bank of Richmond has used a literary analogy that may serve here to introduce one of the most timely, complex, and controversial topics in the new world of commercial banking: the introduction, evolution, status, and potential future of Electronic Funds Transfer Systems (EFTS). The writer recalls Mary Shelley's classic, *Frankenstein,* and points out that the scientist who created the monster could not guide or control it. When Dr. Frankenstein failed to cope with the consequences of his creation, disaster ensued.[1] The monster in the author's metaphor is the electronic payments mechanism and, in particular, Automated Clearing Houses (ACHs). He views the ACH as an invention that, like Dr. Frankenstein's, has failed to live up to expectations and is beset by problems that may prevent it from ever attaining its potential.

The analogy is valid only up to a point. The disparity between Dr. Frankenstein's monster on the one hand, and EFTS applications and techniques on the other, deserves more attention than the supposed similarity. The former had no success whatever and proved disastrous to all concerned; the latter, considered in the broadest sense, has had some notable positive accomplishments in its relatively brief history and holds the promise of still more in the future.

The analogy in the referenced article might be more appropriate if it focused on the situation that gave rise to EFTS in the first place. If that were the scenario, we could draw a parallel between the scientist who created the monster with high hopes for it but found he was doomed to disappointment and the commercial bankers.

Historical Background

A substantial portion of the commercial banks' marketing effort has always portrayed the paper check as the ideal payment medium. Annual growth in check volume, resulting at least partly from this effort, was manageable.

When that growth accelerated, technological improvements, such as the introduction of magnetic ink character recognition MICR to make check data machine readable, enabled the banks—the custodians of demand deposits and therefore the only institutions against which customers could draw checks directly—to cope reasonably well with the increases they had encouraged.

The continued expansion of the U.S. economy meant, however, that the volume of annual check usage grew beyond expectations. As businesses grew in size and number, their need for checks to pay their suppliers and employees increased. Furthermore, the entry of many major banks that had formerly been wholesale in nature into large-scale retail marketing added millions of consumers to the ranks, with a corresponding explosion in check usage. Between 1940 and 1970, the nation's annual volume of checks increased by 1,100 percent, and despite any inroads that substitute forms of payment have made to date, over 100 million checks per day must still be processed by the banking system. The total costs of that processing are estimated to exceed $20 billion per year.[2]

The combination of tremendous growth in volume and steadily escalating labor costs naturally led to concerns over whether the banking industry could continue to cope. Other industries (e.g., brokerage firms) had done such an excellent job of developing new business that they found themselves swamped with a quantity of paper beyond their processing ability. Several well-known firms were forced into liquidation as a result, and bankers logically wondered if a similar fate was in store for them.

Unfortunately, as systems experts, data processing specialists, and consultants worked with the bankers to devise less costly, more efficient payment vehicles, a basic assumption was made; over the course of time, it came to be accepted by many bankers, and its terminology became widely used in their lexicon. The assumption was that a *checkless society* would evolve, in which electronic debit and credit entries to checking accounts would completely replace paper checks. There appears to have been a widespread belief that every segment of the economy would quickly and enthusiastically embrace the new technology and would therefore discontinue all use of paper checks.

At best, that forecast has been fulfilled only to a very limited extent. At worst, it is now regarded as totally unrealistic. A less-check society, in which paper check usage is reduced but not eliminated, is already here; a totally checkless society is, as one observer has noted, unacceptable to every category of bank customers.[3] I do not say this to minimize the banks' early successes in persuading customers to adopt various types of EFTS. Those positive accomplishments should be viewed as a step in the right direction. Mention must equally be made, however, of the many failures and frustrations that have been encountered:

> Check volumes have continued to grow 5 percent per year over the last five years. . . . less than 15 percent of payroll transactions today are EFT direct deposit.[4]
>
> Corporate-to-corporate electronic funds transfer (EFT) . . . has shown relatively little in the way of results. . . . The total volume was less than 3,000 transactions in all of 1984. This was truly a trickle in a river of billions of payments.[5]
>
> When automated clearing was first conceived, a checkless society was predicted as a near-term result. Now, ten years [later] . . . the full potential of automated clearing has only begun to be tapped. . . . *American Banker* recently observed that "ACH volume has barely made a dent in the check world."[6]
>
> Half of those who have tried automated teller machines (ATMs) say they still prefer handling routine business through tellers' windows.[7]
>
> Most of the world-be customers of these advanced systems now seem to be perfectly happy with things the way they are.[8]
>
> The "cashless" and "checkless" societies have not arrived. Checks continue to increase and are now expected to do so until at least 1990. . . . The videotex profit and loss statement is all cost and no revenue. And even home banking is way behind schedule. Present customers can be counted in the thousands rather than millions.[9]

This chapter presents as completely balanced an overview as possible, addressing each aspect of the state of the art in EFTS. The new technology is a critical element in the future of commercial banking in the United States, and an awareness of all its ramifications requires a realistic understanding of what has already been done, what the problems and challenges are, and what appears most likely to occur. Therefore, failures and successes in the total EFTS scenario receive equal attention as I discuss the banks' efforts to market the new technology under five headings:

1. Automated Teller Machines (ATMs),
2. Point-of-Sale Terminals (POS),
3. Home Banking Systems,
4. Systems for Direct Deposit,
5. Systems for Direct Debits and Preauthorized Payments.

Automated Teller Machines (ATMs)

The discussion of global banking in chapter 4 made the point that certain bank services, although they were traditional and basic, were now being offered to customers in different ways. No single aspect of activity in the arena of financial services has undergone such drastic change as the process of delivery: the point of interface between the provider of service and the user, the format of a transaction, and the application of modern technology.[10]

Instead of telephoning a bank to obtain balance information, a client may use a microcomputer or terminal for the same data. Instead of visiting an imposing brick-and-mortar edifice to request a loan, a consumer may apply by telephone or go to a storefront-type loan production office. Instead of a batch of canceled checks, returned in random order with a bank statement, the customer may receive pure information in the form of a computerized list, in check number sequence, of all paid items; the checks are microfilmed for storage by the bank.

The key word *delivery* is nowhere more applicable than in the area of EFTS. How can delivery of information or documents to the customer be effected at reduced cost with more efficiency? Where will customer transactions be initiated? Which types of transactions can most readily be handled on an automated basis? Based on the most recent statistics, ATMs represent the one application of EFTS that has most effectively answered these questions. The use of ATMs by consumers, to the extent that it has increased despite disappointments and negative reactions, represents the greatest success the banks have had in bridging the gap between their objectives and customer desires through implementation of the new technology.

The machines that are known as ATMs today originated in 1971 in Atlanta as limited-function machines, known as cash dispensers, installed by Citizens and Southern National Bank.[11] They served the dual purpose of giving the bank's customers 24-hour, 365-day access to funds and reducing the bank's check-cashing costs.[12] ATMs were initially marketed as an innovative convenience to consumers. For many banks, they provided a differentiated product, and 83 percent of the institutions that installed them before 1975 described their objective as increasing market share, while 31 percent reported that the introduction of ATMs was simply a response to competition.[13] The first units, and most of those that have subsequently been installed, were built through the wall of an existing branch, and as of 1984 70 percent of all on-premises ATMs fell into that category, as opposed to lobby or drive-up facilities.[14]

The original rationales for offering ATMs have been broadened to include possible replacement of brick-and-mortar branches by sophisticated stand alone units, located wherever the consumer population is. The Arizona

Bank estimates that thirteen years are required for a new full-service branch to repay its original investment as opposed to a three-year payback time frame for an off-premises ATM.[15] Alternatively, if ATMs did not succeed in replacing branches, they could serve to reduce the continuing demand for tellers. Bank of America eliminated some 1,400 teller positions by expanding its number of ATMs and imposed a surcharge whenever customers chose to use tellers for transactions that could have been handled through ATMs.[16]

Growth

At year-end 1984 an estimated 59,300 ATMs were in operation in the United States,[17] representing a growth rate of 450 percent since 1978.[18] Ninety-one percent of all commercial banks with deposits of $1 billion or more now provide access to ATMs for their customers, and 93 percent of banks in the $500 million to $1 billion range do so.[19] Average usage per machine per month in 1984 was 5,856 transactions, of which 1,394 were simple balance inquiries.[20]

Using an ATM to obtain information on one's bank balance, coupled with the evidence that off-premises ATMs are increasing at a faster rate than through-the-wall or lobby versions, reinforces the point that basic bank services are now being delivered in new ways. The shopping center and supermarket now account for one-half of all off-premises ATM transactions, indicating that users are extremely responsive to the added convenience of handling at least part of their banking business in frequently visited, high-traffic environments. In 1970 an estimated 90 percent of consumers' checking account transactions were handled at branches; by 1980 that percentage had dropped to 80, and one projection states that it will fall to 60 percent in 1990.[21]

In a relatively new development, many banks have assumed a lead role in installing ATMs in employees' work environments (office buildings, factories, hospitals), in residential buildings, and in college and university facilities. In these cases, the convenience factor is increased tremendously. Tenants in an apartment house, for example, enjoy not only the luxury of having around-the-clock access to account information and funds but also the security of banking inside the building. ATMs at universities now average about 10,000 user transactions per month,[22] making them among the highest performers, and when an employer is induced to allow an ATM on the premises, the bank that markets this service is immediately given new opportunities to sell direct deposit of the employee payroll and to obtain individual accounts from the employees.[23]

The Executive Vice-President for Consumer Services at Citibank, N.A. cites his bank's experience to refute any assumption that proliferation of ATMs necessarily brings about reductions in a bank's number of branches and the size of its branch staff. Citibank reportedly operates thousands of ATMs to serve its 1.5 million consumer customers but still finds it necessary to maintain 270 branches in the New York City area, with a staff of over 7,000 dedicated to consumer services. The same author claims that 70–80 percent of Citibank's consumer customers use the ATMs—a percentage more than double the nationwide average.[24]

ATM Networks

Citibank's system is believed to be the nation's largest proprietary ATM program (i.e., only Citibank cardholders can access it). In contrast, sharing of ATM facilities and the joining of large numbers of banks in local, regional, or national networks have become commonplace and have sprung up in every part of the United States. A study in 1985 indicated that 83.4 percent of all commercial banks with deposits of $1 billion or more were network members; among thrift institutions of that size, the percentage was 68.1.[25]

One reason for the popularity of networks lies in the costs inherent in purchasing a modern ATM, providing facilities to house it, and arranging for annual maintenance. These costs may total $50,000–$75,000. The network concept allows customers of one bank to use the ATMs of many other banks and thus to obtain cash at many locations.[26] The Federal Reserve has specifically authorized such sharing, subject to the laws of individual states.[27]

In early 1985 over 200 networks, handling some 180 million ATM transactions per month for 50 million cardholders, were identified. For example, Internet, in the Washington, D.C. area, serves customers of 110 banks, S&Ls, and credit unions.[28]

In March 1985 six commercial banks and one of the largest savings banks in New York City joined with a commercial bank in Stamford, Connecticut, to form the New York Cash Exchange (NYCE).[29] Banks in the New York–New Jersey–Connecticut area subsequently became participants. As a result, some 3.5 million customers gained access to almost 1,000 ATMs at 650 locations. Any holder of a Visa, MasterCard, or bank card issued by any participant can withdraw cash from checking or savings, obtain a cash advance, or determine the status of an account through an ATM operated by any other participant, without paying a fee for the service.[30]

The PLUS system evolved from a joint venture of three Colorado banks, originally known as the Rocky Mountain BankCard system. By 1985 it had grown to include over 1,400 member banks with 26 million customer accounts in forty-eight states.[31]

Nationwide advertising in 1985 for CIRRUS, the major competing system, claimed that its member banks in 2,600 locations in the United States provided access to 8,400 ATMs for 31 million cardholders.

The four largest commercial banks in Alabama joined in 1985 to form a statewide shared network of ATMs at a cost of $750,000 each. Again, cardholders from any of the four participants can use their cards in any of the 400 terminals operated by members. The four banks found this joint venture less expensive than expanding their individual proprietary ATM systems.[32]

The same logic was cited by the Independent Bankers Association of America (IBAA), which has over 7,500 members, in announcing that it had entered into an agreement with Telecredit, Inc. of Los Angeles, covering a comprehensive range of payment-related services for participating IBAA members at reduced costs. Telecredit, Inc. will provide them with access for their Visa and MasterCard cardholders to all ATMs that are linked to the two systems and will supply card authorization and check guarantee services to merchants and data-processing support to the banks.[33]

State law in Texas prohibits full-scale branch banking but, paradoxically, allows financial institutions (including the state's 1,400 commercial banks) to place ATMs in supermarkets, airports, and shopping centers. Shared networks in that state have displayed steady growth in recent years, giving consumers at least part of the convenience of brick-and-mortar branches.[34] The two major systems in Texas, PULSE and MPACT, have joined to form the nation's largest regional network, handling 3.8 million transactions in December 1984.[35] The same anomaly in Texas laws has led to the formation of MoneyMaker EFT Services, a third party operating some 1,000 shared ATMs throughout the state. The terminals accept VISA, MasterCard, and American Express Cards.[36]

The last-named network further exemplifies the trend toward operation of an ATM network by a third party for the benefit of various types of financial institutions. For example, Switched Transaction Services is an EFT-related company operating 130 leased machines in grocery and convenience stores throughout Georgia. The ATMs dispense cash to participants' cardholders but cannot accept deposits.[37] Similarly, Publix Super Markets, Inc. has invested about $15 million to place 335 terminals in its 285 stores throughout Florida. These handle about 2 million monthly transactions for cardholders from 175 banks, S&Ls, and credit unions.[38]

Shared networks may also consist of joint ventures of bank and nonbank participants. Norwest Corporation, a Minneapolis-based bank holding company has agreed to share ATMs with Tyme Corporation, a nonbank third party operating 700 ATMs in three states (Wisconsin, Michigan, and Illinois). Norwest, prior to the agreement, operated 365 Instant-Cash machines in eight states.[39]

Credit Systems, Inc. is a data-processing firm in Kansas City. The terminals it operates in five states will accept any card issued by one of the forty-five participating banks.[40]

Interstate Banking through ATM Networks

The topic of allowing commercial banks to extend their various operations across the artificial and anachronistic boundaries created by federal laws is discussed in detail in chapter 12. In the present context, it suffices to say that many observers believe that interstate banking, at least in part, is de facto already here. The numerous examples of ATM networks cited in the foregoing section as crossing state lines lend some degree of credence to that viewpoint.

If a customer of Chase Manhattan can use an ATM, operated in Los Angeles by Bank of America, to withdraw funds from his or her account in New York, to initiate a funds transfer, or to obtain a cash advance, the ATM is equivalent to a Chase branch in that consumer's mind, and geography becomes unimportant. The extent to which he or she might do so is also irrelevant; the point is that it is possible, and the potential could become the actual at the touch of a few buttons. Federal bans on full-scale brick-and-mortar branching and interstate deposit taking remain, but as additional service enhancements to ATM networks are implemented, consumers can be expected to become even more indifferent to the statutes.

In establishing shared interstate networks, commercial banks have been quick to point out that they are merely trying to be more competitive. For example, the Federal Home Loan Bank Board has given approval for all S&Ls under its jurisdiction to place their ATMs anywhere in the United States.[41] Similarly, American Express has placed its dispensers in major cities and at airports so that its cardholders can obtain its Travelers Cheques. The American Express card can also be used to activate some 4,000 ATMs throughout the country if the holder wishes to obtain cash; alternatively, the card can be used for check-guarantee purposes or to obtain a supply of cash at about 1,200 American Express Travel Service Offices.

In 1974 an interpretation of federal law by then Comptroller of the Currency James Smith led to prolonged litigation and intense controversy. It was his opinion that because sophisticated terminals did not exist when federal prohibitions on interstate branching were enacted, national banks, over which he has jurisdiction, could ignore the statutes and establish ATMs anywhere they wished. Six lawsuits were instituted in challenging this interpretation, and the Comptroller was ordered to retract it. The decisions on this point by the U.S. Courts of Appeals left all jurisdiction on ATMs to the states; therefore, if a state classifies terminals of branches, its restrictions on branching automatically apply. In such cases each ATM would be required to meet the same capital requirements as a brick-and-mortar installation.[42]

Anyone seeking unanimity on the question of whether an off-premises ATM is a branch or on the status of interstate ATMs owned or shared by more than one bank will do so in vain. For example, in 1985 a federal court ruled that an ATM is not necessarily a branch of a national bank, even if that bank's customers use it, provided the bank does not own the machine or rent it from a third party. Thus, customers can use ATMs in locations where branching is forbidden, provided the terminals are owned by some other entity.[43]

The 1985 ruling coincides with the judgment of those twenty-four states that have held that off-premises ATMs are not branches; the remaining states either have contrary opinions or have not specifically addressed the question. Many bankers and lawmakers have sought Congressional action to standardize the matter and achieve conformity among all fifty states; however, any such laws would fly in the face of the many court decisions and statutes that affirm the rights of every state to regulate branching within its borders.[44]

ATMs in Supermarkets

The question of whether off-premises ATMs should be legally considered as branches and regulated as such is particularly relevant if one considers the extent to which individual banks or bank consortia have placed terminals in supermarkets. A later section of this chapter discusses the use of terminals such as Point-of-Sale units that debit customers' purchases directly to accounts. Even when the machines function on a much more limited scale, however, the impact is significant and the banks' activities in installing them are noteworthy.

In the state of Washington, five banks have placed some 1,100 ATMs in various supermarket chains[45]; First Nationwide Savings (San Francisco) has installed ten units in K-mart stores in California and is adding thirty-five[46]; Heritage Bank (Atlanta) operates fourteen terminals in Kroger Supermarkets in Georgia[47]; U.S. National Bank (Portland, Oregon) is establishing a network of 263 ATMs in stores in that state and in Washington[48]; and Seafirst Bank (Seattle) has placed twenty-one terminals in food stores in California.[49] The nation's largest chain of convenience stores, 7-Eleven, has ATMs in over 5,000 of its 7,500 stores.[50] In each of these instances the bank(s) involved have capitalized on state rulings to the effect that off-premises ATMs are not branches. Any future ruling to the contrary would prove disastrous to the banks, which have made extensive capital investments in the networks.

Consumer Perceptions of ATMs

At year-end 1982, 71 percent of all U.S. households had at least one account at a financial institution that offered access to one or more ATMs.[51] A consumer in Florida may now use over 2,000 terminals, Ohio has over 1,600 units, and the increases in ATM placement in heavy traffic areas such as shopping centers and employees' places of work create still more accessibility.

The facilities and technology clearly are in place. All that is needed is usage. Cumulative evidence exists, however, that ATMs, although their level of acceptance has been higher than that generated by other forms of EFTS, have created substantial disappointments for the planners—and, in particular, for those who predicted the total demise of paper checks.

A Senior Vice-President of a Los Angeles bank states that "there are already too many ATMs, too many systems, and too many people saying 'go nationwide'."[52] The President of MoneyMaker EFT Services, a third-party provider referred to earlier, has blamed the banks for their lack of effective marketing and cites a survey performed by his company, showing that less than half of the adult population of the Dallas–Fort Worth area has ever used an ATM.[53] The same survey indicated that much of the ATM usage in the 7-Eleven stores was simply transferred from usage at banks; that is, transactions were merely cannibalized from less convenient locations, and the net effect was zero. A Group Vice-President in an Atlanta-based financial-planning firm claims that interstate and nationwide ATM networks add very little in value, since cardholders will not "generally perform substantial transactions across state lines or more than fifty miles from home."[54] The survey of 1,000 adults performed for the *American Banker* in 1985 revealed that 52 percent had never used an ATM and supplied some noteworthy examples of the underlying reasons for consumer negativism:

> "We don't have to use one. We have plenty of time to bank with a teller."
>
> "I don't trust a computer to handle my money."
>
> "I have no need to use one."[55]

Earlier studies cited other consumer concerns, including fears that unauthorized parties would gain access to accounts or that the user would be robbed immediately after having obtained cash from an ATM.[56] Other surveys elicited comments such as "I know machines; I know computers; and I prefer people" and "I'd rather deal with a person."[57]

A survey commissioned by the Association of Reserve City Bankers (a trade group consisting of the 150 largest banks) and performed in 1985 by Arthur Andersen & Company indicated that the CEOs of those banks felt that 57 percent of the U.S. consumer population would be using ATMs by the 1990s.[58] If this projection is to be realized, a tremendous task faces bank marketers. Several writers have described an imaginary 33 percent wall—a tendency for the number of active ATM users to plateau at that percentage of the total consumer base.[59]

At mentioned earlier, the average transaction volume per ATM per month in 1984 was slightly less than 6,000. This represented a decrease over the previous year's figure, chiefly because the increase in the number of units exceeded the increase in the level of consumer acceptance. Since a bank may not achieve real savings in internal costs until the monthly usage at each of its ATMs exceeds 8,000, the challenge is formidable.

Promotions and Fees

As the title of Daniel Hertzberg's article ("If Carrots Don't Persuade People to Use ATMs, Banks Go for Sticks") suggests, banks are using both the carrot and the stick to induce customers to use ATMs. Some have offered various forms of sweepstakes and rewards to ATM users, including chances to win trips to Hawaii, cars, and television sets; others have given customers preferential monthly fees on their checking accounts if they take advantage of ATMs for transactions. In other cases, banks have encouraged ATM usage by discouraging the alternative, as Boston's Shawmut Bank and Cleveland's Central National Bank have done.[60] Direct-mail campaigns, coupled with extensive use of radio and television commercials, have been used to persuade customers that ATMs have been installed for their benefit and convenience rather than the bank's.

The effort to promote greater usage of ATMs is intended to drive down a bank's operating costs and possibly to enable it to reduce its number of brick-and-mortar branches. In addition to these benefits, however, many institutions are also seeking direct fee income as a means of offsetting part of the fixed costs involved in providing ATMs to the public. Of the 110 banks responding to a study conducted by the Bank Administration Institute in 1985, more than half placed a direct service charge on ATM usage; of those, 59 percent assessed the fee on each transaction. In many cases, fees were charged only if the user's account balances fell below a predetermined level.[61]

A bank that allows its customers access to the ATMs owned by others, such as third-party operators, is usually assessed a transaction fee by that party or by another bank that is the owner. This fee covers use of the network interchange and compensates the ATM operator or owner. This fee is typically in the $0.50 to $0.75 range. In view of the widespread trend in banking to charge explicit pricing, one would expect each bank to pass any such costs along to its customers.[62]

Most banks recognize the difficulty of imposing fees on ATM users at a time when everything possible is being done to increase usage, however. As of the first quarter of 1985, only 3 percent of banks with deposits in excess of $500 million charged an explicit fee to customers who used the banks' own terminals, and only 22 percent of those banks passed along the fees charged by other banks or third-party operators.[63] Banks in Florida and Texas appear to have taken the lead role in levying direct charges for ATM usage, when the transaction takes place in a foreign environment, in particular—that is, when a customer of one bank uses a terminal operated by another.[64]

One additional incentive that banks are providing to market ATM usage capitalizes on the enhancements in the terminals now offered by many manufacturers. For example, in 1984 IBM introduced a Full-Service ATM that can dispense both coins and currency and cash checks, and the Omron Company (Dallas) began offering an ATM that would give the customer a hard-copy printout of information on each transaction.[65]

Point-of-Sale Terminals (POS)

In the utopian world of the checkless society, a consumer could leave his or her home, fill the car with gasoline, make small purchases, enjoy lunch at a restaurant, and shop for groceries on the way home without using any cash or checks. POS systems constituted a major part of this new world; they would be activated by the bank cards carried by the new breed of sophisticated consumers, and the use of currency and checks would gradually disappear because all purchases would be immediately debited to accounts.

As with many other aspects of EFTS, some successes have been reported. As with the other EFTS applications, progress in implementing the POS concept unfortunately has been slow, and despite the fact that almost twenty years have passed since the Bank of Delaware introduced the first POS pilot project, the degree of interest remains disappointingly low. In a survey conducted for the Bank Administration Institute among 1,006 consumers, 395 merchants, and 257 financial institutions in late 1984, 62.7 percent of the consumers, 51.7 percent of the financial institutions, and 70.4 percent of the merchants stated that they had no interest in POS.[66] Similarly, in a study sponsored by *Bank Systems & Equipment* in 1985 among 413 commercial banks and thrift institutions, only 19.3 percent of the respondents with deposits of $500 million or more were participating in POS systems; only 7.9 percent of respondents of smaller size were doing so.[67] Many of these institutions had plans to begin participation within two years, however.

As with many applications of EFTS, the putative advantages to all parties were obvious. The consumer would no longer have to carry cash or use checks, and the purveyor of services or goods would benefit both from the immediate availability of funds (the seller's account at a financial institution would receive credit on the day the transaction took place) and from the elimination of the chronic problem of bad checks. Terminals in a store could be designed to provide detailed sales records and inventory controls. Optimally, they could also lead to in-store banking, since consumers could transact much of their banking business without the need for visiting a branch.

The early history of POS systems reveals that several commercial banks and thrift institutions experienced failures with them, leading in each case to abandonment of the entire project. Frauds, high operating costs, and the lack of a technological structure to support the activity were the causative factors.[68]

Conversely, a major success with a POS program in 1974 gave rise to many similar systems involving supermarkets, either with individual banks or with consortia. Hinky Dinky, a major supermarket chain in Nebraska, placed the terminals of an S&L in its stores so that customers could use the cards issued by the S&L to pay for purchases. The results were immediately gratifying to both parties. The supermarket chain reported increased sales, reduced its losses on bad checks, and received immediately available funds in its account; the S&L showed a gain of over $600,000 in deposits, of which almost one-half came from new customers who found in this innovation a convenience that none of the local commercial banks could match.[69] The terminals were subsequently enhanced so that shoppers, in addition to using them to pay for grocery purchases, could make cash withdrawals and deposits through them. The S&L found that its transaction costs when the terminals were used were less than half of those it incurred at tellers' windows.[70]

Both the Nebraska Bankers Association and the State Attorney General brought lawsuits against the supermarket and the S&L, charging them with infringement of banking functions, but the state courts ruled in favor of the defendants.[71] Based on that legal precedent and the success of the Hinky Dinky program, several supermarket chains in California, Kansas, Kentucky, and Iowa soon entered into POS agreements, either with individual financial institutions or with members of networks.[72]

The intense competition existing among supermarkets indicates that installing a POS terminal might lead to additional business by providing a competitive edge; at the same time, the low profit margins these chains traditionally report would tend to indicate that elimination of, or reductions in, their losses on bad checks would have a very positive impact. An additional inducement for supermarkets to become involved in POS is that, if the system created reductions in checkout time, the supermarket would have an important marketing plus that would become an element in customer loyalty.

Supermarkets normally operate what is, in effect, a free check-cashing service for customers, yet they incur substantial bank charges, directly or indirectly, for the large volumes of checks they deposit.[73] For competitive reasons, they do not pass those bank costs along to customers. The Senior Vice-President and Controller of the nation's largest supermarket chain, Safeway Stores, Inc., has addressed this point in discussing the negative side of POS:

> Since Safeway typically does not charge customers a fee for paying by check, they have little incentive to use debit cards instead. . . . [There is also] the perennial point-of-sale problem: which party pays for the system.[74]

Some supermarket chains have been among the pioneers in POS. For example, Publix, which had already invested $11 million in ATMs for its stores, spent an additional $9 million for POS terminals in forty-three of its Florida stores.[75] The chain presently incurs $750,000 in annual check-processing costs levied by its banks; to offset those costs, it will charge banks $0.40 for any cash withdrawal made through its units and $0.15 for each POS transaction.[76] Southland Corporation has placed POS terminals in 200 of its 7-Eleven stores in Florida,[77] and Marine Bank (Milwaukee), a member of the Tyme statewide shared network, reports a high degree of consumer usage of the POS terminals it has placed in grocery stores.[78] Florida is also the site of the Honor System, owned by the nine largest banks in the state and operating approximately 1,000 terminals in direct competition with the Publix system.[79]

Offsetting these success stories again is evidence of the negativism that pervades much of the total EFTS picture. The Food Marketing Institute has estimated the cost of a check transaction to a supermarket at $0.42 versus $0.15 for a cash or POS transaction,[80] yet the director of that trade group concedes that less than one-half of 1 percent of all U.S. supermarkets had installed POS units on their premises by late 1984.[81] In spite of the presumed advantages awaiting them through POS, 18 percent of the supermarket operators in the Bank Administration Institute survey cited earlier continued to express no interest in such systems.[82]

The same survey also disclosed the reasons consumer respondents gave for opposing POS. These paralleled the arguments they have used against other forms of EFTS. The most frequently cited reasons were the lack of canceled checks for record purposes (85.5 percent of those who were not interested), concern over computer errors (73.6 percent) and the system's security (66 percent), and loss of float benefits (55.5 percent); the most affluent respondents most frequently cited the last-named objection.[83]

The question of float is critical if attempts are made to project the future of POS. A consumer who might be willing to have his or her account debited directly for a bag of groceries or for small purchases at a retail store will not accept a POS system that charges the account immediately for a larger amount, while giving the vendor immediately available, potentially interest-earning funds. The larger the dollar amount involved in the sale, the more vehement the customer's opposition to POS and its system of direct debiting.

Perhaps the experiences of the nation's largest oil companies illustrate this degree of sophistication in consumer buying habits and payment preferences. Purchases at the nation's 220,000 retail gasoline outlets lend themselves ideally to the POS concept: the dollar amounts are relatively small (typically under $15), the retailer is anxious to reduce the costs inherent in a paper-based card system, the financial institutions seek economies of scale through increased POS usage, and the customer demands value at the lowest price. The manager of all retail business development for the U.S. operations of the Exxon Corporation looks on POS as a cheaper alternative to the $0.40–$0.06 per gallon costs involved in use of the company's credit cards and believes that consumers will use POS if savings are passed along to them, if processing time is kept to an absolute minimum, and if locally, regionally, or nationally accepted cards are used to debit accounts.[84]

Senior management at Exxon evidently has supported this manager's belief by making a major commitment to the future of POS. In 1985 Exxon participated with MCorp, the Texas-based bank holding company responsible for MPACT, in installing terminals in 450 of its gas stations and planned eventually to have 17,000 Exxon stations in a nationwide POS system.[85] Similarly, the Mobil Oil Corporation invested $20 million to place POS terminals in its stations and expected to have 2,500 of these on line by December 1985.[86] Because Mobil underwrote the entire cost of the system, it refuses to pay transaction fees to any of the banks whose cards may be used for direct debiting.

Through the Honor System in Florida, 350 Mobil stations and twenty-five Shell Oil stations went on-line for POS in 1985,[87] and Shell anticipated eventual installation of POS in its 4,000 stations. Atlantic Richfield (Arco), Gulf Oil, and Sun Oil (Sunoco) also planned to install pilot systems for POS in 1985.[88]

Bank of America, First Interstate, Crocker National, Security Pacific, and Wells Fargo joined forces in California to form a POS system that would act as a switch between them and their merchant customers to provide volume, speed, and security. In 1985 this system, known as Interlink and designed to handle 500 transactions per second, was marketed to gas stations throughout the state.[89]

Innovation in designing and marketing POS systems is not the exclusive province of the nation's largest banks and corporate giants. In some cases far smaller financial institutions have identified and capitalized on opportunities and have reaped relatively greater benefits than the industry leaders. The Cornelia Bank (Georgia), a $70 million institution, serves as an example. It implemented a system of franchising its concept, trademarked Supermarket Bank, to other banks, placed twenty-two modular units in supermarkets, achieved excellent results in terms of deposit growth and customer acceptance, and planned to add thirteen more units in 1986.[90]

The history of the successes and failures in POS systems since their inception in the 1970s conveys the strong impression that some basic issues remain unresolved and must be addressed if more progress is to be made. For example, it is not clear whether supermarkets and gas stations will eventually agree to pay part or all of the implementation costs or whether banks will absorb those expenses as part of their budgets for business development. The net effect of POS on the consumer has not been fully analyzed, and there is no consensus among banks regarding universal accessibility; retailers will not tolerate multiple terminal systems in their stores for multiple-access cards, yet the financial institutions seemed uncertain in 1985 about whether fully cooperative, limited-sharing, or individual proprietary systems provided the best solution.[91]

A resort report prepared by the investment banking firm of Salomon Brothers summarizes the problems of POS:

> A significant number of customers must prefer it to cash, check, or credit card payment; it must become available at a large number of retail outlets; and retailers and banks must develop workable, long-term agreements on cost sharing.[92]

Home Banking and Videotex

As part of the original scenario that forecast the advent of the completely checkless society, banking at home was envisioned as a major contributor, whether delivery of data to consumers and their initiation of transactions took place over telephone lines or through two-way cable television systems. Under the optimum scenario, the consumer would use a personal computer to instruct a bank to pay bills by directly debiting an account. Funds would be immediately transferred to any of the hundreds of authorized payees listed by the bank. The consumer would be able at any time to call up a current bank statement on the computer screen so that all debits and credits and online balance information were available. The system would also allow for instantaneous transfers of funds from one account to another and would handle a variety of preauthorized payments such as insurance premiums and home mortgage or loan payments.

The potential benefits to both banks and their customers were significant. One study estimated that bank costs of $0.72 for a check payment could be reduced to $0.22 for a terminal-initiated electronic payment.[93] Banks would enhance existing relationships, attract new ones, gain fee income, create a favorable image as high-tech innovators, and reduce traffic in branches.[94] From the consumer's standpoint, time saving and convenience were identified as primary benefits.

An American society in which some 18 million households had installed some type of video game, 35 percent of all homes had cable television, and 98 percent possessed telephones theoretically created an ideal market, and the increased degree of sophistication of the average consumer appeared to make him or her an excellent prospect for home banking.[95] A study conducted in 1983 by the consulting firm of Booz Allen Hamilton predicted such widespread acceptance of home banking that the banks would generate revenues of $32 billion by 1995.[96]

The commercial banks were not alone in their optimistic forecasts of the potential for delivery of various services directly to the nation's households. Under the generic name of *videotex,* organizations such as IBM, Honeywell, AT&T, CBS, and Sears, Roebuck began to devise systems that would provide advertising, news, weather, travel information, and educational programs to home computers attached to television sets.[97]

During the early 1980s several joint ventures, some of which included banks as participants, were formed in efforts to appeal to the consumer market. In 1983 Knight-Ridder Newspapers joined with AT&T to offer a service known as Viewtron in Florida at a total cost of some $20 million. Since then, IBM joined CBS and Sears, Roebuck to develop a nationwide videotex system accessible through personal computers[98]; Chemical Bank and Bank of America formed a joint venture to offer home banking, including brokerage services[99]; and the InterFirst Bank of Fort Worth entered into an arrangement with that city's Star-Telegram to provide a complete menu of banking services, news, stock prices, and airline flight schedules to customers.[100]

Innovations have been introduced as additional marketing tools. The original home banking services have been modified so that small business have access to revolving credit and credit-paying services,[101] and Citibank has introduced a service that allows customers of its Direct Access to transfer data from their bank accounts directly into popular spreadsheet software packages.[102] In addition, Citibank in 1985 introduced a terminal that fits into a jacket pocket and, substituting for the home computer, can be used with any modular telephone jack to pay bills and obtain balance information.[103]

According to the senior planning executive at Bank of America, the average U.S. household generates about thirty noncash transactions per month, twenty of which involve checks and ten are through some form of credit card. Of the check transactions, eight are for bill payment, nine are for POS business, and three are for payments between individuals and for cash. In his view, approximately 10 billion of these transactions could be transferred to home banking.[104]

Given the size and sophistication of the total consumer market, its increasing demands for greater convenience and for anything that provides more effective use of time, and the need for banks to reduce their operating costs, one might expect that the story of home banking would consist of evidences of continued growth, widespread acceptance, and escalating involvement of banks in implementing the new technology. In actuality, after years of effort and the commitment of many millions of dollars, the banks can report only mixed results.

At mid-1985 twenty-eight video banking services were in operation. Twenty-six commercial banks, thrifts, and credit unions were offering these, and twenty-three additional financial institutions were conducting pilot programs. The number of users at that time was estimated at 58,000, with

Chemical Bank's Pronto service accounting for 23,000 individual and 4,000 small-business customers.[105] By the end of 1985, 75,000 consumers and small businesses were believed to be users of various home banking systems.[106]

An innovative bank service that attracts 75,000 users would ordinarily be considered successful. However, if one considers that twenty-five financial institutions offered it and that a single New York bank garnered over one-third of the total users, or that 15 million U.S. households with computers were viewed as potential customers, the figures are discouraging. Indeed, there is evidence of reduced, rather than increased, customer acceptance of the concept of home banking.

In a survey conducted by the *American Banker* in 1984, 62 percent of the respondents said they would seriously consider using home banking; one year later, that percentage had dropped to 51. Forty-five percent of those replying to the 1986 questionnaire said they would not seriously consider the service, versus 33 percent in the 1984 study.[107]

Unfortunately, reports of failures far outnumber the success stories. In 1985, three banks (Dadeland Bank, Miami; First Interstate Bank, California; and Crocker National Bank, also in California) canceled their home banking projects.[108] Crocker National Bank, in announcing its decision, stated that it could not justify a financial commitment to a system that would create losses for at least two years and that it had no plans to test or offer home banking in the near future.[109] A California-based consulting company conducted a research study in which 60 percent of the group tried home banking; only 4 percent of those participants continued to use the service after testing it.[110] And although Chemical Bank has become the nation's largest provider of home banking, its number of users must be considered minute in relation to its 1.15 million retail customers.[111]

Extensive research among customers clearly reveals many of the same objections they have expressed regarding other applications of EFTS. Many of them feel that home banking is overdesigned, providing them with features that enable them to manage stock portfolios or create spreadsheets for household budgets when these are unnecessary.[112] Others point to the fact that home banking, despite its benefits, cannot provide for deposits or cash withdrawals.[113] Those who have tested the service and subsequently dropped it make comments such as "It was more trouble than it was worth," "It took twice as long to enter data into a PC," and "It was faster to do checks by hand."[114] Fears of computer crime, in which unauthorized parties gain access to an account, and complaints regarding consumer shutdowns and complicated, confusing instructions have also been noted.[115]

In other cases, the fees charged by banks for the service have created consumer objections. These fees typically range from $5 to $15 per month; however, the customer at Bank of America who finds that it is costing $8 per month to make five payments through the home terminal undoubtedly questions the value of home banking. When the costs of a modem or other special attachment required to access the system are superimposed on the monthly charges, that question becomes even more important.[116] This problem was highlighted in early 1986 at a conference sponsored by the Inter-Financial Association, where speakers pointed out a classic catch-22 dilemma: customers will not subscribe to video banking until fees are reduced, but banks will not offer low-cost services until the mass market proves it will support them.[117]

Regulation E

In 1978 Congress passed the Electronic Funds Transfer Act (EFTA), primarily for the protection of consumers' rights. The major provisions of the EFTA were incorporated by the Fed into Regulation E, which requires that all financial institutions offering EFTS services disclose beforehand the terms and conditions under which those services are provided. Regulation E also mandates periodic statements of account activity, restricts unsolicited issuing of cards for use in ATMs, establishes limits on a consumer's liability for unauthorized transfers, and requires that financial institutions establish and maintain procedures for resolving any errors.[118]

In considering home banking, the Fed's Board of Governors made the decision to exempt financial institutions from the section of Regulation E that requires that every consumer use of EFT facilities be documented by a receipt. Use of video banking, then, does not provide what the consumer has been accustomed to receiving. The lack of hard-copy records of every debit and credit may create a further obstacle to widespread acceptance of the service.

Direct Depositing and Debiting

One of the cornerstones upon which the checkless society was to be built was the Automated Clearing House (ACH), which would perform the same function as traditional clearing houses except that paper checks would be replaced by magnetic tape containing all essential data. One of the largest contributors to the ACH movement was to be the transfer of the deposit function to an electronic basis so account crediting would consist of computer-generated entries. At the same time, the forecasts predicted that customers of every deposit size and type would permit their financial institutions to charge their accounts for a wide range of preauthorized electronic payments.

The Subcommittee on Paperless Entries (SCOPE) began operating the first ACHs in California in 1972.[119] They and the thirty-two ACHs that followed them were created chiefly to prevent paper-based payments from overwhelming the back offices of banks and other financial institutions. They do not appear to have been aimed at specific market needs and cannot be described as customer-oriented[120]; rather, their formation seems to have been based on the same assumption that has been identified elsewhere—that is, that both debtors and creditors would quickly embrace the new system for all types of payments. Forecasts predicted direct depositing of payroll (the largest single component of U.S. check volume), direct corporate-to-corporate trade payments, and automatic debiting of recurring obligations such as insurance premiums, with corresponding electronic crediting to the payee.

Projected Benefits

Those who foresaw widespread use of the ACHs and acceptance of the entire concept had excellent reasons for their projections. For an employee, direct depositing of pay would provide maximum convenience, complete security, an end to check-cashing costs, a guarantee by the receiving financial institution of timely crediting, and access to other services. For the issuer, the expense and time involved in preparing individual checks could be substantially reduced; a magnetic tape containing all the necessary information could be prepared, sent to an originating bank, and forwarded through ACHs to any financial institution at which the employee maintained an account. For the banks participating in the system, even greater benefits were possible. Escalating labor costs in check processing and in deposits handled by tellers, the explicit pricing mandated by the 1980 Monetary Control Act for all checks handled by the Fed, the possibility of opening accounts for payees, and the opportunity for selling other banking services to those payees combined to create strong motivation for the banks to market the program. As an illustration of the cost factor, a Social Security check deposited with a teller was estimated to create an expense for the bank of $0.24 in 1981; when the payment was made through EFT, the cost was $0.07.[121]

Similar substantial savings were projected for corporations issuing large volumes of checks in payment of trade obligations, dividends, and pensions. The anticipated savings included the elimination or reduction of postage expenses incurred in mailing checks.

Federal Government Programs

The bellwether in the program of EFT credits was the federal government, and at no time in the history of the system has it been responsible for less than one-half of the total ACH volume. For example, in 1984, 264 million government payments were processed through ACHs; all other originators accounted for only 201 million.[122]

The decision to begin implementing paperless payments was made in

Washington, D.C. at a time when in-house costs for every issued check were $0.18, when the volume of payments to all payees was growing at an explosive rate, and when the Treasury Department was attempting to cope with over 1 million claims per year from individuals whose checks were reportedly lost or stolen. In the words of an official in the Fiscal Service Unit,

> We had no palatable alternative to the development of a better means of coping with continually increasing workloads. At the same time, we needed a more positive payment delivery system. And lastly, it has become more difficult to attain higher productivity and reduce consumption of resources under the check disbursement system.[123]

It may be noted parenthetically that the traditional medium for government payments of every type—income tax refunds, Social Security disbursements, veterans' payments, and civil service and railroad retirement payments—has long been the familiar, though cumbersome and expensive, card check, designed for processing on keypunch equipment. It was not until 1986 that this payment vehicle gave way to less expensive paper for use in those cases where EFT was not being applied.

The program of direct depositing of Social Security payments stands out as by far the greatest single success in the entire EFT program. Unlike many other aspects of EFT, it has more than lived up to expectations, as is evidenced by the cost reductions experienced by both the banks and the government and by the high degree of satisfaction expressed by payees. Personnel in all branches of the armed forces have become participants in similar government programs, and the possibility of placing all income tax refunds and payments on government debt has been explored.[124]

Corporate Electronic Payments

No similar success has occurred in the private sector. The projected adoption of direct deposit of payroll and of corporate electronic payments has simply not taken place to the extent that was originally forecast; indeed, an executive of General Motors Corporation has categorically described corporate EFT as a "market failure,"[125] and the total volume of 500 million ACH transactions in 1984 represents only one-eightieth of U.S. check activity.[126] During the entire year 1984 fewer than 3,000 corporate trade payments (CTPs) were processed through ACHs.[127]

In view of the extremely optimistic forecasts regarding the ultimate success of ACH transactions, questions must naturally arise about the reasons for the lack of progress. In the case of direct deposit of payroll, banks do not appear to have been able to overcome the skepticism of workers who feel that it is nothing more than another means of gaining benefits for employers and banks at the employees' expense.[128] Other research has identified employee opposition based on a perceived lack of security and personal control and an invasion of the individual's privacy.[129] In addition, those employees who do not maintain checking accounts at any financial institution see no reason for changing their financial lifestyle, which would be required under an EFT program.[130]

An employer who wishes to implement direct deposit of payroll must realize that employees' cooperation may not be readily forthcoming. Since the inception of EFTS, participation has been optional, and in 1978 the Financial Institutions Regulatory Act (Title IX) prohibited compulsory programs. At the same time, employers have expressed objections to direct deposit of pay on the grounds that they still must prepare all current and year-to-date records of employees' earnings, deductions, and taxes.

An additional objection to the system, as voiced by employers, reflects the benefits of float to the issuer of checks. On the one hand, issued checks represent nothing more than entries in a disbursement register until such time as they have been sent to drawee banks and debited to accounts. On the other hand, a corporation that converts to an EFT mode for disbursements is aware that its bank account is charged immediately when its magnetic tape is presented to its bank.

As is discussed in chapter 8, devoted to Cash Management, many disbursement systems have been designed specifically to capitalize on float through the use of remote drawee locations. In this way the presenting and debiting require additional time, and the sophisticated financial officer puts this time to advantage by investing funds until the last possible moment.

Because the Federal Reserve provides the mechanism through which most checks are processed, and because the Fed gives the sending banks credit for those checks before it actually has presented them to drawees and obtained settlement funds, it has an average daily float figure far higher than that of any bank. This figure peaked at $6.7 billion in 1979. Since then, the Fed has acted aggressively to reduce its float. It has opened Regional Check Processing Centers (RCPCs) throughout the United States and has substantially reduced the time allowed for a drawee to examine checks presented to it and pay the Fed for them. As a result, the 1979 figure was reduced to $400 million in 1984.[131]

The efforts of the Fed to reduce float in the banking system may induce employers to look more favorably on ACH payments, since their previous benefits have decreased proportionately.[132] Nevertheless, 61 percent of the treasury managers in a survey conducted in 1985 by the National Automated Clearing House Association (NACHA) still maintained that the loss of float was a major obstacle to converting to electronic payments.[133]

Other employer objections include concerns over computer fraud, questions about ACH dependability and reliability, and bottom-line economic justification.[134] On the latter point, a study conducted in 1983 under NACHA auspices indicated that full-scale implementation of EFTS might cost as much as $100,000 for a major corporation.[135]

The Fed and the Private Sector

Ever since the first regional ACHs were linked in the 1970s, the Federal Reserve has handled virtually all the processing of electronic payments for them. However, the banking industry voiced fears that the Fed would exercise a monopoly over the system and establish fees—comparable to those in its program of explicit pricing for other services—so high that they would inhibit further progress. As a result, competition from the private sector has sprung up.

A subsidiary of General Electric Corporation, General Electric Information Services Company (GEISCO), has become a leader in this field. In 1985, it obtained a contract for electronic transaction processing from the Calwestern ACH Association and subsequently was selected to handle West Coast payments sent directly to it by Chase Manhattan Bank.[136] This competition may force the Fed to reduce its per-item fees.

This action by Chase Manhattan, coupled with its decision to break away from the New York Automated Clearing House to form its own ACH, is especially important. The New York ACH is the only automated facility not operated by the Federal Reserve; Chase Manhattan formerly accounted for 72 percent of its volume. In addition, Chase is the largest private sector originator of ACH payments in the nation, with 25 percent of government and 12 percent of all ACH volume.[137] By establishing its own proprietary ACH, Chase planned to offer customers electronic payments at lower costs.

Direct Debits and Preauthorized Payments

Aside from the federal government's programs for direct deposit, there is only one significant success story in the total EFTS picture. It is found in the acceptance consumers have given to certain programs for direct preauthorized debits to their accounts (excluding POS transactions) when important recurring payments must be made on predetermined dates. An insurance premium or the monthly payment on an installment or mortgage loan exemplifies this category of payments. By 1982 over 4 million monthly debits were being processed on a paperless electronic basis, with the insurance industry as the leader in the field.

Direct debits to meet those fixed obligations the consumer cannot afford to neglect or postpone offer many advantages to the debtor, the payee, and the processing bank. For the payee, the work and expense incurred in receiving, examining, and depositing paper checks are eliminated, as are the follow-up dunning letters on delinquencies. For the remitter, benefits include assurance of payment on the specified date, elimination of check costs and postage expense, and convenience. The bank reduces its processing costs and is able to offer the payee quicker availability of funds since checks are not being held up in the collection system.

The application of direct debits to insurance premiums originated with a joint venture of the Equitable Life Assurance Society and Chase Manhattan Bank. The insurer implemented a system of mag tape transmission to the bank, containing all the necessary data to identify the insured, the amount due, and the account to be debited, wherever that account might be domiciled. Chase then credited Equitable, charged the accounts of those policyholders who were among its customers, and forwarded the remaining tape data through ACHs to some 1,500 financial institutions throughout the country.[138] More recently, estimates have shown that some 150 companies have adopted similar programs with the cooperation of their customers and that a single company accounts for about 1 million monthly payments.[139]

Many banks have marketed the concept of direct debits in cases where they are the payees—for example, in the commercial, installment, and mortgage loan areas. Consumers are usually favored with preferential interest rates if they agree to have their accounts automatically charged each month for the payments on their installment loans.

That the program of direct debits has not achieved greater success is explained by the long-standing objections of many consumers. Loss of control over one's financial affairs, fears of unauthorized debits and computer misposts, and again, awareness of float benefits have repeatedly been identified.[140]

The types of payments that have gained acceptance directly reflect the consumer's willingness to authorize direct debits. The program succeeds with those payments that represent critical obligations, are repetitive in nature, and are for fixed amounts. Conversely, consumers are unwilling to pay bills rendered by department stores, card issuers, and public utilities without having carefully examined them and, in many cases, capitalized on the maximum time frame allowed for payment.

These objections have largely been overcome in many other countries where the GIRO system, or a variation of it, is widely accepted, for example, in Great Britain, France, the Netherlands, Sweden, Germany, and Austria.[141] Through use of a standardized invoice form, often designed to be machine readable, the payee, amount due, payee's bank, and payee's account number are identified; the remitter's signature on the form authorizes a direct transfer of funds from account to account.[142] The consumer thereby maintains full personal control over payments yet eliminates check and postage costs.

Summary

It is unfortunate that an overview of the total EFTS picture, compiled in 1986, necessarily included so many accounts of failures, negativism, and problems encountered by the banks in their efforts to lead the public toward the checkless society. It would have been gratifying to report that the various types of paperless systems that the banks have attempted to market for almost twenty years have been widely accepted by all parties concerned and to state that the United States is well on the way toward that society, replacing the usage of some 100 million checks per day by computer-generated debits and credits. Just as government statutes call for truth in lending, however, literary ethics require truth in writing, and the EFTS success stories are undeniably far less numerous than the accounts of program cancellations and corporate and consumer antipathy or hostility. When all the evidence has been analyzed, one basic truth clearly surfaces: EFTS programs cannot be sold to a marketplace that sees so little advantage in them, distrusts them, and has so many other fears and concerns about them.[143]

The banks' marketing efforts are offset by many reports of new failures. For example, California consumers learned that during the 1985 Christmas season National Transaction Systems (NTS), the operator of some 450 ATMs in Safeway and 7-Eleven stores, suddenly closed down the entire network because of financial losses.[144] An in-depth study of ACH transactions in seven midwestern states through the Mid-America Payments Exchange showed that only 18 companies accounted for 45 percent of the total monthly volume and that preauthorized debits to pay insurance premiums and utility bills comprised 44 percent of the originated items.[145]

Theoretically, ATMs offer significant benefits to consumers in terms of 24-hour convenience; yet a 1978 research study showed that 42 percent of the respondents claimed ATMs were "not needed,"[146] and seven years later only 11 percent of the adult population was using them.[147] From the banks' standpoint, the results have been extremely disappointing; distribution costs have not been reduced enough to offset the capital costs of the terminals, and branches—contrary to the earlier hopes—must still be kept open.[148]

Theoretically, systems for direct deposit, in particular for use with payrolls, should gain wide acceptance. They can wholly or partly eliminate losses and thefts of salary checks and costs of check cashing. In theory, employers should welcome a system that reduces check purchase and issuance expense. Nevertheless, employees have raised a host of personal objections to direct deposit, and employers have not displayed any marked enthusiasm.

Theoretically, corporate-to-corporate payments, made through an ACH, represent a major improvement over check payments, but the record is one of virtually total failure. The issue of float appears to be a major obstacle to further progress. The typical corporate treasurer welcomes a system that allows him or her to improve funds availability on incoming payments but naturally opposes one that debits a bank account immediately.

Theoretically, systems that require preauthorized debits or use POS terminals can provide the young, upwardly mobile, affluent segment of American society with convenience, thus enabling these individuals to take greater advantage of leisure time. Again, however, with the basic exceptions cited earlier, these systems, too, have never lived up to the early forecasts of those who were responsible for the vision of a checkless society.

Because he became identified as one of the foremost proponents of electronic banking during his tenure as a Chase Manhattan executive, and since then as a consultant, the comments in 1986 of George C. White are relevant. In discussing the failure of EFTS to attain the objectives that were foreseen for it, he stated:

> One of the real failures today is that the electronic options are not better than the check system. . . . There's a lot of focus on getting rid of the check, but not looking to see if the user is getting a real benefit. . . . Only 1½ percent of payments are [being made] electronically, . . . I overestimated that financial institutions would work together, . . . [and] I have found it very disappointing. . . .[149]

Notes

1. Bruce J. Summers, "Dr. Frankenstein and the ACH," *Journal of Cash Management,* November/December 1985, p. 25.
2. "The Evolving Financial Services Industry: Competition and Technology for the '80s," *HBS Case Services* (Harvard Business School no. 183–007, 1983), p. 4.
3. Checkless Society Still Just a Vision," *American Banker,* November 25, 1985, p. 5.
4. Ralph W. Clark, "A Talk with IBM," *The Bankers Magazine,* March–April 1985, pp. 29–30.
5. Theodore O. Johnson and Steven F. Maier, "Making the Corporate Decision: Paper Checks to Electronic Funds Transfer," *Journal of Cash Management,* November/December 1985, p. 30.
6. John F. Lee, "Modern-Day Lessons about Automated Clearing," *The Bankers Magazine,* September–October 1985, p. 74.
7. David LaGesse, "Wooing Customers to ATMs: Beyond Puppy Love," *American Banker,* November 12, 1985, p. 1.
8. John Parry, "Bank Technology's Big Task: Convincing People to Use It," *American Banker,* April 9, 1985, p. 2.
9. Richard S. Braddock, "Bridging the Gap between New Technology and Customer Desires," *American Banker,* June 28, 1985, p. 4.
10. James H. Donnelly, Jr.; Leonard L. Berry; and Thomas W. Thompson,

Delivering Financial Services (Homewood, Ill.: Dow Jones-Irwin, 1985), excerpted in "The Tentacles of Technology," *American Banker,* December 12, 1985, p. 24.

11. Linda Fenner Zimmer, "ATMs: Time to Fine-Tune and to Plan," *Bank Administration,* May 1982, p. 20.

12. In 1981 one major West Coast bank reported its costs as $0.26 for a cash withdrawal through an ATM as against $0.55 for a teller to cash a check (Leo P. Hardwick, "What Role Will the ATM Play," *The Bankers Magazine,* May–June 1981, p. 49). More recently, the Bank Administration Institute reports the respective costs as $0.21 and $0.52 (Daniel Hertzberg, "If Carrots Don't Persuade People to Use ATMs, Banks Go for Sticks," The *Wall Street Journal,* February 21, 1985, p. 35).

13. James B. Moore, "Banks Install ATMs to Compete," *Bank Systems & Equipment,* May 1985, p. 101.

14. Thomas E. Reynolds, "Electronic Banking: Current Status/Trends," *Mid-Continent Banker,* June 1985, p. 33.

15. Stephanie Nowack, "How to Market ATMs with Style," *Bank Administration,* December 1984, p. 29.

16. Hertzberg, op. cit.

17. Michael Weinstein, "ATM Makers Perceive Opportunities Despite Signs of Saturation," *American Banker,* December 19, 1984, p. 14.

18. Reynolds, op. cit.

19. Richard D. Dart, "ATM Services—1985," *American Banker,* December 4, 1985, p. 15.

20. Michael Weinstein, "Survey Predicts Growth in Off-Site Cash Dispensers," *American Banker,* June 26, 1985, p. 8.

21. Reynolds, op. cit.

22. Ibid.

23. Linda Fenner Zimmer, "ATMs 1983: A Critical Assessment," *Bank Administration,* May 1984, p. 28.

24. Braddock, op. cit.

25. Dart, op. cit.

26. Jerry Adams, "Can Cash from Machines Hit the Small Town Spot?" in "Machine Banking USA," *American Banker,* December 3, 1985, pp. 12–13.

27. Federal Reserve Bank of New York, "Electronic Funds Transfers," Circular 8669, October 29, 1979.

28. Eric Gelman, "How America Pays the Tab," *Newsweek,* January 7, 1985, p. 40.

29. Richard W. Stevenson, "Big New York Banks Link Teller Machines," *The New York Times,* March 7, 1985, p. D1.

30. Lesta Cordil, "Cashing in on Convenience," *White Plains Reporter-Dispatch* (Gannett Westchester Newspapers), March 24, 1985, p. K1.

31. Randy Welch, "PLUS: The Evolution of a National Electronic Network," *American Banker,* June 3, 1985, p. 1.

32. Michael Weinstein, "4 Alabama Banks Forming ATM Network," *American Banker,* May 28, 1985, p. 3.

33. Jay Rosenstein, "Program Puts Credit Cards, ATMs Within Reach of Small Banks," *American Banker,* December 18, 1985, p. 18.

34. *"Tapping a Cash Machine Bonanza," Business Week,* October 12, 1981, p. 136.

35. Reynolds, op. cit.

36. Jim McTague, "Money Machines Magnify Cash and Carry Concept," *American Banker,* December 3, 1985, pp. 14–15.

37. Peter Mantius, "An Eye to the Cash Dispensers," in "Machine Banking USA," *American Banker,* December 3, 1985, pp. 23–24.

38. David Satterfield, "Stop, Cash, and Shop: The Market-Run ATM," in ibid., pp. 18–19.

39. Michael Weinstein, "Norwest and Tyme to Share ATMs," *American Banker,* December 11, 1985, p. 13.

40. "Electronic Networks Springing up All Over," *American Banker,* March 19, 1982, p. 2.

41. "Savings Unit Automation," *The New York Times,* August 7, 1981, p. D5.

42. John G. Heimann, in "Banking in Transition," *The Bankers Magazine,* September–October 1978, p. 22; and in "A Conversation with the Comptroller," *The Bankers Magazine,* January–February 1979, pp. 28–29.

43. Michael Weinstein, "Federal Court Says ATM Is Not a Branch," *American Banker,* March 1, 1985, p. 1.

44. Robert A. Bennett, "Banks Will Link Cash Machines," *The New York Times,* April 8, 1982, p. D1.

45. "It's Time to Start Thinking about Redeploying ATMs," *ABA Banking Journal,* September 1985, p. 53.

46. "First Nationwide Savings and K-mart Exceed Deposit Goals in Joint Venture," *American Banker,* December 12, 1985, p. 32.

47. "ATMs and Branches in Kroger Supermarkets," *American Banker,* April 9, 1985, p. 3.

48. "Oregon Bank to Install ATMs in 154 Supermarts," *American Banker,* April 9, 1985, p. 3.

49. "Seafirst to Install Cash Machines in 21 Food Stores," *American Banker,* April 9, 1985, p. 15.

50. Michael Weinstein, "Coming at 7-Elevens: Electronic Shopping Terminals," *American Banker,* June 12, 1985, p. 9.

51. Frederick J. Schroeder, "Developments in Consumer Electronic Funds Transfers," *Federal Reserve Bulletin,* June 1983, p. 396.

52. Gil Davenport, in Nancy Meyers, "ATM Networks Turn Co-Op," *Computers in Banking,* June 1985, p. 48.

53. Scott L. Engle, in ibid.

54. In Reynolds, op. cit.

55. In LaGesse, op. cit.

56. Olin J. Pugh and Franklin J. Ingram, "EFT and the Public," *The Bankers Magazine,* March–April 1978, p. 47.

57. In Hertzberg, op.cit.

58. Laura Gross, "New Andersen Survey Predicts More Nonbank Competition," *American Banker,* December 11, 1985, p. 1.

59. Bruce A. Birchfield, "Case Studies in Marketing ATMs Effectively," *Bank Administration,* November 1984, p. 28; and Hertzberg, op. cit.

60. Birchfield, op. cit.

61. Weinstein, "Survey Predicts Growth in Off-Site Cash Dispensers."

62. Lynn C. Goldfagen and Gerald P. Hurst, "Regulatory Responses to Changes in the Consumer Financial Services Industry," *Federal Reserve Bulletin,* February 1985, p. 78.

63. Dart, op. cit., pp. 19–20.

64. Michael Weinstein, "Levying Fees for Use of ATMs Spreads," *American Banker,* February 14, 1985, p. 1.

65. Dart, op. cit., p. 19.

66. Marjolijn van der Velde, "Point of Sale: Attitudes and Perceptions of Financial Institutions, Merchants, and Consumers," *Bank Administration,* April 1985, p. 42.

67. Joan B. Goldberg, "POS Gains Ground in '80s . . . ," *Bank Systems & Equipment,* April 1985, p. 43.

68. Wray O. Candilis, *The Future of Commercial Banking* (New York: Praeger, 1975), p. 126; and Susan A. Anderson, "Taking a Second Look at Point-of-Sale Banking," *American Banker,* June 2, 1981, p. 17.

69. "An S&L Puts the Teller in the Supermarket," *Business Week,* April 20, 1974, p. 88.

70. Peter D. Louderback, "Who's Afraid of EFT?" *World,* Peat, Marwick, Mitchell & Co., Autumn 1977, p. 48.

71. Alan Richman, "Court Upholds Hinky Dinky EFT Service," *Bank Systems & Equipment,* September 1974, p. 8.

72. Eric N. Compton, *Inside Commercial Banking,* 2nd ed. (New York: John Wiley & Sons, Inc., 1983), pp. 168–169.

73. Clark, op. cit., p. 29.

74. "Safeway Controller Sees Marginal Role for Use of Debit Cards in Supermarkets," *American Banker,* April 9, 1985, p. 16.

75. Satterfield, op. cit.

76. "Debit Cards Go Shopping," *Fortune,* February 4, 1985, p. 23.

77. Michael Weinstein, "Coming at 7-Elevens."

78. Helene Duffy, "Direct Debiting at Point of Sale," *American Banker,* December 3, 1985, p. 24.

79. Ibid.

80. Michael Weinstein, "Supermarkets Eye Electronic Banking Warily," *American Banker,* November 1, 1984, p. 1.

81. Michael Weinstein, "Supermarkets Question Feasibility and Cost of POS," *American Banker,* May 29, 1985, p. 8.

82. van der Velde, op. cit., p. 47.

83. Ibid.

84. Karl R. Fink, "A View of POS Applications in the Oil Industry," *American Banker,* November 1, 1984, pp. 13–14.

85. "Exxon Unveils Point-of-Sale System; MCorp to Be First Participant," *American Banker,* September 26, 1985, p. 3.

86. Michael Weinstein, "Mobil, Citing a Good Start, Revs up Its Point-of-Sale Plans," *American Banker,* January 4, 1985, p. 3.

87. Michael Weinstein, "Shell to Test Debit Cards in Florida," *American Banker,* September 11, 1985, p. 7; and Gelman, op. cit.

88. M. William Friis, "Is POS Approaching Critical Mass?" *ABA Banking Journal,* September 1985, p. 51.

89. Lisa McCann, "Building California's Interlink," *United States Banker,* January 1985, p. 41.

90. "Banks Finds a Niche Franchising 'Branches'," *ABA Banking Journal,* January 1986, p. 6.

91. Douglas D. Anderson, "Point-of-Sale Benefit Flows and Pricing Relationships," *Bank Administration,* September 1985, pp. 28–29.

92. In Mary-Margaret Wantuck, "Push-Button Banking," *Nation's Business,* September 1985, p. 50.

93. "Are Banks Really Ready for Home Banking?," *ABA Banking Journal,* January 1984, p. 80.

94. Robert B. Willumstad, "A Home Banking Case Study," *The Bankers Magazine,* November–December 1984, pp. 41–45.

95. John A. Farnsworth, "Technology Report: Home Banking—Part of a Bigger Picture," *United States Banker,* July 1983, p. 65.

96. Robert A. Bennett, "Banking Goes into the Home," *The New York Times,* December 7, 1983, p. D1.

97. John S. Davidson, "A Technology Searches for Its Destiny," *Telecommunication Products + Technology,* April 1985, pp. 21–22.

98. Davidson, op. cit.

99. David O. Tyson, "Chemical, BankAmerica Join in Videotex Venture," *American Banker,* June 4, 1985, p. 1.

100. Michael Weinstein, "Fort Worth Bank and Newspaper Join to Market Home Banking Service," *American Banker,* June 5, 1985, p. 8.

101. Jeffrey Marshall, "Home Banking Gaining Converts," *American Banker,* June 10, 1985, p. 9.

102. David O. Tyson, "Citibank Integrates Home Banking with Spreadsheet Package," *American Banker,* September 11, 1985, p. 7.

103. Michael Weinstein, "Citibank's Pocket Terminal: The Next Wave in Banking?," *American Banker,* November 4, 1985, p. 3.

104. David O. Tyson, "Home Banking Is Next Frontier, Says BankAmerica Planner," *American Banker,* July 3, 1985, p. 8.

105. Marshall, op. cit.

106. David O. Tyson, "Expert Estimates 75,000 Use Video Banking," *American Banker,* January 14, 1986, p. 9.

107. David LaGesse, "Bright Future of Video Banking Is Still There, but Further Away," *American Banker,* November 8, 1985, p. 1.

108. Marshall, op. cit.

109. David O. Tyson, "Crocker Drops out of Home Banking," *American Banker,* May 29, 1985, p. 1.

110. Scott Cook, "Research Finds Home Banking's Key Benefit," *ABA Banking Journal,* November 1984, p. 120.

111. Philip Elmer-De Witt, "Brave New Piggy Bank," *Time,* July 15, 1985, p. FT8.

112. Ellen Benoit, "The Hard Sell," *Forbes,* November 5, 1984, p. 222.

113. Elmer-De Witt, op. cit.

114. Cook, op. cit.

115. Elmer-De Witt, op. cit.

116. Bennett, op. cit.

117. David O. Tyson, "The Chicken, the Egg, and Video Banking's Unfulfilled Promise," *American Banker,* January 22, 1986, p. 11.

118. Goldfaden and Hurst, op. cit., pp. 76–77.

119. "California's Step Toward Checkless Banking," *Business Week,* September 9, 1972, p. 56.

120. John F. Lee, "Modern-Day Lessons about Automated Clearing," *The Bankers Magazine,* September–October 1985, p. 74.

121. Robert Trigaux, "Direct Deposit Benefits to Institutions Found Substantial," *American Banker,* April 13, 1981, p. 1.

122. "ACH Report," *ABA Banking Journal,* April 1985, p. 101.

123. Les Plumly, Paper presented at the Cash Managers' Conference, New York, April 12, 1978.

124. Robert O. Thompson, Paper presented at the 9th Annual Payment Systems Symposium, Atlanta, April 20, 1980.

125. B.K. Woo, "Why Corporate America Has Not Embraced Electronic Corporate Trade Payments," *Journal of Cash Management,* November/December 1985, p. 41.

126. Tom Ferris, "Network May Process Clearing House Payments," *American Banker,* February 25, 1985, p. 3.

127. Johnson and Maier, op. cit.

128. Alfred L. Hunt, *Corporate Cash Management and Electronic Funds Transfers* (New York: AMACOM, 1978), pp. 150–151.

129. In *Bank Systems and Equipment,* November 1972, p. 54.

130. Carl M. Gambs, "Automated Clearing Houses," *Economic Review* (Federal Reserve Bank of Kansas City), May 1978, p. 4.

131. Johnson and Maier, op. cit.

132. Dale R. Sorenson, "ACH Payment Methods More Alluring as Fed Shrinks Float," *Cashflow,"* June 1985, pp. 47–50.

133. Theodore J. Gage, "Surveys, Expert Predict Increased Electronic Funds Transfer Use," *Cashflow,* September 1985, p. 86.

134. Woo, op. cit.

135. Johnson and Maier, op cit.

136. Tom Ferris, "Chase Clearing House Gets Fed Link," *American Banker,* December 20, 1985, p. 1.

137. "Chase Manhattan Builds Its Own ACH," *ABA Banking Journal,* April 1985, p. 105.

138. George C. White, Jr., "Electronic GIRO Payments," *American Banker,* October 14, 1976, p. 5.

139. Mary L. King, *The Great American Banking Snafu* (Lexington, Mass.: Lexington Books, D.C. Heath, 1985), p. 106.

140. Louderback, op. cit. p. 47.

141. King, op. cit., p. 42.

142. George C. White, Jr., "Electronic GIRO or Credit Transfer Payments," *United States Investor,* October 4, 1976, p. 17.

143. Paul Nadler, in "Banking in Transition," *The Bankers Magazine,* September–October 1978, p. 28.

144. Michael Weinstein, "Backer Pull-Out, Big Bank Chill-Out Blamed for ATM Network's Demise," *American Banker,* January 13, 1986, p. 1.

145. Tom Ferris, "Study Shows a Few Firms Dominate ACH Volume," *American Banker,* January 6, 1986, p. 6.

146. Pugh and Ingram, op. cit.

147. Denis G. Gulino, "Federal Reserve Study of US Currency Can't Determine Where Most Cash Is," *American Banker,* February 7, 1986, p. 10.

148. Richard J. Roll, "Targeting Markets in Consumer Banking," *The Bankers Magazine,* January–February 1986, p. 46.

149. In Tom Ferris, "Some Static Electricity to Jolt EFT Acceptance," *American Banker,* April 7, 1986, pp. 18–20.

6
The New World of Consumer Banking

In New York City in 1950 only two commercial banks, one of which was a small, union-owned institution, actively marketed monthly-payment unsecured loans to the average working person, and only a handful of banks offered the so-called special checking account that did not require a minimum balance. Individuals who applied for home mortgage loans were referred to a thrift institution, usually one that was a correspondent. Passbook savings accounts were limited in number and usually were opened only as a convenience for individuals who had substantial corporate connections and/or already maintained personal checking accounts. The savings account marketplace was left, with those exceptions, to the mutual savings banks, which by law could pay higher interest than the commercial banks. CDs were also few in number and were not issued in negotiable form. Newspaper advertising for banks was confined to modest, black-bordered announcements, indicating, for example, that "Our Trust Department will welcome your inquiries." Television and radio commercials were virtually nonexistent.

This scenario did not exist in New York City alone; in many parts of the country, commercial banks lived up to their name by focusing almost entirely on relationships with businesses, government agencies, correspondent banks, and institutions. Bank of America, which may be considered a leader in the entire area of consumer banking, was a notable exception. For many institutions, the size and potential value of the consumer market were ignored. Aggressive selling, as has been frequently noted, was anathema to many bankers who considered the word *salesperson* to have highly pejorative connotations. The emphasis on wholesale banking was so widespread that the term *benign neglect* has been used to describe the banks' view of large-scale retail banking.[1]

To the individual who today finds himself or herself besieged constantly with radio and television commercials for banks, who constantly receives mail solicitations from banks offering their magic pieces of plastic, whose installment loan activity is eagerly solicited, and who finds it incredibly easy to shop among banks for the best available rates on modest accounts under a variety of names, the 1950 scenario may appear farfetched, but it is historically true. Only in the post–World War II period, and more accurately, since the 1960s, has the consumer become the prime target of the commercial banks. Not until then did the latter group realize the extent to which thrift institutions and credit unions were growing at their expense; not until then did mass marketing come into play as the banks belatedly tried to convince John Doe and Mary Jones of their desirability as customers.

The transition from a largely wholesale posture to one that was also retail was perhaps most obvious in New York City. The former Chase National Bank, the former Hanover Bank, the former Bankers Trust Company, and the former Chemical Bank and Trust Company all entered into mergers with other institutions (Bank of the Manhattan Company, Manufacturers Trust Company, Public National Bank, and Corn Exchange Bank respectively) as a means of obtaining an existing network of branches with a consumer base.

This concept of Full-Service banking, extending services across the broadest possible spectrum of the market, was largely a reaction to the phenomenal growth the thrift institutions achieved in the post–World War II period. It is axiomatic that a vacuum in the area of financial services can never exist for a lengthy period of time; if one type of financial institution, for whatever reason, fails to meet the needs of a market segment, another will quickly step in to fill the void. When millions of Americans shed their World War II uniforms and returned to civilian life, they immediately needed installment loans, low-balance checking accounts, and home mortgage loans. By failing, in many cases, to meet those needs, the commercial banks left the field open to the mutual savings banks, S&Ls, and credit unions. All these institutions had always been oriented toward retail services and were willing and able to capitalize on the opportunities.

Thrift Institutions

The settlers who migrated to the United States from Europe in the nineteenth century brought with them a tradition of dealing with three types of financial institutions that dealt exclusively with wage earners of modest means. The first mutual savings bank, for example, had been established in Scotland in 1810, and by 1819 there were over three hundred such banks in England, Ireland, and Wales.[2] Earlier, institutions known as "penny banks" had sprung up in England; these banks received weekly deposits of coins from individuals, invested those deposits, and paid periodic dividends.

Mutual savings banks are legally permitted in only sixteen states, with by far the highest concentration in the northeastern part of the country. Total deposits at savings banks in Massachusetts, New Hampshire, Maine, and

Connecticut have regularly exceeded the savings and time deposits at the commercial banks in that area.[3]

Today's S&Ls are the successors to the building societies that had been established in Europe to offer residential mortgage loans. The funds used to make those loans came from the deposits of individuals. S&Ls in the United States operate under either federal or state charters and are the second-largest category of financial intermediaries, with total assets in October 1985 of $1.049 trillion, outranked only by the commercial banks ($2.4 trillion).[4] Deposits at S&Ls are insured by the FSLIC.

The importance of the S&Ls and savings banks as home mortgage lenders is evident from the 1985 statistics. In the third quarter of that year, outstanding mortgage loans on 1-to-4 family homes totaled $786.2 billion. Of that amount, the S&Ls held $446 billion and the savings banks held $119 billion; therefore, these institutions were involved in 71.8 percent of the total debt.[5]

The credit unions in the United States number approximately 20,000 (as contrasted with some 3,300 S&Ls and 400 mutual savings banks) and in 1985 held total assets of $114.8 trillion.[6] They are nonprofit, cooperative organizations that are composed of individuals with a common bond who lend to and borrow from one another. The common bond required for membership is usually occupation or place of employment but can also be based on union, church, or society affiliations. Because credit unions are mutual in nature—that is, owned by members—deposits are classified as shares in the organization, and interest paid on deposits is classified as dividends. Credit unions enjoy an exemption from federal and state income taxes and operate under either a federal or state charter. As of 1983, their total membership numbered over 48 million individuals.[7]

The degree of penetration of the consumer market achieved by savings banks, S&Ls, and credit unions in the post–World War II years is reflected in table 6–1, which shows the growth pattern of financial intermediaries in selected years from 1950 through 1979.

The Crisis of the 1980s

The position of the nation's S&Ls and savings banks in the field of home mortgage lending, while it helped them to achieve their growth in the postwar period at the expense of commercial banks, also was the principal factor in the financial crises they experienced in the early 1980s. Those mortgage loans were traditionally long term, with fixed rates of interest. A lending institution that had granted a home mortgage loan in 1954 at the then prevailing rate of 4.5 percent was still receiving that yield in 1980, when the rates it was competitively forced to pay on deposits exceeded 15 percent. The prime rate (i.e., interest charged by commercial banks to their largest, most creditworthy

Table 6–1
Total Assets of Financial Intermediaries, Selected Years from 1950 to 1979
(in billions of dollars)

Institution	*1950*	*1955*	*1960*	*1965*	*1970*	*1975*	*1979*
Commercial banks	169	211	258	377	576	965	1,480
S&Ls	17	38	72	130	176	338	579
Savings banks	22	31	41	58	79	121	163
Credit unions	1	3	6	11	18	38	66

Source: United States League of Savings Associations, *Savings and Loan Fact Book '80* (Chicago, 1980), p. 46.

corporate customers) rose to an unheard-of 21.5 percent in late 1980 and remained at the 20 percent level through 1981. Of necessity, banks were paying extremely high interest rates on deposits to fund their operations. The negative spread between interest income and interest expense created losses totaling over $6 billion for the nation's S&Ls in 1981,[8] and the ninety-two state-chartered savings banks in New York State reported aggregate losses of $634 million during six months of 1982.[9] In a great many cases, survival of individual banks or S&Ls was clearly impossible, and during this critical period, federal agencies assumed an activist role in bringing about mergers and in providing substantial funding. The rationale for the FDIC and the FSLIC to intervene, spending millions of dollars to assist in mergers and otherwise keep institutions alive, lay in the fact that it would have been infinitely more expensive for the federal insurers to allow the financial institutions to fail, thereby incurring the burden of paying the depositors.

Disintermediation

In addition to being the victims of negative profit margins on their operations, the thrift institutions in the late 1970s and early 1980s faced a problem that, in this instance, was shared with the commercial banks. In 1972 brokerage firms introduced the money-market funds, a form of mutual funds designed to use the small deposits of individuals, pool them, and generate yields that those individuals could not otherwise obtain. The new funds offered liquidity since there was no fixed maturity and withdrawals did not incur penalties. The investor was assured of interest rates that fluctuated with the market, and during an era when rates rose steadily, this proved to be a most important advantage.

Both thrifts and commercial banks found that the core deposits on which they had traditionally relied were deserting them in favor of these new investment vehicles. Within ten years of their introduction, the money-market funds totaled almost $200 billion.[10] During a Congressional hearing, Walter

Wriston noted that within 24 months Merrill Lynch's money-market funds had exceeded Citibank's total domestic deposits, which had been built up over the course of 160 years.[11]

Merrill Lynch's Cash Management Account proved especially attractive since it combined a brokerage account with overnight investment of funds at prevailing rates, a Visa card, a checking account with overdraft privileges, and the right to borrow at any time against the value of the securities held in the account. No commercial bank or thrift was able to offer any such combination of benefits in a single relationship.

As detailed in chapter 1, the Monetary Control Act of 1980 had attempted to create competitive equity among the various types of financial institutions and had given S&Ls and federally chartered savings banks expanded loan and investment powers. The Garn-St Germain Act of 1982 supplemented this expansion and took particular note of the need for commercial banks and thrifts to have a new type of account that would enable them to compete with the money-market funds. In addition, it granted additional lending powers to the thrifts.

Both the Monetary Control and Garn-St Germain Acts also included provisions specifically designed to assist credit unions. For example, the former authorized them to make share drafts available to their customers; these are negotiable checklike instruments that can be used for payment purposes. The Garn-St Germain Act gave credit unions expanded lending powers on mortgages.[12]

Recent Developments

The typical thrift institution today differs in two important respects from those of prior years. The first difference is that it remains the primary lender in the home mortgage field, but the loans it makes are on a different basis. Instead of the traditional fixed-rate terms, the mortgage loan is now frequently on an adjustable-rate basis so that the lender can change the interest rate according to money-market conditions. Adjustable-rate mortgages (ARMs), also known as variable-rate mortgages (VRMs) have had a major impact on the thrifts' former problems and have given them a flexibility they never possessed in the 1960s and 1970s.

The second significant change is particularly apparent among the large thrifts. Through the Garn–St Germain Act, they were allowed, for the first time, to engage in commercial lending, and many of them have achieved a degree of penetration of that market. They have found the yields on commercial loans to be higher than those on residential mortgages in many cases. In addition, the corporate borrower, who can change the price of a product to meet market conditions, is usually receptive to adjustable-rate loans; the individual who has no ability to cope with rate increases is far less amenable.

As of November 1985, the nation's commercial banks had total commercial and industrial loan outstandings of $492.8 billion.[13] By comparison, the $12.85 billion in similar outstandings at all FSLIC-insured thrifts may not appear significant[14]; yet readers must remember that the thrifts have had only three years in which to achieve that figure. During 1985, their commercial loans grew by 60 percent,[15] and among the 100 largest thrifts the rate of increase was 73 percent.[16]

Interstate Banking

Although a section in chapter 12 is devoted to interstate banking, I must note here that the financial crises of the 1980s among the thrifts led to a breakdown of the legal barriers on acquisitions and mergers across state lines. At the outset, these were confined to the same segment of the overall financial services industry; that is, the FDIC or the FSLIC helped to bring about the acquisition of a troubled thrift institution by another institution of the same type. Later, a commercial bank in a particular state was allowed to acquire a thrift in the same state as a means of preventing the latter's liquidation. This precedent, set in Minnesota in 1982,[17] was soon followed by federal permission for an interstate takeover, as the Federal Reserve approved the acquisition of the $3 billion Fidelity S&L (San Francisco) by Citicorp.[18]

Does interstate banking, de facto, exist today, despite federal and state restrictions? That question was posed in chapter 5 as part of the discussion of nationwide ATM networks. It has even greater validity in the present context as numerous and large-scale takeovers across state lines continue to take place. Many of these takeovers appear to have accomplished two simultaneous objectives:

1. They have given the acquiring bank a foothold in a geographic area it could not otherwise have legally entered and an existing base of retail customers.
2. They have averted the failures of several thrifts and the consequent payout costs to federal insurers and have at least partly lessened further public concerns about industry strength and viability.

A BHC can acquire a federally insured thrift only with the joint approval of the Federal Reserve and the insurer. The speed of approval is usually a direct function of the severity of the thrift institution's problems. The acquirer can take advantage of the thrift's intrastate (and, in some cases, interstate) freedom to branch and its beneficial tax status.[19] The acquiring bank also gains the ability to diversify into areas of potential profit.[20] A specific example is California, where state law allows thrifts to place an unlimited amount of assets into service corporations. These corporations may engage in real estate ventures and other activities prohibited to the thrifts.[21]

Nineteen eighty-five was a year of particular crisis in Ohio and Maryland, where several substantial thrift institutions, not insured by any federal agency, experienced such severe financial problems that direct state intervention became necessary. At one point the Governor of Maryland assumed control of 102 privately insured thrifts in that state and imposed dollar limits on withdrawals of funds by their customers. The ultimate solution in both Ohio and Maryland lay in permitting out-of-state commercial banks—for example, Chase Manhattan—to acquire the troubled thrifts with the objective of eventually converting them into full-scale commercial banks.[22]

If, therefore, one construes the term *interstate banking* to mean that many commercial banks and thrifts are already conducting business across state lines, the facts clearly support its existence. For example, at year-end 1985 Citicorp was conducting either thrift or commercial banking operations in New York, California, Illinois, Florida, Maryland, and Nevada and was negotiating to acquire the fifth-largest commercial bank in Arizona.[23] By early 1986 Chase Manhattan had added the former Park Bank of Florida (St. Petersburg) to its previous acquisitions in Maryland and Ohio and was taking over an Arizona bank.[24]

Many major thrift institutions were also aggressively expanding in various areas. For example, the nation's largest thrift, Home Savings of America, with deposits of $19.5 billion,[25] is headquartered in Los Angeles and operates also in Texas, Missouri, Florida, and Illinois.[26] CityFed Financial Corporation (the parent of City Federal S&L in Palm Beach, Florida) has 123 thrift offices in that state and in New Jersey, plus 160 consumer loan, mortgage, and financial service facilities in twenty-seven states.[27]

Trends in Branch Banking

As the change in traditional philosophy became more widespread and many major banks decided to enter the retail market, it became evident that the growing army of consumers, with their broader spectrum of personal financial needs, could be served only if substantial expansion of branch networks could take place. The post-World-War II exodus from the cities to the suburbs meant that banks necessarily had to follow their customers by placing facilities wherever the latter might be, such as in a shopping center or a newly expanding suburban area. Despite the obvious need for such facilities, however, the banks that wished to open networks of branches often found their options limited.

They could either pay the price—often including a substantial premium—to acquire an existing bank, its branches, and its customer base, or they could adopt the even more expensive course of establishing *de novo* locations. The four major New York City banks whose mergers were mentioned earlier exemplify the former course; yet in many cases mergers alone were not necessarily the answer because of the plethora of federal and state restrictions and regulations that affect commercial banks. A bank that saw its marketplace as existing beyond the purely geographic boundaries of a city or county might find that the laws of its particular state precluded expansion beyond those limits. If the bank's marketplace logically extended into the territory of another state, federal laws prevented interstate branching; even if no such barriers existed, the bank would still be constrained by the branch banking regulations of the state.

The right of every individual state to prohibit or restrict branch banking within its borders has been repeatedly upheld at every level of the judicial system, including the U.S. Supreme Court. Despite the intensive lobbying that commercial banks have conducted in their quest for additional freedom, and despite the fact that one of their major financial competitors, the S&L industry, is not shackled by any comparable restrictions, state laws that ban or limit full-scale branching persist.

A series of state legislative actions in the late 1970s and early 1980s have tended to make branch banking easier; however, the most recent statistics indicate that seven states (Illinois, Colorado, Kansas, Missouri, North Dakota, Texas, and Wyoming) still operate as *unit* banking entities; that is, full-scale branching is prohibited within their borders. Commercial banks in those states are therefore called *unit banks,* operating entirely from a single location. In addition, eighteen states have statutes that in some way restrict branching—for example, to contiguous areas or within a single county. Therefore, it remains true that as of 1986 over half the states do not allow full-scale branch banking.[28]

Where state laws originally favored statewide branching, and in those states that have liberalized their statutes in recent years, the movement toward more retail banking offices was dramatic. New York State, for example, twice revised its laws to permit increased branching; as a result, there were 1,390 branches in the state in 1950 and 3,414 in 1977—even though the number of banks decreased from 635 to 239 during that period.[29]

Among the many voices that have been heard on this subject, John Heimann's was prominent. During his tenure as Comptroller of the Currency, he stated that restrictions on branch banking create inequities,[30] and two Presidential Commissions subsequently reported that removal of those restrictions might well be in the public interest.[31] In today's environment, when so many nonbank companies (e.g., Sears, Merrill Lynch, Beneficial Corporation, and GMAC) aggressively compete with commercial banks without regard for state boundaries, those opinions assume even greater validity.

In contrast, however, many associations of small, independent banks in various communities throughout the country continue to raise the spectre of the undue concentration of power that would accrue to the money-center giants through interstate or intrastate branching expansion, and their opposition to any liberalization of existing statutes evidently is uppermost in the minds of many legislators at both the federal and state levels.

In 1984 and 1985, in particular, there was strong evidence of a trend toward reductions in branch networks at some of the major commercial banks, thereby reversing the earlier pattern. One reason for this reversal is found in the proliferation of nonbank facilities at which consumers can conduct their various financial affairs. In 1974 a member of the Federal Reserve Board of Governors posed the rhetorical question, "Once a man can cash a check at a local supermarket, what does he need a branch for?"[32] His prescience was remarkable, anticipating as it did the thousands of ATMs that now dot the countryside and, in particular, that are housed in so many grocery chains. The brick-and-mortar networks of the post–World War II period simply are redundant today in many parts of the country.

The second reason for the reduction in branch networks goes directly to the question of operating costs:

> Faced with slimmer profit margins compared to five or ten years ago, bankers are looking for ways to cut costs. They view their extensive branch networks—there are some 40,000 commercial bank branches around the country—as a prime area for retrenchment.[33]

Three of the nation's more prominent institutions have made public their plans for such retrenchment. Late in 1983, Bank of America, which had achieved appropriate recognition as a pioneer in statewide branching and which was for many years the nation's largest commercial bank in both assets and deposits, announced that its network of 1,071 branches would be reduced in 1984 to 950 "or less."[34] In fact, it closed 132 branches during 1984 and reduced the size of 53 others; over a three-year period, its California work force shrank from 40,000 employees to 32,000.[35]

During 1985, Manufacturers Hanover Trust, with 190 branches in the New York area, embarked on a major advertising campaign with the objective of persuading consumers not to use those branches. This magazine, television, and billboard campaign highlighted the bank's telephone, mail, ATM, and home banking capabilities and services as substitutes for branches; implicit in this approach was the possibility of reductions in the latter if consumers would follow the suggestions.[36]

In Columbus, Ohio, Bank One (lead bank in the Banc One holding company) began testing a new type of branch, with fewer staff members but increased emphasis on technology, in 1985; John Fisher, Senior Vice-President of the bank and the holding company, foresaw an eventual closing of 10–15 percent of the branches, with size reductions to take place in other locations.[37] Since then, he has outlined plans for the redesigned branches and has repeated the prediction that some facilities that have proved unnecessary must be closed.[38] A Senior Vice-President of BancOhio National Bank, also in Columbus, commented on the closing of 19 of his bank's 250 branches in 1985 and expressed the opinion that many offices should have been closed several years earlier.[39]

The combination of escalating labor and occupancy costs with a technology that helps to make brick-and-mortar locations unnecessary contributed to a nationwide trend toward fewer branches in the early 1980s. In 1980 banks opened 1,430 branch offices and closed 248—a ratio of 5.77 to 1.[40] By 1983 the ratio had shrunk to 1.89, and in 1984 closings in the San Francisco and Cleveland Federal Reserve districts actually outnumbered openings. Stephen Brobeck, Executive Director of the Consumer Federation of America, has predicted even greater increases in the number of branch closings in the future.[41] Despite this prediction, however, the number of branches of U.S. commercial banks at year-end 1984 stood at 41,773.[42]

Whatever the rationale behind them, branch closings cannot be implemented without a bank's consideration of the implications of the Community Reinvestment Act (CRA), passed by Congress in 1978 in reaction to the charges of redlining that had been brought against some institutions. That term refers to their alleged practice of drawing red-ink boundaries on maps to delineate those neighborhoods in which they would restrict lending because of what they perceived as excessive risks.[43] As a result of this Act, every bank can be evaluated according to what it has done, or is accused of having failed to do, in meeting the credit needs of the community in which it is based. The public is invited to comment on a bank's performance in this respect. All such comments become part of the bank's file, maintained by regulatory agencies, and a file that contains detrimental data may persuade those agencies to deny requests for expansion of services or additional branch powers.

Therefore, profitability alone cannot determine a bank's decision to close branches; opposition from residents in the affected neighborhood must also be considered. Protests from community activists, aside from any legal recourse they may seek, often occur. An informative campaign of public relations, explaining the bank's reasons for a closing and suggesting possible alternatives for those affected by it, may help forestall such protests.

Whether or not future closings outnumber openings, one fact is clear: federal and state regulatory constraints have brought about a geographic and functional fragmentation of the retail market. The absence of an integrated nationwide system of branches places the U.S. consumer at a real disadvantage when he or she is contrasted with counterpart individuals in Sweden, the Netherlands, Germany, the United Kingdom, or Canada.[44] In Sweden, for example, the coverage per person provided by branch offices is 38 percent higher than the U.S. figure, and France and Germany have about twice as many branches per person.[45]

Pricing and Service Strategies

Before the Monetary Control and Garn–St Germain Acts, commercial bankers sought deregulation to abolish inequities in competition. In retrospect, they can scarcely be blamed if the legislation has caused them still more dissatisfaction. Their competitors, for example, received far greater benefits through the two Acts. All credit unions were allowed to offer share drafts as payment vehicles, thereby reducing commercial banking's share of the market. Reserves against the new Super-NOW accounts permitted by the Acts were set at only 4 percent for thrifts versus 12 percent for commercial banks, thereby giving the former group an additional advantage. Deregulation has conferred relatively fewer benefits to commercial banks.

In contrast to the financial services industry of the past, where lines of demarcation between types of financial institutions were clearly drawn and payments of interest to depositors were severely restricted, we now have an industry in which open competition has blurred the former distinctions. Interest ceilings on many types of deposits are disappearing, and new, explicit pricing of many retail services has become a widely observed phenomenon. The shock waves from these changes have been deeply felt throughout the consumer marketplace.

An 80/20 relationship was historically common in banking; that is, 80 percent of total deposits came from 20 percent of the customer base, while 80 percent of the depositors provided only 20 percent of the deposits. The earnings generated from use of the balances provided by large depositors subsidized the small customers and kept service charges to a minimum.[46]

Regulation Q, rather than competition, set the cost of retail funds in many instances, and the price of money to borrowers on the retail side was capped by usury statutes and indexed to the prime rate. The bank's spread between the cost of funds and its price structure was "stable, substantial, and predictable."[47] The combination of deregulation and new competition—for example, the efforts of Sears, Merrill Lynch, and others to attract retail deposits—in an environment of widely fluctuating interest rates has forced many commercial banks to make an agonizing reappraisal of their pricing structures for a wide range of consumer accounts and services and to rethink their strategies as interest-free deposits continue their relative decline.

When rate deregulation brought about increases in the costs of funds, many banks simply began charging new or increased fees and/or requiring higher account balances to make the 80 percent of their customer base more profitable. Consumers who had previously enjoyed nominal service charges suddenly found that their accounts had become much more expensive to maintain. Their complaints grew in number and vehemence and quickly came to the attention of legislators.

The customer who is charged $20 by a bank for a small overdraft or who finds that the bank's service charges on a modest savings account exceeded the interest is outraged.[48] The individual who must face an annual interest rate of 19 or 20 percent on credit card outstandings at a time when the same bank is paying only 5.5 percent on a savings account—and is simultaneously calling for a minimum balance of $500 or $1,000 to keep the account at all—feels unjust discrimination. In a March 1986 study by the New York State Banking Department, twenty-seven commercial banks and thrift institutions were found to be charging at least 19 percent on card outstandings; many of these had an additional annual charge just to have the card.[49] In the same survey, eighty-one New York State commercial and savings banks were charging $7 or more for a Stop Payment Order, with several using $12 or more as the standard. Minimum balances of $1,000 and $1,500 for checking accounts were required in many cases.[50]

The trend toward higher pricing for accounts and services has been evolving for several years. From 1978 through 1983, for example, fees levied on credit cards and checking accounts at the nation's ten largest banks rose from $8 per $1,000 of total income to $11.80.[51]

These policy actions may have been responsible for driving some consumers completely away from the banks; in other cases, they created a perceived need on the part of many legislators for a mandated set of so-called lifeline services, to be provided either to certain groups or to all consumers at little or no cost. In 1985, in particular, pressures from consumer advocates increased, on the grounds that the banks were depriving many lower-income individuals and senior citizens of the basic services they needed.[52]

At year-end 1985 the controversy on this point continued, with many bankers taking the position that legislation that compelled them to offer services at no cost or at drastically reduced cost was discriminatory, since banks were being singled out as prime targets for this type of regulation. The CEO of a $1 billion bank in Delaware rhetorically asked whether basic insurance and brokerage services might be added next to the "mandatory free" list,[53] and his counterpart at a Virginia bank stated flatly that he questioned anyone's right to obtain banking services without paying for them.[54] At the same time, state officials, members of Congress, and consumer groups have maintained that depository institutions are inherently obligated to "subsidize" the young, the poor, and the old.[55] Class action suits have been brought to prevent banks from charging "unconscionable and overreaching" fees for returned checks, and legislation has been introduced to prevent their collecting charges from those who fail to maintain minimum balances in checking accounts.[56] The bankers' view of fairness in pricing clearly differs from the consumers'.

On the one hand, there are documented instances in which banks have raised fees and service charges to levels that consumers perceive to be excessive; these have certainly resulted in protests. On the other hand, a survey of 1,500 banks in 1985 indicated that 75 percent of the respondents were already offering no-cost checking accounts to senior citizens, and bank policies that do not penalize the individual who maintains a small checking account deserve equal mention.[57] In contrast to the evidence of protests over bank pricing, the President and CEO of a corporation that conducts hundreds of consumer surveys each year reports that his firm's research identifies a consumer willingness to pay more for a demonstrably superior product or service and a consumer stress on leisure time and convenience rather than on price alone.[58]

Although their strategies may vary, the banks' actions are indicative of their awareness of the size and potential value of the total consumer market. For example, the pool of retail deposits has been variously estimated at $1 trillion–$1.5 trillion, with net revenues from consumer financial services in excess of $200 billion.[59] Despite deregulation and the many attractive investment opportunities that are readily available, some $300 billion is still held in passbook and statement savings accounts, and Federal Reserve statistics disclose an average balance of $3,500 in those accounts.[60] For those account holders the payment of high explicit interest, as permitted by deregulation, is not necessarily of primary concern. The customer's tax bracket may be such that higher interest becomes relatively meaningless. In this case the bank's strategy for retaining his or her business may take the form of offering less traditional services such as investment planning, insurance, and financial counseling.[61]

In the face of a perception among consumers that the quality of bank service is deteriorating and that bankers are concentrating on profitability, a bank that emphasizes the quality of its delivery and its concern for the satisfaction of its customers may find itself differentiated from competitors. Thus, quality control may offset the institution's pricing policies.[62]

The term *relationship planning* has become far more widely used among banks in the 1980s. It refers to the concept that a customer's total use of the bank's services should be taken into account in applying the institution's policies and in its marketing approach. An existing satisfied depositor usually is the best source of additional business; selling an added service to him or her may cost the bank as little as one-third of the expense involved in marketing to a prospect. The national average, however, indicates that commercial banks and thrifts have only 1.3 accounts per customer. Given the lower cost and added value of cross-selling, the development by the bank of detailed CIFs (Customer Information Files) is a needed and logical step.[63] CIFs are vital in both marketing and price setting, since they provide a picture of the entire relationship and can be used to indicate opportunities for targeting an expanded product line at existing customers.[64] An individual's CIF is a portrait of his or her financial life cycle and an indication of needs the bank can address through selective marketing.[65]

The word *selective* reflects a significant policy change among those banks that, for many years, determined that they would endeavor to be all things to all people. In contrast, the emphasis today is frequently placed, on the retail side of banking, in particular, on market segmentation. This emphasis enables the bank to concentrate its entire marketing approach on the most likely profitable areas of the total marketplace so that it is offering the right services to the right customers at the right time in the right locations at the right price.

Merrill Lynch, a firm whose operations are detailed in chapter 10, has chosen to rephrase the bankers' traditional policy. Its Consumer Markets Director, John Steffens, has outlined plans to be "all things to *some* of the people"[66]:

> Today, the establishment of multiple profitable relationships with desirable customers . . . is not an option, it is an imperative. The more services, the more loyalty; the more services, the greater the profit; the more services, the larger the preexisting market for even broader services, which will, of necessity, be offered in the future.[67]

The strategy that has been announced by Security Pacific Corporation is an application of the policy of segmentation. Vice-Chairman William Ford admits that the effort will not be aimed at being all things to all people[68]; however, the corporation's various units, which have more than 500 offices serving some 3 million customers in forty-six states, will offer a matrix of consumer-oriented products for those individuals who appear most likely to generate profits for the organization.

Consumer Debt

Any stigma that was attached to personal borrowing in the years before World War II has now disappeared, and the banks, right or wrong, have been chiefly responsible for eliminating it. Consumers today, whose predecessors felt that incurring debt was a sign of weakness, have no reluctance to borrow, whether to meet an emergency need or simply to enhance their lifestyle. The banks, by not merely tolerating the steady growth in consumer debt but also aggressively encouraging it, have assuredly helped to raise the American standard of living. Home improvements, cars, appliances, and luxuries such as vacation trips have been made available under the pay-later philosophy.

At the same time, questions must arise about the culpability of the banks in making it too easy for too many individuals to incur too much debt. Bankers who do not act to discourage or control consumer borrowing because they are concerned over its growth, the effects of a possible recession, or the increase in personal bankruptcies cannot expect their customers to display restraint. As long as the banks continue to make credit so easily available, "keeping up with the Joneses" by borrowing is not likely to decrease.

The gradual change in the policy of major commercial banks regarding unsecured, monthly-payment installment loans has been remarkable. At year-end 1945, this type of loan accounted for only 7.5 percent of total bank portfolios; within twenty-five years that percentage had tripled.[69] In 1945, the ratio of consumer debt to disposable personal income was less than 2 percent; by 1955 it had reached 11 percent, and in 1985 it approached 18 percent.[70] The latter represents an all-time high and, as two prominent economists have noted, makes consumers especially vulnerable should an economic downturn occur, with a corresponding rise in unemployment.[71]

From 1983 through October 1985, consumer installment credit grew by 38 percent and amounted to $530.2 billion. Perhaps the most significant point—one that has been historically true throughout the post–World War II period—is that the commercial banks, which at one time completely neglected the consumer as a borrower and left the satisfaction of his or her borrowing needs to finance companies, are by far the principal lenders. Commercial banks were responsible for $242.2 billion of the total (45.7 percent), while finance companies generated 22.4 percent, credit unions 14.5 percent, and thrifts 10.4 percent.[72] By March 1986, the total figure had increased an additional 3.6 percent and stood at $549 billion.[73]

Once the commercial banks rejected their traditional policy and began to engage in consumer lending on a large scale, the results fully justified their strategy. Installment loans are almost invariably discounted; that is, the interest for the full life of the loan is collected in advance so the bank gains the use of that amount at once. As rates have steadily increased in the 1980s, this feature has taken on additional meaning.

That interest-rate increase has not served to reduce the propensity of consumers to avail themselves of bank credit. The strong demand for installment loans has given bankers no incentive whatever to reduce their charges. Many are puzzled by the consumer's willingness to pay 19 or 20 percent on loans while savings earn only 7 or 8 percent; at the same time, they are gratified at the contribution that installment lending makes to overall bank profits.[74]

Many banks, concerned over the rising costs of funds and cognizant of the problems that arose among thrift institutions because of fixed-rate loans, have changed the traditional structuring of installment loans and now make them on a fixed-payment, variable-rate basis. In these cases the dollar amount of each monthly payment does not change, but the maturity is extended or shortened whenever the rate is adjusted to reflect conditions in the money markets.

In increasing numbers, commercial banks have added to their consumer-debt portfolios the so-called home equity loan, made on a second-mortgage basis. Upscale, affluent individuals who have already built up substantial equities in their residences find it easy to borrow on this basis. The loans are attractive to the banks because default levels are low, administrative costs vary little from those on smaller loans, and the yield reflects the second-mortgage risk the bank is assuming.

The statistics on consumer debt mentioned up to this point have omitted the single most important component: home mortgages. As of the third quarter of 1985 the total amount owed on 1-to-4 family homes was $1.4 trillion, of which S&Ls held 56.7 percent and commercial banks held 26.4 percent.[75] The latter figure is remarkable in that there was no large-scale involvement of commercial banks in the home mortgage field until 1913.

Mortgage lending, like some types of installment lending, has assumed new forms through the extending of a variety of terms that protect the lender against fluctuations in money-market conditions. Variable-rate or adjustable-rate mortgages have become common. In some cases the original loan is made for a relatively short term (three to five years) and can be renewed automatically at revised rates; in others the borrower's payments are graduated, starting on a low level but increasing as his or her income and the value of the property climb.

In the installment lending field, many banks have developed a set of point systems, on which credit decisions are based. The prospective borrower's income, length and type of employment, current debt, and home ownership are key factors.

A host of federal and state regulations affects banks in the lending process and is designed to protect the consumer. For example, the APR (Annual Percentage Rate) on installment loans must be conspicuously stated. All forms of discrimination in lending are prohibited. If a loan is declined, the applicant can ask for an explanation of the decision and is entitled to see the credit information on which it was based. Collection procedures must conform to certain standards. State usury laws may set the maximum interest rates on consumer loans, but some lending banks have circumvented this restriction by establishing units in states that have no such laws—for example, South Dakota.

S&Ls, taking advantage of the expanded powers granted by the Monetary Control Act, have become much more important than before as suppliers of consumer credit. Between 1982 and February 1985 their outstandings doubled,[76] and by October 1985 they had surpassed retailers, with $40.4 billion as compared with the latter group's $37.8 billion.[77]

Bank Cards

What factors can we cite to account for the steady growth in consumer debt? How can we explain continuing sharp increases? The following list may provide a partial answer.

1. Individuals have displayed a willingness to incur additional debt burdens as a means of acquiring possessions and meeting personal needs.
2. There is a consumer perception that borrowing during a period of inflation means that future repayments will be made with cheaper dollars and that increases in personal disposable income will more than offset those repayments.
3. Lenders of all types have become increasingly aggressive in marketing, and have relaxed some of the former credit criteria.[78]
4. Maturities on automobile loans have been lengthened, thereby reducing monthly payments and making borrowing more acceptable.
5. Bank cards have proliferated.

Evidence exists to support the view that the proliferation of bank cards is the most important single factor. No development in consumer lending since the 1950s has had as permanent and revolutionary an effect. Despite its humble beginnings and the problems that marked its early years, the bank card has become an integral part of the consumer's way of life and a necessity rather than a luxury. From the banks' standpoint, it is an indispensable element in their efforts to market ATMs and POS systems.[79]

The average number of cards per U.S. household now exceeds five, and almost 75 percent of all households possess at least one such card.[80]

The 25–34 and 35–44 age groups, upwardly mobile and marked by high rates of family formation and spending, jointly make up the nation's largest borrowing class. For their households, the mean debt is $3,842, and in both groups over 73 percent of those households are in debt to a greater or lesser extent.[81]

> The baby boom generation has grown up. With so many people in a prime age for family formation (typically a time of heavy borrowing), the U.S. population now has a structural tilt toward acquiring debt.[82]

Senator Alfonse M. D'Amato (R, N.Y.) has predicted that American consumers will charge over $300 billion during 1986 and will pay an average interest rate of 18.6 percent on outstandings.[83] Much of that activity will take place among the 2 million merchants who now accept bank cards.

The nomenclature that is most appropriately used in this world of plastic is significant. When commercial banks first offered cards, the term *credit cards* was used because these, like the cards of American Express, gasoline companies, and retailers, were used to obtain goods and services on credit. The merchant who accepted them deposited sales slips with a bank; the issuer eventually billed the cardholder; and the cardholder subsequently made payment.

More recently, the plastic has taken on a dual identity. It serves as both a

Table 6–2
Bank Card Statistics

	1983	*1984*
Usage ($ billions)		
Visa	47	61
MasterCard	37	50
Number of cardholders in the United States (millions)		
Visa	72	77
MasterCard	58	60

Sources: 1983 figures: Michael Weinstein, "'83 Figures Show Year of Strong Growth at Visa, MasterCard," *American Banker,* May 23, 1984, p. 10. 1984 figures: Monci Jo Williams, "The Great Plastic Card Fight Begins," *Fortune,* February 4, 1985, p. 21.

credit *and* a debit card; for example, when a cardholder obtains cash through an ATM by using it or makes a POS purchase, the cardholder's account is charged at once. Given the marketing efforts of the banks in these two aspects of consumer usage, the generic term *bank card* today is more accurate than *credit card.*

Table 6–2 indicates the statistics for MasterCard and Visa, the two major systems, for 1983 and 1984. As of June 1985, the outstandings on MasterCard were estimated at $28 billion—an increase of $17 billion since 1983.[84]

In addition to Visa, which is jointly owned by over 17,000 financial institutions, and MasterCard, owned by an association of over 25,000, many banks issue their own proprietary cards. Foremost among these is Citibank, which uses a subsidiary of Citicorp (Citicorp Retail Services) for this purpose and is reported to handle over $2 billion per year in receivables from consumers.[85]

Evolution of Bank Cards

Gasoline companies and retailers introduced the first charge cards during the 1920s; Diners Club introduced the entertainment-and-travel-card concept in 1950; and American Express began its card program in 1958. The successes achieved by these issuers led many commercial banks to enter the field in the mid-1960s. At that time, disintermediation was having a severe impact on the banks, and the shift of deposits toward interest-bearing accounts created increasing pressure to develop new types of high-yielding services. At the same time, advances in computer technology enhanced the banks' ability to deal with the volume of paper that cards create.

The introduction of cards ideally would simultaneously serve several purposes. For example, cards would generate substantial income from cardholders through interest on outstanding balances; they would provide new accounts or increased deposit activity from the merchants who accepted them; they could be used as a means of attracting new consumer accounts; and they would provide banks with additional income from interest charged to cardholders who obtained cash advances and discounts on each sales slip deposited by merchants. Each of those benefits still exists, and when banks are in the position of having to pay 7 percent or less on time and savings deposits while charging 18 percent or more on card outstandings, the attractiveness of the world of plastic increases.

The early history of bank card plans is one of large losses, however—often the direct result of the banks' carelessness and shortsightedness in introducing cards to the public.[86] In many cases, banks either discontinued their card operations or decided not to enter the field. The imposition of strict controls over card issuance and processing, including the use of credit criteria and the introduction of security measures, proved beneficial, and following the appearance of MasterCard and Visa in the late 1960s, levels of profitability began to appear. Losses in 1979 through 1981 resulted from the huge increases in the banks' cost of funds at a time when interest rates on outstandings were restricted by state laws.

More recently, banks have taken a series of actions to enhance profitability. They have implemented new or increased fees for cards, begun to charge interest from the posting date, and raised interest rates on outstandings wherever state usury laws have been liberalized. Where strict usury laws remain in force, banks have moved their card operations to more favorable locations; for example, twelve banks now use Delaware for that purpose.[87]

To attract new cardholders and achieve greater economies of scale through increased volume, many banks have embarked on nationwide marketing campaigns; Citicorp's 1984 program cost $150 million–$200 million.[88] RepublicBank (Dallas) and Continental Illinois have also engaged in nationwide marketing.

In rebutting consumer protests over card charges, the banks have pointed out that processing costs on card operations are ten to twelve times higher than those on installment loans.[89] In addition, the banks realize that sophisticated cardholders are taking full advantage of the time frame allowed for repayment of outstanding balances without incurring interest charges. The sales slip deposited by a merchant is treated exactly like a check: the merchant's account is credited at once. As many as forty-five days, however, may elapse before the bank receives payment from the cardholder. As a result, the banking industry incurs average daily float of $10.7 billion; using 9 percent as the cost of funds, this float has a value of almost $1 billion per year.[90] Unless remedial action can be taken, increases in transaction volume could, according to one consultant, double that figure by 1989.[91]

Fraud and the Smart Card

Ever since the widespread introduction of bank cards, fraud has been a chronic problem. In 1982 MasterCard International and Visa reported worldwide losses of $130 million. Lost or stolen cards that were fraudulently used accounted for the largest portion of these losses.[92] One year later, the President and CEO of MasterCard admitted to losses in the United States alone of some $20 million.[93]

Repeated efforts have been made by individual banks and by the American Bankers Association to educate the public regarding protective measures against fraud and to motivate merchants to become more security-conscious. Many individuals today make it a practice to remove and destroy the carbon copies of the charge slips they have signed.

Instead of relying on cardholder or merchant awareness, however, card issuers and equipment manufacturers have sought to promote the so-called smart card. This card contains an embedded microprocessor, into which an incredible amount of personal identification and financial information can be programmed. The most notable success achieved to date through the smart card has taken place in France, where it was invented in 1974 and where 3 million are now in use. Estimates call for 17 million smart cards to be in the hands of French cardholders by 1989; the cards can be used to make funds withdrawals through ATMs in post offices, banks, and stores and to activate the terminals used in home banking.[94]

The potential of the smart card appears limitless. Because the microchip embedded in it is completely programmable, a highly sophisticated security system can be implemented to set a preestablished dollar limit, to control the number of transactions, and to recognize a PIN (Personal Identification Number). Signatures, fingerprints, or voice characteristics can also be programmed into the microchip.[95]

In 1985 MasterCard International announced plans to test 50,000 smart cards in the Washington, D.C. area for use in some 200 special terminals in stores and service establishments.[96]

The potential of the smart card rests not only on the security it can provide but also on the fact that it can pave the way for far greater consumer acceptance of the POS concept. If individuals can be persuaded to use it to obtain funds through ATMs and to pay for merchandise in stores, check volume will begin to decrease significantly. Merchants will also benefit because their fears of fraud will diminish. J.C. Penney, American Express, and General Electric are among the corporations that have expressed interest in promoting use of the card.[97]

Nonbank Competition

The financial services industry today is highly fragmented; the exclusivity once possessed by banks has disappeared completely, and while the entire topic of competition from nonbanks is treated at length in chapter 10, one manifestation of it deserves mention here. Whenever the term *credit card* is used, one may immediately think of Visa, MasterCard, one of the several types of cards issued through Citicorp, or the traditional American Express card. One additional name, not mentioned up to this point, must be included; for some bankers this name appears to present the major threat to their card operations. The name is Sears Roebuck. As of 1985 60 million of Sears's proprietary (i.e., usable only in Sears stores) cards were in the hands of the public. Twenty-eight million of those cards were in active use and created 1984 billings of $13.6 billion.[98]

The former Chairman and President of Sears, Edward Telling, has stated, "Our goal is to become the largest consumer-oriented financial-service entity."[99] As part of the corporate strategy aimed at achieving that goal, Sears completed acquisition of Greenwood Trust Company, a Delaware bank, in 1985 and announced plans to offer a new card, to be called *Discover,* for a variety of credit and financial services.[100] With a huge data-processing network already in place to handle transactions for cardholders, with the largest unilateral base of cardholders in the world, and with the capacity to have terminals in all its stores throughout the country, Sears enjoyed many basic advantages. Some questions were raised, however, over whether merchants who viewed Sears as a competitor would accept the new card.[101]

In the light of subsequent developments, the concerns seem to have been unjustified. The Discover card has achieved wide acceptance. Sears has claimed that national merchants with 100,000 outlets have signed up; American Airlines, Holiday Inns, Budget Rent-a-Car, and Hospital Corporation of America are among the national companies that have agreed to accept the card and offer discounts to its users. Because the card is bank issued (Greenwood Trust), Sears can negotiate access to any ATM network and believes that cardholders will eventually be able to bank electronically at 5,000 machines.[102]

An outstanding feature of the Discover card, and therefore one that has a potentially severe impact on banks, lies in the synergy it offers to cardholders through the entire family of Sears financial services. The holder can use the card not only to transfer funds among all types of accounts at Greenwood Trust but also to cash personal checks up to $250 at Sears stores, and it ties together his or her use of Allstate (insurance), Dean Witter (brokerage and IRA accounts), and Coldwell Banker (real estate mortgages), all of which are Sears entities. Edward Brennan, who succeeded Telling as President of Sears, has said "Discover is the glue that will pull together our banking, insurance, brokerage, and real estate products. We're going to change the way people think about plastic."[103]

One problem Sears must address is the same one that has plagued card-issuing banks for many years: losses related to lending on credit cards. In the first quarter of 1986, the Citicorp report showed $303 million in net charge-offs on loans, with three-quarters of this volume attributable to card operations. The Citicorp earnings report commented that card products were the fastest growing segment of its business but that card products historically have had a higher loss experience.[104]

Individual Retirement Accounts (IRAs)

When Congress approved the Keogh Plan (H.R. 10) to permit self-employed individuals to set aside part of their annual income, on a tax-exempt basis, toward retirement, it also authorized Individual Retirement Accounts (IRAs) for those salaried workers not covered by qualified pension plans. In 1981 the Economic Recovery Tax Act liberalized the former regulations so that individuals could open IRAs even if they were already covered by such plans. Intense competition for IRAs developed immediately and remains manifest today. Thrift institutions, insurance companies, and brokerage firms vie with commercial banks in efforts to attract IRAs, which generate a steady inflow of stable funds. Despite that competition, the commercial banks as a group have done extremely well in this aspect of consumer banking.

Of the $148.4 billion in IRAs reported by commercial banks and thrift institutions as of December 31, 1985, the former group held $59.2 billion (40 percent); Bank of America, Citibank, and Wells Fargo each reported over $1 billion in IRA deposits.[105] Commercial banks attracted 27.4 percent of all the new IRAs that opened in 1985.[106]

In 1981 the DIDC authorized all depository institutions to offer time deposits of eighteen months or more with no interest-rate ceilings for use in IRAs.[107] More recently, many banks have begun offering self-directed IRAs, often linked to a discount broker's services. In this type of IRA relationship the customer can move funds from money-market accounts into mutual funds, CDs, or stocks and bonds. Offering self-directed IRAs not only gives the banks a competitive edge but also typically provides them with additional fee income for the services.[108]

One survey in 1986 disclosed that 31.4 percent of all U.S. households now have IRAs; among those households that reported annual incomes of over \$40,000, the percentage was 63.8.[109] IRAs will clearly continue to represent a most desirable type of activity among those institutions that are heavily involved in consumer banking.

Summary

The New World of consumer banking is one in which individuals, particularly the "upscale" or affluent, now find themselves the targets of a very significant portion of the banks' total marketing efforts. The range of services offered to them has broadened tremendously, but the fees charged to them have also increased, in recognition of the banking principle that all customers should pay their fair share of the expenses that their transactional activity creates. Those banks that have continued to remain wholesale—that have few branches and a focus on corporate, institutional, and government business—have avoided the high costs of doing business with the mass market. They remain in the minority, however. A bank may determine that it does not wish to be all things to all people, but in the current environment it will nevertheless, if it is typical, do everything possible to attract and retain those aspects of consumer financial services that prove most profitable. In the face of aggressive competition from all the other entities that offer those services, and despite the maze of federal and state regulations that inhibit nationwide growth, retail banking and the new emphasis on the consumer as a desirable customer will continue to expand, if for no other reason than the ability of the banks to serve the needs of over 200 million Americans.

Notes

1. Robert J. Rogowski, "The Financial Services Industry and the Consumer: Competition, Innovation, and Technology," *Survey of Business,* Spring 1985, p. 19.
2. American Institute of Banking, *Savings Banking Today* (New York, 1979), p. 14.
3. Donald T. Savage, "Depository Financial Institutions," in Richard C. Aspinwall and Robert A. Eisenbeis, eds., *Handbook for Banking Strategy* (New York: John Wiley & Sons, Inc., 1985), p. 195.
4. *Federal Reserve Bulletin,* February 1986, pp. A18 and A26.
5. Ibid., p. A39.
6. Ibid., p. A26.
7. Douglas K. Pearce, "Recent Developments in the Credit Union Industry," *Economic Review* (Federal Reserve Bank of Kansas City), June 1984, p. 13.
8. William D. Marbach, "The Fidelity Takeover," *Newsweek,* April 26, 1982, p. 68.
9. Robert A. Bennett, "Heavy Losses Continue at State Savings Banks," *The New York Times,* November 20, 1982, p. 29.

10. Robert A. Eisenbeis, "Inflation and Regulation; The Effects on Financial Institutions and Structure," in Aspinwall and Eisenbeis, op. cit., p. 91.

11. In Carol J. Loomis, "The Fight for Financial Turf," *Fortune,* December 28, 1981, p. 62.

12. Pearce, op. cit., p. 9.

13. *Federal Reserve Bulletin,* February 1986, p. A18.

14. L. Michael Cacace, "Thrifts Surge Ahead in Commercial Lending," *American Banker,* March 10, 1986, p. 1.

15. Ibid.

16. Lisabeth Weiner, "S&L Executives Enthusiastic about Corporate Business," *American Banker,* March 10, 1986, p. 1.

17. Robert J. Cole, "Bank, Thrift Unit Merge in Minnesota," *The New York Times,* February 23, 1982, p. D5.

18. Linda W. McCormick and Robert E. Norton, "Fed Lets Citicorp Acquire Fidelity Savings & Loan," *American Banker,* September 29, 1982, p. 1.

19. Thomas P. Vartanian, "If You're Thinking of Acquiring a Thrift," *ABA Banking Journal,* November 1983, pp. 70–74.

20. James R. Butler, Jr., "New Appeal in S&Ls," *Mortgage Banking,* December 1984, pp. 75–78.

21. Kenneth B. Noble, "U.S. Curbs Thrift Units that Enter New Fields," *The New York Times,* November 29, 1983, p. D2.

22. The details of the crises in Maryland and Ohio may be found in "Another Time Bomb Goes Off," *Time,* May 27, 1985, pp. 56–59; and "Washington Wrangles as the Thrift Crisis Deepens," *Business Week,* May 27, 1985, pp. 128–129.

23. John P. Forde, "Citicorp Gets Full-Service Bank Charter in Nevada with Takeover of Failed Thrift," *American Banker,* November 15, 1985, p. 1.

24. "Chase Gets Jump on Its Rivals by Buying Failed Florida Bank," *American Banker,* February 19, 1986, p. 1.

25. L. Michael Cacace, "Assets Grow 75% More than Deposits at Thrifts in 1984," *American Banker,* February 28, 1986, p. 1.

26. "Interstate Thrifts," *American Banker,* April 4, 1984, p. 14.

27. "CityFed Expects Long Wait on Its Branching Request," *American Banker,* January 2, 1985, p. 11.

28. Savage, op. cit., p. 186.

29. Eric N. Compton, *Inside Commercial Banking,* 2nd ed. (New York: John Wiley & Sons, Inc., 1983), p. 236.

30. In "Banking in Transition," *The Bankers Magazine,* September–October 1978, p. 22.

31. Edward W. Reed; Richard V. Cotter; Edward K. Gill; and Richard K. Smith, *Commercial Banking* (Englewood Cliffs, N.J.: Prentice-Hall, Inc., 1976), pp. 33–34.

32. In Martin Mayer, *The Bankers* (New York: David McKay Company, 1974), p. 180.

33. Michael Weinstein, "The New Bank Branch," *American Banker,* February 19, 1985, p. 22.

34. Joan Fitzgerald, "B of A Plans 10% Branch Cut," *American Banker,* December 8, 1983, p. 1.

35. Andrew Pollack, "Coast Bank Sets Retail Revamping," *The New York Times,* February 27, 1985, p. D5.

36. Laura Gross, "Hanover Introduces Bankless Banking," *American Banker,* February 22, 1985, p. 1.

37. Weinstein, op. cit.

38. "Banc One's Blueprint for Future Branches," *ABA Banking Journal,* March 1986, pp. 98–99.

39. Michael White, "Close the Losing Branch," *United States Banker,* April 1985, p. 39.

40. Blanca Riemer, "Liberty, Justice, and Bank Accounts for All," *Business Week,* July 1, 1985, p. 68.

41. In White, op. cit.

42. Board of Governors of the Federal Reserve System, *71st Annual Report: 1984,* p. 249.

43. Donald T. Savage, "CRA and Community Credit Needs," *The Bankers Magazine,* January 1979, p. 51.

44. A detailed study comparing the retail systems of ten major countries may be found in Dimitri Vittas and Patrick Frazer, "Retail Banking in the United States," *Bank Administration,* November 1983, pp. 29–34.

45. Mary L. King, *The Great American Banking Snafu* (Lexington, Mass.: Lexington Books, 1985), p. 61.

46. Jim Cairns, "The Abstraction We Call Banking," *Illinois Banker,* April 1985, p. 17.

47. Dr. Thomas W. Thompson, "Pricing: The Silent 'P' of Bank Marketing," *United States Banker,* November 1984, p. 7.

48. William E. Blundell, "As Basic Institutions Like Phones and Banks Change, Public Chafes," *The Wall Street Journal,* February 5, 1985, p. 1.

49. "Consumer Guide to Bank Services," March 3, 1986.

50. Ibid.

51. "The Revolution in Financial Services," *Business Week,* November 28, 1983, p. 88.

52. Philip T. Sudo, "Survey Pinpoints a Growing, Upscale Bank Market," *American Banker,* May 28, 1985, p. 1.

53. "Everyone Has a Place in Banking's Line," *ABA Banking Journal,* April 1985, p. 37.

54. Ibid.

55. Thompson, op. cit., p. 8.

56. Philip T. Sudo, "Chemical's Increases Fuel Bank-Fee Debates," *American Banker,* March 2, 1983, p. 3.

57. Cairns, op. cit.

58. Andrew J. Brown, "The Changing Financial Customer," *American Banker,* November 8, 1985, p. 30.

59. Donald Shoultz, "Rate Ceilings Go on Passbook Accounts," *American Banker,* March 23, 1986, p. 24.

60. Ibid.

61. Peter J. Elmer, "Developing Service-Oriented Deposit Accounts," *The Bankers Magazine,* March–April 1985, p. 60.

62. Deborah Colletti, "Service Quality: It Can Be Your Competitive Edge," *Bank Administration,* February 1986, pp. 38–39.

63. Richard J. Roll, "Targeting Markets in Consumer Banking," *The Bankers Magazine,* January–February 1986, pp. 47–48.

64. Yvette D. Kantrow, "The Price Is Right," *Computers In Banking,* February 1986, pp. 30–31.

65. Douglas Hile, "Marketing Focus in Personal Banking," *Bank Administration,* January 1986, pp. 20–22.

66. Richard L. Stern and Lisa Gubernick, "Financial Services—Who Owns the Future?" *Forbes,* February 24, 1986, p. 91. (emphasis added)

67. In Roll, op. cit., p. 47.

68. Laura Gross, "Security Pacific to Test 1-Stop Finance Center," *American Banker,* April 7, 1986, p. 1.

69. Howard D. Crosse and George H. Hempel, *Management Policies for Commercial Banks,* 2nd ed. (Englewood Cliffs, N.J.: Prentice-Hall, Inc., 1973), p. 176.

70. Charles A. Luckett and James D. August, "The Growth of Consumer Debt," *Federal Reserve Bulletin,* June 1985, p. 390.

71. Barbara Rudolph, "Mounting Doubts about Debts," *Time,* March 31, 1986, p. 50.

72. *Federal Reserve Bulletin,* February 1986, p. A40.

73. Rudolph, op. cit.

74. Robert A. Bennett, "High Rates, Hefty Borrowing," *The New York Times,* May 24, 1985, p. D1.

75. *Federal Reserve Bulletin,* February 1986, p. A39.

76. Lucket and August, op. cit.

77. *Federal Reserve Bulletin,* February 1986, p. A40.

78. Lynn C. Goldfaden and Gerald P. Hurst, "Regulatory Responses to Changes in the Financial Services Industry," *Federal Reserve Bulletin,* February 1985, p. 75.

79. Reed et al., op. cit., p. 370.

80. Andrew J. Brown, "Getting a Fix on the Consumer Attitude-Behavior Kaleidoscope," *American Banker,* November 13, 1985, p. 6.

81. Luckett and August, op. cit., p. 399.

82. Edward J. Frydl, "The Challenge of Financial Change," in Federal Reserve Bank of New York, *Seventy-First Annual Report* (1986), p. 8.

83. Letter to constituents, April 1986.

84. Rudolph, op. cit.

85. Warren Strugatch, "Private-Label Credit Cards," *American Banker,* February 4, 1986, p. 9.

86. Irwin Ross, "The Credit Card's Painful Coming of Age," *Fortune,* October 1971, pp. 108–111; and Harold Taylor, "The Chicago Bank Credit Card Fiasco," *The Bankers Magazine,* Winter 1968, pp. 49–52.

87. Michael J. Hosemann, "Bank Card Report," *ABA Banking Journal,* September 1984, pp. 135–136; and Michael Weinstein, "RepublicBank Plans to Market Credit Cards Across the Nation," *American Banker,* July 22, 1985, p. 2.

88. Williams, op. cit.

89. Steve Cocheo, "Bank Card Report," *ABA Banking Journal,* September 1985, p. 46; and Janice Fioravante, "Processing Bank Cards for Profits," *Computers in Banking,* May 1985, pp. 65–69.

90. Tom Ferris, "Credit Card Float Costs Banking Industry $965 Million a Year," *American Banker,* April 9, 1985, p. 16.

91. Patricia L. McFeely, "Two Card Processing Studies," in Fioravante, op. cit.

92. Bill Streeter, "Going after Card Counterfeiters," *ABA Banking Journal,* August 1983, p. 53.

93. "Terminal Detects Counterfeits," *Bank News,* January 15, 1985, p. 14.

94. Christian H. Loviton, "Smart Card Moves Ahead in Europe," *ABA Banking Journal,* April 1986, pp. 38–40.

95. David E. Sanger, "Technology: Now, 'Smart' Credit Cards," *The New York Times,* April 18, 1985, p. D2.

96. Michael Weinstein, "MasterCard Will Test 'Smart Cards'," *American Banker,* February 22, 1985, p. 1.

97. Julia E. Dvorkin, "What You Ought to Know about the Smart Card," *The Bankers Magazine,* March–April 1984, pp. 44–49.

98. Williams, op. cit.

99. In Winston Williams, "A Money Fund Next for Sears," *The New York Times,* September 2, 1981, p. D1.

100. Jeffrey A. Lieb, "Sears to Broaden Credit Card," *The New York Times,* February 21, 1985, p. D4; and Michael Weinstein, "Golden Days of Credit Card Business May Be Fading As Sears Enters Market," *American Banker,* October 7, 1985, p. 1.

101. "MasterCard, Visa, and the New Kid," *ABA Banking Journal,* August 1985, pp. 45–48.

102. John Morris, "Sears Plans National Rollout of Discover Card," *American Banker,* January 8, 1986, p. 1.

103. In James E. Ellis, "Mighty Sears Tests Its Clout in Credit Cards," *Business Week,* September 2, 1985, p. 62.

104. In Bart Fraust, "Asset Quality Down in Quarter at Most of Top 10 Bank Firms," *American Banker,* April 25, 1986, p. 1.

105. "Top 25 Banks in IRA Deposits," *American Banker,* April 14, 1986, p. 32.

106. Philip T. Sudo, "Are IRAs Hitting Participation Barrier?," *American Banker,* April 24, 1986, p. 1.

107. *Federal Reserve Bulletin,* October 1982, p. A8.

108. Philip T. Sudo, "Financial Institutions Catch IRA Fever Again," *American Banker,* January 28, 1985, p. 1.

109. Sudo, "Are IRAs Hitting Participation Barrier?"

7
The New World of Commercial Bank Lending

The use of the words New World in connection with commercial bank lending may be questioned by those who recall that loans have been an integral part of banking since time immemorial and who point to the fact that federal legislation takes specific note of this relationship. Indeed, Section 2(c) of the Bank Holding Company Act defines a bank as "any institution which accepts demand deposits and makes commercial loans." A bank that is not a lender is a theoretical, as well as a legal, impossibility. What aspects of bank credit, of the ways loans are made, or of the bank-borrower relationship are sufficiently new to justify the term New World?

The lending process can be traced back over 4,000 years to the time when a Babylonian farmer found it necessary to borrow funds to meet his expenses until the harvest; moneylenders (e.g., Shylock in *The Merchant of Venice*) have never disappeared from the business scene; and various forms of credit have always been part of society. However, the New World in bank lending is found in new types of loans, new analytical approaches to credit, new structuring of banks to meet the credit needs of their markets, and inevitably, new problem areas and failures.

The New World of commercial bank lending is one in which new competition has emerged to reduce the banks' market share. The comptetitors include thrift institutions, which are capitalizing on the enhanced powers and authorities granted to them through the legislation of the 1980s. Insurance companies and brokerage firms such as Merrill Lynch, which has announced plans to enter the area of commercial lending, are also active. Perhaps most important, companies that traditionally were among the banks' best customers have now become their aggressive competitors in lending.

General Electric Credit Corporation, originally a captive finance company that financed sales of the parent's appliances, is now a $21.5 billion organization that lends to corporations for major projects, transportation facilities, and real estate and manages a $250 million commercial paper program for BMW Credit Corporation.[1] At year-end 1984 it showed receivables of $15.3 billion.[2]

General Motors Corporation has become the nation's second-largest mortgage lender as a result of its 1985 purchases of two mortgage servicing companies that had $18.4 billion in assets. Its automotive financing subsidiary, General Motors Acceptance Corporation, generated profits of $1.021 billion in 1984; those profits represented over one-quarter of the total profits reported by the parent and were $200 million greater than those of Citicorp, the nation's most profitable banking organization. Indeed, Chairman Robert Murphy has pointed out that his corporation is already "the fifth largest bank in the country."[3]

Similarly, the Ford Motor Company has acquired First Nationwide Financial Corporation, and the Chrysler Corporation now owns both E.F. Hutton Credit Corporation and Finance America, which was purchased from BankAmerica Corporation. Through these entities, both Ford and Chrysler have diversified into new areas of lending, in addition to their traditional activities in auto financing.[4]

In the New World of commercial lending, governments and corporations develop new ways of obtaining funds without using their traditional bank relationships. By issuing commercial paper, of which over $300 billion may be outstanding at any time, they bypass the banking system and raise money on an independent basis.

It is a New World in which many major banks have shifted the emphasis from granting loans to selling loans. The steady increases in asset size that banks formerly sought through portfolio expansion no longer seem as desirable. By selling portions of those portfolios to smaller correspondent banks or other financial institutions, a bank reduces the asset size of its balance sheet and thereby lessens the pressures on it for greater capital adequacy.

It is a New World of commercial lending in which bank holding companies use existing or establish new factoring, leasing, and capital markets units so that they can respond to every opportunity for financing instead of merely offering traditional forms. This change may also be accomplished through acquisition, as in the case of Manufacturers Hanover's purchase of the multibillion-dollar nationwide CIT Corporation.

The New World of commercial bank lending resembles every other that preceded it, however, in that it continually tries to learn from the mistakes from the past and to fortify itself against further credit shocks. Every loan write-off represents an expensive lesson that may in time be justified if it serves to prevent future losses. In that connection, banks are increasingly adopting a back-to-the-basics policy. This policy is sharp contrast to those of the 1970s, when many of the fundamentals of credit appear to have been neglected in the banks' quest for greater profits, to be achieved by accommodating as many borrowers as possible.

The Lending Process

The bank lending process essentially consists of five steps:

1. Loan application and interview;
2. Credit analysis and risk evaluation;
3. Decision-making; loan-structuring; rate-setting;
4. Loan review;
5. Collection

Throughout this process, there are ongoing applications of the bank's fundamental credit policy, established by the Board of Directors and senior management.

The process logically begins with a request for a specified sum of money. The application and interview, and the two subsequent steps in the process, form part of the responsibilities of the individuals who typically are called *lending officers* or *loan officers.* Some institutions have chosen to use the terms such as *account officer* or *relationship manager* instead, in recognition of the fact that credit is often only a part of the total bank relationship with the customer. For purposes of this text, however, the traditional and more familiar term *loan officer* describes the activities and responsibilities of the individual that are part of the lending process.[5]

First and foremost among loan officers' responsibilities is that of knowing the customer and the industry and understanding the loan. He or she must then monitor the credit to ensure that no deterioration in the borrower's situation has occurred.

The application and interview requires that the applicant answer certain obvious question at the outset. What is the requested amount? What is the purpose of the proposed loan? Is that purpose legal and in conformity with bank policy? What is the identifiable source of repayment? Is there any type of safety factor for the company and bank to fall back on if projected profits do not materialize?

Loan officers are responsible for obtaining periodic financial statements from the borrower. Visits to the company and regular meetings with management are a vital source of information. All economic and industry trends, especially in those cases where technological developments, competition, and public taste (e.g., in fashion or style) create a high degree of vulnerability, must be closely watched.

The loan officer's knowledge base helps to provide a foundation for the interview process. Indeed, a study cited lending based on too little knowledge and placing excessive reliance on the credit analyses performed by other banks as leading causes of the loan losses of the 1970s.[6] "In extending credit, what you don't know *can* hurt you. Information is lending's fuel. There are no surprises, only ignorances."[7]

The borrower's overall relationship with the bank is always a factor in the consideration of a loan request. A company that has maintained good balances with the bank for a number of years, uses the bank for other services, and has borrowed in the past feels that it has a legitimate claim to credit in time of need. It expects to have priority over companies whose accounts are relatively new and less meaningful, or whose accounts are being solicited with credit as the tool.

Credit Analysis and Risk Evaluation

At various times, individuals have sought a foolproof, magic system that would always automatically remove all risk from the lending function and would guarantee the outcome of a loan. This formula or set of guidelines, this Eldorado, Utopia, or Holy Grail, can never be devised. With the exception of those few loans that are fully secured by liquid assets of unquestioned creditworthiness (e.g., passbooks or U.S. government bonds), risk is ever-present in the lending process. Since a bank can never eliminate risk entirely, it must seek to mitigate risk wherever possible.

One guarantee, however, does exist. If banks do not follow certain safeguards and procedures, then problem loans are almost certain to result, and losses will increase.

The Committee on General Terminology of the American Risk and Insurance Association has defined risk as "uncertainty as to the outcome of an event when two or more possibilities exist."[8] Lenders must always be concerned about the uncertainties in the borrower's operations; even then, losses may take place because of totally unpredictable events. A corporation that has had an unblemished record of success and enjoyed an excellent credit standing may become the sudden victim of economic events beyond its control, of competition, of an act of carelessness by an employee in one of its major facilities, or of an act of God (e.g., an earthquake or tornado destroying its factory). An individual borrower who has worked for a major corporation for many years and achieved a measure of financial well-being may suddenly become unemployed because the employer embarks on a program of cost-cutting and staff reductions; the employee's home mortgage, personal loans, and bank card outstandings then become collection problems.

Banks, in turn, face operating risks that reflect the nature of their customer base. A major oil company finds that decisions made thousands of miles away by OPEC members have a severe impact on its business; this, in turn, directly affects the company's relationship with its banks.

The lending process, then, must involve *risk analysis,* which in essence is nothing more than a systematic attempt to answer the question, "What could go wrong?" The danger, of course, is that the loan officer or credit analyst who tries to develop every possible worst case scenario will find so many answers to that question that no loan will ever be approved. Analysis must assign probabilities. Prudence and experience teach that failure to focus on those risks that appear most probable can lead only to a failure to make loans that will stand the test of time.

The majority of commercial bank loans are made to manufacturers. A comprehensive listing of every risk that manufacturers face may be almost limitless; however, certain risks are inherent and can always be considered. The real test of the manager's ability assesses the degree to which they understand those risks and have acted to offset them wherever possible.

The manufacturing process always involves four steps in a recurring cycle. Raw material is converted into work in process. This becomes finished goods. A demand for the finished goods results in sales; these create accounts receivable (because most sales are made on credit terms) which must be collected. The risks in the cycle are therefore classified as *supply, production, demand,* and *collection* risks. In the New World of commercial lending, banks are analyzing these risks in more detail and paying more attention to them than ever before.

To reduce supply risk, the company's management may provide for alternate sources of raw material wherever possible, ensuring that the right quantities will be on hand in the right place at the right price at the right time. If the production risk has been addressed, the company has all the necessary facilities to do the required processing; its plant is efficient, its energy costs under control, and its workers sufficiently productive. Management may address the demand risk through diversification, so that the entire financial success of the company does not depend on a single product, and through ongoing market research, so that a change in style or public taste will not cause adverse effects and so that there is an awareness of competition. Commitments to research and development are also important in this regard. Finally, the manufacturer should follow a risk-analysis process like that of the bank. Sales on credit terms should be made only to those buyers whose accounts are most likely to be settled according to agreed-on terms.

This approach to risk analysis differs somewhat from the pure, traditional emphasis on statement analysis alone. Today, banks recognize that while the borrower's statements are essential in that they reveal past performance and thereby provide clues to the future, they cannot alone form the basis for credit decisions. The banker can never neglect the data from a company's balance sheet and income statement, but should view them as the net results of what management has done or failed to do. They are a measure of the managers' success in understanding the risks that affect the business and in acting to offset them, totally or in part.

Just as the prudent banker must try to identify the risks in a loan situation and to mitigate them through devices such as personal guarantees, collateral, or protective covenants, so a prudent manager must act to protect the business, its creditors, and its stockholders against harm.

Loan Policy

The policy documents of a bank set forth the general framework of the desired level of conservatism in evaluating risks. They then address specific policy matters, such as, "We will not entertain loan requests that finance hostile takeovers" or, "We will consider requests for real-estate construction loans only when permanent mortgage financing provides a firm takeout for us." The bank's policy manual may also set forth the approval process for all commercial loans, including the amounts of lending authority given to officers at various levels and the committee structure through which loan requests must pass. Loan officers in banks are charged with implementing policy. They sometimes see a conflict between that responsibility as it pertains to risk management and their mandate to bring in new loan business. Any such perceived conflict can be resolved if the emphasis is placed on adding quality loans to the portfolio, rather than merely increasing quantity. Higher risks may create an expectation of higher yields, but in the New World of bank lending they are unacceptable.

Reports at several large banks have exemplified some inadequacies in managing loan risk during the 1980s. In some cases, members of the banks' senior management have been forced out of office by federal regulators because of their overly aggressive loan policies,[9] and concentrations of problem loans in several areas have given rise to fundamental questions of capital adequacy and the need for much more rigid credit supervision.[10]

Loan policies are subject to revision whenever rates in the money markets or federal or state regulations change. If a combination of state usury laws on mortgage loans and the bank's funding costs has made such loans unattractive, policy precludes offering them; if funding costs drop, and state laws become more liberal, the bank will reenter the market.

The unfortunate truism is that many of the losses banks have experienced in recent years were avoidable if appropriate loan policies had been in place and if loan officers had diligently followed them. Proper procedures for managing risk form a major part of every loan officer's responsibility.

Financial pressures on some major corporations and banks have compelled the former to sell their headquarters buildings and the latter to reduce their investment portfolios. Non-recurring incidents such as these, reported in financial statements, can be warning signals of imminent risk. The sale of real property by a major airline as a means of generating the income needed for continuing operations was an indication that no alternative existed. Survival under this type of scenario is questionable.

Smaller banks, which may not have a headquarters building that can be sold or an investment portfolio that can be liquidated, are far more vulnerable. During a four-year period (1980–1984) the average return on assets (ROA) of the nation's smaller banks declined 41 percent and their average return on equity (ROE) fell 45 percent; for the banking system as a whole, the comparable percentage declines were 14 percent and 17 percent, respectively.[11]

Loan Officers

Inadequate management of risk in the lending function is often nothing more than failure by loan officers to carry out their responsibilities. It is also true that their failures can be compounded by the bank's lack of a thorough process of loan review that detects earlier mistakes or omissions, and by management policies that emphasize short-term income for the bank at the expense of long-term safety and prudence, blandly assuming that no untoward events will take place.

Loan officers must always be aware of industry concentrations. Experience indicates that firms in the same industry create interrelated loan defaults and experience simultaneous similar problems. A bank with a substantial portfolio of loans to such firms is inherently weak. The same logic may be applied to loan portfolios that display a concentration of credits in a single geographic area.[12]

The loan officer's tasks are far easier, as are the customer's, if he or she has literally grown up with an account—that is, has been assigned to it for a long period of time and become thoroughly familiar with the managers, their plans for the future, the problems facing their industry and company, and their ability to handle adversity. The number of such officers unfortunately has been substantially reduced in recent years because of rotation, job mobility, and promotions. A high degree of officer turnover provokes many complaints from customers who must start over again in educating their new loan officers.[13]

Assuming a favorable decision on the borrower's request, the loan officer must negotiate the method of compensation to the bank that will be tied to the credit facility. Lines of credit (e.g., expressions of willingness by the bank to make specified amounts available for a stated period) traditionally called for certain compensating balances to be kept on deposit. Ten percent was a normally accepted requirement in these situations. Actual use of the line, or direct borrowings, would call for a 15 or 20 percent compensating balance. Demand deposits were the usual vehicle for compensation, thereby providing a source of funds for the bank's further use.[14]

Both bankers and borrowers have had recent problems with this technique. The banker often finds that the compensating balance, intended to support an extension of credit, is being double counted, or used to cover the company's use of other bank services. For this reason, many banks have moved to the so-called unbundling of relationships so that each aspect of the total relationship is addressed separately and each service is covered by adequate compensation.

By the same token, many corporate borrowers recognize the value of balances that might be freed up and invested and are aware that a system of compensating balances actually creates a significant increase in the stated interest rate. They wish instead to obtain credit on an all-in-the-rate basis in which interest is calculated without any regard for balances.

An alternative calls for the use of a non-interest-bearing time deposit as compensation. Because reserve requirements on such deposits are substantially lower than those on demand deposits, the bank gains the use of additional funds for its own purposes and the customer's required figure may be reduced accordingly.

Corporate borrowers have also cited the advantages of paying direct fees for loans as a business expense, thus making the costs fully tax deductible. Compensating balances provide no comparable benefit.

Financial Statement Analysis

Statement analysis, which has been equated with risk evaluation, is part of the second step in the lending process. It is usually based on a perception of the borrower as an ongoing business enterprise and therefore includes pro forma balance sheets and income statements, projecting cash flow over a future time frame. Many banks now use desktop computers to develop and store actual and projected spread sheets.[15] Alternatively, the analysis may contain elements of a worst case scenario, showing the effects of possible liquidation.

In the case of loans that will extend for periods beyond one year (in the United States, most banks arbitrarily classify all such loans as *term* loans), in particular, the analysis of future cash flow is important as a means of determining whether the company will have sufficient cash to meet its need for payments to creditors. Using the borrower's history and present status as guidelines, the bank may assume several varying situations.

In the first of these situations, the borrowing company is in a mature phase of its life cycle. There is little or no expectation of large-scale growth. In this case, retained earnings can be assumed to finance any projected future gaps between the company's current assets and current liabilities; noncash charges for depreciation will be sufficient to maintain fixed assets; short-term loans will be repaid without lengthening trade payments and without refinancing; and dividends and the current portion of any long-term debt will be handled without additional borrowing.[16] Alternate scenarios can be created on the grounds that the company has paid excessive dividends in the past, has financed its ongoing operations by lengthening payments to suppliers, is introducing new products that will require additional working capital and/or plant capacity, or is facing significant supply, production, or other risks.

Statement analysis should always be active and forward-looking rather than merely descriptive and passive. It should synthesize the information that has been obtained, organized, and evaluated so that a clear-cut recommendation becomes the end result.

The sources of that information are numerous. The bank's credit files provide a logical starting point. These files contain the entire history of the customer relationship, including official memos, financial statements, reports of contacts with the firm's management, newspaper magazines and articles regarding the company, and reports of past borrowings, average balances, and account profitability. Significant customer involvement with areas of the bank such as trust and cash management should also be noted.

The benefit of other banks' experience with the company should be obtained wherever possible; this is done on the basis of full reciprocity and is an accepted part of the analysis process. In addition, the company's trade suppliers, and possibly its competitors, may be contacted. Economic and industry studies and reports from credit agencies may be used.[17] The exchanging or even the obtaining of information from the borrower's other banks is more difficult in the United States than in other countries, simply because of the large number of banks with which a major company can deal. A business of that caliber, due to restrictions on full-scale interstate branching, may have accounts with a large number of banks in various parts of the country. Each of these banks maintains its own credit files, and each becomes part of the investigative and evaluative process.

In the actual analysis, the financial strength of a company can be summarized under six principal headings. While these, like all purely mathematical and nonjudgmental criteria, cannot provide all the answers, they highlight the firm's liquidity, its leverage, and its profitability; thus, they provide clues about the effectiveness of management in putting assets to work, handling debt obligations, and managing ongoing operations. Three ratios (current assets to current liabilities, net income to sales, and debt to tangible net worth) and three rates of annual turnover (receivables, inventory, and payables) provide a quick summation of the company's position and can be measured against comparable figures for the industry.[18]

The actions or inaction of the company's management regarding its supply, production, demand, and collection risks, which were mentioned earlier, must also be highlighted. If there are any indications that management ignored those risks or failed to protect against them wherever possible, the lending bank is also unprotected and the loan proposal becomes unacceptable. Again, the loss experiences of several large banks in 1985 and early 1986 suggests that lending officers never asked what could go wrong when they were approving substantial loans.

Although the reports of banks in the southwestern United States for the first quarter of 1986 were particularly distressing, the problems were not confined to that area. Citicorp's net charge-offs of $303 million for the first three months of 1986 rose 55.4 percent from the comparable 1985 period; Bank of America, whose net income declined 50.8 percent, charged off $257 million in loan losses; and Manufacturers Hanover reported net charge-offs up 25 percent, to $100 million.[19]

These reported losses on loans are an integral part of the New World of commercial bank lending; because of them, federal bank regulators have sought additional authority from Congress to cope with failing and failed banks and thrifts. From 1982 to 1985, the number of bank failures rose from 42 to 120—by far the worst figures since the Great Depression. In April 1986, Chairman William Seidman of the FDIC said that his organization's watch list of problem banks included 1,196 institutions, several of which were "very large."[20]

Regulatory concerns over the risk exposure of U.S. commercial banks are readily justified if one examines nothing more than the loan-to-deposit ratios over a period of time. For example, table 7–1 shows those ratios for selected years in the post-World War II period, and table 7–2 shows them for eleven months of 1985.

The enormous expansion of loan portfolios as a percentage of the banks' total deposits is viewed with alarm in many quarters. A typical commercial bank in the United States today will earn one-half of 1 percent to 2 percent on its gross revenues. These figures represent approximately 3 percent (average) as a spread over the cost of money. If a bank loans $100,000 for one year at the rate of 20 percent, gross revenue is $20.000 and net income is $400. Default on that one loan, resulting in a loss of $100,000, means that the bank

Table 7–1
Loan to Deposit Ratios, All Commercial Banks, Selected Years from 1950 to 1982

Year	*Ratio*
1950	33.7
1960	51.2
1970	65.2
1974	72.3
1982	80.6

Source: *Federal Reserve Bulletin,* various issues.

Table 7–2
Loan to Deposit Ratios, All Commercial Banks, 1985

Month	*Total Loans (\$ billions)*	*Total Deposits (\$ billions)*	*Ratio*
February	1466	1620	90.5
March	1476	1628	90.7
April	1492	1639	91.0
May	1495	1662	90.0
June	1512	1660	91.1
July	1534	1685	91.0
August	1534	1677	91.5
September	1547	1683	91.9
October	1558	1706	91.3
November	1591	1744	91.2
December	1615	1764	91.5

Source: *Federal Reserve Bulletin,* March 1986, p. A18.

would have to make 250 other loans of $100,000 for one year to recover, through net income, the principal amount of the bad loan (250 × $100,000 × 0.20 × 0.02).

Corporate Debt

The total structure of corporate debt in the United States and the total risk exposure of the commercial banks cannot be fully realized from the banks' published reports. For example, the increases in outstanding commercial paper—short-term unsecured promissory notes, issued by major corporations of excellent credit standing, sold by dealers in the open market or placed directly with investors, and sometimes backed by letters of credit issued by banks—from 1980 through 1985 are shown in table 7–3. The $303 billion reported as outstanding in December 1985 is an additional obligation of the corporate borrowers, yet it was used as a means of obtaining funds while bypassing direct borrowing from banks.

Far more significant in the New World of commercial bank lending is the amount of so-called off-balance-sheet commitments. As of December 1985, these were believed to total $1.5 trillion at the nation's twenty-five largest banks alone. That figure represents a one-third increase since September 1983, when the quarterly Schedule L reports filed by those banks were first publicized.[21]

These commitments by banks—commitments that they hope will not have

Table 7–3
Commercial Paper Outstanding, 1980–1985
(in billions of dollars)

Year	*Amount*
1980	124.4
1981	165.8
1982	166.4
1983	188.3
1984	239.1
1985	303.1

Source: *Federal Reserve Bulletin,* April 1986, p. A23.
Note: Figures are as of December in each year.

to be honored and are not funded, as loans are—include standby letters of credit, in which the obligations of borrowers to specified third parties are guaranteed; interest-rate swaps; foreign-exchange contracts; note issuance facilities; options; and currency swaps. Federal regulators have expressed frustration over the fact that the banks' balance sheets do not disclose these items, and investors and analysts complain about the difficulty of determining the actual dollar total of risk exposure of so many banks.[22] One analysis of the Schedule L reports indicates that for seven of the largest commercial banks, the ratio of off-balance-sheet items to total assets ranged from a high of 2.96 (Bankers Trust) to a low of 1.66 (Manufacturers Hanover), with an average ratio of 2.11.[23]

Superimposed on the problem of sheer magnitude, reflected in the fact that these commitments are more than double the total assets of seven of the nation's largest banks, is that of the amount of compensation they are receiving for the risks they assume. For competitive reasons, many banks have steadily reduced their fees and rates on off-balance-sheet commitments.

The response of the Federal Reserve to this overall problem has created much controversy among bankers. The Fed is pressuring for inclusion of all such commitments in the banks' published balance sheets. It also seeks corresponding increases in bank capital to reflect the risk exposure. The Fed's proposals are opposed by those bankers who claim that appropriae credit criteria are being used whenever these commitments are made.[24]

Interest Rates

When a loan has been approved, the bank determines the appropriate interest rate, within legal limits. Interest—money charged for the use of money—is a reflection of four factors:

1. The *availability* of funds. Conditions of supply and demand help establish the price of borrowing.
2. The perceived degree of *risk*. Lenders who are less conservative and more willing than others to take chances expect to be compensated accordingly.
3. The *time* factor. Loans made for long periods of time usually call for high rates because of the extended period of exposure and uncertainty and the impact on liquidity.
4. The lender's *cost of funds*.

These factors have an impact on nonbank lenders as well as the commercial banks. The latter, of course, because of the fundamental change in their deposit base and the corresponding increase in interest expense, must watch their profit margins more carefully than ever before. Nonbank lenders, such as finance companies, are willing to assume risks that are not always acceptable to banks, but they cannot attain the degree of leverage that banks can. They structure their loans in an effort to cope with both these problems at the same time. General Electric Credit Corporation, referred to earlier in this chapter, has achieved exemplary success in that effort. It now ranks among the nation's twenty-five largest banks in loan volume yet has achieved a return on equity of over 20 percent, higher than that of any major bank or finance company.[25]

The words *prime rate* have been used—and perhaps abused—by commercial banks for many years. They were used traditionally to describe the fact that the most creditworthy customers who had maintained long-standing satisfactory relationships were given preferential rate treatment, paying less than borrowers of lesser stature. The assumption has been that if the quoted prime rate is 10 percent, the largest corporations will be charged on that basis while all other borrowers will pay higher rates.

Lending banks have justified this situation on the grounds that the credit standing of prime borrowers warranted it. For example, the loan agreement of one major bank that was involved in litigation over the meaning of the term contained this definition: "The bank's commercial loan rate, from time to time in effect on unsecured 90-day loans to its most responsible and substantial corporate borrowers."[26]

Several class action lawsuits have been brought against banks on the grounds that the prime rate as quoted by them and publicized in the media has been ignored in the daily realities of doing business. There is some evidence that the large-scale entry of foreign banks into the commercial lending field in the United States in the 1970s caused some U.S. banks to undercut their stated prime in the competitive effort to retain or attract creditworthy customers. The borrower who agreed to pay interest at a rate of *x* percent above prime, when the latter presumably represents the best available loan rate, has grounds for litigation if he or she can establish that certain customers of the bank paid a lower rate.[27]

The interest rates set by banks for their various categories of borrowers usually reflect the *discount rate,* which is charged by the Federal Reserve on loans it grants to banks and other financial institutions. The discount rate is comparable to the widely quoted rates of the Central Banks in other countries. Table 7–4 shows the fluctuations in the discount rate during a thirteen-year period. It illustrates the point that the rate is one of the major tools of monetary policy at the Fed's disposal. By raising or lowering the discount rate, it can make bank credit more difficult or easier to obtain. At the same time, the Fed retains the right to reject applications from any financial institutions that, in its sole judgment, may be abusing the borrowing privilege.

Loan Classification

In accordance with the requirements of federal regulators and for internal control purposes, banks subdivide their loan portfolios into several headings. Management information systems can then make all the data for each category available throughout the institution and for use in call reports at any time.

One common system of loan classification uses four basic categories:

Table 7–4
Discount Rates of Federal Reserve Banks, 1973–1985

Year	*Rate at Year-End*	*Number of Rate Changes during Year*
1973	7.5	
1974	7.75	4
1975	6	9
1976	5.25	4
1977	6	4
1978	9.5	12
1979	12	7
1980	14	12
1981	12	4
1982	8.5	14
1983	8.5	None
1984	8	5
1985	7.5	2

Source: *Federal Reserve Bulletin,* March 1986, p. A6.

1. *Commercial and industrial loans.* This is the largest of the categories and can be further subdivided according to maturities, loan collateral, and industry code.
2. *Consumer loans.* This category includes home improvement, automobile, and all other types of personal loans, plus all card outstandings and uses of consumers' revolving credit.
3. *Real estate loans.* The usual subdivisions in this category show construction loans, which are usually short term and unsecured but which provide for payback through permanent mortgage financing, and mortgage loans, which are long term and are secured by the value of the property.
4. *Interbank loans.* This category includes federal funds transactions and all direct extensions of credit to other banks.

Under the broad umbrella of commercial and industrial loans, the subdivision by maturities is extremely important because of the twin considerations of risk and liquidity. The general policies of lending banks in the United States differ from those in other countries in that most loans in the United States are unsecured, and the largest single subdivision shows the total amount of *seasonal* loans, which are short-term advances made to provide the borrower with working capital. These loans are also described as self-liquidating; that is, the repayment comes from the conversion of a company's current assets into cash at the completion of a business cycle. A toy manufacturer, for example, needs to finance an increase in inventory to prepare for the Christmas season. The ultimate conversion of the accounts receivable into cash should provide the funds for payback to the bank. This type of loan has traditionally formed the backbone of the commercial banks' portfolios.

In contrast, term loans are used to provide businesses with the funds required for plant and equipment needs. Here, the assets that are financed by the loan will not be converted into cash; repayment comes from the projected cash flow of the business over a period of time.

The basic classification of loans as outlined here permits of considerable variation. Banks in agricultural areas, for example, necessarily add a category that totals all outstanding farm loans. Other banks, which are actively involved in loan participations, may wish to include these as a separate category.

Participations are syndicated extensions of credit by two or more banks to a single borrower. They arise for several reasons. Each bank has a legal lending limit, showing the maximum amount of unsecured credit it can extent to a single obligor; 15 percent of total capital and surplus is a commonly used figure. When a loan request exceeds that figure, two or more banks share the credit. Participations often result from requests to the lead bank for loans in excess of that institution's legal limit; in other cases, the borrower wishes to divide the credit among several banks with whom relationships have been established, or the lead bank simply wishes to diversify its portfolio by giving its correspondents a portion of the total credit facility.

Whatever system of classification is used, the bank must take care to avoid any duplication or overlapping. It must place every loan in one category only. For example, a single large loan to a nationally known company, made for the purpose of building a new headquarters facility, is simultaneously a commercial loan, a term loan, a real estate loan, and possibly a participation. It must be definitely categorized so that no distortion of figures occurs.

As mentioned earlier, industry classification of loans is extremely important in identifying excessive concentrations of credit. In the New World of bank lending, banks must identify those industries that are highly vulnerable to global developments, economic trends, and new competition. Management can monitor risk effectively only if it is aware of the bank's total exposure to each of these industries.

Country Risk Analysis

Because of the increased attention that global lending has attracted, the twin concepts of portfolio classification and risk analysis are united in the systems of country risk analysis that most major banks have found it necessary to implement.

During the late 1970s, federal regulators reacted to the steady growth in the dollar amounts owed to U.S. banks by foreign borrowers by introducing reporting requirements, compelling the banks to identify loan outstandings by countries.[28] Their concerns stemmed not only from the magnitude of the exposure but also from the fact that the legal lending limits imposed on U.S. banks in their domestic activities did not affect loans they might make to the public and private sectors in other countries. A major bank in New York, San Francisco, Dallas, or Chicago theoretically could lend any amount it wished to a foreign government or corporation.

At the same time, an increased emphasis on risk awareness created the need for better management information systems that would capture and synthesize all the relevant data on cross-border lending. As the extent of the global debt crisis became apparent, the banks recognized the necessity of knowing their exposures in specific areas of the world. This knowledge, in turn, would facilitate determinations of future courses of action in policing existing debt and in considering requests for further credits or for restructuring.

Country risk, as defined, results from all the political, social, and economic factors within a country that might affect the ability of the public and private sectors to make repayment in the currency of the loan. The latter phrase is especially significant. For example, if all payments of interest and/or principal must be made in a currency other than that of the debtor country, that country's reserves of foreign exchange might prove inadequate.

Country risk focuses on the possibilities and probabilities of internal and external conditions that might lead to default.[29] It assists management in establishing country limits, setting forth the maximum exposure the bank is willing to permit. It assesses the economic and financial policies of governments, the perceived willingness of a country's leaders to make repayment, the political trends and degree of stability of the country's government, and the resource base. Included in the last-named aspect of the analysis are the natural (e.g., minerals, oil), human (worker productivity, literacy, skills, and health), and financial (rate of inflation, reserves of foreign exchange, types and effectiveness of financial institutions) resources through which obligations can be honored.[30] Country risk analysis must also take into consideration the strategies and objectives of the political leaders: their fiscal and monetary policies and the effects these may have on short- and long-term economic growth.

The number of factors that can be considered in country risk analysis is almost limitless. For example, in trying to assess the political risk in a given situation, a bank may estimate the probabilities of civil war, a declared moratorium on all debt repayment, nationalization of industries, assumption of power by a new party, and official repudiation of existing debt—all these on a short- and medium-term basis. The bank may also attempt to evaluate the characteristics of the local government (dictatorship, military junta, monarchy, family rule, social democracy), its alignment with the world's major powers, and its overall relationships with U.S. banks.[31]

The Export-Import Bank (Eximbank), an independent agency of the U.S. government, established in 1934 to assist in financing U.S. exports, extends over $8 billion per year in guarantees, loans, and insurance. It has developed a checklist for the analysis of country risk that includes 16 critical factors (e.g., natural resource base, balance of payments, economic growth and size) and uses a number of statistical elements (e.g., external debt as a percentage of gross domestic product, reserves of gold and foreign exchange) to make comparisons among various countries.[32]

Analyzing country risk, therefore, is inherently far more complex than analyzing corporate risk for the analyst. If he or she begins with the basic question, "What could go wrong?," the range of possibilities in an international lending situation becomes far wider and the interrelationship of all the risk factors far more detailed. One axiom that has traditionally been included in credit training programs states that no bank has ever had a charge-off or workout situation that resulted from too much knowledge of the borrower; losses typically result from not knowing enough, from not asking relevant questions, and from failing to analyze all the relevant data. This axiom has even more application in global lending.

Rather than a set of bland assumptions that the agricultural or oil or mineral resources of a nation will automatically generate a source of repayment and that a foreign government is stable and will never repudiate its obligations, the concepts of country risk analysis in the New World of commercial bank lending state that foreign loans should be made only after due consideration of every individual factor that has an impact on the financial and economic future of a country, its business enterprises, and its citizens.

Enhanced management information is one of the keys to reduced losses in global lending. If a thoroughly up-to-date and comprehensive information system is developed to show the bank's cross-border exposure according to types of loans, risk rating (updated periodically), maturities, and current status of each outstanding obligation, the ability of management to police the portfolio and make decisions regarding restructuring or further commitments will be significantly improved.

The management information system that is so important in the overall process of country risk analysis must also make a distinction between the debts of the private sector in a given country and all those incurred by a government or by various government agencies and entities. This information is vital in the event the bank ever wishes to exercise its right to setoff against funds the government may have on deposit with it. Table 7–5 provides an example of this statistical breakdown.

Commercial banks are not alone in their efforts to consolidate and compile information on a global basis. In 1985 Merrill Lynch announced the formation of a Debt Transactions Group to track the firm's activities throughout the world in the areas of private placements, foreign currency transactions, floating-rate issues, and underwriting.[33]

Table 7–5
Public and Private Sector Obligations, Selected Countries, 1984
(in billions of dollars)

Country	*Public Sector Obligations*	*Private Sector Obligations*	*Total*
Argentina	0.6	0.3	0.9
Brazil	1.7	1.1	2.8
Mexico	1.3	0.4	1.7
Venezuela	0.9	0.4	1.3
Total	4.5	2.2	6.7

Source: The Chase Manhattan Corporation, *1985 Annual Report,* pp. 34–36.

Asset-Based Lending

Companies finding it necessary to pledge their receivables, inventory, or other assets so that they could borrow were historically looked on unfavorably by many banks, as if such pledging were a last-ditch effort to avoid bankruptcy and a sign of financial weakness in the business. In the New World of commercial bank lending, the perception is entirely different. Banks and other commercial lenders have expanded their facilities for secured lending, and there is no longer any stigma attached to this form of borrowing. Corporations, especially those in the so-called middle market, use asset-based borrowing as a means of raising funds without resorting to equity sources; they thus avoid both the costs of underwriting in a public offering and the demands of investors for a share of the profits.

The receivables (assuming they are of satisfactory quality) and inventory (assuming it is readily saleable) of a company that operates through a succession of cycles represent future value, often at points in time when the company's need for cash is immediate. These current assets can be converted, through asset-based lending, into a ready source of working funds to resolve the problem.

Asset-based lending is predicted on certain basic principles. First, collateral alone does not justify a loan. The need for determining the customer's creditworthiness remains, and the collateral, whatever its nature, should not be a substitute for repayment. Loans should be repaid from self-liquidation of assets (e.g., collection of accounts receivable) or from the borrower's profits rather than from the forced liquidation of any collateral that has been pledged. Whenever a bank is forced to take possession of and sell collateral, it is a demonstration of a loan that was not entirely sound in the first place. It has been said that good collateral, of and by itself, does not make a good loan; rather, it strengthens a credit situation by helping to mitigate the lender's risk.[34]

Second, asset-based lending must provide protection to the lender in the form of *margin*. This is achieved by establishing a safety factor, protecting the bank against the possible deterioration of the pledged assets. For example, a bank may choose to lend no more than 80 percent of the face value of quality receivables or 50 percent of the appraised value of inventory.

The third basic principle is that, in all lending situations, the bank should seek to obtain seniority, protection, and control. These factors are even more important in asset-based lending than in other types of lending.

> *Seniority* is a term used to indicate the bank's priority position vis-à-vis that of other creditors of the same borrower. If the bank cannot be sure that it ranks first on the list of creditors, it can at least make sure that no

others outrank it. The lender's security interest in the pledged assets must be perfected by the filing of all appropriate documents as specified under the Uniform Commercial Code.

Protection is gained through the margins used in the various types of secured lending. The lender must be continually on guard against declines in the value of the pledged assets.[35]

Control can be achieved through frequent reviews of the borrower's financial condition and, again, the status of the pledged assets. If, for example, accounts receivable are involved, the lender must have ongoing knowledge of their rate of turnover and their aging. Regular visits to the company's offices and factories and requests for its cash flow projections are routine methods of providing control.

Especially for weak companies and those in industries that are vulnerable to sudden change, the bank should insist on monthly financial statements and forecasts of income and expenses for the coming year. A business that is unable to generate these figures cannot be considered a desirable borrower. Financial statements can be compared with those of other firms in the same industry; Robert Morris Associates and Dun & Bradstreet are among the publishers of this type of industry study.[36]

Loan Agreements

Because those involved in the New World of commercial bank lending are making a conscious effort to learn from the mistakes of the past, they are paying more attention than ever before to the matter of adequate loan documentation. Borrowers may object to the complex agreements banks ask them to sign, but they must understand that a clearly written contractual document is in the best interests of both parties. Inadequate agreements have been responsible for many loan problems in previous years, and those lacking in specifics may lead to different interpretations by the bank's staff, the borrower, and the courts.

The standard form of agreement sets forth all the details of the loan itself (interest rate, repayment schedule, collateral, size, and terms of participation if more than one lender is involved) and the identities and legal status of the contracting parties. It sets forth conditions that must be satisfied before the payout to the borrower takes place. For example, the borrower may attest to the fact that the financial statements it has supplied are correct and that no material adverse change has occurred since the date of their preparation.

The question of what constitutes default, and what actions the lender can take in the event of default, is extremely important. Delinquencies in payment, changes in ownership, insolvency, or evidence of misrepresentation by the borrower may be listed as situations that will allow the lender to exercise legal rights to accelerate the repayment schedule or to call the entire loan.

Loan agreements typically include a set of covenants, which may be affirmative, negative, or both. Affirmative covenants state the obligations to which the borrower agrees; for example, a specified current ratio or amount of working capital is to be maintained at all times and the borrower will furnish the bank with quarterly financial statements. Negative covenants set forth conditions or events that the borrower will prevent from occurring; for example, the borrower agrees not to incur any additional debt beyond a specified figure, not to change the basic nature of the business, not to sell capital assets, and not to enter into mergers or acquisitions. Although covenants may appear to the borrower to be unduly restrictive, they are designed to give the bank additional safeguards during the life of the loan.

Bank Investments

Safety and income are always prime considerations in a bank's program for funds management. Nevertheless, liquidity is what banks think of first since it is absolutely essential for the continued operations of the institution. Liquidity provides the bank's wherewithal to meet anticipated withdrawals of funds and to satisfy the demands of its long-standing, creditworthy corporate customers, who have a legitimate claim on it.

Most banks determine their liquidity needs by calculating a deposit floor and a loan ceiling. The former estimates a level below which deposits will not drop during the period; the later projects a maximum dollar amount, to which the portfolio will increase during the same time frame. By measuring both of these against the current figures, the bank establishes the amount of liquidity it requires.[37]

A bank's cash on hand, its funds on deposit with the Fed, and its balances with correspondent banks constitute its *primary* reserves. Since they can be obtained at a moment's notice, they are the basic and immediate source of liquidity; however, they do not produce any income. Banks also carry *secondary* reserves, typically consisting of U.S. Treasury bills or other highest quality instruments. Because of their ready marketability, these reserves add to liquidity but have the additional advantage of generating income.

The management of bank funds is always accomplished on a priority basis. Liquidity needs are determined first; only after that process has been completed can the bank turn its attention to those investment opportunities permitted within legal limits. The essential point here is that investment planning occupies a lower priority in the overall management process than does liquidity in general or loans in particular. In its various investment activities, the bank must be constrained not only by certain statutes but also by principles of credit risk and market risk.

As in the lending process, *credit risk* tries to establish the degree of probability that an investment will be repaid at maturity and that during its life there will be a flow of funds sufficient to give investors an annual rate of return. *Market risk* addresses a different issue—namely, the fluctuations in money-market conditions that may have an impact on the selling price that an investment would bring if its holder wished to dispose of it.

The difference between the two types of risks is exemplified by the types of obligations—bills, notes, and bonds—issued by the U.S. government. These instruments carry no credit risk whatever, since there is no question about the ability of the federal government to honor them at maturity. Whatever must be done to repay those obligations will always be done by the government.

Market risk, in contrast, poses a problem because interest rates are so volatile. If a bank holds a quantity of government bonds that will not mature for seven years and that were issued with a 5 percent coupon, it may find that the market price of these bonds has deteriorated significantly because so many other instruments, with different maturities and higher yields, are readily available to investors. The market risk in this case is that of a distressed sale, in which the seller is forced to suffer a loss in comparison to the purchase price.

Legislative Constraints

During the Roaring Twenties, commercial banks in the United States enjoyed a great deal of freedom in making investments and in entering the securities underwriting business. The collapse of the stock market wiped out the face value of their portfolios and contributed largely to the demise of many institutions.

One of the major objectives of the Glass-Steagall Act of 1933 was to ensure that the commercial banking functions would be divorced from those connected with the securities business, whether as investors or underwriters. This legislation, as of 1986, still prevents banks from placing their surplus funds in any common stock issues for investment purposes and prohibits their underwriting of any bond issues except those known as general obligations—that is, backed by the full faith and credit of the state or local government that stands behind them. The taxing power of that municipal entity provides the source of repayment. Revenue bonds, therefore—those used for turnpike or bridge construction, for example—remain outside the purview of commercial banks, and litigation continues as to whether the public would benefit if banks were allowed to underwrite them or otherwise to become more broadly involved in the securities business.

Required Investments

In many cases, banks make investments because they are legally required to do so. Many states, to ensure still further protection for their funds on deposit (above the coverage by the FDIC), require that the depository banks hold and segregate a quantity of federal or state obligations. Similarly, the trust operations of banks have very significant impacts on retired persons, beneficiaries of estates, widows, and minors, and for the protection of those parties, the trust powers granted to the banks compel them to set aside federal and state debt issues to back up the pension, profit-sharing, and trust funds they manage.

Bank investment portfolios, aside from the holdings required by various statutes, are divided into two parts. The securities held for the bank's purposes—that is, to yield income with due regard for safety and liquidity—constitute the actual investment account. In addition, many banks establish a trading account, in which they "make a market" by assuming positions in federal and state or city obligations as a means of serving their customers.

Especially in major banks, the composition of the investment account may change substantially from day to day. Conditions in the money markets and liquidity needs may require that the bank sell some of its holdings, even if losses result, so that other priorities in funds management may be satisfied.

The triple objectives of funds management in commercial banks—liquidity, safety, and income—are achieved in the investment account through diversification and spacing of maturities. For example, a typical portfolio of U.S. government obligations will be divided among those issues maturing within one year, those with one- to five-year maturities, those that extend to seven years, and a limited quantity of those whose maturities fall in the seven-to-ten-year range.

Two obvious exceptions exist to the provision of the Glass-Steagall Act that prohibit investment of bank funds in any issues of common stock. Member banks in the Federal Reserve System are legally required to buy and hold stock in the district Fed. Bank holding companies are allowed to own stock in their subsidiaries.

For those investments that are legally permitted, there is a limitation on the extent to which any single security may be purchased and held. This restriction is comparable to the bank's legal lending limit. Again, there is an exception: a bank is allowed to hold unlimited amounts of U.S. government obligations.

Municipals

The generic term *municipals* describes the bonds issued by any government or government agency other than the federal. A state, city, county, town, or other entity of local government raises the funds it needs for its operations by issuing various forms of long-term debt. The full faith and credit issues referred to earlier are backed by the revenue-raising powers of the government agency involved; conversely, revenue bonds are issued on the assumption that the cash flow and profits from a specific project will generate the funds needed for payment of interest and principal.

Reciprocity between the federal and state governments on the subject of taxation of the income from debt issues is a long-established legal tradition. The states cannot levy income tax on any income derived from federal obligations; similarly, all municipals issued in accordance with federal laws provide the holder with an exemption from federal income tax on the income they generate. They may also be exempt from state and local income taxes, depending on the investor's domicile relative to the municipality that issued them. Issues of municipals are usually accompanied by a statement from the issuer's legal advisors, ensuring the investor of this exemption.

Investments in municipal issues serve two purposes for banks. Although their credit and market risk factors are higher than those of the federal government or its agencies, their tax-exempt yield is highly attractive. In addition, they provide evidence of the bank's support of the communities in which it operates.

At year-end 1985 the nation's commercial banks reported holdings of $413.6 billion in their investment portfolios. Of this, $249.9 billion (60.4 percent) represented investments in all forms of federal government and federal agency obligations, while $163.6 billion (39.6 percent) was invested in other securities, most of which were the debt issues of various municipalities.[38]

Summary

The New World of commercial bank lending is one in which many of the fundamentals of credit still apply but are being adjusted and restated in the face of new forms of financing, loan-to-deposit ratios, risks, and competition. Unusual equity-participation instruments, bonds with warrants or put options attached, adjustable-rate convertible bonds, and debt issues of municipalities, backed by bank standby letters of credit, are among the many types of financing vehicles that have appeared in the 1980s, and the banks must take careful note of these as well as of the increased competition that has arisen from both domestic and foreign lenders.[39]

On the global scene, hindsight now makes it clear that the large-scale buildup of bank claims against the public and private sectors in many foreign countries was excessive in the late 1970s and early 1980s and that it took place without proper attention to the risk factors involved. New approaches to the analysis of country risk have become necessary, and there can be no doubt that the process of partial or total recovery of the loans outstanding to less-developed countries will be slow and painful.

On the domestic scene, hindsight again compels the banks to implement new lending policies and new methods of analysis so that they can reduce losses. This is a never-ending process, and the most troublesome question in the entire lending process asks whether experience has actually proved to be a teacher.

During the years immediately preceding the Great Depression, banks capitalized on the euphoria that existed throughout the country; in many cases, they also contributed to it. Loans were made without adequate analysis of repayment sources. Common stocks were purchased with bank funds, for the institutions' investment purposes, on the assumption that the market would continue to climb. The prevailing feeling seems to have been that nothing could go wrong. Catastrophic losses resulted. Almost fifty years later, in 1974, over $2 billion in loan losses had to be written off, including some $382 million by the nation's five largest banks alone.[40]

Ten years later, loan losses at many banks reached alarming proportions, and federal regulators sought to impose more stringent requirements to bolster public confidence in the banking system. In 1986, the fact that almost 1,200 banks were on the FDIC's watch list relates directly to a combination of questionable lending policies and inadequate analyses of the risk factors involved.

One result of these latest losses has been a revised approach to traditional methods of credit analysis, in which financial statements were overemphasized as the determining factors in credit decisions. The more modern analysis process looks at the borrower's balance sheet and income statement and recognizes their importance but places more stress on the fact that the figures are nothing more than reflections of the skills of the company's management in identifying the risks entailed in the operation of the business and mitigating them wherever possible.

Liquidity, safety, and income remain the objectives of all programs in the management of bank funds, but the experiences of recent years indicate that safety may have received less attention than an emphasis on short-term profits or a sheer buildup of asset size. It is to be hoped that the policies of commercial banks in the future, as determined by their senior officers and directors and implemented by their line officers, will correct this and any other weaknesses that may have existed in the past. A sounder banking system inevitably will result.

Knowledge is the watchword in the New World of bank lending: knowledge of the management of a borrowing company, knowledge of the risks it faces, knowledge of the industry of which it is a part, and knowledge of the many factors that affect its prospects for future growth and profitability.

By tradition, under standard operating policy, and in accordance with the Community Reinvestment Act, the primary obligation and basic function of a commercial bank is to serve the legitimate credit needs of its marketplace. Investments occupy a lower priority than loans, and only those funds that are not required for liquidity (including expansion of the loan portfolio) or are pledged to secure public deposits can be used for income purposes.

Because of legal restrictions, a bank's investment portfolio consists almost exclusively of federal government or federal agency obligations and municipals. With the exception of those municipalities whose financial problems have been publicized in recent years, the credit risk in investments does not apply to the same extent as in loans; however, the higher safety must be measured against the factor of market risk.

Investment portfolios normally offer more flexibility than loan portfolios in that daily adjustments can be made through purchases and sales. By spacing maturities and diversifying the holdings, the bank achieves both liquidity and income.

Banks that are experiencing periods of high profits increase their investment portfolios, specifically through tax-exempt bonds issued by state and local governments. During 1985 Morgan Guaranty Trust, believing that interest rates would decline so the costs of funding its deposits would drop, doubled the size of its portfolio and, through municipals, effectively achieved a spread of 9 percent.[41] As a group, the 1,000 largest commercial banks during that same year increased the book value of their municipal holdings by 45 percent, from $71.9 billion to $104.3 billion, although banks in states that were suffering severe economic problems reduced their portfolios.[42]

Notes

1. Matthew Crabbe, "Inside the New In-House Banks," *Euromoney,* February 1986, pp. 24–28.

2. General Electric Credit Corporation, *Annual Report 1984,* p. 31.

3. Paul A. Eisenstein, "Here Come the Auto Companies," *United States Banker,* March 1986, pp. 32–33.

4. Ibid., p. 34.

5. Edward I. Altman, "Managing the Commercial Lending Process," in Richard C. Aspinwall and Robert A. Eisenbeis, Eds., *Handbook for Banking Strategy* (New York: John Wiley & Sons, Inc., 1985), pp. 476–478.

6. "The Quality of Credit is Strained," *Business Week,* June 26, 1971, pp. 70–74.

7. P. Henry Mueller, "Factors Influencing Contemporary Bank Lending," *Journal of Commercial Bank Lending,* November 1985, p. 5.

8. Robert I. Mehr and Emerson Cammack, *Principles of Insurance,* 5th Ed. (Homewood, IL: Richard D. Irwin, Inc., 1972), p. 19.

9. Thomas C. Hayes, "Ailing Bank Jolts Oklahoma," *The New York Times,* April 29, 1986, p. D1.

10. Robert O. Blomquist, "Managing Loan Portfolio Risk," *Journal of Commercial Bank Lending,* December 1984, p. 2.

11. G. Christian Hill, "Smaller Banks Have Difficulty Coping with Increasing Number of Bad Loans," *The Wall Street Journal,* February 5, 1985, p. 4.

12. Mark J. Flannery, "A Portfolio View of Loan Selection and Pricing," in Aspinwall and Eisenbeis, *op. cit.,* pp. 462–464.

13. Randy Welch, "Effective Commercial Lenders Must Understand Clients' Needs," *American Banker,* October 30, 1985, p. 24.

14. Thomas Ulrich, "Are Compensating Balance Practices Declining?," *Bank Administration,* January 1985, pp. 48–52.

15. Jim Ludlow, "Using Microcomputers to Ease Credit Analysis," *Credit & Financial Management,* November 1984, pp. 26–28.

16. A more detailed description of cash flow analysis may be found in Altman, op. cit., pp. 488–495.

17. William G. Dearhammer, "Improving Credit Information Exchange," *Journal of Commercial Bank Lending,* June 1984, pp. 17–21.

18. William L. Stone, "Financial Statement Analysis—A Two-Minute Drill," *Journal of Commercial Bank Lending,* November 1983, pp. 11–19.

19. Eric N. Berg, "Bonds Spur Banking Profits," *The New York Times,* May 1, 1986, p. D1.

20. In Henry T. Simmons, "Bridge over Troubled Water," *Financial World,* May 13, 1986, p. 14.

21. Suzanna Andrews and Henny Sender, "Off-Balance-Sheet Risk: Where Is It Leading the Banks?," *Institutional Investor,* January 1986, p. 111.

22. Joseph F. Sinkey, Jr., "Regulatory Attitudes Toward Risk," in Aspinwall and Eisenbeis, op. cit., pp. 357–359.

23. Andrews and Sender, op. cit.

24. "Opinion Survey: How to Handle Off-Balance-Sheet Items—Lenders' Reactions," *Journal of Commercial Bank Lending,* January 1986, pp. 23–28.

25. Robert A. Bennett, "General Electric's Amazing Money-Making Machine," *The New York Times,* May 25, 1986, p. 3–1.

26. "Hanover Sued on Prime Rate Charges," *American Banker,* May 8, 1984, p. 2.

27. Tamar Lewin, "Accord in Suit Against Manufacturers Hanover," *The New York Times,* May 3, 1985, p. D2.

28. "A New Supervisory Approach to Foreign Lending," *Quarterly Review* (Federal Reserve Bank of New York), Spring 1978, pp. 1–6.

29. Ingo Walter, "Country Risk," in Emmanuel N. Roussakis, ed., *International Banking: Principles and Practices* (New York: Praeger, 1983), p. 19.

30. J. Alexander Caldwell, "Assessing Country Creditworthiness," *Journal of Commercial Bank Lending,* July 1983, pp. 9–17.

31. John B. Morgan, "Assessing Country Risk at Texas Commerce," *The Bankers Magazine,* May–June 1985, pp. 23–28.

32. Howard Turk, "How Eximbank Analyzes Country Risk," *ABA Banking Journal,* October 1985, pp. 129–132.

33. Andrew Albert, "Merrill Lynch Creates Global Coordinating Unit," *American Banker,* March 7, 1985, p. 3.

34. Howard D. Crosse and George H. Hempel, *Management Policies for Commercial Banks,* 2nd ed. (Englewood Cliffs, N.J.: Prentice-Hall, Inc., 1973), pp. 170–174.

35. Walter Macur, "Asset-Based Lending: A Performance Evaluation," *Credit & Financial Management,* December 1984, pp. 11–14.

36. Jay M. McDonald and John E. McKinley, *Corporate Banking: A Practical Approach to Lending* (Washington, D.C.: American Bankers Association, 1981), pp. 224–226.

37. George W. McKinney, Jr.; William J. Brown; and Paul M. Horvitz, *Management of Commercial Bank Funds,* 2nd ed. (Washington, D.C.: American Bankers Association, 1980), pp. 220–232.

38. *Federal Reserve Bulletin,* March 1986, p. A18.

39. Robert A. Taggart, Jr., "Recent Developments in Business Financing," in Aspinwall and Eisenbeis, op. cit., pp. 163–165.

40. "The Great Banking Retreat," *Business Week,* April 21, 1975, p. 78.

41. Gary Hector, "Morgan Guaranty's Identity Crisis," *Fortune,* April 28, 1986, p. 64.

42. Matthew Kreps, "Irresistable [*sic*] Yields . . . Spurred Most Big, Profitable Banks to Buy Municipal Bonds in 1985," *American Banker,* June 10, 1986, p. 6.

8
The New World of Cash Management

In 1947 one of the nation's best known corporations asked two of its banks if they could design a service that would expedite the inflow and processing of its payments from customers. The first lock box plan was implemented shortly thereafter. In the early 1950s a Big Three automobile manufacturer contacted the bank on which it drew a very heavy volume of payroll checks and asked the bank's cooperation in providing a sequential sorting and listing of the paid items. The first account reconcilement service went into operation as a result. Also in the early 1950s, major banks began to work their large corporate customers to design wire transfer programs for the quick and efficient movement of funds to and from accounts throughout the country. New departments, with names such as Money Mobilization, Specialized Corporate Services, Transcontinental Banking, and Cash Flow began to be listed in bank telephone directories. Finally, in 1973 a New York bank was the first to establish a terminal-based information system so that financial officers among its corporate clients could access the bank's data base to obtain the status of their accounts and details of the prior day's debits and credits.

The four developments mentioned in this historical synopsis form the genesis of the New World of cash management services, now used by thousands of businesses and offered by hundreds of banks throughout the United States. In some cases, variations of the original services, especially in the field of terminal-based information, have been modified to serve customers. The basic laundry list of former years has been expanded to include zero-balance and controlled-disbursement accounts, payable-through drafts, and other services. In addition, the first services offered have been updated and enhanced in many ways. The net result is that financial officers of businesses of every size and type, units of government, and not-for-profit entities now have available to them an integrated family of techniques to help them manage their funds.

In the New World of corporate cash management, four factors have had an impact on the evolution of the services, the acceptance they have received, the banks' marketing approach, and the overall corporation-bank relationship.

1. As in other areas of banking, competition has intensified. In some cases corporations have bypassed the banks and implemented services in-house; in others, companies that were once considered the banks' best customers now compete with them by offering cash management services to other corporations. Those banks that were originally lukewarm regarding the value of the services now emphasize the marketing of cash management.
2. A literal explosion of technology has taken place. Use of microcomputers has grown by leaps and bounds, cash management has become global, and service capabilities exist in 1986 that were entirely unknown in 1981.
3. The regulatory climate, chiefly as a result of the Monetary Control Act, has changed. Banks, as providers of services and custodians of relationships, have necessarily changed in reaction to it.[1]
4. Corporate interest in the range of available services has grown dramatically—sometimes as a result of changes in interest rates, sometimes as a result of the exchange of knowledge among those individuals who have responsibility for the cash management functions in their businesses or organizations. The stature of those cash managers has been substantially upgraded, even as their numbers have grown. Cash management is a universal business activity, and because it is so basic to the financial health of every corporation, institution, and government agency, doing it well is now accepted as an integral part of the overall functioning of the business entity.

Attendance at the 1984 annual meeting of the National Corporate Cash Management Association was seven times the 1980 figure, and many of the attendees reported that their new titles reflected the recognition given to them in their corporate hierarchies. Controlling disbursements, handling incoming payments, and managing bank balances may once have been considered menial clerical tasks; today they are under the jurisdiction of individuals whose titles are Manager of Banking and Finance, Assistant Treasurer, or Manager of Bank Relationships. The corporation's Chief Financial Officer cannot but be aware of the bottom-line value of the work these staff members perform.[2]

Definition

The term *Cash Management* creates semantic problems at the outset, since it may mean different things to different people. A member of senior management in one of the largest insurance companies considers the term to be self-contradictionary; he uses all the services offered by banks yet actual cash is never involved. The insurer's entire inflow of payments consists either of checks (processed by banks) or electronic debits to policyholders accounts; all disbursements are computer-generated and monitored; all funds transfers are initiated through terminals in the company's offices and processed electronically; and surplus funds each day are automatically invested. No one in the corporate headquarters ever sees cash; daily information from all the banks is the key to the entire Treasury operation.

The homemaker may define cash management as the process of budgeting the family income against household expenses. Consumers may define the term similarly as they do their personal financial planning. The corporate financial officer thinks of the term as describing a combination of forecasting and managing cash flows, monitoring and controlling bank balances, and investing surplus funds. These services are viewed as being completely interdependent. The cash management services offered by banks play a critial part in this entire process since they emphasize three aspects:

1. speeding up collections;
2. controlling and monitoring disbursements;
3. knowing where funds are domiciled, their amount, and the ways in which any excess funds can be put to profitable use.[3]

The growth in usage of various cash management services is an integral part of the change in the deposit structure at the nation's commercial banks in recent years. External and internal disintermediation has taken place as non-interest-bearing demand deposits have been shifted, in ever-increasing proportions, to income-producing vehicles. The individual in a corporation who has been able to transfer sterile balances at banks into bottom-line income has very often been able to do so with the direct help of the banks' services, and for this reason cash management poses a dilemma for the commercial banks.

The marketing of cash management services makes the corporate financial officer more knowledgeable and sophisticated in methods of expediting collections, delaying and monitoring payables, and gathering information on all his or her accounts. It is perhaps unreasonable for the banks to expect that this individual, whose knowledge base has been broadened, will remain so naive that he or she will leave large surplus balances, earning no interest, on deposit. Despite the progress that has been made in the New World of cash management, some bankers, who point to reductions in demand-deposit balances among the users, still look at it askance. Their opinions of the value of cash management in the overall client-bank relationship are minority views but must be taken into consideration in the overall treatment of the subject. Indeed, the question about whether the banks or their customers have been the greater beneficiaries of all the marketing of cash management that has been done for some forty years is moot. The principle that permits of no argument is this: cash management services, offered by banks, are unquestionably here to stay and can be expected to be more widely offered and used in the future.

That prediction not only stems from the continuing demands of customers for new, more, and better services but also is predicated on the banks' concern with narrowing profit margins on their loan portfolios. By offering cash management services and requiring those services to be profitable on a stand-alone basis, they shift the emphasis to make transaction-driven business a more important contributor to income. Paul Nadler has cited a study by Greenwich Research Associates,[4] indicating that many banks had implemented profit-center concepts and were evaluating each service offered to customers independently, so that they would not provide a service if it did not sell at a profit. The President of Philadelphia National Bank has gone on record to say that this is the policy at his bank as regards all cash management services.[5]

Just as conditions in the money markets have been major contributors to the shrinkage in demand deposits at banks, they have had an impact on the usage of cash management services. The financial officer who had little interest in the subject when interest rates were 4 percent, and therefore could earn only $111 by investing $1 million dollars for one day, became far more interested in funds management as rates rose and the same overnight investment at 9 percent yielded $250 or $389 when rates rose to 14 percent.

Float

When the corporation cited in the first sentence of this chapter first sought a bank's help in speeding up the receipt and processing of its incoming remittances, its need arose from the fact that over 90 percent of all payments in the United States are made by check and that the biggest anomaly in our banking system allows "money"—contrary to all logic—to be in two places at the same time. Checks are not "money"; the only real money is the legal tender issued and backed by the government. Checks, instead, are claims to money; they are negotiable orders to pay and are nothing more than pieces of paper until such time as their payees can convert them into usable funds.

U.S. banks handle deposited checks by giving their customers immediate, but provisional, credit; that is, the customer's balance increases on the day of deposit, even though the bank realizes that time must elapse before the drawee bank makes its decision about whether the item should be honored. Therefore, the issuer's bank balance is not reduced until the check has been presented to his or her bank and actually debited to an account; yet at the same time the recipient's account has been credited. *Float* represents the dollar amount of checks that have been deposited and credited to accounts but that are in the process of collection. It amounts to billions of dollars each day.

The life cycle of a check typically involves mail time, which is required for the item to reach its payee; deposit time, which represents the recipient's time frame in presenting it to a bank to be deposited; and collection time, required for it to reach the drawee and be honored. Every delay in this cycle works to the advantage of the drawer of the check by delaying its actual charging to an account; if the process can be slowed up, he or she can invest the funds pending completion of the process.

Conversely, the payee of a check wishes to have float reduced so that he or she can utilize uncollected deposited funds. The New World of cash management embraces a spectrum of services that attempt to meet the requirements of the recipient in some cases and the issuer in others.

The dollar amount of float is even more important to the Fed, through which the largest volume of check collection activity takes place. The Fed has traditionally operated on a basis of scheduled availability. When a sending bank gives the Fed items to be collected, it is given credit by the Fed in a maximum of two days, even though the process of presentment to the drawee and receiving settlement for each check may take several additional days.

Prior to passage of the Monetary Control Act of 1980, total Fed float averaged over $6 billion per day.[6] The Act directed all Federal Reserve Banks to implement measures to cut that figure and to levy charges against the sending banks in those cases where Fed float was not eliminated or reduced.[7] As a result, the figure was reduced to $3.4 billion in 1981,[8] and efforts to bring about further reductions continue.[9]

Lock Box

To meet a client's needs for speedier collection on incoming checks, the first lock box was implemented in 1947. Under this service, the time required for receiving, processing, and depositing remittances is substantially reduced; the clerical work and expense required to handle those payments is also reduced; and information on each payment is supplied to the client in any of several configurations.

As agent for its customer, the lock box bank establishes a post office box in the customer's name and arranges for its messengers to pick up all mail from the box at frequent intervals throughout the day. Thus, the mail time that is part of the life cycle of a check is shortened. The bank's personnel examine checks for negotiability, route them by the quickest means to drawees to gain maximum availability of funds, prepare the daily deposit, and furnish a record of every deposited item. Most lock box customers traditionally have accepted photocopies of all deposited checks from the bank for posting to their accounts receivable; more recently, automation has become more important, and the daily detail is often furnished to the client in the form of magnetic tape, either delivered or transmitted directly from computer to computer. As of 1985, over three hundred U.S. banks were offering lock box service in various forms.

When major banks first began offering lock box service, the emphasis was on increased availability and corresponding reduction of float. Therefore, the optimal clients were those who received a relatively small number of incoming checks each month but whose checks were for large dollar amounts. A bank's processing charges for a $10 check are no different from those involved in a $10 million check, but the benefits to both the bank and the user are far greater in the latter case if the check can be converted into available funds more quickly.

The same emphasis on reduced mail time and better availability led many major corporations to conduct studies, showing the originating points for their remittances. Those with nationwide operations established lock boxes with their banks in money-market cities in the areas where most of their customers were located to keep incoming mail time to a minimum; hence, New York, Atlanta, Chicago, Dallas, and San Francisco became the typical locations.

As competition among banks has increased, many changes have taken place in the original concept and implementation. New technology has made it possible for several banks to establish large-scale operations for the processing of hundreds of thousands of payments for so-called retail lock box users such as utilities, insurance companies, department stores, and those oil companies that issue credit cards.[10] In these retail lock box operations, the marketing approach by the bank stresses the client's potential reduction in clerical work and expense rather than the reduction in float. The average check amount is obviously far lower than the amount seen in the wholesale lock box service. The bank and its retail client can work together to design invoices with data that optical scanners can read so that the entire document-handling process is automated and tape output is automatically generated.[11]

A second major change has occurred in the methodology used by a corporation to determine the optimum sites for lock boxes and the strategies devised by banks to capture a larger share of the market. The questionnaires developed by the Bank Administration Institute to assist a company in selecting its lock box banks no longer have the same impact, since those businesses that formerly determined that four or five regional lock boxes were best suited to their needs were compelled to deal with that number of banks.[12] Today, many banks are offering to provide lock box services on an integrated, nationwide basis so that the client need deal with only one bank.

First National (Chicago) and Mellon Bank are among the banks that have established sites for receiving and processing payments in various parts of the country, and Continental Illinois picks up mail at post offices in eighteen cities and flies it back to Chicago for processing.[13] Wachovia Bank (North Carolina) has opened processing centers in Atlanta and Dallas,[14] and other banks have joined in networks that provide corporate treasurers with lock boxes in several key locations, operating through a single bank account.[15]

These techniques, which are actually a form of interstate deposit taking, have not gone entirely unopposed, especially in Georgia. In 1985, both houses of that state's legislature approved a bill that would compel out-of-state banks to close their lock box centers in Atlanta.[16] Banks in that city, led by Citizens and Southern (which reportedly handles about $4 billion in lock box volume per month and annually earns some $500,000 in fees and $50 million in compensating balances through the service), helped initiate the legislation.[17]

The retail lock box operation is characterized by very large volumes of incoming checks, typically for relatively small dollar amounts. This operation is highly capital-intensive because it requires sophisticated paper-handling machines and data-processing units; as a result, many banks have avoided establishing departments to process retail payments. A solution—one that illustrates the dynamics of change in banking services—has been provided by the J.C. Penney Company, whose Credit Services subsidiary was already processing 12 million payments per month for the parent.[18] Commerce Union Bank (Nashville) entered into an agreement whereby it would market a high-volume, low-dollar lock box service to customers, receive the incoming payments, and forward them at once to the Orlando, Florida, processing center of J.C. Penney Credit Services. All remittances are returned to the bank on the same day for deposit and clearing.[19]

In the area of wholesale lock box, Chase Manhattan Bank and the Equitable Life Assurance Society established a five-location network (Atlanta, Chicago, Dallas, San Francisco, and New York) so that the remittances of the bank's corporate customers who required lock boxes in those geographic areas would be processed by Equitable's facilities.[11]

Other Deposit Services

Automated Depository Transfer Checks (DTCs) represent another cash management technique for attracting and retaining deposits. DTCs are preprinted, no-signature instruments prepared by banks that are concentrating funds for their customers. One bank, on its customer's behalf, receives daily input regarding all the deposits made by that customer's local sales offices, regional lock box banks, or other receiving points. The concentration bank creates DTCs drawn on each depository and makes a single deposit to the customer's account.

One advantage of DTCs lies in the fact that they are far less expensive than transfers made by wire. More recently, deposits through *Automated Clearing Houses* (ACHs) have been marketed to corporations for direct deposit of payroll or for payments to suppliers and other companies; these are even less costly than DTCs and provide the user with detailed payment information.[21]

Disbursement Services

When the first *Account Reconciliation* plan was implemented in the early 1950s, the objective was simple. The bank developed a means of sequentially sorting and listing all the paid checks for a major customer so reconciling the check register became far simpler and less time-consuming and expensive. Card checks, keypunched before issuance with the necessary data, were a necessity for this service. The report furnished to the customer showed the check number, date of payment, and dollar amount of every paid item; the development of a list of outstanding checks remained the customer's responsibility.

Several developments in the intervening years have refined and expanded the original concept. The introduction in the 1960s of Magnetic Ink Character Recognition (MICR) enabled customers to use fully encoded paper checks instead of the more expensive and cumbersome card checks and allowed the banks to reconcile accounts through computer equipment instead of the special keypunch machines they had formerly used. This process alone made Account Reconciliation more feasible for both parties.

In a second major development, banks began to work with their large-volume customers so that some form of input (magnetic tape, check copies, or some form of issued-check register) would be supplied to the bank, listing all issued checks by date, number, and dollar amount. The bank could then perform a matching job so that it could list all outstanding, as well as paid, checks for the customer.

Under full reconciliation, many additional reports can be generated for the customer's use in issuing checks and managing the cash position. Because the bank has all the necessary data to compare the date each check was issued with the actual date of its debiting to an account, it can provide float reports in a variety of forms.[22]

In a further development, many banks have introduced a retention service, which avoids the need to return paid items to the customer with each reconciliation. Since the bank has gone on record as to the date of payment and dollar amount of each item, the actual paid checks serve no real purpose for the issuer and can create problems of storage and access over a period of time. Under a typical agreement with the customer, the bank holds the paid checks for a stated period of time and then destroys them; in the meantime, it microfilms each check. A copy of the front and back of any paid item can be developed from the bank's microfilm and made available to the customer at any time.

This retention service (microfilm/archival) serves the interests of both parties. The bank avoids all the clerical work and postal or messenger expense of returning thousands of paid checks to customers; the latter no longer need to store those checks and to spend time and incur costs in locating specific checks for audit or tax purposes. The service has been given the stamp of approval by the accounting and legal professions.

I may note parenthetically that retention of paid checks has been made a matter of policy by many U.S. banks in their handling of consumer checking accounts. The individual who wishes to have his or her checks returned with the bank statement incurs a service charge for this special handling; otherwise, retention by the bank is automatic. European banks have followed this practice for several years.

Controlled Disbursements

As pressures have increased on corporate cash managers to take advantage of float wherever possible and to monitor bank balances more closely so that any excess funds can be invested, the banks have developed special techniques to lengthen the time required for issued checks to be presented to drawees for actual debiting to accounts and to provide timely data on all checks paid. The accounts used for this purpose were originally known as *remote disbursement accounts,* since they were opened with institutions at remote locations outside the mainstream of commercial banking. Corporate checks drawn on banks in New Mexico, Montana, and Alaska began to appear in large numbers. By using those banks as drawees, the corporate cash manager delayed the presenting of the checks and used this extended time frame to make investments of excess funds.

The corporations that did so were, of course, taking full advantage of the Fed float referred to earlier in this chapter. Regardless of the actual time required to present checks to drawee banks in remote locations, the Fed always gives the sending bank credit for the items in a maximum of two days, and availability of funds to the payee is not affected. If four, five, or six days are actually consumed in the Fed's collection process, the Fed absorbs the float. For this reason, the Fed has instructed banks to curb their marketing of so-called remote accounts and to avoid references to Fed float in discussing the service with their corporate customers.

As a result, the special disbursement accounts, which cannot be used for any payments to individuals, are now known as *Controlled Disbursement* relationships, and the banks emphasize the benefits of up-to-the-minute control of corporate funds rather than the longer time frame that results. New York banks, for example, have established facilities in upstate locations and in Delaware, against which corporate checks for accounts payable can be drawn. By noon each day, they notify their customers of the exact dollar amount of checks presented against the special accounts. The corporate cash manager then replenishes the account (which is in technical overdraft) by transferring from the company's concentration account with the same bank or by Fed funds transfer from another source. No positive balances are ever maintained in the Controlled Disbursement account.

In further reaction to the increased use of these accounts, the Fed instituted a program in 1985 known as High-Dollar Group Sort (HDGS). It calls for all financial institutions that receive $10 million or more in checks per day through the Fed to be subject to a second, later presentment each day. Controlled Disbursement accounts thus lose some of their effectiveness since checks included in the later presentment cannot be part of the early-morning report to the user.[23]

Zero-Balance Accounts

Controlled Disbursement Accounts are merely refinements of the Zero-Balance system that has been widely used by customers for many years. Under that system, balances are not maintained in a number of accounts with a single bank. The subsidiary (or satellite) accounts issue checks as necessary; however, the bank agrees to handle each of these accounts on a zero-balance basis. Checks presented to the drawee and posted to those zero-balance accounts create overdrafts that are wiped out on the same day by transfers from the client's concentration account at the same bank. The use of zero-balance accounts is not confined to major corporations. One large city, for example, has opened a large network of these accounts with its main bank for all the agencies and departments that must issue checks every day. No positive balances ever exist in those accounts. All overdrafts are eliminated each night by credits that are offset by a single debit to the city's concentration account. Balances in the latter are maintained at a level sufficient to compensate the bank for all credit and transaction services, and the funds that otherwise would have been tied up in a large number of checking accounts are invested until the issued checks reach the bank and are posted to the satellite accounts.

Although the use of zero-balance accounts has been accepted, both in the banking system and by regulatory authorities, for many years, the U.S. Justice Department has indicated that it will be examining all such arrangements more closely as a result of the abuses that have received wide publicity in the

E.F. Hutton case (1985). An Assistant Attorney General in that department has commented that "Float-extending disbursement techniques . . . can be construed as a scheme to defraud, *under certain circumstances*"; therefore, there will be more pressure on corporations to be more circumspect in their financial practices and on the banks to ensure that no such procedures are accepted until and unless the risk aspects have been fully understood.[24] In this respect, the bank must understand the risk implications of both zero-balance and controlled disbursement accounts. All funding that is used to replenish these accounts and thereby to restore them to zero balances must come from available funds on deposit with the concentration bank or from transfers, of guaranteed value, from another bank. Checks on other banks, especially those located out-of-town, cannot be accepted for funding purposes.

In 1985 Security Pacific (Los Angeles) introduced what it described as the first nationwide corporate disbursement plan. This system enabled the bank's customers to initiate all their payments (checks, ACH transactions, and wire transfers) through terminal-based data transmission. Security Pacific's service reportedly analyzes the payment requests, considers the float factors on each, determines the best account to be used (North Carolina, Ohio, Texas, and California bank accounts are involved), generates the checks, and mails them. Although acceptance of this innovative service has been low, with only four customers on-line as of May 1986, Security Pacific continues to entertain great expectations for it. The clients' reluctance to adopt it has been attributed in part to concerns over any cash management techniques that might, in the wake of E.F. Hutton, prompt action by the U.S. Justice Department.[25]

Consulting Services

A corporation considering the adoption of lock box services or the implementation of some type of controlled disbursement account makes its decisions on the basis of one or more studies of its geographic patterns of inflow and outflow of funds. On the one hand, these studies may be performed in-house; on the other hand, several major banks have developed an expertise in consulting and are aggressively marketing this service. They are in a position to work closely with the client in performing all the necessary analyses and making recommendations for the systems that will best achieve the desired objectives.

For example, all receivables payments may be analyzed by having the bank's professional consultants record the mail and bank collection time required to convert them into usable funds. Computer models can then provide the client with the optimal configuration for the number and locations of lock boxes to reduce mail and collection time and improve availability, alternate configurations of lock box sites, the costs of maintaining a network of collecting banks, and the dollar amount of increased availability, under different rate scenarios, to be gained in each case. Remitters who are using controlled disbursement accounts in an effort to generate positive float for themselves can be easily identified.

On the disbursement side, the bank's consultants can develop a data base showing the number of days that elapse between the issuing of a check and its debiting to an account under the client's existing programs. They can also provide schedules for direct sendings to drawee banks that can affect the time frame and can present the complete Federal Reserve schedules for timing shipments of checks and granting availability.

Certain companies possess characteristics that make them excellent candidates for cash management consulting:

They are experiencing rapid growth.

They are contemplating changes in their systems of centralization or decentralization of receipts and/or disbursements.

They are appraising the effectiveness of their existing cash management techniques.

They are concerned over the opportunity costs of not establishing cash management programs.

They are simply updating their state-of-the-art knowledge of cash management services.

For these companies, detailed diagnostic studies can be made. These are usually offered in modular form, so that the client may decide on any one module or any combination. The studies may cover receivables, disbursements, funds concentration, banking relationships and their related expenses, and balance reporting and control. The cost of these diagnostics is usually more than justified through the bottom-line benefits the client can gain.

The bank's expenses in establishing and maintaining a consulting unit are substantial. Effective consulting services can be offered to corporations interested in cash management only if the bank's staff includes specialists with broad experience in treasury management, credit, operations, systems design, float studies, and product development. The fee structure for the various consulting services must reflect these expenses.

Information Services

Earlier in this chaper, an executive in one of the largest insurance companies was quoted because of his opinion that the term *cash management* is a misnomer. Treasury functions in his company do not involve cash; financial decisions and transactions each day are based on a daily flow of data from the banks with which it deals.[26] Semantics aside, his viewpoint reflects the attention banks have been paying to the third major area of cash management services: supplying information.

From the implementation of the first lock box in 1947 until the early 1970s, cash management servicec concentrated on customer needs in the deposit and disbursement aspects of everyday operations. Services under both those headings remain popular today and are being enhanced and marketed on an ongoing basis. Nevertheless, deposit and disbursement services, no matter how sophisticated and efficient, can no longer serve the corporate customer's overall purposes unless they are integrated with a system that answers the basic questions. Financial decision makers in corporations, correspondent banks, government agencies, and not-for-profit organizations seek to know, early each day, how much money they have, where that money is, and how much of it can be used for investment, loan reduction, or other purposes.

Information has become the key to maximizing the profitable use of corporate funds. It has helped the cash manager become an important cog in his or her organization's treasury operations. As a result, the cash manager now finds increased promotional opportunities that recognize the increased responsibilities and contributions to bottom-line income.

The New World of technology in banking has made it possible for customers to use an ever-widening range of information services. John Yaecker, Manager of Banking at J.C. Penney, uses a group of these services to "pull together the whole picture" of the corporation's treasury functions and has commented that some of the tools he now employs in information gathering were unavailable five years ago.[27] The broad spectrum of cash management and disbursements, desk terminals and microcomputers that answer all the financial officer's needs to know.

The correlation between information services and the changed deposit structure of banks is clear. Because the cash manager can now obtain early-morning information on the status of all bank accounts, excess balances can quickly be put to profitable use and investment decisions can be made before the usual 11 A.M. (New York) market peak. Transfers of funds from demand deposits to interest-bearing accounts can be routinely made with speed and accuracy, at reduced cost. Regardless of the client's size, the flow of financial information can be tailored to meet specific needs on a cost-effective basis.[28]

The banks have registered trade names such as Cash Connector, Transsend, Centrics, ChemLink, MARS, and Infocash for the systems that generate that flow of information. The methods of delivery and the range of services differ, but certain basics are common.

Through a simple terminal in the user's office, a hard-copy printout is generated, showing the bank's book, collected, and available balances and the specifics of all debit and credit transactions posted to the client's account(s) on the previous business day. Access to the bank's data base takes place under strict security procedures, guaranteeing that no unauthorized party can obtain information. Telephone lines transmit all the data to the terminal. The client typically requests the information at the earliest possible time each morning. Customers who have personal computers in their offices can use them as information-gathering and transaction-initiating devices, so a separate terminal is unnecessary.

If the client wishes to access the system again in the afternoon, all details of lock box credits, checks paid, money transfers in or out, and securities bought or sold through the bank account will print out. Using the information obtained either through morning or afternoon access, the client can initiate money transfers through the terminal. In addition, the customer may authorize other banks to report their balances, debits, and credits to the institution providing the service so that there is consolidated information on the status of every account.

Customers at the large banks can obtain additional terminal-based information services. Foreign exchange rates, current yields on key investment vehicles, and details of DTCs, EFTs, and all preauthorized payments are examples.

The advances in technology that have led many corporations to install networks of Treasury Work Stations or Treasury Management Stations readily find a parallel among those banks that use microcomputer technology to make the cash management interface simpler, even faster, and more comprehensive and cost-effective. The banks' sophisticated microcomputer capabilities allow users to bring up on a screen, in virtually any desired format, an entire worksheet: bank balance and investment portfolio data, cash flow reports and projections, investment and debt maturities and scheduled payments, and money transfers or EFTS transactions stored for the future. The microcomputer may also contain report-generating and work-processing elements and may give the client the ability to initiate or amend letters of credit.

Risks in Cash Management

The efforts of the Federal Reserve to reduce its daily float position, including the High Dollar Group Sort, have reduced the level of disbursement float that corporations were formerly able to enjoy under the system of controlled disbursement accounts. The bank's ability to provide timely information for the user's control purposes has been correspondingly reduced.[29] Therefore, for the fifty or more commercial banks that offer this type of account, the risk factors mentioned earlier in this chapter are less significant. Nevertheless, they cannot be ignored.

A bank offering controlled disbursement accounts must consider the possibility, however remote, that the corporate client will not have a sufficient balance in a concentration account to provide the necessary funding on a given day. The bank should draw up a course of action to provide for this contingency. If the funding is done by wire transfer of funds from another bank, the risk is that inadvertent delays or errors in transmitting, receiving, or posting the credit will create a substantial dollar overdraft; again, the bank should anticipate that possibility. The typical contingency plan under this scenario calls for the immediate dishonoring of checks drawn against the controlled disbursement account.

Considerations of risk must also enter into a bank's agreement to implement a system of zero-balance accounts for a customer or to offer a service module in which funds transfers can be made directly through a terminal without the knowledge of a bank staff member. In the latter case the risk can be lessened if a daily debit limit is established for all outgoing transfers requested by a corporation. Any such requests that exceed the intraday debit limit are referred by the bank's money transfer department to the account officer for specific approval.

The basic question, What could go wrong?, is as valid here as in the discussion of lending. For example, in the case of a corporate bankruptcy, statutes prohibit a bank from acting unilaterally to recover funds. If the customer has been allowed to incur overdrafts or draw against uncollected funds and files for bankruptcy, any funds that may be on deposit are frozen for a period of time, and the bank cannot exercise the right of setoff.[30] The foregoing highlights a basic principle: bankers who in the past saw no connection between cash management services and credit risk must revise their thinking, identifying the areas of potential exposure and acting to lessen the risks wherever possible.

The processing through a lock box of a customer's incoming checks may, at first glance, not appear to create any risk for the bank. However, advising the client of a substantial lock box deposit can entail risk if no one monitors daily reports of drawings against uncollected funds. Checks that were included in the day's deposit may be returned by drawees for any reason. If the customer has been allowed to withdraw funds prematurely, recovery may be difficult.

Even direct deposit of payroll—again, a bank service that may not have been viewed as having risk implications—can create exposure. From the time a bank processes the tape sent to it by its customer, posts the credits to those employees who have accounts with it, and forwards the tape through ACH facilities for sending to other financial institutions until the time it receives available funds from the customer, it is at risk. In effect, there is a two-day commitment by the bank to fund the customer's payroll, and bankruptcy would pose a serious problem of recovery.[31]

One of the time-honored axioms in commercial banking states simply, "Know your customer." Relationship managers, cash management marketing representatives, and product managers can work together in evaluating the creditworthiness of a prospective customer, understanding the degree of risk that a cash management service may create, and establishing contingency plans that will protect against the risks.

Marketing and Compensation

Closely allied to the technological changes and expanded range of services that have characterized cash management since 1947 is a revised marketing approach. It parallels those used in other areas of commercial banking in that it identifies a customer base and specific client needs, tailors services to meet those needs, and ensures that the bank is compensated adequately through balances, fees, or both for the services it provides.

Among the relatively few banks that aggressively used cash management as a marketing tool, the effort was originally confined to the largest corporate customers. For example, lock box service was offered only to those major firms receiving a small number of high-dollar remittances. Account reconciliation was made available only to those customers who used large quantities of monthly checks. The so-called middle market—that is, companies with annual sales of less than $250 million—was usually neglected.

This thinking was certainly valid. A service that could reduce the mail-deposit-collection time cycle on the largest checks, thereby reducing float and accelerating availability, was of real benefit to both the user and the bank. By the same token, companies that used thousands of checks for payables, dividends, and payroll were the major beneficiaries of account reconciliation. These companies were frequently among the banks' largest account relationships, and cash management was a logical extension of the credit, international, and trust services they used.

In the New World of cash management, the entire universe of businesses, including specifically the middle market, not-for-profit organizations, correspondent banks, and entities of government, is the market. There are several reasons for this new marketing approach. Thirty-nine banks in various parts of the country have been identified as leaders in the cash management field. A survey of companies with annual sales exceeding $250 million determined that the typical company used eight of those banks for one or more cash management services and was being solicited by six additional banks.[32] For these customers, it is extremely difficult to provide differentiated services that will persuade them to change bank relationships. Many of them necessarily have developed internal systems covering all areas of treasury management; they are interested in innovations in the field (e.g., microcomputers) but usually look to their existing banks to supply these. Their needs for the spectrum of cash management services may not be as great as those of smaller companies.

Conversely, the demand for cash management services has shown steady growth among middle-market and even smaller companies. Unlike their larger counterparts, they may not have made heavy investments in the latest computer technology, but they represent an untapped market for the more traditional products. There is no valid reason why a company with sales of $10 million or $20 million cannot use lock box service, for example.[33]

When account reconciliation was introduced as a service, the customer was forced to use card checks to gain the benefits. At the same time, the bank providing the service had to make heavy investments in the keypunch equipment that would sort, list, and total the checks and generate reports. With the advent of magnetic ink character recognition, no such equipment is needed, and ample time is available on the bank's computers to reconcile smaller volumes of checks for companies.

As part of the new marketing approach in cash management, banks should follow the same steps that have proved successful in other areas of bank marketing and among many nonbanks. Building complete profiles on customers and prospects is an essential first step. Their size in terms of annual sales, the geographic distribution of those sales, the industry type, the rate of growth, and the location of offices and factories all contribute to the bank's knowledge base, from which a call program can be developed.

A second step in the process requires the communication of cash management knowledge from the specialists in that field to the account officers, who will usually open the doors for specialized cultivation. All appropriate training media can be used for this purpose. It may be helpful for the cash management unit to build a library of product profiles so that other staff members can understand the selling features and benefits. Videotapes on cash management may also be used for training and education.

Knowledge of the competition is a third requirement for successful marketing of cash management. If a corporation's existing bank relationships and the extent to which those banks have successfully provided cash management services are known, solicitation becomes far easier. Any intelligence that can be gleaned regarding the strengths and weaknesses of competing banks with whom the company is dealing will be of value.

If the marketing program in cash management is to succeed, the bank must make a commitment to devote the necessary resources to product development. New or enhanced product features differentiate a bank from its competitors, and this differentiation may be more easily achieved in cash management than in credit, although the latter always remains the key in banking relationships with customers.[34]

Innovation is particularly important in the case of terminal-based or microcomputer-related products. Cash management is moving steadily in the direction of supplying clients with as much real-time information as possible, so banks are increasingly in the information business. Transaction-driven services, such as lock box and account reconciliation, are therefore receiving less attention. In steadily growing numbers, businesses of all sizes (and their counterparts in governments, correspondent banks, and institutions) have come to recognize the fact that information about money can be at least as important as the money.

The number of banks that have gained additional business as a result of cash management has increased in recent years. Of the 1,255 financial executives responding to the 1985 survey cited earlier, one-half said they had rewarded banks with additional activity because of cash management marketing and quality performance in rendering cash management services.[35]

There is no reason why the past practice of neglecting certain segments of the marketplace should continue. For example, one prominent consultant in the cash management field feels that less than one-third of the potential market among federal, state, and local governments has been tapped, and the range of services that these agencies can use is no different from that of the corporate market.[36] The smallest state government is actually a high-ranking, *Fortune*-sized company, and the various units of governments at every level generate a volume of transactions that immediately qualifies them as prospects for lock box service (e.g., for tax collections), account reconciliation, wire transfers, and all terminal-based information products.

The final element in the new approach to cash management addresses the question of compensation to the banks for their services. In previous years, those services were looked on as less important aspects of overall relationships with the bank's largest customers, and the balances that supposedly served to support credit facilities were also accepted as covering the cash management activity. Any cash management unit within the bank was considered to be a cost center rather than a profit center. The corporate trend toward reducing bank balances to an absolute working minimum had not developed; relatively few corporate financial officers requested regular monthly analyses from their banks so that they could monitor balances, activity, and the profitability to the banks of each relationship.

> Banks initially viewed cash management services simply as an accommodation—part of the credit relationship with a corporation. At best they were subsidized by the balances maintained by a customer; at worst they were simply given away free.[37]

The Monetary Control Act forced the Federal Reserve to use explicit pricing for its services; banks, in turn, have reacted by unbundling their relationships, so the profits on individual services were specifically identified on a stand-alone basis. Increases in operating costs, reduced spreads on loans, and a need for increased fee income have all played a part in the new policy and strategy regarding cash management. At the same time, corporate financial officers have displayed increasing interest in using direct fees, rather than demand deposits, as a means of compensating the banks for various cash management services. There are several reasons for this trend.

If balances are used as a form of compensation, the required level will fluctuate with each change in money-market rates. The amount the bank requires is a direct function of the earnings credit it allows, and the latter is tied directly to prevailing conditions in the marketplace. Therefore, a demand deposit of $1 million at a time when interest rates were in the 15 percent range would support far more in bank services than it would when rates dropped to 7 percent. The account officer, when the latter event took place, would naturally call on the customer to raise the level of compensation. This request would, in turn, require negotiation, which at least in some cases, might prove difficult and detrimental to the overall relationship.

The corporate financial officer today knows the value of money. If, by paying direct fees, he or she can avoid questions of balances as compensation, that officer can free up funds for investment or other purposes and, in doing so, take advantage of rates more favorable than those the banks use for earnings-allowance purposes. Negotiations over the level of balances then become unnecessary.

A classic example is in the rate fluctuations that occurred between 1980 and 1985. The earnings credit rate at thirty large banks (i.e., the allowance, based on balances, that can be used to offset expenses) in the former year was 13.64 percent; by the end of 1985, it had dropped to 7.28 percent.[38] As a result, a service that required a compensating balance of $100 in the earlier year needed $370 in 1985 even if the price of the service remained unchanged.

Fees paid to banks in exchange for services immediately become business expenses for the corporation and, therefore, are a tax deduction.

The value of deposits and balances can never be denied or minimized; nevertheless, there is much to be said for a system of fee compensation. Through it, direct income can be measured against the total cost of supplying each cash management service, and the cash management unit can become a profit center. Fees constitute a valuable source of bottom-line income for banks, particularly when disintermediation is taking place as customers reduce balances and place funds in various yield vehicles.

Corporations contemplating a change in their cash management practices or the implementation of new services with new banks commonly use questionnaires, sent to several institutions and requesting specific information on the per-item price of every transaction and the level of compensation, whether in fees, balances, or a combination of the two, that the bank expects. If the bank is willing to accept a non-interest-bearing time deposit as compensation so that it can benefit from the lower reserve requirement, it should indicate this option. Those units of government that are opening up areas of cash management services follow this practice by sending Requests For Proposals (RFPs), detailing the specifications of the required services and asking the bank to outline its methods of expected compensation.

Summary

From humble beginnings in which very few services were marketed to a very limited number of corporate customers, cash management as a specialized aspect of commercial banking has made steady progress. Its growth was most notable when corporate financial officers, capitalizing on the high interest rates of the late 1970s and early 1980s, took advantage of every available technique to put funds to work, maximizing their early-morning knowledge of the status of every bank account and reducing excess demand deposits in their banks.

The degree to which the total marketplace has been penetrated is remarkable if one considers the statistics that show the number of banks that have made a commitment to provide cash management services. That number represents only a small fraction, roughly 2 percent, of the nation's 14,500 banks. Of those, only one in ten has been identified as a leader in the field.

In a 1985 survey of 1,255 companies with sales of over $250 million, however, 95 percent of the cash managers received computerized data from their banks through terminal-based systems, and 70 percent used those terminals to initiate money transfers. Over two-thirds used zero-balance and/or controlled disbursement accounts, and 56 percent used lock boxes.[39] The banks' services to large corporations have clearly been effectively sold and supplied. While comparable statistical studies apparently have not been done among not-for-profit organizations and banks, experience in the New York City area indicates that these, too, are active users of various cash management services.

To ensure a future for cash management as successful as its past, two essentials exist. First, the so-called middle market must be exploited. Banks can no longer afford the luxury of focusing only on the largest firms. The needs of companies with sales of less than $200 million are at least as great. Because these smaller companies deal with fewer banks—typically no more than four—an institution that learns all it can about the nature of their business, employs the services of knowledgeable officers to cultivate them, and targets its services to meet their specific needs has an excellent opportunity to improve its market share at the expense of competitors. Cash management can provide the motivation for a smaller company to change its bank relationships; the industrial giants are far less likely to make such a change since any services they may need can readily be obtained from any of the major banks with whom they deal.

Second, traditional cash management services can continue to be marketed, but much more emphasis must be placed on the full range of information products. Little can be done to enhance further the basic lock box and disbursement systems if a bank wishes to differentiate itself from its competitors. Conversely, much can be done to increase the completeness and timeliness of microcomputer-based and terminal-based services to satisfy the demands of the marketplace. Issues related to float and geography will become less significant as the emphasis on technology and delivery systems increases.

It is somewhat ironic that one of the best examples of a multibillion dollar corporation's use of a host of cash management services is one that bypasses the commercial banking system wherever possible. R.J. Reynolds Industries, Inc., with annual sales of over $12.9 billion in 1984, has created a Financial Company (FinCo) to monitor all receipts in some eighty currencies, manage liquidity and bank balances, and report foreign exchange exposure. As a result, the parent has been able to reduce the number of its worldwide bank relationships from 600 to 50, has reduced bank fees by over $2 million per year, and has consolidated information from some 145 global offices and subsidiaries. The excess deposits that the system has effectively removed from Reynolds Industries' banks have been used for short-term investments and currency trading.[40] The number of large multinational corporations with the ability to implement similar plans may be small; nevertheless, in their marketing strategies the banks must be aware of all developments paralleling this one.

Notes

1. Frederick T. Sauer, "Like a Chameleon, Cash Management Keeps Changing," *ABA Banking Journal,* November 1984, p. 114.
2. Claire Makin, "Cash Managers Come of Age," *Institutional Investor,* December 1984, p. 273.
3. David I. Fisher, *Cash Management* (New York, The Conference Board, 1973), p. 25.
4. "The Banking Scene: Cash Management and Relationship Banking," *Journal of Cash Management,* November/December 1985, p. 20.
5. Richard S. Ravenscroft, in Tom Ferris, "Trends in Cash Management: Information and Cost Effectiveness," *American Banker,* January 4, 1985, p. 20.
6. George C. White, Jr., "After a Decade, Where Is EFT Headed?," *ABA Banking Journal,* May 1980, p. 88.

7. Federal Reserve Bank of New York, *Annual Report 1981,* p. 26.

8. Ibid.

9. Paul J. Beehler, *Contemporary Cash Management: Principles, Practices, Perspectives* (New York, John Wiley & Sons, Inc., 1983), p. 418.

10. Dr. James B. Moore, "Moore on EFT," *Bank Systems & Equipment,* January 1985, pp. 53–56.

11. Sandra G. Carcione, "Electronic Cash Management: The Corporate Toy Grows Up," *Bank Marketing,* February 1981, p. 16.

12. Fred S. Wayland, "How to Select a Bank: Lockbox Guide," *Cashflow,* December 1985, p. 26.

13. "The Many Keys to Lock Box Success," Operations & Automation Report, *ABA Banking Journal,* March 1986, p. 98.

14. Tom Ferris, "More Banks Open Remote Lockboxes," *American Banker,* July 23, 1985, p. 1.

15. Tom Ferris, "7 Banks Unveil a Nationwide Lockbox System," *American Banker,* March 7, 1985, p. 1.

16. "Georgians Vote to Lock out Out-of-State Banks' Atlanta Remittance Centers," *Corporate EFT Report,* March 6, 1985.

17. "End of Out-of-State Lockboxes in Ga.?," *American Banker,* March 21, 1985, p. 3.

18. "J.C. Penney Joins the Lockbox Game," Operations & Automation Report, *ABA Banking Journal,* March 1986, p. 102.

19. Michael Weinstein, "Bank to Buy Lockbox Services from Penney Unit," *American Banker,* December 18, 1985, p. 3.

20. Tom Ferris, "Lockbox Networks Growing Rapidly Around the Nation," *American Banker,* November 13, 1984, p. 16.

21. Sauer, op. cit., p. 118.

22. Beehler, op. cit., pp. 128–130.

23. Sauer, op. cit., p. 116.

24. Barbara Donnelly, "Cash Management: Where Do You Draw the Line?," *Institutional Investor,* September 1985, p. 76. Emphasis added.

25. Tom Ferris, "Customers Slow to Accept Security's Nationwide Payment Service," *American Banker,* May 21, 1986, p. 11.

26. Robert Field, in Suzanne Wittebort, "The Frantic New Pace of Cash Management," *Institutional Investor,* June 1981, p. 183.

27. In Makin, op. cit., p. 274.

28. Allen M. Cohen, "Electronic Financial Services: A Battleground for Survival," *Bank Administration,* January 1985, p. 19.

29. Daniel M. Ferguson and Steven F. Maier, "Reducing the Risk in Corporate Disbursement Systems," *Bank Administration,* June 1984, pp. 29–32.

30. Christine G. Dea, "Needed: Control of Cash Management Operating Risk," *ABA Banking Journal,* December 1984, pp. 89–90.

31. Harold S. Overholt, Jr., "Managing Risk in Cash Management," *The Bankers Magazine,* July–August 1985, pp. 62–65.

32. Tom Ferris, "Corporations Exhibit a Penchant to Buy New Services in the Cash Management Products Market, Survey Finds," *American Banker,* October 9, 1985, p. 13.

33. John J. Stack, "Profits from Cash Management Products Will Accrue to the Astute," *American Banker,* December 11, 1985, p. 8.

34. Tom Ferris, "Ace Card for Banks: Cash Management," *American Banker,* November 13, 1984, p. 1.

35. Ferris, "Corporations Exhibit a Penchant to Buy New Services," p. 13.

36. Marshall D. Sokol, in Tom Ferris, "Consultant Believes City, State, U.S. Governments Are Potentially Lucrative Markets for Operational Services," *American Banker,* April 25, 1986, p. 16.

37. Sauer, op. cit., p. 114.

38. Tom Ferris, "Cash Management Fees Leveling Off, Survey Says," *American Banker,* May 27, 1986, p. 1.

39. Ferris, "Corporations Exhibit a Penchant to Buy New Services," p. 13.

40. Jerry Adams, "R.J. Reynolds Saves Millions by Bypassing Banking System with Its Own 'Near Bank'," *American Banker,* December 12, 1985, p. 34. Because of its acquisition of Nabisco, the company is now known as RJR Nabisco, Inc.

9
The New World of Competition

The reply of Willie Sutton to the question, "Why do you keep robbing banks?," has become part and parcel of U.S. folklore: "Because that's where the money is." In terms of access to coin and currency for a bank robber, his answer remains as valid today as it was twenty years ago. In terms of consumer services, however, it has become increasingly clear that the banks are not where those services are to be found. In fact, the commercial banks' share of the total financial marketplace, with emphasis on retail banking, has been steadily shrinking.

Changes in market share for commercial banks vis-à-vis some of their major competitors from 1950 to 1980 are shown in table 9–1. Since 1980, many other nonbank companies have joined those competitors. While nonbank companies differ in type and size, they have this in common: unhampered by the plethora of federal and state regulations that hamstring commercial banks, they have assumed steadily increasing importance in the fragmented financial services industry. In addition, a new type of entity, the limited-service (nonbank) bank, has entered the fray, causing controversy and litigation.[1]

An accepted fact of financial life in the United States is that no vacuum in services is ever permitted to exist. If one type of institution cannot or will not meet a real, perceived, or created need, some other type of financial intermediary will soon do so. The examples are numerous.

Individuals in many cases could not meet the commercial banks' requirements on high-yielding, negotiable CDs; therefore, the money-market funds were organized. For many years, commercial banks displayed little or no interest in residential mortgages; therefore, the thrift institutions assumed a dominant role in that field—a preeminence they have never relinquished.

Consumers today are more knowledgeable in financial matters than their predecessors and far more willing to move their relationships from one type of institution to another if, in doing so, they gain better yield, find greater convenience, or have access to more services. Therefore, whenever the banks choose to neglect an area of retail banking or are prevented by statutes from

Table 9–1
Market Shares of Selected U.S. Institutions, 1950–1980
(volume, in billions of dollars; share, in percent of total assets)

Institutions	1950		1960		1970		1980		*Annual Growth, 1970–1980*
	Volume	*Share*	*Volume*	*Share*	*Volume*	*Share*	*Volume*	*Share*	
Commercial banks	149.6	50.6	228.3	37.4	504.9	36.7	1,360.9	35.4	10.4
S&Ls	16.9	5.7	71.5	11.7	176.2	12.8	629.8	16.4	13.6
Credit unions	1	0.3	6.3	1	18	1.3	69.6	1.8	14.5
Life insurance companies	62.6	21.2	115.8	19	200.9	14.6	456.1	11.9	8.5

Source: Board of Governors, Federal Reserve System, *Flow of Funds*.

offering certain services, competitors will quickly capitalize on the opportunity to fill the void.

Historically, bankers who worried about competition were concerned only with the actions of other commercial banks. The U.S. Supreme Court shared this narrowness of thinking. Its ruling in the case of *United States* v. *Philadelphia National Bank*[2] established the principle that commercial banks constituted a unique line of business and that they therefore competed only with one another:

> Commercial banks are the only financial institutions in which a wide variety of financial products and services . . . are [*sic*] gathered together in one place. The clustering of financial products and services in banks . . . makes possible access to certain products or services that would otherwise be unavailable.[3]

At the time of the decision (1963), many bankers found it extremely difficult to accept[4]; in today's environment, any logic that may have led to it has lost all meaning. Bankers note with alarm the growth of S&Ls and savings banks as more active competitors with expanded powers; however, if the focus remains restricted to those institutions and to other banks, another, potentially much more serious type of competition, is ignored: nonbank companies in several fields are aggressively marketing all their services for consumers, and the new nonbank banks (often owned by retailers, industrial conglomerates, or brokerage firms) are also using their relative freedom to attract customers. If commercial banking ever constituted a unique line of business, it certainly has no such franchise today.

Indeed, in 1981 Henry C. Wallich, then member of the Federal Reserve Board of Governors, described the commercial banks:

> They face intensive competition across a rapidly broadening scope of product and geographic markets from . . . thrifts and nonfinancial firms. . . . They are experiencing an all-out invasion from both traditional and new competitors.[5]

His comments were perceptive and relevant in 1981 and are even more so today. Financial transactions that were handled on bank premises in 1981 may now take place in supermarkets, the new Sears Financial Centers, or brokerage firm offices. The regulatory distinctions among the various types of financial intermediaries, and markets that were protected by geography, no longer exist as such. They are irrelevant to the consumer, and equally irrelevant to the authorities and legislators who seem intent on preserving anachronisms while ignoring reality in the marketplace.

The financial services and the information products businesses are fast becoming a single entity. Technology and competition have combined to give consumers a new freedom of choice among the suppliers of that entity. One bank consultant made this comment in the *Economic Review,* published by the Federal Reserve Bank of Atlanta: "Are banks getting disenfranchised? . . . I would have to say "yes." The trend increasingly is for nonbanks to develop bank-like relationships with banking clients."[6] In the dynamics of change in the financial services industry, all this has been made possible by the definite advantages that the banks' competitors enjoy:

1. Unlike commercial banks, nonbank companies can operate across state lines and enjoy unlimited branching privileges within the borders of every state. Neither the McFadden Act nor any state regulation on branching affects them.
2. Unlike commercial banks, they need not maintain reserves on deposit with the Fed or with the Fed's member banks; thus, they have far greater opportunities to put their funds to profitable use.
3. Because they are not banks, they are not subject to the host of constraints that have been imposed on banks over the past 200 years; their ability to offer completely integrated financial services is limited only by their innovativeness, their willingness to commit the necessary resources, and their strategies for further expansion.
4. Because they are not saddled with portfolios of long-term, low-yield mortgages and are not faced with the problem loans that are part of the global debt crisis, they are more able to generate profits and less constrained to place large sums in loan-loss reserves.
5. Many of them enter the financial services arena from an extremely advantageous starting point, in that they have tremendous data bases that are composed of files on their existing customers. Individuals who already shop with them, finance cars with them, are their policyholders, use their credit cards, buy and sell securities through them, or establish retirement fund accounts with them represent ideal targets for cross-selling. Even the largest banks have no comparable data bases.

As charter-free competitors continue to establish themselves at the banks' expense and explore new markets, the need for legal and regulatory approaches to the financial services industry becomes ever more apparent. A Vice-Chairman of the Chase Manhattan Corporation has suggested a future scenario that is predicated on the banks' inability to gain regulatory relief:

> There will be far fewer banks in the United States than the present 14,000. . . . Many banks and thrifts will simply not be able to compete with Merrill Lynch, American Express, Sears, and other financial institutions which are already putting more banking and banking-related products through the vast coast-to-coast infrastructures they already have in place.[7]

The proliferation of services offered by nonbanks and the resulting overlapping of functions have led to what has been called

> A confused, even inequitable, regulatory environment. . . . This may very well have increased the total risk in the overall financial system by allowing previously segregated institutions to engage in new markets but in a hit or miss way. The need for a legislative rationalization of this confusion grows clearer and more pressing.[8]

Deregulation

The clamor raised by the nation's commercial bankers in their quest for greater freedom to compete has grown increasingly strident in recent years. Each new incursion of a competitor into an area of service in which the banks once enjoyed exclusivity, and each new announcement of a service that banks cannot legally offer, prompts additional lobbying for change. However, every banker's request to "make the playing field more level" meets opposition from those who fear greater concentration of power in the hands of the money-center giants, who point to the highly leveraged position that already exists in the system as a whole, and who bemoan the increasing number of bank failures.

Opponents of deregulation (as the commercial bankers interpret the term) often cite the near insolvency of Continental Illinois, conveniently ignoring the fact that the problems of that bank had nothing to do with diversification into new lines of business or geographic expansion. Deregulation, or increased authority to enter nonbank business, did not make a federal agency's bailout of Continental Illinois a necessity; weaknesses in the loan portfolio did, and the massive withdrawals of funds from that bank by large depositors cannot be attributed either to federal or state statutes or the lack of them.[9]

The commercial banks' quest for deregulation, combined with the problems of the thrift institutions, increasing attrition of banks from the Fed system as a means of freeing up reserves, and the massive disintermediation that was caused by the money-market funds, led to the passage of the Depository Institutions Deregulation and Monetary Control Act of 1980. Its stated objectives were twofold:

> To improve the effectiveness of monetary policy by making the fulcrum on which that policy operates more stable . . . [and]
>
> To provide competitive equity among financial institutions which, given uniform reserve requirements, will be placed on a more equal footing and, given new authorities, will be able to offer more equivalent services to their customers.[10]

Among its specifics,[11] the Monetary Control Act subjected all depository institutions to reserve requirements, increased the maximum FDIC coverage, addressed the question of Fed float, implemented explicit Fed pricing for all services, and gave S&Ls and credit unions significantly increased powers. The commercial bankers found little benefit in these provisions. The *deregulation* mentioned in the Act's complete title did nothing to create the "more equal footing" for them that had been stated as an objective.

Similarly, the Garn–St Germain Act of 1982 was considered a further step toward deregulation. It directed the establishment of a new type of insured deposit relationship, with rates that fluctuated with money-market conditions and thus facilitated competition with the funds. Again, thrift institutions were the major beneficiaries of the Act. The newly authorized MMDAs and Super-NOW accounts at commercial banks have indeed attracted billions of dollars; yet these accounts in many cases have done nothing more than cannibalize the same banks' demand deposits.[12] The net effect is a growth in interest expense and a further shift in the overall deposit structure.

The Garn–St Germain Act did provide for deregulation of rate ceilings and removed the interest-rate differentials that had existed between commercial banks and thrifts. In the New World of competition, however, it is *product* and *geographic* deregulation that commercial bankers seek. The Monetary Control and Garn–St Germain Acts, by providing *rate* deregulation, did much to make thrift institutions more competitive with money-market funds and commercial banks but did little or nothing to make the latter more competitive with those nonbanks that were and are offering so many financial services in so many places with so few restrictions, thereby succeeding so handsomely. For example, the 1983 profits ($8 billion) from financial services of thirty nonbank companies represented a 19 percent increase over their 1981 results in the same area and were more than half the combined profits of all U.S. commercial banks.[13]

Any exclusivity the commercial banks enjoyed as holders of demand deposits and primary forces in the payments system began to disappear in 1972, when thrift institutions in New England introduced the first NOW accounts. These were interest-bearing relationships against which checklike instruments could be issued. Since 1982, all depository institutions have been empowered to offer NOW and Super-NOW accounts and MMDAs.[14] Similarly, the nation's credit unions, discussed later in this chapter, are authorized to offer share drafts. These checklike negotiable instruments are used as a payment medium by members.

The desire of commercial bankers to expand geographically and through additional lines of business is intensified by their awareness of the size and potential profitability of the retail market. They recognize the increasing trend among their major corporate customers to bypass them in seeking credit (e.g., by using the commercial paper market) and to place less reliance on them for certain services. At the same time, the bankers identify the growth and affluence of the consumer population.

A survey conducted in 1985 by a market research firm studied that population in detail.[15] It determined that more than 8 million U.S. households (10.3 percent of the total) had incomes of over $50,000 or a net worth of over $200,000 and predicted that this market segment would more than double within ten years. Every such household typifies the so-called upscale market the banks would like to serve more completely and has the potential to generate annual profits of over $1,500 per household for those banks.

Can we categorize the universe of providers of financial services? Although much overlapping occurs within the subdivisions, the competitors of commercial banks can be divided into two basic groups:

nonbank companies,

nonbank banks.

Credit unions, since they are financial institutions that closely resemble banks in so many ways, constitute a third category of much lesser magnitude.

The first category can be arbitrarily subdivided into five groups:

financial conglomerates (e.g., American Express),

industrial companies with a heavy emphasis on financial services to consumers,

brokerage firms (e.g., Merrill Lynch),

insurance companies (e.g., Prudential Bache),

retailers.

The second category comprises those institutions that have evolved in recent years as a specialized type of hybrid in the financial services industry.

One can grasp the importance of the nonbank companies as competitors for commercial banks from a single statistic. Of the thirty largest participants in the financial services industry in the mid-1980s, twenty would fall under that heading.[16] Many of them have expanded their traditional, basic activities to include commercial loans, IRA and Keogh accounts, mortgages, mutual funds, and direct loans to consumers.

This is not to suggest that the commercial banks, as a group, have experienced drastically reduced profits because of the new competition; relative to nonbanks of all types, they have suffered to some extent but, even in the face of all the constraints under which they operate, have displayed a good deal of resilience in attempting to cope.[17] More important than other considerations is the opportunity cost—that is, the net income that could have been earned had the commercial banks been able to compete fully and freely. If the existing regulatory climate continues, that opportunity cost can only increase with each passing year as the competitors become more solidly entrenched in the marketplace. The repeated use of terms such as *nonbank* and *nonbank bank* leads logically to a question: Exactly what is a bank?

Definition of a Bank

Section 2(c) of the Bank Holding Company Act of 1956, amended in 1970 [70 Stat. 133 as amended, 12 U.S.C. Section 1841(c)] establishes the legal principle:

> A bank is any institution which (1) accepts deposits that the depositor has a legal right to withdraw on demand, *and* (2) engages in the business of making commercial loans. (Emphasis added)

This definition was incorporated into Federal Reserve Regulation Y, which governs the operations of all bank holding companies. The converse of the definition is most pertinent here, however.

If an institution performs only one of the two specified functions—for example, handles demand deposits but does not make commercial loans, or vice versa—it does not fall under the strict definition and therefore is not subject to the regulations governing banks. If the acquirer of a bank should divest it of either function, the institution legally becomes a nonbank and, again, avoids bank regulatory constraints. In this way a new term, the *nonbank bank,* has been added to the lexicon of the financial services.

In 1984 the Federal Reserve, responding to the sharp increase in the number of institutions and very much aware of their relatively high degree of freedom in offering various financial services, amended Regulation Y and redefined its original terminology. The amendment stated that an institution offering NOW accounts and/or dealing in commercial paper would, per se, come under the definition of a bank. The Fed stated that its action fell within the "plain purpose" of regulating all institutions that were "functionally equivalent" to banks.[18]

The U.S. Supreme Court overturned this amendment in a landmark decision rendered on January 22, 1986 by ruling that the Fed had exceeded its statutory authority and could not restrict the activities of nonbanks (also known as limited-service banks). It was the Court's feeling that any revisions in the Bank Holding Company Act to protect the public interest should be initiated by Congress and not by the Federal Reserve.[19]

The Senior Legislative Counsel to the American Bankers Association has described the Court's action as the granting of an "unrestricted mandate" to the nonbank banks[20]; however, as of mid-1986 Congress had not addressed the issue. Chapter 10 discusses the nonbank banks, their functions and activities, and their current legal status.

Credit Unions

In the mid-nineteenth century, an organization was formed in Germany to provide low-cost financing for a group of urban workers and merchants. This so-called credit society enabled members to obtain loans without having to resort to the usurers who had been preying on them. The first credit union in the United States was organized in Manchester, New Hampshire, in 1909, and the movement has grown steadily since that date.

Today there are over 17,600 credit unions, with over 52 million members; at year-end 1985, total assets of these organizations were $118 billion.[21] Each credit union is either federally or state chartered. Largely as a result of the powers granted to them by the Monetary Control and Garn–St Germain Acts, credit unions can compete to a meaningful extent with commercial banks as providers of various financial services to consumers. The former Chairman of the National Credit Union Association has claimed that, as a group, credit unions have at least 5 percent of the total consumer market.[22]

The legal, traditional requirement for membership in a credit union is a common bond. Members may work for the same employer; belong to the same religious, professional, fraternal, or social group; live in the same geographic area; or serve in the same branch of the armed forces. For example, the Navy Federal Credit Union, with assets in excess of $2 billion, is the nation's largest, and its members are Navy or Marine Corps personnel and their families.

Credit unions have always specialized in small loans to members. More recently, they have begun to use their expanded authority to offer mortgage, automobile, and small business loans. They may also participate with other financial institutions in ATM networks.[23]

Each credit union enjoys a significant advantage in competing with banks: it is exempt from all federal taxation on its net income. Members of credit unions can either deposit funds or purchase shares; typically, they can at the same time receive a higher return on their deposits or shares than they would find at a bank and pay a lower rate on loans. In addition to their tax-exempt status, credit unions also benefit from free or low-cost office space and clerical help provided by a corporate employer or unit of government (e.g., a municipal workers' credit union).[24] At year-end 1985 the nation's credit unions listed total members' savings and shareholdings at $106 billion; outstanding loans to members amounted to over $73 billion.[25]

Financial Conglomerates

Any attempt to categorize the various nonbank companies that constitute the commercial banks' major competition is at best arbitrary. The lines of distinction between these companies are often blurred, and many of them could arguably be placed in a group other than the one in which they are listed here. General Electric Credit Corporation, for example, was referred to in chapter 7; it could easily be called a conglomerate in its own right yet is grouped under the heading of industrial companies because of the orientation of its parent.

Among the names arbitrarily listed as financial conglomerates, a great deal of diversity exists. They range in size from the prototype, American Express Company, with its total assets of over $61 billion at year-end 1984, to a company known as Kinder-Care Learning Centers, Inc., based in Alabama, with 1985 revenues of $192 million. Yet the latter, through its 1986 acquisitions of an insurer and a thrift institution, intends to have at least 20 percent of its 1987 earnings stem from its activities in insurance, mutual funds, CDs, mortgages, IRAs, and college savings plans.[26] That objective and range of services qualify Kinder-Care as a financial conglomerate, despite its relatively small size.

The choice of American Express as the prototype for this group reflects both its size and the completeness of its product line in the overall financial services industry. The company invented travelers' cheques in 1891 and sold over $15 billion of them in 1984. Over 20 million American Express cards are in circulation, and in 1984 these were used to buy some $50 billion worth of services and products in 150 countries. The subsidiaries of American Express provide travel-related, insurance, investment, and international banking services and provide consumer banking services on U.S. military bases in foreign countries. American Express Leasing Corporation offers financing for equipment. In 1986, the company added two limited-service (nonbank) banks, American Express Centurion Bank (Newark, Delaware) and IDS Trust Company (Minneapolis), to the Boston Safe Deposit & Trust Company, which was already owned through a subsidiary. These institutions will not accept demand deposits but will provide credit facilities to American Express cardholders and investors.[27] First Data Resources, Inc., of which an American Express subsidiary owns 75 percent, offers transaction processing for businesses. American Express International Banking Corporation (AEIBC) offers private banking and merchant banking facilities through seventy-five offices in thirty-nine foreign countries and handles an average of $6 billion per day in global money transfers.[28]

Through its acquisitions of Shearson Lehman Brothers (formerly Shearson Loeb Rhoades), Investors Diversified Services (IDS), and Fireman's Fund Insurance Company, American Express meets a wide range of services in every aspect of the financial services industry and achieves a high degree of synergy among all its subsidiaries. Table 9–2 shows the size of these entities and their contributions to the overall net income of $610 million achieved by American Express in 1984. The extent to which American Express has become involved in the lifestyle of American consumers is further evidenced by its ownership of Warner Amex Cable Communications, which owns 104 cable and TV systems in twenty-one states, serving over 1 million households; two-thirds of MTV Networks, Inc.; and 19 percent of Showtime/The Movie Channel.

Because of its lower tax rates on corporate income and the fact that it imposes no rate restrictions on card outstandings, Delaware has become a favored state for the operations of many banks (Morgan Guaranty, Chase Manhattan, and Citicorp are among those that have established facilities there) and financial conglomerates. Beneficial Corporation, headquartered in that state, ranks high in the latter group. It has diversified from its former finance company status into a host of other financial services. It owns a commercial bank, has established a nonbank in Delaware, and owns a $2 billion S&L in Texas.[29] Beneficial has become the largest finance company in the second-mortgage field, with $3.1 billion in receivables in 1985.[30] Beneficial Corporation also owns a multibillion-dollar firm and a mail-order merchandising company and has acquired a bank in the United Kingdom with sixty branches.[31] It operates 2,000 domestic offices, and twenty-six states have granted it authority to accept deposits from consumers using those offices. They are connected by an on-line electronic network for transfers of funds.[32] Beneficial Mortgage Corporation extends first-mortgage financing; Beneficial Insurance Company offers life insurance, annuities, casualty and accident insurance, and underwrites the insurance on card outstandings and consumer loans; and Beneficial's bank subsidiary has acquired the card outstandings of two other commercial banks.[33] Among all independent finance companies—that is, those not owned by or affiliated with corporate entities or banks, Beneficial ranked third in 1985, with capital funds of $1.1 billion, receivables of $5.8 billion, and net income of $101 million.[34]

Larger in terms of capital funds, receivables, and net income than Beneficial, but possibly less diversified as a provider of the full spectrum of financial services, Household International Corporation is a financial conglomerate that, like Beneficial, had its origins as a finance company. Its principal subsidiary, Household Financial Corporation, has over 1,100 offices in forty states, which make second-mortgage loans and other personal loans and, to a lesser extent, are engaged in commercial financing and leasing. The parent owns both a commercial bank and thrift institution in California. Its classification here reflects the stated objectives of its President: "Our particular goal is to become a consumer bank. We will offer a broad range of financial services, loans, demand and time deposits, insurance services, and income tax services."[35]

Another subsidiary, Alexander Hamilton Life Insurance Company,

Table 9–2
American Express Company

Component	*Operations*	*Revenues ($ millions)*	*Net Income ($ millions)*	*Comments*
Card and travel-related services	Credit cards, travel agency operations, travelers cheques	3,600	387	Total assets, $12.5 billion
American Express International Banking Corporation	Global banking network	522	156	Total assets, $13.9 billion
Shearson Lehman Brothers	Investment banking, underwriting, brokerage	2,280	103	Total assets, $22.7 billion
IDS Financial Services	Financial planning, insurance, Keogh and IRA plans, life insurance	1,576	62	Assets owned or managed, $19.3 billion; life insurance in force, $13.8 billion
Fireman's Fund Insurance Companies	Property, liability, life, accident, and health insurance	4,025	43	Total assets, $7.7 billion; life insurance in force, $23 billion

Source: American Express, *Annual Report* (1984).

markets both ordinary life and credit life insurance. At year-end 1985 consolidated figures for Household International showed capital funds of $1.4 billion, receivables of $6.9 billion, and net income of $143 million.[36]

Each of the organizations listed in this category has nationwide distribution facilities, enabling it to market financial services without regard for state boundaries. In addition, they are characterized by their aggressive cross-selling campaigns, through which they can build integrated portfolios. For example, the holder of an American Express card at once becomes a target for the brokerage, insurance, financial planning, and money-market-fund services that are available through the parent's various subsidiaries.[37]

Industrial Companies

As distinguished from the financial conglomerates, the banks' competitors in the industrial companies category are companies whose names appear on the *Fortune* 500 list because of their basic product lines, not because of their financial services. Although not all of them offer all the same services or aim at the same market segments, as a group they have made tremendous inroads in the industry. The Big Three of the automotive industry and companies such as Gulf + Western, IBM, and ITT may not be thought of as competitors for the commercial banks in supplying financial services, but in fact their strong capital base, active marketing programs, and nationwide operations make them forces to be reckoned with now and increasingly important entities in the future. In the Pavel and Rosenblum study,[38] the authors noted that the profits from financial activities of a group of thirty nonbank industrial companies increased 19 percent from 1981 to 1983, to an aggregate net of $8 billion. This profit was more than half that reported by all the U.S. commercial banks.

The category of industrial companies can be subdivided, again arbitrarily. General Motors, Ford, and Chrysler comprise one subset; their captive finance companies, huge though they originally were, are rapidly diversifying into additional areas of financial services. General Electric Company, both because of the activities of its Credit Corporation subsidiary, referred to earlier, and its 1986 acquisition of Kidder, Peabody and Company, constitutes a competitor deserving of standalone listing. The third grouping includes other major corporations that have actively entered the arena.

General Motors Corporation

Heading the 1985 *Fortune* 500 listing, with global sales of $96 billion and total assets of $63 billion, General Motors (GM) regained that leadership position, which it had held twenty-seven times (out of a possible thirty-two) in the past.[39] Its size as a corporation and its stature in the automotive industry are universally known; however, the contributions to its success of its finance subsidiary, General Motors Acceptance Corporation (GMAC), may be less widely recognized. I have frequently made the point that whenever one type of financial institution neglects some area of consumer service, another will step in to fill the void. GMAC owes its origin (1919) to the fact that commercial banks were not interested in financing purchases of GM vehicles.[40]

The year-end 1985 figures for GMAC showed total assets of $75.4 billion and net receivables of $66 billion; its net income of $1.02 billion was not only larger than that of any commercial bank but also represented one-quarter of its parent's consolidated bottom-line profit of $4 billion.[41] If GMAC were legally classified as a bank, which it is in everything but name, it would rank fifth largest in the United States in terms of total assets, slightly ahead of Morgan Guaranty. Its capital funds of $5.1 billion at year-end 1985 were double those of Merrill Lynch.[42] Morgan Guaranty ranked as the most profitable bank in 1985 on the basis of Return on Equity (ROE), which was $18.06 per $100; GMAC achieved ROE of $22.30 per $100 in the same year, and the mean ROE for fourteen major money-center banks was $13.[43] Forty-one percent of all GM dealer sales in 1985 involved GMAC financing in one form or another.[44]

In addition to all its financing of GM sales and leases and its direct loans to GM dealers, GMAC has diversified into two unrelated areas of financial services that add significantly to its stature as a bank competitor. In April and May 1985, GMAC acquired the $11 billion Northwest Mortgage Company (Minneapolis) and Colonial Mortgage Services Company, based in Philadelphia and servicing mortgage assets of $7.4 billion.[45] Through these acquisitions, GMAC immediately became the second-largest mortgage banker in the United States.

GMAC is also involved in commercial lending. At year-end 1983 it held $11.4 billion of such loans in its portfolio, a figure that was approximately equal to the commercial and industrial loans in the Chase Manhattan portfolio for the same year.[46]

One other GMAC acquisition deserves mention here. Electronic Data Systems (EDS), the data-processing and computer giant founded by H. Ross Perot, is now part of GMAC and provides it with a network of centers, linked by satellite or telephone lines and capable of supplying a wide range of services to all types of customers, including financial institutions. In the world of the future as GMAC visualizes it, a customer's order in a dealer showroom will initiate a complex, related program, all controlled by EDS computers. Under this scenario, financing can be arranged, parts ordered and shipped to assembly lines, instructions relayed to the automated facilities that do the actual manufacturing, and the vehicle shipped to the correct dealer. GMAC President Robert Murphy has also announced a pilot program that would allow dealers to enter credit data in the showroom so that the system would conduct automatic credit checks and rate the customer's creditworthiness. The response to the dealer would be almost instantaneous.[47]

GMAC has no intention of resting on these laurels. President Murphy has outlined an additional scenario in which the company becomes a provider of cash management services, both to consumers and middle-market companies. For example, as dealers generate cash GMAC could automatically invest it in its own commercial paper.[48] As the next step, President Murphy foresees the possibility of offering the GMAC money-market fund (now available only to GMAC employees) to its 6.5 million customers:

> It would be a money market fund with draft and checking privileges, and we could do direct deposit of payroll. And if we can offer a money fund, then we can offer a mortgage . . . [and] life, homeowner, and mortgage insurance.[49]

He has no reservations about GMAC's ability to lend to the corporate middle market: "If we can grant loans to a medium-size business like an auto dealership, we can do it in other areas."[50]

In addition to all the advantages outlined earlier, GMAC has a capability that further enhances its role in the area of financial services. It enjoys ready access to domestic and global capital markets and can raise funds through innovative instruments (e.g., long-term zero-coupon bonds) with a wide range of maturities. This helps GMAC protect itself against rate changes while it still offers fixed-rate auto loans.[51]

Ford Motor Company

The automotive industry, with its millions of workers, thousands of suppliers, and army of stockholders, is a bellwether of the entire U.S. economy. Accompanying its size and importance, however, is an extremely high degree of vulnerability. Pressures of foreign competition, changes in public taste regarding sizes and types of vehicles, or a sudden swing in fuel prices can create earnings fluctuations of major proportions.

Like General Motors and GMAC, the Ford Motor Company and Ford Credit Company have tried to offset that vulnerability and cyclic pattern through various forms of diversification. Although it is only about one-half the size of GMAC, Ford Credit still ranks as the second-largest finance company. Its 1985 figures disclose net receivables of $30.2 billion, net income of $441 million, and capital funds of $3.3 billion.[52] Its 1985 ROE was $19.30 per $100; again, compare this figure with those of the major money-center banks.[53]

Ford Credit has 142 branch offices throughout the country, but most of its retail financing originates through the parent company's 6,000 dealerships.

It also provides, directly or through subsidiaries, leasing, credit insurance, auto and disability insurance, and a broad range of home improvement, personal, home equity, and commercial and industrial loans.[54]

In its most important single move toward diversification, the Ford Motor Company acquired First Nationwide Financial, parent of the nation's eighth-largest thrift institution, in 1985 for $493 million.[55] First Nationwide was a consolidation of three former troubled thrift institutions in New York, Florida, and California and had been acquired in the early 1980s by the then National Steel Corporation (now National Intergroup, Inc.) when the latter sought to ameliorate the problems of the steel industry (highly labor- and capital-intensive, sensitive to environmental issues, and vulnerable to foreign competition) by diversifying.[56] The synergy of First Nationwide and Ford Credit means that a consumer's two largest purchases, a home and a car, can be financed through a single entity. In commenting on that synergy, Chairman James W. Ford of Ford Credit said:

> We saw an affinity between auto financing and the finance of housing. It was a natural extension . . . . You qualify people on almost the same basis. We think consumer finance in general is something we can do.[57]

The 180 branches of First Nationwide in New York, California, Florida, and Hawaii serve 2 million customers. Through a subsidiary, TransSouth Financial Corporation, it operates a network of 144 consumer finance offices in seven southeastern states. Ford Motor Company already owned two companies, Ford Aerospace and StarNet; these two satellite communications systems can participate with First Nationwide in the creation of a nationwide financial network. Such a network is one of the parent company's stated objectives.[58]

The acquisition of First Nationwide by Ford did not go entirely unnoticed in banking circles. One President of a savings bank, in particular, took strong exception to it; he differentiated it from those takeovers of failing thrifts that had taken place elsewhere and noted that First Nationwide, with assets of $11 billion, was in no financial difficulty. He saw the takeover pessimistically as a possible first step in the overall restructuring of the U.S. financial system. His fears that the Ford acquisition might presage similar takeovers of thrifts by major industrial corporations were linked to his comments on the ability of the new entity to offer consumers a combination of services (e.g., insurance and securities) prohibited to the banks.[59]

Chrysler Corporation

Just as the Chrysler Corporation ranks third among the Big Three auto manufacturers, its captive finance company, the Chrysler Financial Corporation, occupies third place among all such lenders. At year-end 1985 it reported net receivables of $14.9 billion, capital funds of $2.8 billion, and net income of $154 million.[60] To supplement its activities in automobile, commercial, and insurance financing, it made two major acquisitions in 1985.

On August 31, Chrysler Financial purchased E.F. Hutton Credit Company for $125 million, and on November 22 it paid $450 million for FinanceAmerica, formerly a financing unit of the BankAmerica Corporation. The latter has since been renamed Chrysler First, Inc., while the former Hutton Company is now Chrysler Capital Corporation. Chrysler Financial is also involved in a substantial joint venture with General Electric Credit Corporation as a lender.[61] Robert S. Miller, Vice-Chairman of Chrysler Corporation, has outlined a business plan that will make these subsidiaries far less dependent on automobile financing and far more active in other profitable areas than they are now. For example, FinanceAmerica has 267 nationwide branches, engaged in upscale-individual and small-business lending. It also includes a state-of-the-art computer system, Impact, which has a retail software program for complete processing of consumer loans. Expansion into fields such as property and life insurance and mortgage banking appear to be definite possibilities for the Chrysler entities.[62]

The pattern of major acquisitions and wide diversification among the nation's three largest automakers and their finance subsidiaries is one that the commercial banks cannot ignore or denigrate. These firms' cash-rich positions, their existing data bases of consumers who represent targets for cross-selling, and their ability to integrate financial services throughout the country all combine to reinforce their role as competitors. It is neither unrealistic nor unduly pessimistic to envision them as changing, at least in part, the way businesses and consumers "borrow, save, and manage their money."[63]

General Electric Credit Corporation

The preceding chapter cited General Electric Corporation (GECC) as a competitor of commercial banks in certain areas of lending. It deserves much more detailed discussion here because of its status as a nationwide provider of a range of financial services that no commercial bank can match.

In the newspaper advertising that announced the acquisition by GECC of the investment banking firm of Kidder, Peabody and Company, Inc., GECC cited its current position as the nation's largest nonbank business-to-business lender and its total assets of $20 billion. Even more important than that mere statement, however, is an analysis of the complete scope of GECC operations in many diversified areas.

From humble beginnings in 1932 as the captive finance company that helped General Electric's sales of appliances, GECC has expanded into commercial, industrial, and real estate financing; leasing; insurance; and commercial and residential real estate financing. Through subsidiaries, GECC also engages in mortgage banking and real estate syndication.[64]

GECC is now part of General Electric Financial Services, Inc. (GEFS), which was formed in 1984 when GECC acquired Employers Reinsurance Company for $1.1 billion. This acquisition added to the existing insurance activities of GECC through its ownership of Puritan Insurance Company (life and property casualty) and Mortgage Insurance Company. General Electric Company, the parent, ranked tenth on the 1985 *Fortune* 500 list with total revenues of $28.3 billion and net income of $2.3 billion. The contribution to those results of GEFS, Inc. (of which GECC is the major component) is extremely significant. It became the second-largest (after power systems) element in General Electric's overall operations, with net income of $406 million, or 17.6 percent of the parent's bottom line. In addition, the depreciation credits GECC derives from leasing real estate and aircraft have helped the parent reduce (or, in some years, avoid completely) its federal tax liability.[65]

In 1984 GECC achieved a Return on Equity of $20 per $100. Again, by comparison, Morgan Guaranty, with a ROE in 1984 of $15.29, made the best showing of any major commercial bank.[66] In describing the financial performance of GECC over the preceding five years as "superb," one analyst pointed to the company's high degree of sophistication, aggressiveness, and flexibility, its ability to raise funds in domestic and global capital markets because of its AAA credit rating, and the fact that almost every loan GECC makes is secured by some form of collateral.[67]

Indeed, 1984 marked the tenth consecutive year in which GECC achieved record earnings. Its management, commenting on those results, restated the corporate objective: "To provide high added-value products to selected segments of the U.S. economy."[68] The company's four major lines of business clearly indicate how far it has come from its original role as a financer of the parent company's appliances. In specialized lending (including the financing of major projects), national financing (including the creation of private-label credit systems for firms such as Apple Computer, John Deere, and Monsanto), asset management (including leveraged buyouts and leasing), and insurance, GECC has achieved an outstanding synergy, superimposed on its original base of consumer borrowers, dealers, and manufacturers.

The acquisition of Kidder, Peabody increased that synergy. In 1985 GECC acted as the manager of financings, which raised over $74 billion for governments, corporations, and tax-exempt entities. Kidder, Peabody enjoys a leading position in futures and equity trading, mergers and acquisitions, and underwriting. Its net income for fiscal year 1985 was $47 million. It provides GECC with the ability to underwrite and market corporate stock issues and debt issues, fund major commercial loans, and become more active than before in the global reinsurance market—specific areas the commercial banks have long sought to enter.[69]

Other Industrial Corporations

This grouping identifies several companies of somewhat lesser size that nevertheless represent competitors of commercial banks in areas of financial services.

Gulf + Western Corporation is a diversified conglomerate that may be best known as the owner of Paramount Pictures, Madison Square Garden, and two major publishing firms (Prentice-Hall, Inc. and Simon and Schuster). For fiscal year 1985, it reported net income of $243.3 million on revenues of $3.1 billion.[70]

Less widely known, however, is the corporation's ownership of Associates Corporation, its financial services sector. This subsidiary contributed net income of $231 million in 1985 on revenues of $1.4 billion; thus, its consumer and commercial lending supplied some 45 percent of the parent's total revenues and an even higher percentage of profits. Associates Corporation has also become active in credit cards, with $800 million in outstandings. It owns Associates National Bank and Heritage Federal Savings and Loan Association, both in California, which supplement the 500 Associates offices in forty-six states.[71]

ITT Corporation (electronics, telecommunications, and consumer products) owns ITT Financial Corporation (630 consumer loan offices in thirty-four states and the Caribbean), ITT Industrial Credit Company (commercial loans, asset-based lending, and equipment financing), and the Hartford Insurance Group. The latter writes life, accident and health, and property-casualty policies and has 10,000 U.S. agents, plus 2,800 outside the country. These subsidiaries' net income of $405 million for 1983 represented 60 percent of ITT's consolidated profit of $675 million.[72]

Control Data Corporation, a multinational computer company, acquired Commercial Credit Company in 1968 as a means of providing a wide range of financial services to consumers and businesses. Commercial Credit offers a wide range of loans to businesses (asset-based lending, equipment and vehicle financing and leasing, and construction loans for real estate); provides consumers with mortgage loans, Visa and MasterCard, and personal loans; and, through an international banking subsidiary, arranges Eurodollar loans for governments, banks, corporations, and utilities. It is also active in the credit, life, health, and property-casualty insurance fields.

Commercial Credit operates 256 deposit-taking offices in sixteen states. These offer NOW, IRA, and savings accounts and MMDAs and CDs. The company also owns four S&Ls and the First National Bank of Wilmington, Delaware. At year-end 1983 these institutions held $1.5 billion in deposits.[73]

Insurance Companies

Insurers—in particular, those involved primarily in providing various types of life insurance—have traditionally been mortgage lenders. In October 1985, life insurance companies held a total of $166 billion in mortgages,[74] and in 1982 the fifteen largest life insurance companies reported holdings of $88 billion in commercial mortgages, while the fifteen largest bank holding companies' holdings were only $25.8 billion.[75]

Since then, the insurance companies—possibly seeking to diversify to offset their substantial underwriting losses in the property and casualty field—have begun to offer a far wider range of financial services and as a group have therefore become important competitors for the banks. Mortgage banking, consumer finance, mutual funds, brokerage services, and cash management have become part of the total package they can offer to the public.

The Prudential Insurance Company, through its 1981 acquisition of the former Bache group, now combines a complete range of insurance with a full spectrum of brokerage services. Cross-selling, achieved by having insurance agents and brokerage account executives join forces in Prudential-Bache, generated over $2 million in investment commissions in 1983. Investment banking and cash management, and commercial loans and leases, are also offered, and the Capital City Bank (Hapeville, Georgia) has become another Prudential subsidiary, offering federally insured time deposits and MMDAs.[76]

The Colonial Penn Group, Inc. (Colonial Penn) is a diversified firm in the field of financial services, with 1.5 million customers and total assets of $1 billion. It considers itself the largest financial services direct-response marketing company in the United States. Most of its accounts are sold, delivered, and serviced by mail or telephone. In 1985 it acquired the Bay Loan and Investment Bank, which does not offer demand deposits and immediately conducted a nationwide campaign in which 400,000 circulars were mailed to consumers, featuring the bank's CDs. Colonial Penn's management has announced the objective of serving consumers throughout the country by accepting their deposits and using them for a variety of loan products and investments.[77]

John Hancock Mutual Life Insurance Company, the nation's sixth-largest insurer, has estimated that over 3 million households in the United States have at least one of its products (life and property-casualty insurance, stock brokerage, investment management, and realty services). In 1985 John Hancock stated its corporate objective: to become a full financial services company; to do this, it acquired a bank in North Hampton, New Hampshire, and announced plans to telemarket the bank's service to policyholders.[78]

The Travelers Corporation subsidiary, First Financial Services, completed arrangements in 1984 with Landmark Bancshares Corporation, a St. Louis–based bank holding company. This is another example of the linkage between an insurer and a bank in the business of financial planning and related services. The combination of the two was announced by Travelers (one of the nation's largest insurers) as part of its strategic plan to become a wholesaler of products and services in the financial field, thereby adding to its existing consumer base. The marketing by the joint venturers will involve a wide range of investment, credit, and insurance products; access to tax, financial, and legal experts; discount brokerage and bond sales; estate planning; and comprehensive financial planning for affluent customers.[79]

Metropolitan Life Insurance Company has entered into a joint marketing agreement with Society Corporation (Cleveland). Under this agreement Metropolitan policyholders (of whom there are 500,000 in Ohio) will be contacted by direct mail and offered a variety of credit card features and interest rates.[80]

Aetna Life and Casualty Company, in addition to its full line of property-casualty, life, health, and pension products, also owns one of the five largest merchant banks in Great Britain. Among its other noninsurance subsidiaries are firms in the fields of real estate development, energy-related services, business communications, money management, and mutual funds.[81]

Brokerage Firms

In their 1986 study of the financial services industry, two FDIC analysts noted that

> The banking industry's role in U.S. financial markets has declined so substantially that the industry most certainly will continue to seek broader authority to more effectively (and more efficiently) compete. . . . That effort may well intensify in light of the continuing decline in their role in recent years.[82]

That decline is clearly the result of the creation of many new hybrids—for example, the so-called financial supermarkets, which combine entire groups of financial services and offer them on a nationwide basis.

Merrill Lynch serves as the ideal prototype of these hybrids. With the exceptions of domestic commercial banking (although it is closely tied to Bank One in Columbus, Ohio) and S&L ownership, Merrill Lynch is active in every aspect of the financial services industry—so much so that the then Chairman of Bank of America commented in 1981 that "We've already got the nationwide banking of the future. It's called Merrill Lynch."[83] Through various subsidiaries, it provides a complete range of brokerage, real estate, insurance, mortgage banking, Eurobond and securities underwriting, money management, and commercial paper services, and its entry into commercial lending was cited earlier in this text.[84] It operates about 800 offices throughout the country and has 5 million clients.

Merrill Lynch's introduction of the Cash Management Account (CMA) in 1977 sent shock waves throughout the banking world by offering the client an integration of financial services that banks could not match. The CMA client has access to a Visa card and check-writing privileges through Bank One, plus overnight investments of excess funds at market rates and complete loan and overdraft privileges. By year-end 1983 there were over 1 million personal and ten thousand business holders of CMAs.[85]

The E.F. Hutton Group, even after the sale of the credit company to Chrysler Financial, remains an active force in the financial services industry. Its 350 domestic and 15 international offices serve over 1 million customers, and in addition to its securities- and investment-related activities, it provides insurance products and financing through various subsidiaries.

The Dreyfus Corporation's acquisition of the Lincoln State Bank in East Orange, New Jersey, in 1982, sparked much of the controversy over nonbank banks. Until that time, Dreyfus had been an investment firm, widely known for its various mutual funds. Through the acquisition, it became the first firm in the securities industry actually to enter the arena of commercial banking, over the opposition of the then Chairman of the Federal Reserve, Paul Volcker.[86] By stripping the bank of its commercial loan portfolio, Dreyfus qualified it as a nonbank bank and renamed it the Dreyfus Consumer Bank. It offers all banking services except commercial loans.[87]

Retailers

In retrospect, the entry of brokerage firms and insurers into diversified areas of financial services might reasonably have been predicted by commercial bankers because of the parallels between the operations of all three types of organizations. Less predictable, however, were the inroads that the largest retailers in the United States made in similar areas, in increasing numbers and with growing impact.

In some instances, these retailers have merely made space in their store locations available to ATM users, and in others they have begun the process of selling a limited range of financial services through the store locations in partnership with local banks. However, the most significant situations are those in which major retailers have become the direct providers of services to consumers, so the basic nature of their business has changed dramatically.

The Kroger grocery chain exemplifies the first-named category. Like several of its competitors who were identified earlier during the discussion of consumer banking (chapter 6), Kroger has placed bank ATMs in twenty-one of its mid-South stores and allowed banks to establish minibranches in fifty-nine Georgia locations. As a result, "bank products become just more items on a grocery shelf for customers."[88]

The K Mart Corporation has taken the additional step of making the financial services of its subsidiary, K Mart Insurance Services, Inc., available to customers in its stores and, more recently, of opening so-called financial kiosks in conjunction with Metropolitan Federal Bank (Fargo, North Dakota). In 1984 it established insurance centers in its Texas and Florida stores and began offering savings accounts, on a test basis, through Standard Federal S&L in three Florida locations.[89] In 1985 K Mart expanded on this plan, reaching agreements to offer real estate brokerage, mortgage, and consumer financing at thirty-one stores and, in San Diego, to offer savings accounts through a California S&L.[90] In 1986, the kiosks were introduced in the Twin Cities area, providing clients with a personal financial counselor, located near an ATM.[91] Each of these annual increments added to a base established in 1974, when K Mart first began offering its subsidiary's insurance to customers in its Dallas–Fort Worth stores. There are some 2,000 K Mart stores in various parts of the country that in time could become mini–financial centers.

In 1974, a member of the Board of Governors of the Federal Reserve posed the rhetorical question, "Once a man can cash a check at a local supermarket, what does he need a branch for?"[92] In 1986, his question has even greater relevance.

The successful entrants into the New World of the financial services industry must meet the needs of consumers in the New World of American society. What are the characteristics of these consumers? As a group, they are better educated, far more sophisticated in financial matters, and more aware of opportunities for yield on their investable funds—of which they typically have more—than their predecessors. In many cases they represent two-income households, making convenience and maximum use of leisure time extremely important to them.

Those providers of financial services who display the greatest ability to satisfy all these demands and needs in the right places, at the right time, at the right price, while requiring the least effort on the part of the users, will reap the rewards. Which entrants have those qualifications?

Commercial banks are constrained by geographic and product limitations. Thrift institutions, while less restricted, have not fully developed the capability to offer a range of deposit, loan, brokerage, debit/credit card, and insurance services in every part of the country, and most of them lack the expertise and financial resources to make the attempt.

The industrial giants and the leaders in the finance company and brokerage categories have no such limitations, and they have steadily assumed a greater share of the consumer market. The firms cited in this chapter have accelerated their competitive thrust and will continue to do so.

There remains one group. Its two major representatives, to an even greater degree than the firms already analyzed, are in a position to become major competitors of the banks in all the service areas. Indeed, to some extent they have already achieved that status.

J.C. Penney Company and *Sears, Roebuck and Company* already meet all the criteria for ongoing success in every aspect of the financial services industry. No commercial bank has the comparable foundations on which to build, a comparable network already in place, a comparable track record in dealing with millions of customers, or the comparable ability to offer a multitude of integrated products in every part of the country.

The consumer today looks for one-stop financial shopping.[93] Until and unless drastic changes are legally permitted in the commercial banking system, the two largest U.S. retailers can be expected to capitalize on their opportunities and effect an even greater erosion of the banks' market share. The bankers who persist in minimizing this possibility do so at their peril and ignore the clearly stated objectives of their rivals.

J.C. Penney Company

In 1964, J.C. Penney formed a Financial Corporation subsidiary to finance retail sales. Subsequently, J.C. Penney Realty and J.C. Penney Financial Services were created. The latter offered life, health, homeowners, and automobile insurance, and in 1983 it acquired the First National Bank of Harrington, Delaware. J.C. Penney Systems Services was established in 1982 to offer nationwide electronic data processing for credit card transactions and quickly secured two major oil companies as clients.[94] J.C. Penney Credit Services, offering lock box processing and ancillary functions, was formed in 1985.

Also in 1985, J.C. Penney entered into a joint venture with Security Pacific Corporation (holding company for Security Pacific National Bank). This venture allowed applicants for personal, mortgage, or auto loans to use

J.C. Penney stores in a test area in California as the originating points for their credit requests. The company conducted an advance solicitation by direct mail to J.C. Penney cardholders in that state.[95]

In November 1985, Executive Vice-President Thomas J. Lyons of the parent company outlined the scope of its activities and the ways in which it can interface with consumers:

> J.C. Penney has over 30 million of its proprietary credit cards in use; it processes some 180 million transactions per year and mails 16 million card statements per month.
>
> The insurance subsidiaries generated over $240 million in 1984 premiums from over 1 million policyholders.
>
> There are 2,000 J.C. Penney store locations in 50 states and Puerto Rico, with more space in suburban shopping malls than any other retailer.
>
> The financial services centers that J.C. Penney has established in partnership with a bank and a savings and loan association have already identified patterns of consumer behavior and have confirmed that there is a preference for financial services that are all available in the same physical environment.
>
> The company's nationwide electronic network, capability in data processing, and existing systems for handling remittances and providing credit card authorizations and settlement equip it to meet the needs of corporations and banks, in addition to serving consumers.
>
> Direct-marketing programs were implemented in 1985, inviting Penney policyholders and cardholders in an Arizona test area to discuss CD and mutual funds needs with their insurance representatives.[96]

To supplement these comments, 1983 reports disclose net income from Penney financial services of $69 million, or 15 percent of the company's consolidated total profits; in that year, consumer receivables were $5.5 billion.[97] If several of the nation's large supermarket chains have the potential to become the financial services centers of the future, how much greater—given its established data base of cardholders, its ownership of a bank, its ties to a thrift, its nationwide locations, its electronic network, and its processing capabilities—is the potential of J.C. Penney?

Sears, Roebuck and Company

Among his many commentaries on financial topics, Paul Nadler has characterized commercial bankers as individuals who would "never do something for the first time."[98] Although his remark may appear unduly harsh, it reflects, at least to some degree, a perception in the public mind of the traditionalism, lack of innovativeness, and parochialism that many bankers have displayed over the years in their management roles. A corollary of those traits may also be an unwillingness to accept the realities of the financial services industry today by recognizing the shrinkage in the banks' market share, the number of competitors, and their resources, capabilities, and objectives. The bankers' posture, over the course of many years vis-à-vis Sears, Roebuck illustrates this.

In 1972 Sears's income from its financial services alone was greater than that of any one bank or bank holding company, and its consumer receivables (resulting from use of Sears cards) at that time could easily stand comparison with the $5.3 billion then outstanding on all bank credit cards; yet Sears was not considered a competitor.[99] By 1980, Sears's financial services generated $477 million in net income, or 77 percent of the annual reported Sears profits of $610 million. Yet a 1983 survey reported that

> In general, community bankers in cities where in-store centers have opened can't imagine ever feeling seriously threatened by Sears—no matter how numerous nor generally accepted such centers might become.[100]

By year-end 1984, Sears had established 302 financial centers offering an integrated package of insurance, brokerage, and real estate services and additional enhancements, in its key stores in forty-two states. In that year, these financial services generated a net income of $704 million, or 48.2 percent of the world's largest retailer's consolidated net of $1.46 billion.[101] In early 1985, however, representatives of three major banks in Chicago, Arizona, and Colorado minimized the importance of Sears as a competitor and downgraded it as a threat.[102]

Chapter 6 mentioned Sears's introduction of the Discover card and its acquisition of a Delaware bank (followed by the 1985 takeover, through Sears's Dean Witter subsidiary, of the Hurley State Bank of Hurley, South Dakota[103]) as evidence of the steps being taken to meet the overall corporate objective. The Hurley acquisition is noteworthy because Dean Witter, which is not a bank holding company, could effect it with impunity, and the bank, as a state-chartered nonmember, is not subject to regulation or examination by the Federal Reserve.

Those who are unaware of Sears's business goals need only refer to the public statements of its top management. In 1985 Robert E. Wood, Vice-President for Corporate Planning and overseer of all Sears financial service centers, restated the objective: "To offer Sears customers nation-wide retail financial services, including deposit-taking and lending."[104] Edward Telling, former Chairman and President of Sears, had frequently used similar language in publicly outlining the company's game plan:

> Our goal is to become the largest consumer-oriented financial service entity. . . .[105]

> Someday every Sears outlet will be a bank, making second mortgages, selling to consumers in their homes via electronic buy-and-bank services, and more. . . .[106]
>
> Eventually all outlets in the Sears family of companies can have the capacity to accept and disburse funds. . . . [107]

The banker who ignores these statements and fails to assess the possibility that Sears will be able to meet its objectives may suddenly experience a rude awakening. This is especially true if he or she represents a relatively small community bank in an area now being served by a Sears financial service center—for example, in a local shopping mall.

Granted, the expertise that has made Sears the world's largest retailer may not prove to be the expertise needed to integrate and manage a group of diverse subsidiaries so that they become the profitable financial supermarkets of the future. Granted, consumers may not respond in sufficiently large numbers to Sears's advertising. The convenience factor may be overemphasized; individuals may not be willing to transact their financial affairs in a Sears store simply because they are visiting it to buy clothing, furniture, or appliances. They may prefer to continue with traditional banking, thereby retaining the benefits of personal, direct contact with the individual bankers who have served the community for many years.

Nevertheless, an analysis of Sears's past, present, and potential future leads to a realistic approach. The company, with its 1984 assets of almost $60 billion, has the resources to make the objectives possible, has the components for future success in place, and has shown a willingness to make large near-term commitments and sacrifices for the sake of future long-term profits.

For example, in 1986 the expenses connected with launching and promoting the Discover card were estimated at $115 million after taxes. Sears accepted that cost.[108] The 1984 decision to expand the Dean Witter firm by adding 1,000 brokers to provide better and broader customer service caused a one-time loss of $33 million. Sears found that loss acceptable.[109]

The Sears network of over 800 store locations is less than half the size of the K Mart chain. Its consumer receivables are only a fraction of those reported by GMAC. It lacks a global banking presence and range of international consumer services. It is not engaged in leasing or lease financing, as is General Electric Credit. In many respects, however, Sears is better equipped to become the consumer bank's more serious—and successful—competitor than any of the companies cited in this chapter. The whole, in effect, can be greater than the sum of its parts. What components in the relatively new Sears corporate structure create the synergy to justify that statement? What is Sears, Roebuck and Company today?

Sears began offering retail credit in 1911. At year-end 1983 it reported consumer receivables of $13.8 billion, and during that same year its credit card volume of $14.1 billion exceeded the combined volumes of Bank of America ($6.2 billion) and Citicorp ($5.6 billion).[110]

Allstate Insurance, the Sears subsidiary established in 1931, has 3,250 sales locations. Its activities in homeowners, life, and automobile insurance accounted for 23.2 percent of total Sears revenue for 1984.[111]

Nearly one-half of the 83 million households in the United States have some form of business relationship with Sears in the form of a credit card, Allstate policy, or record of having purchased merchandise through the Sears catalogue. Approximately 26 million Sears cards are in active use.[112]

The 1981 acquisitions of Dean Witter (formerly Dean Witter Reynolds, Inc.) and Coldwell Banker at a total cost of $812 million have made Sears a major force in the fields of real estate finance, securities trading, and investment management. These two entities have over 1,300 local sales offices and are key components in the new Sears financial service centers.

Allstate Insurance provides insurance coverage on Dean Witter's active assets and regular brokerage accounts. The various savings instruments offered by the Sears Savings Bank (a former California S&L with over 100 branches and $5.3 billion in assets[113]) are available through Dean Witter brokers and, more recently, through the financial service centers.

In 1984 Sears Mortgage Securities Company, another subsidiary, introduced the first privately packaged, publicly offered securities backed by adjustable-rate mortgages. The offering was aimed initially at institutional investors and required a minimum purchase of $1 million; however, a Sears spokesman indicated that additional offerings could be marketed to the individual investor.[114]

The company has established the Sears Communications Network to sell various communications services, including transmission of computer data. Through Sears's affiliation with MCI Communications (a strong competitor of AT&T), MCI customers can charge long-distance calls to their Sears bill. Sears has also begun a joint venture with IBM and CBS to provide home information services that will combine banking, bill paying, and shopping.[115] The nationwide communications networks will also link the ATMs in Sears stores and provide customers with a so-called credit account that can be used to make payments for home mortgage loans, insurance premiums, or card outstandings.[116]

The Discover cardholder can obtain a line of credit with participating retailers, deposit funds into an account at a Sears financial institution, and obtain instant cash from participating ATMs, many of which will be in Sears stores.

The possibilities for synergy among all the Sears entities are virtually limitless. Completely integrated financial handling through Sears may not have arrived in 1986, but there can be no doubt that the company is doing everything possible toward that goal. Sears spokesman Robert M. Gardiner has said:

> We intend to establish long-term relationships with the 36 million American households who shop at Sears and to serve those families' changing needs. . . . We want them to look first to Sears when a need for financial, banking, insurance, or real estate services arises.[117]

No other financial conglomerate has the potential to meet such an ambitious objective.

Consider the hypothetical example of a family that moves from one part of the country to another. Coldwell Banker sells the former house, helps the family find a new one, and arranges the mortgage financing through Sears Savings Bank. Allstate provides every category of insurance for the family home, car, and members. CDs and money-market accounts at Sears Savings Bank are arranged through Dean Witter, which also handles all the family's retirement accounts and investments and serves as the contact if a home equity loan is needed. The Discover card provides access to merchants and services throughout the country and helps the family obtain instant cash through ATMs. Perhaps most important, virtually all these transactions can take place in the financial service centers in Sears stores while the family is doing its shopping. If there is a utopian combination of convenience, accessibility in every part of the country, range of services, and long-standing reputation for quality and dependability, Sears has that combination, and no commercial bank, large or small, can match it.[118]

During his tenure as Chairman of Citicorp, Walter Wriston saw the Sears potential and complained that the company was free to enter the banking business, while Citibank, because of federal and state regulations, was not able to be fully competitive. At the same time, Paul Volcker stated bluntly, "We don't want Sears, Roebuck in the banking business."[119] In retrospect, it appears that Walter Wriston's comment was entirely valid then and is even more valid now, while Paul Volcker's statement missed a most significant point. Sears at that time was already in the banking business; it certainly is now, and will continue to be, and it presents perhaps the most formidable single challenge to banks in the evolving financial services industry.

Summary

Those bankers who today look back wistfully over their shoulders and long for the good old days deserve at least an ounce of sympathy from the public, along with the many pounds of criticism to which they may be subjected. It is only natural that the bankers yearn for a return to the era when they were the exclusive providers of services connected with the payments function, and their nostalgia reflects a time when they held the largest market share in all financial services.

Any criticisms the bankers face because of their failure to recognize the potential of the huge consumer market and their inertia in trying to meet its needs and demands must be tempered by a realization of the limitations that regulatory agencies have placed on their geographic expansion and lines of business. It was never legally possible for banks to do everything their competitors now do throughout the country, even had they wished to do so.

It remains true, however, that in many cases the banks could have done much to preserve their competitive position. They could, for example, have become much more active in the areas of home mortgage, personal, and automobile loans and in developing integrated financial planning for the affluent individuals whom they now so avidly cultivate. They might have, at a much earlier time, recognized the need for and value of advertising the availability of their permitted services and therefore formed the integrated marketing units on which so many of them have come to depend (in 1971, commercial banks spent ten times as much on all types of advertising as in 1950[120]). The banks' strategies for expanding their retail banking systems could have been developed sooner. The question is whether any or all of these actions would have served to inhibit the growth of the nonbank companies whose activities this chapter has detailed.

Whether one blames the banks for their lack of foresight, is completely sympathetic to them because of the constraints that inhibit them but that do not affect their competitors, or feels an ambivalence in the overall situation, one cannot ignore the hard facts. The former captive finance companies of many industrial giants have become giants in their own right and are offering services that bear no relation to sales of their parent companies' products. They and the major retailers, both by capitalizing on their inherent advantages and, in several cases, by buying financial institutions, have also become the nationwide purveyors of comprehensive packages of consumer services. Today's consumers, far more concerned about convenience and more aware of opportunities and yields than their predecessors, have thus turned to the nonbank entities and thrift institutions in steadily growing numbers.[121]

None of the foregoing should be construed as a gloom-and-doom scenario for the entire commercial banking industry. Indeed, for the largest money-center banks, in terms of 1986 dollars of profit, it may be among the best of times. Despite the global debt crisis, the problems created by their loan portfolios, and the losses they have incurred in expanding their card business, the commercial banks not only have survived but also have been able to show improved earnings.

For the thousands of much smaller, community-oriented banks, however, it may be among the worst of times. More than their large counterparts, they are in a position to dispute the 1963 Supreme Court decision. They know that they are not part of a unique line of commerce and that what they are legally unable to do, Sears, Merrill Lynch, General Electric Credit, Prudential, and GMAC are doing and will continue to do.

The sheer size of the money-center giants makes them far less vulnerable than the small community institutions, especially as regards competition from the thrift institutions. Many small banks are experiencing difficulties simply because the S&Ls have expanded aggressively in recent years, offering both consumer and commercial loans at lower rates and bidding at higher rates for deposits. In some cases, the weaker thrift institutions have emphasized the latter course of action; that is, they have attempted to solve their problems by a form of growth based on deposit rates.

The small banks, which in many cases are primarily installment lenders and lack a broad base of corporate business, have also been the chief victims of the unrelenting pressure of the automakers' finance subsidiaries. It is literally impossible for the small institution to compete for auto loans with the GMACs, the Ford Credits, and the Chrysler Credits when the latter are offering financing terms at rates far lower than the small banks are paying for deposits.[122]

If real relief is to be granted to the banking industry so that the playing field becomes more level, only two alternatives readily suggest themselves. The first would take the form of direct Congressional action, forcing the nonbank entities to divest themselves of those products and services that might be considered closely related to the business of banking. This is not a viable alternative, however. Any proposal that Congress force the huge nonbank companies to give up the consumer activities they have worked so diligently, and expended such large sums, to build up would be rejected out-of-hand.

The second possibility would also require Congressional action, but in this case it would give the commercial banks greater latitude to compete more effectively—for example, by allowing them to cross state lines and/or to offer additional services. This added authority would be granted only to those banks that demonstrated a sound financial condition and adequate capital and that were not creating antitrust situations. Lacking this form of Congressional relief, the Fed might seek to ameliorate the current problem.

In 1986 there was some evidence that the Fed would adopt the latter course and that the courts would also be supportive of the banks' efforts. For example, in California the U.S. Court of Appeals for the Ninth Circuit ruled that banks could sell commingled funds for IRAs. The court decision effectively overcame objections from the Investment Company Institute, a mutual fund trade group.[123] During the same year, the Federal Reserve cleared the way for banks to sell shares of unit investment trusts and mutual funds through subsidiaries; again, this Fed ruling was made over the opposition of the securities industry.[124]

In addition, the Federal Reserve has gone on record with Congress by recommending that legislative action be taken to establish a new statutory definition of *bank, thrift institution,* and *powers for state-chartered banks.*[125] In 1985 the Board of Governors of the Fed approved six additional activities for bank holding companies, including tax preparation services performed in a nonfiduciary capacity, providing authorization services on credit cards, and servicing student loans.[126] While the effect of these additional authorities is minimal, the Fed's action represents a step in what the bankers believe to be the right direction.

Until such time as the commercial banks receive real freedom to compete more freely and effectively in the overall financial services industry, the comments made several years ago by Kenneth A. Randall, then Chairman of the FDIC, will continue to summarize the banks' problem:

> In our imperfect world, there is the branch that we may want to start but that branching laws will not permit, the banking market that we can't reach because it's just into the next state or county, . . . and the financial service that has not been approved by the Federal Reserve.[127]

Mr. Randall's comments apply to none of the nonbank companies.

Notes

1. Peter W. Bernstein, "Not-Quite-Banks May Be Good Business," *Fortune,* November 26, 1984, p. 151.
2. 374 U.S. 321 (1963).
3. Ibid.
4. For selected criticisms of the decision, see F. Jay Cummings, "Commercial Banking as a Line of Commerce," *Economic Review* (Federal Reserve Bank of Dallas), September 1982, p. 12.
5. Walter A. Varvel and Henry C. Wallich, "Evolution in Banking Competition," *Economic Review* (Federal Reserve Bank of Richmond), March–April 1981, p. 3.
6. Peter Merrill, in Eric Gelman, "How America Pays the Tab," *Newsweek,* January 7, 1985, p. 40.
7. Robert R. Douglass, "The Outlook for Nationwide Expansion," *The Bankers Magazine,* November–December 1984, p. 7.
8. Edward J. Frydl, "The Challenge of Financial Change," in Federal Reserve Bank of New York, *1985 Annual Report,* p. 17.
9. See Alan Gart, *Banks, Thrifts, and Insurance Companies* (Lexington, Mass.: Lexington Books, 1985), pp. 19–20.
10. Board of Governors, Federal Reserve System, *The Monetary Control Act of 1980* (Washington, D.C., June 1981), p. 1.
11. The *Federal Reserve Bulletin,* June 1980, pp. 444–453, quotes the detailed provisions of the act.
12. Charles P. Alexander, "A Big Brawl in Banking," *Time,* January 17, 1983, p. 34.
13. Christine Pavel and Harvey Rosenblum, "Financial Darwinism: Nonbanks—and Banks—Are Surviving," Working Papers, Staff Memorandum 1985-5 (Chicago: Federal Reserve Bank of Chicago), p. 5.

14. Harvey Rosenblum and Christine Pavel, "Banking Services in Transition: The Effects of Nonbank Competitors," in Richard C. Aspinwall and Robert A. Eisenbeis, eds., *Handook for Banking Strategy* (New York, John Wiley & Sons, 1985), p. 238.

15. Payment Systems, Inc., *The Affluent Market Fact Book,* in Donald Shoultz, "Financial Services Told to Heed Affluent Market's New Strength," *American Banker,* June 17, 1986, p. 20.

16. "The Financial Services Scene: An American Banker Scorecard," *American Banker,* January 4, 1985, pp. 10–11.

17. Christine Pavel and Harvey Rosenblum, "Banks and Nonbanks: The Horse Race Continues," *Economic Perspectives* (Federal Reserve Bank of Chicago), May/June 1985, p. 15.

18. Charles G. Daley, "Before the Courts," *American Banker,* February 11, 1986, p. 5.

19. *Board of Governors of the Federal Reserve System* v. *Dimension Financial Corp. et al.,* U.S. Supreme Court 84-1274.

20. Philip S. Corwin, "Nonbank Banks Endanger the Banking System," *ABA Banking Journal,* May 1986, p. 17.

21. *Federal Reserve Bulletin,* June 1986, p. A26.

22. Mark Basch, "The Market Heft of Local Change," *American Banker,* June 16, 1986, p. 13.

23. Mary L. King, *The Great American Banking Snafu* (Lexington, Mass.: Lexington Books, 1985), p. 137.

24. Mark J. Flannery, *An Economic Evaluation of Credit Unions in the United States* (Boston, Federal Reserve Bank of Boston, 1974), p. 7.

25. *Federal Reserve Bulletin,* June 1986, p. A26.

26. Pete Engardio, "Kinder-Care Will Mind Your Money, Too," *Business Week,* June 9, 1986, p. 34.

27. Laura Gross, "The American Express Banker," *American Banker,* June 11, 1986, p. 1.

28. Robert M. Garsson, "American Express Bank Restructures to Focus on Three Key Business Lines," *American Banker,* June 18, 1986, p. 13.

29. Laura Gross, "Beneficial Gets Approval to Start Bank," *American Banker,* May 19, 1983, p. 1. See also M.W. Caspersen, "Whither the Finance Company in a Dynamic Environment," *American Banker,* May 6, 1982, p. 7.

30. L. Michael Cacace, "Beneficial Leads Finance Companies in Second Mortgage Loans," *American Banker,* June 13, 1986, p. 1.

31. Michael Wines, "The Financial Supermarket Is Here," *National Journal,* November 21, 1981, p. 2059.

32. Caspersen, op. cit.

33. Pavel and Rosenblum, "Financial Darwinism," p. 36.

34. "36th Annual Survey of the Finance Company Industry," *American Banker,* June 13, 1986, p. 15.

35. Robert A. Bennett, "Banks and Retailers Report High Losses on Consumer Loans," *The New York Times,* February 13, 1981, p. D1.

36. "36th Annual Survey of the Finance Company Industry."

37. Jon C. Poppen, "Demystifying the Nonbank Financial Supermarket," *Bank Administration,* April 1985, pp. 58–60.

38. Pavel and Rosenblum, "Financial Darwinism," p. 5.

39. Alex Taylor III, "Thin Profits in a Lean, Mean Year," *Fortune,* April 28, 1986, pp. 182–183.

40. Paul A. Eisenstein, "Here Come the Auto Companies," *United States Banker,* March 1986, p. 32.

41. "36th Annual Survey of the Finance Company Industry."

42. Beth McGoldrick, "The Carmakers that Would Be Bankers," *Institutional Investor,* February 1986, p. 176.

43. "1985 Performance of Top U.S. Banking Companies," *American Banker,* June 20, 1986, pp. 22–24.

44. Robert M. Garsson, "Big 3 Automakers' Lending Units Post Record Earnings for '85," *American Banker,* February 18, 1986, p. 31.

45. McGoldrick, op. cit., p. 176.

46. Pavel and Rosenblum, "Financial Darwinism," p. 27. The Chase figures are for domestic loans only.

47. Robert M. Garsson, "GMAC Takes Giant Steps into Business of Banks," *American Banker,* December 27, 1985, p. 16.

48. Ibid., p. 15.

49. Robert M. Garsson, "Auto Makers Veer into Financial Services Traffic," *American Banker,* December 26, 1985, p. 1.

50. Ibid.

51. Rosenblum and Pavel, op. cit., p. 222.

52. "36th Annual Survey of the Finance Company Industry."

53. Garsson, "Big 3 Automakers' Lending Units," p. 31.

54. Pavel and Rosenblum, "Financial Darwinism," p. 24.

55. Mark Basch, "Ford Motor Company Agrees to Buy 1st Nationwide," *American Banker,* August 2, 1985, p. 1.

56. Details of the consolidation and acquisition can be found in Lydia Chavez, "National Steel's Financial Arm," *The New York Times,* January 4, 1982, p. D1; Thomas Hayes, "First Nationwide: A New Era," *The New York Times,* November 19, 1981, p. D1; and Subrata Chakravarty, "Blast Furnace Banker," *Forbes,* October 26, 1981, p. 95.

57. In L. Michael Cacace, "Automakers Carve Out Bigger Pieces of Financial Services Pie," *American Banker,* June 13, 1986, p. 18.

58. Eisenstein, op. cit., pp. 34–35.

59. Stephen C. Hansen, "Why Ford Shouldn't Be Your Banker," *The New York Times,* March 2, 1986, p. F2.

60. "36th Annual Survey of the Financial Services Industry," p. 14.

61. McGoldrick, op. cit., p. 176.

62. Eisenstein, op. cit., p. 38; and ibid., pp. 176–177.

63. Garsson, "Auto Makers Veer into Financial Services Traffic."

64. Pavel and Rosenblum, "Financial Darwinism," pp. 19–20.

65. Marilyn A. Harris, "Can Jack Welch Reinvent GE?," *Business Week,* June 30, 1986, p. 65.

66. Andrew Albert and Robert M. Garsson, "General Electric Emerges as a Financial Power," *American Banker,* April 28, 1986, p. 3.

67. Gail Landis, in Robert M. Garsson, "Shrewd Management of Risk Makes GE Credit the Envy of Competitors," *American Banker,* July 8, 1985, p. 1.

68. General Electric Credit Corporation, *1984 Annual Report,* p. 2.

69. Albert and Garsson, op. cit.

70. Robert A. Bennett, "The Orderly World of Martin Davis," *The New York Times,* February 23, 1986, p. F8.

71. Ibid.

72. Pavel and Rosenblum, "Financial Darwinism," pp. 23–24.

73. Pavel and Rosenblum, "Financial Darwinism," p. 22.

74. *Federal Reserve Bulletin,* March 1986, p. A26.

75. Rosenblum and Pavel, op. cit., p. 231.

76. Pavel and Rosenblum, "Financial Darwinism," p. 50.

77. Laura Gross, "Colonial Penn Unveils National Mail-Order Financial Services," *American Banker,* October 21, 1985, p. 8.

78. Lynn Brenner, "John Hancock Prepares for Leap into Banking," *American Banker,* December 20, 1985, p. 1.

79. Lynn Brenner, "Travelers Sells Bank Financial Planning Wares," *American Banker,* December 24, 1984, p. 1.

80. Michael Weinstein, "Society Corp. to Issue Credit Cards to Clients of Metropolitan Life," *American Banker,* July 1, 1986, p. 23.

81. Pavel and Rosenblum, "Financial Darwinism," pp. 47–48.

82. Alan S. McCall and Victor L. Saulsbury, "Perspective on Banks' Declining Market Share," *American Banker,* June 26, 1986, p. 4.

83. In "The Savings Revolution," *Time,* June 8, 1981, p. 59.

84. Carl J. Loomis, "The Fight for Financial Turf," *Fortune,* December 28, 1981, p. 57.

85. Pavel and Rosenblum, "Financial Darwinism," pp. 34–35.

86. Lisa J. McCue, "Volcker Hits Loophole Letting Commercial Firms Own Banks," *American Banker,* December 2, 1982, p. 1.

87. Robert A. Bennett, "Dreyfus Buys Bank in New Jersey," *The New York Times,* December 28, 1982, p. D1.

88. "Kroger to Put Bank Branches in Stores," *American Banker,* May 28, 1985, p. 8.

89. "Financial Services at K Mart," *The New York Times,* January 13, 1984, p. D2.

90. "K Mart to Provide Financial Services," *The New York Times,* January 22, 1985, p. D4.

91. "Twin Cities K Marts to Host Metropolitan Financial Kiosks," *American Banker,* June 17, 1986, p. 20.

92. In Martin Mayer, *The Bankers* (New York, David McKay Company, 1974), p. 180.

93. Veronica Bennett, "Consumer Demand for Product Deregulation," *Economic Review* (Federal Reserve Bank of Atlanta), May 1984, pp. 28–40.

94. Pavel and Rosenblum, "Financial Darwinism," p. 9.

95. Laura Gross, "Penney Probes Financial Services," *American Banker,* November 14, 1985, p. 1.

96. In "J.C. Penney's View of the Financial Marketplace," *American Banker,* February 6, 1986, p. 4.

97. Pavel and Rosenblum, "Financial Darwinism," pp. 12 and 16.

98. In Herbert V. Prochnow and Herbert V. Prochnow, Jr., eds. *The Changing World of Banking* (New York, Harper & Row, 1974), p. 381.

99. Rosenblum and Pavel, op. cit., p. 207.

100. In "The Only Thing We Have to Fear Is Sears Itself," *ABA Banking Journal,* October 1983, pp. 58–60.

101. Steven Greenhouse, "Sears: A Giant Grows Bigger," *The New York Times,* May 2, 1985, p. D1.

102. "Bankers Say Sears Causes Little or No Pain," *ABA Banking Journal,* April 1985, p. 70.

103. Richard Ringer, "Dean Witter Buys Dakota Bank to Aid Sears Card," *American Banker,* May 20, 1985, p. 3.

104. Steve Cocheo, "How Sears Mixes Finance, Retailing," *ABA Banking Journal,* April 1985, p. 51.

105. In Winston Williams, "A Money Fund Next for Sears," *The New York Times,* September 2, 1981, p. D1.

106. In Laura Gross, "Sears Outlets Cashing Checks," *American Banker,* June 17, 1982, p. 1.

107. In John Morris, "Sears Promises to Have a Bank at Every Outlet," *American Banker,* February 26, 1982, p. 1.

108. John Morris, "Sears Plans National Rollout of Discover Card this Month," *American Banker,* January 8, 1986, p. 1.

109. Greenhouse, op. cit., p. D12.

110. Pavel and Rosenblum, "Financial Darwinism," p. 15.

111. Greenhouse, op. cit.

112. Jonathan Hakim, "A New Awakening," *The Economist,* March 24, 1984, p. 10.

113. Molly Hooper, "Sears Thrift Offers Low-Cost Checking," *American Banker,* November 2, 1984, pp. 56–57.

114. David LaGesse, "Sears Mortgage Subsidiary Marketing Securities Backed by ARMs," *American Banker,* December 26, 1984, p. 3.

115. John S. DeMott, "Sears' Sizzling New Vitality," *Time,* August 20, 1984, p. 86.

116. Gart, op. cit., pp. 56–57.

117. In Lisabeth C. Weiner, "Sears Positioned for Growth," *American Banker,* April 26, 1984, p. 1.

118. Philip T. Sudo, "Sears: A Boon to Competitors?," *American Banker,* November 1, 1984, p. 3; and Lesta S. Cordil, "New Look in Financial Services," *White Plains Reporter-Dispatch,* March 25, 1984, p. J1.

119. In DeMott, op. cit., p. 85.

120. "Now Banks Are Turning to the Hard Sell," *Business Week,* June 24, 1972, p. 78.

121, Pavel and Rosenblum, "Banks and Nonbanks," pp. 3–5.

122. Sanford Rose, "Random Thoughts," *American Banker,* July 15, 1986, p. 4.

123. Dennis P. O'Connell, "Fed and Appeals Court Answer Challenges to New Bank Powers," *American Banker,* July 14, 1986, p. 9.

124. Ibid.

125. Board of Governors of the Federal Reserve System, *72nd Annual Report* (1985), p. 158.

126. Ibid., p. 181.

127. In Prochnow and Prochnow, eds., op. cit., p. 324.

10
The New World of Nonbank Banks

During 1984, a commercial message on television stations in New York City asked the public to distinguish carefully among the types of financial institutions and seek "real bankers," only at "real banks." The fact that the "real banks" felt this commercial was necessary is testimony to their concern over the nonbank banks that have begun to proliferate in the 1980s.

As mentioned in chapter 9, these hybrid institutions, also known as *consumer* or *limited-service* banks, have created controversy and litigation and, less important, complaints from those who dislike the nomenclature. The continued existence of nonbank banks establishes them as competitors, not only for local commercial banks but also for those retailers, securities firms, insurers, and finance companies that are vying for retail business.

There is an important distinction between the nonbank banks that have been acquired or formed by companies outside the banking industry and those that, if approved, would become part of existing bank holding companies (BHCs). In the former case, the purpose is merely to add a financial institution to the parent's overall structure to provide facilities for check processing, ATMs, credit/debit cards, or handling certain types of deposits. Since the parent is legally not a bank, and since its nonbank component does not meet the criteria of the Bank Holding Company Act, unrestricted geographic and/or product expansion is legally possible. When a BHC seeks approval for one or more nonbank banks, however, the objective and regulatory impact are quite different. For example, in 1984 approximately twenty BHCs, many of which were among the nation's largest, filed for such approval. In the vast majority of these cases, the requested nonbank banks were to cross state lines. Thus, the clear purpose was to gain an interstate presence, using the loophole in the Bank Holding Act as a means of escaping the restrictions of the McFadden Act.[1]

Historical Development

The nonbank bank movement, although the years following 1983 brought it to national prominence, had actually begun in 1981 with an application by Associates First Capital Corporation (a subsidiary of Gulf + Western) to acquire a small national bank in California and divest it of its commercial loan portfolio. The Comptroller of the Currency, whose approval was required because a national bank was involved, ratified the request in the absence of any objection or adverse ruling from the Fed and approved other similar applications during that year.

In February 1984 the Fed reluctantly approved the application of United States Trust Company (New York) to convert its trust subsidiary in Florida into a so-called consumer bank that would not make commercial loans.[2] That decision by the Federal Reserve opened the floodgates. During the remainder of 1984 the Office of the Comptroller of the Currency processed 332 requests for nonbank banks, of which 326 were submitted by BHCs.[3]

If the full competitive potential of a Sears, a Merrill Lynch, a General Electric Credit, or a Beneficial Corporation did not cause widespread consternation among bankers in the nation's small communities, the actions of the BHCs—especially when the large money-center banks were involved—quickly and surely did. At one point during 1984, the file of pending applications for nonbank banks included fifty-four for Florida alone, and bankers in that state protested vehemently.[4] Bank of Boston, in seeking approval for seven such institutions in Florida, conceded through a spokesperson that its applications might help to induce Congress to ease the restrictions on full-scale insterstate banking.

In other parts of the country at the same time, local bankers raised the spectre of potential Citibank, Bank of America, Mellon Bank, Security Pacific, and Chase Manhattan nonbank banks on every corner of their communities. The concept of a mass invasion of a town or city by the money-center giants aroused far more local opposition than the prospect of a Sears financial center.[5]

The Independent Bankers Association, representing over 7,500 smaller banks throughout the United States, joined with a trade group and a Florida bank in a 1984 lawsuit, seeking a court injunction against the Comptroller of the Currency. They requested that he be ordered to revoke all the preliminary approvals his Office had granted and that he be enjoined from approving any new applications for nonbank banks.[6] The lawsuit stemmed from the fact that the Comptroller had given preliminary approval (pending ratification by the Fed) for twenty-nine such nonbank banks to be opened across state lines by thirteen BHCs.

Because of the controversy and confusion surrounding the issue, it is relevant to examine the logic underlying both the litigation and the Comptroller's actions. The injunction was requested on the grounds that nonbank banks cannot be banks; therefore, a federal regulator of banking can neither sanction their existence nor have any jurisdiction over them. C. Todd Conover, Comptroller, did not address that specific question but justified his preliminary approvals on the grounds that the nonbank banks were "legal under existing law."[7] In a November 1984 decision, the Fed's Board of Governors used the same language to explain its approval (by a 5–2 vote) of five nonbank banks in Florida and Washington, D.C. The Board held that these institutions were "technically consistent with current law."[8]

While the Independent Bankers' lawsuit was pending, the Board of Governors, which had sought to broaden the legal definition of a bank and thereby halt the entire acquisition process, also extended indefinitely the timetable it had set for registration of nonbank banks, stating that

> This action is being taken in view of the continued uncertainty of congressional and judicial action regarding the bank definition. The extension will be effective until legal issues regarding the "bank" definition are resolved by Congress and the courts.[9]

Again, the thinking of the Board paralleled that of the Comptroller. In his remarks of December 19, 1984, Conover said his approval of 134 nonbank banks (most of which were owned by retailers, insurers, and securities firms) had been intended to persuade Congress to resolve the basic question—that is, the legal definition of a bank. He also took official cognizance of the fact that the Board of Governors had not yet ruled on 130 pending applications from BHCs for the formation of nonbank banks.[10]

One further development in 1984 added to the controversy. Also in December of that year, Great Western Financial Corporation, of Beverly Hills, California, a holding company for thrifts, sought approval for sixteen nonbank banks that would offer demand deposits but would not make commercial loans.[11]

The historical record makes it clear that 1985 developments, instead of resolving the problem, perpetuated it. The close of that year saw no change in Congressional inertia, in spite of the pressures exerted on legislators from various directions and the precedents contained in court decisions.

Early in 1985 a federal district court in Jacksonville, Florida, in responding to the 1984 petition of the Independent Bankers Association and others, ordered the Comptroller not to issue any final approvals for nonbank banks. The court agreed with the plaintiffs that such institutions, which it called "clearly an anomaly," should be authorized only through Congressional action and suggested that the Comptroller seek this action. The court made no mention of the Comptroller's 1984 rulings, which had been aimed at inducing Congress to provide the definitive answer.[12]

Industrial Banks

Any confusion among the public over the legal definition of a bank and the insured status of depositories was compounded by the existence in eighteen U.S. states of yet another hybrid financial institution, the so-called industrial bank, which is neither a bank nor a thrift. Industrial banks are chartered by the states and do not offer depositors any form of federal insurance. Their loan portfolios often contain high-risk credits on which interest of 20 percent or more may be collected. As a result, the investment certificates, or thrift certificates, they issue to customers normally have far higher yields than bank CDs. The risks inherent in dealing with industrial banks were brought to public attention on "60 Minutes," and in a recent three-year period the failures of thirteen such institutions resulted in losses of over $250 million to their depositors—who may have assumed that they were clients of an insured bank or thrift.[13] Although many industrial banks are owned by nonbank companies (e.g., Household International), several have been acquired or established by major BHCs (e.g., BankAmerica Corporation, Citicorp, Chemical New York Corporation, First Pennsylvania Corporation, and Manufacturers Hanover Corporation).[14] Since industrial banks restrict the categories of deposits they will accept, they can be categorized with all other nonbank banks.

The decision handed down by the federal district court early in 1985 was reaffirmed later that year, when the same court made it clear that the injunction preventing the Comptroller from giving final approval to nonbank banks applied to all cases and was not confined to Florida.[15] The court's feeling was that Congress, in adopting the Bank Holding Company Act with its definition of a bank, had never intended the Act to apply to institutions that dealt only in consumer banking.[16]

In hearings before a House Banking subcommittee in April 1985, Chairman Paul Volcker of the Federal Reserve Board called for Congressional action to close the "nonbank bank loophole"; at the same time, Representative St Germain spoke in support of that objective. As of that date, 382 applications for nonbank banks had been submitted, and 277 of these had received preliminary approval from the Comptroller.[17]

The Florida Decision

A key development in the entire chronology occurred in May 1985, when the U.S. Court of Appeals for the Eleventh Circuit overturned the 1984 decision of the Federal Reserve. The Fed had approved a request from United States Trust Company for the conversion of its Florida trust subsidiary into a nonbank bank. As noted earlier, that Fed ruling was made reluctantly; the two dissenting members of the Board of Governors noted that

> Although approval of this proposal presents a serious potential for undermining the policies of the [BHC] Act, the Board is constrained by the definition of bank in the Act to approve the [U.S. Trust] application.[18]

The Court of Appeals, in reversing the Fed ruling, held that the clear intention of Congress, through the BHC Act, had been to prohibit the creation of interstate deposit-taking networks without specific state authorization and that the Fed, therefore, should not have approved the original request. Later in 1985, the Supreme Court was asked to review the Court of Appeals decision; in view of that pending action by the nation's highest court, Congress took no action during the year to change the definition of a bank or to clarify the status of nonbank banks and their acquisition or formation by BHCs or nonbank companies.[19] At year-end 1985, the Fed Board of Governors noted that

> The framework for legislative action should include . . . new statutory definitions to clarify what is a bank . . . . New definitions of the terms "bank" and "thrift institution" are urgent to . . . establish clearly the competitive rules for the various segments of the financial service industry.[20]

The most important 1986 development regarding the question of nonbank banks took place in January, when the U.S. Supreme Court overturned a specific ruling of the Federal Reserve. In an 8–0 opinion (with Justice White abstaining), written by Chief Justice Warren Burger, the court held that the Fed had not acted "within its statutory authority in defining banks as it did."[21]

The Dimension Case

The litigation arose from an attempt in 1983 by Dimension Financial Corporation (at that time a subsidiary of Valley National Savings & Loan Association, Hutchinson, Kansas) to build a network of thirty-one limited-service banks in twenty-five states. Dimension, targeting the affluent market, intended to offer all banking services except commercial loans, and its application represented the most ambitious effort on record to create an interstate network of nonbank banks.[22] In its opinion, the Supreme Court cited Section 2(c) of the 1956 Bank Holding Company Act as amended—namely, the definition of a bank as "any institution which (1) accepts deposits that the depositor has a legal right to withdraw on demand, and (2) engages in the business of making commercial loans."[23]

In 1984 the Fed had ruled that nonbank banks "offering the functional equivalent of traditional banking services" would thereafter be regulated as banks. The Fed claimed that nonbank banks were circumventing the legal definition and its statutory restrictions by offering NOW accounts and/or dealing in commercial paper. Therefore, it amended Regulation Y so that institutions providing these services would, per se, fall under the definition.[24]

The Fed specifically attempted to bring NOW and similar types of accounts under the umbrella of demand deposits and also redefined the original description of a commercial loan. In the former instance, the Fed added certain key words that became the focal point of the eventual Supreme Court ruling:

> Deposits that the depositor has a legal right to withdraw on demand . . . means any deposit with transactional capability that, as a matter of practice, is payable on demand and that is withdrawable by check, draft, negotiable order of withdrawal, or other similar instrument.[25]

The term *commercial loans* was also redefined to mean

> Any loan other than a loan to an individual for personal, family, household, or charitable purposes, and includes the purchase of retail installment loans or commercial paper, certificates of deposit, bankers acceptances and similar money market instruments, the extension of broker call loans, and the deposit of interest-bearing funds.[26]

The Supreme Court upheld a prior decision of the U.S. Court of Appeals for the Tenth Circuit. The latter, in its original ruling against the Fed, had held that the Fed exceeded its authority when it made the foregoing amendments. Chief Justice Burger's opinion made the following point:

> The statute may be imperfect, but the Board has no power to correct flaws that it perceives in the statute it is empowered to administer. Its rulemaking power is limited to adopting regulations to carry into effect the will of Congress. . . . If the Bank Holding Company [Act] falls short of providing safeguards desirable or necessary to protect the public interest, that is a matter for Congress, and not the Board or the courts, to address.[27]

The Supreme Court decision has been cited at length here because of the two effects that were immediately predicted to follow. The decision was considered likely to prompt Congress to act on the question of nonbank banks and to encourage additional requests for nonbank bank charters.[28] In fact, neither effect occurred.

By the time the Supreme Court rendered the decision, Dimension Financial was financially unable to take advantage of it. In the immediately preceding years, the company had incurred legal fees of $1.5 million and had lost its CEO and its legal counsel. In addition, its original parent (Valley National S&L) had sold it, and Dimension lacked the $54.5 million in capital that would be legally required for the formation of a thirty-one-bank network.[29]

The decision also failed to produce the expected increase in charter applications or approvals. As of July 1986, only twenty nonbank banks were in operation, and the court injunction that prevented the Comptroller from granting final approvals remained in effect.[30]

As for impacting Congressional progress, which the final sentence in the preceding quote clearly called for, the Court decision did nothing to expedite passage of any legislation on the subject of nonbank banks. It may have established an important precedent for the Fed and the Comptroller, but despite the fact that Representative St Germain, on the day it was announced, promised prompt action to "close the door" on a "plethora of new hybrid banking institutions,"[31] no definitive action was taken in the ensuing six months.

In June 1986, Senator Jake Garn introduced a bill that would allow commercial banks to underwrite securities and that would address the question of nonbank banks. Paul Volcker, appearing before the Senate Banking Committee, urged approval of the additional authority for banks[32]; however, he was highly critical of one section of the bill that would allow nonbank companies or banks to acquire failing thrift institutions.[33] As of mid-July, the Senate continued to listen to the often conflicting views of all the interested parties. While awaiting passage of some form of legislation, the Fed, monitoring the activities of the existing nonbank banks, levied its maximum fine of $600,000 on Household International, Inc., on the grounds that its consumer bank subsidiary, the former Valley National Bank of Salinas, California, had continued to make commercial loans in violation of its charter.[34]

Summary

The initial appearance of the institutions known as nonbank banks went virtually unnoticed in 1981. However, since 1984, when the Fed gave its reluctant approval to the request of United States Trust Company, the controversy, confusion, and litigation have been virtually continuous. Throughout that period, commercial banks, nonbank companies, regulatory authorities, and the Supreme Court have repeatedly importuned Congress to take appropriate action to clarify the situation.

E. Gerald Corrigan, President, Federal Reserve Bank of New York, has been particularly outspoken on this subject:

> Bankers and bank supervisors have a strong common interest in the pressing—indeed urgent— need for the Congress to enact broad-based new banking legislation. The case for legislative reform is powerful. . . . The understandable compulsion of institutions to seize every loophole in law and regulation to achieve some strategic business purpose threatens to reach a point of *de facto* restructuring of the financial marketplace such that even

> the most basic of doctrines—such as the separation of banking and commerce—may be irreversibly breached. . . . Our federal banking laws are in desperate need of reform and we need to get on with that task promptly. New legislation must incorporate contemporary definitions of banks and thrifts.[35]

One year later, in 1986, he repeated these thoughts:

> In the Supreme Court ruling in the so-called "nonbank bank" case two weeks ago . . . the Court seemed to me to be saying that . . . the proper remedy was legislative, not judicial—which, of course, has been the Fed's position all along. Hopefully, the Court's ruling will serve as a catalyst for federal legislation.[36]

When the 1985 Congressional session opened, Representative St Germain introduced a bill, in the hope that the House would act without delay, to close out all nonbank banks that came into being after July 1, 1983. The American Bankers Association announced its support of this bill. Eighteen months later, no legislation on the subject had been passed.[37] Therefore, the basic questions remain unanswered:

1. What is the legal definition of a bank?
2. Should the existing so-called nonbank banks be allowed to continue to operate? If so, under whose jurisdiction?
3. Should the pending approvals for nonbank banks be finalized?
4. If nonbank banks are to be legally permitted, what specific financial services should they be allowed to offer?
5. Assuming their legality, should nonbank banks be allowed to cross state lines?

In all the literature describing the nonbank bank movement, the word *loophole* has been repeatedly used to indicate how these institutions have capitalized on the language of the Bank Holding Company Act. Given that such a loophole exists, it has become abundantly clear that no authority other than Congress can render the final word on whether it should be closed by definition. Only Congress, similarly, can determine what should be the fate of the 300 charter applications for nonbank banks that remain pending.

All interested parties to the financial services industry hope that the legislators will resolve these questions in the immediate future to avoid further costly litigation and eliminate all doubts. Should that happen, additional commercial messages, inviting the public to conduct its financial affairs only at real banks, will not be necessary.

Notes

1. See Alan Gart, *Banks, Thrifts, and Insurance Companies* (Lexington, Mass.: Lexington Books, 1985), pp. 22–24.

2. Bart Fraust, "Financial Firms Took Full Advantage of Nonbank Bank Loophole in 1984," *American Banker,* January 4, 1985, p. 20.

3. Marilyn Much, "Are the 'Real' Banks Worried?," *Industry Week,* November 26, 1984, p. 73.

4. John Taylor, "Why Nonbank Banks Strike Fear in the Hearts of Florida Bankers," *Florida Trend,* December 1984, p. 76.

5. Blanca Riemer, "The Two Trailblazers Leading Banking to the Promised Land," *Business Week,* December 17, 1984, p. 100.

6. Leon Wynter, "Comptroller Is Sued in Attempt to Stop New Charters for Limited Service Banks," *Wall Street Journal,* December 18, 1984, p. 12.

7. Much, op. cit.

8. Jay Rosenstein, "Fed Approves Five Nonbank Banks," *American Banker,* November 6, 1984, p. 5.

9. In Andrew Albert, "Fed Board Cancels Nonbank Deadline," *American Banker,* December 26, 1984, p. 1.

10. Lynn Brenner, "Conover Hopes Nonbank Banks Will Spur Congress to Act," *American Banker,* December 20, 1984, p. 3; and Office of the Comptroller of the Currency, News Release 84-77, December 21, 1984.

11. David Barnes, "Nonbank Bank Bids Made by 2 Thrifts," *American Banker,* December 20, 1984, p. 17.

12. "Limited-Service Bank Approval Hits Court Snag," *Wall Street Journal,* February 19, 1985, p. 3.

13. "As Good As Their Word," *Forbes,* February 25, 1985, pp. 52–53.

14. Karen W. Arenson, "A Bank Bridge over State Lines," *The New York Times,* April 20, 1979, p. D1.

15. Bartlett Naylor, "Florida Judge Upholds Ban Against Charters of All Nonbank Banks," *American Banker,* April 9, 1985, p. 1.

16. Peter J. Wallison, "Court Rules on the Loophole that Never Was," *American Banker,* April 11, 1985, p. 4.

17. Bartlett Naylor, "Volcker Says Congress Should Close Nonbank-Bank Loophole," *American Banker,* April 18, 1985, p. 2.

18. The complete text of the Court of Appeals decision can be found in *American Banker,* May 24, 1985, pp. 4–6.

19. Philip T. Sudo, "Nonbank Bank Issue Dominates Court Activity," *American Banker,* December 20, 1985, p. 1.

20. Federal Reserve Board of Governors, *72nd Annual Report 1985,* p. 158.

21. Bartlett Naylor, "High Court Overrules Fed in Nonbank Case," *American Banker,* January 23, 1986, p. 1.

22. Bart Fraust, "Dimension's Future Dim Despite Court Victory," *American Banker,* January 27, 1986, p. 1.

23. 12 U.S.C. §#1841(c).

24. Charles G. Daley, "Before the Courts," *American Banker,* February 11, 1986, p. 5.

25. Board of Governors of the Federal Reserve System, Regulation Y as revised effective February 3, 1984, 12 C.F.R. §# 225.2(a)(1)(A).

26. Ibid., §# 225.2(a)(1)(B).

27. The full text appears in *American Banker,* January 23, 1986, pp. 9–11.

28. Stuart Taylor, Jr., "Fed Loses Nonbank Bank Case," *The New York Times,* January 23, 1986, p. D1.

29. Fraust, "Dimension's Future Dim."

30. Nathaniel C. Nash, "Fed Fines Household $600,000," *The New York Times,* July 1, 1986, p. D1.

31. Naylor, "High Court Overrules Fed," p. 11.

32. Bartlett Naylor and Robert M. Garsson, "Vote on Garn's Bill Postponed Amid Intense Lobbying," *American Banker,* July 21, 1986, p. 1.

33. Bartlett Naylor, "Volcker Raps S&L Ownership by Nonbanks," *American Banker,* July 24, 1986, p. 1.

34. Naylor, "Fed Fines Household Over Nonbank Unit," *American Banker,* July 7, 1986, p. 13.

35. Remarks before the Fifty-seventh Annual Mid-Winter Meeting, New York State Bankers Association, January 31, 1985, in Federal Reserve Bank of New York, *Quarterly Review,* Spring 1985, p. 5.

36. Remarks before the Fifty-eighth Annual Mid-Winter Meeting, New York State Bankers Association, January 30, 1986, in Federal Reserve Bank of New York, *Quarterly Review,* Winter 1985–86, p. 3.

37. Jay Rosenstein, "Outset of 99th Congress Marked by Flurry of New Banking Bills," *American Banker,* January 4, 1985, p. 3.

11 The New World of Deregulation

The observer who studies the banking systems that exist among the major nations in the free world quickly identifies a twofold uniqueness in the U.S. structure. For example, in Canada, Great Britain, France, and West Germany, a relative handful of giant banks dominates the financial scene. Names such as Royal Bank of Canada, Barclays Bank, Crédit Lyonnais, and Deutsche Bank come to mind at once; these are among the world's twenty-six largest banks as of year-end 1985.[1] The second distinguishing feature is found in the fact that these, and other major banks, in the named countries operate networks of branches that extend from border to border.

Since its inception, the U.S. banking system has been entirely different in both these respects. An individual who has found branches of a Canadian bank thousands of miles apart in Nova Scotia and Vancouver or a British bank with a branch in a seaport town on the English Channel and another near the border of Scotland will look in vain for any comparable organization in the United States. The U.S. system has always been fragmented, both in terms of geography and in the fact that there are over 14,000 commercial banks in the United States, in contrast to the six or eight dominant banks in other countries (see table 11–1).

The Regulatory System

Commercial banks in the United States may be national or state. They may be unit banks (i.e., with no branches) or branch banks. They may or may not be Federal Reserve members (more than half are not), and they range in size from a Citicorp, with deposits of $105 billion at year-end 1985, to a small community bank one-thousandth that size. In every case, they are part of a regulatory system that makes them the most thoroughly and frequently controlled, examined, and restricted of all U.S. industries.

Although bankers accept the premise that they cannot expect to function

Table 11–1
Bank Structures in the United States and Other Major Countries

Country	*Number of Commercial Banks*	*Number of Banking Offices*	*Population per Bank Office*	*Deposit Share Held by Five Largest Banks (Percent)*
Canada	11	7,425	3,296	77.7
United Kingdom	35	14,000	4,004	56.8
Japan	86	13,420	8,836	34.5
France	206	40,200	1,347	76.1
West Germany	243	41,000	1,506	61.8
United States	14,451	54,235	4,177	19.2

Source: "The New England Experiment in Interstate Banking," *New England Economic Review,* March/April 1984.

without regulation, the scope and the frequent overlapping of that regulation cause concern. For example, all national banks (numbering about 4,500) are under the direct jurisdiction of the Comptroller of the Currency, who charters, regulates, and audits them; yet they must also belong to the FDIC and the Federal Reserve. Both of the latter agencies may also examine them at any time if necessary, and if the national bank is a member of a BHC, the Fed has additional regulatory authority over it. If the bank or BHC is a publicly owned corporation, the Securities and Exchange Commission is involved. Should it wish to expand across a state line, the McFadden Act (and possibly the Douglas Amendment to the Bank Holding Company Act) immediately restrict it, and the Justice Department has the right to review any acquisition or merger affecting it if antitrust statutes appear to pertain.

State-chartered member banks must also belong to the FDIC; they are regularly examined by the Fed and the state but also are under the jurisdiction of the FDIC, which can audit them at any time. Again, the regulations and laws of all these Acts and organizations may affect these banks' operations and restrict their growth. State nonmember banks, if insured by the FDIC, fall under the joint supervision of the FDIC and the state. Fewer than 300 banks are in the fourth (nonmember, noninsured) category, and these are under direct state supervision.

Because banks can choose either national or state chartering and can subsequently convert from one type to the other (as several hundred did during the 1970s),[2] the system, aside from what Senator William Proxmire described as "overlapping and burdensome duplication,"[3] has also been characterized by the same Senator as one that "leads to competition in laxity, with regulation at the lowest common denominator level."[4]

Conflicts among the three federal regulatory agencies—the Comptroller, the Fed, and the FDIC—are common. There are philosophical differences among them, in addition to areas of disagreement on important issues such as global lending, nonbank banks, expansion of services, and interstate banking.[5] Bankers become confused over all the differing regulations, and one agency may try to limit the authority of another.[6] The presence of fifty state banking departments, establishing laws that are far from standardized, is superimposed on the federal involvement.

The historical overview in chapter 1 traced the evolution of U.S. commercial banking, starting with the unregulated climate created by free banking laws and the colonists' insistence on minimal government intervention. Bank failures, money crises, the affirmation of states' rights, and recurring fears of undue concentration of economic power in the hands of a few money-center giants have all played a part in the formation of the present regulatory system. In the New World of commercial banking, it is a system that has come under increasingly strong criticism from those who see it as duplicative in authority, anachronistic, excessively restrictive, and discriminatory (in that it inhibits the banks' efforts to compete effectively with unregulated providers of financial services). Indeed, the National Bank Act, the Federal Reserve Act, the McFadden Act, and the Glass-Steagall Act were reactive measures, designed entirely to overcome weaknesses, strengthen the industry, rebuild public trust, and solve the perceived problems existing at the time. The crucial question is whether all the restrictions imposed on the current banking environment are necessary.

For many years, banks have functioned under an unspoken form of agreement with the federal government. As the lenders of last resort to U.S. business, the instruments of federal economic policy, and the holders of huge deposits, they have been given certain privileges and the government's ultimate insurance, through the FDIC, of at least part of their liabilities. At the same time, they have necessarily been subject to many restrictions on their operations. Their freedom to carry out their institutional strategic plans was and is constrained by legislation divorcing commercial from investment banking, prohibiting full-scale interstate branching, and otherwise limiting the range of services they can offer.[7]

Therefore, in the New World of commercial banking, *deregulation* is the most frequently heard watchword. If the observer from the first paragraph in this chapter had noted branches of Citicorp Savings in California or Florida, had seen the television commercials advertising Bank of America's discount brokerage service (through a subsidiary), or had charted the pattern of recent regional banking agreements, he or she might feel that deregulation had already taken place. However, many leading spokespersons contend that much more legislation is needed as regards geography, products, or both. If further deregulation does not come about by act of Congress, the banks' only alternative is to circumvent existing statutes wherever possible through one loophole or another, embarking on courses of action in the hope that the courts will not subsequently direct the banks to stop.

Chain and Group Banking

Because the rights of each state to regulate branching within its borders have repeatedly been upheld, two different types of organizational structuring have been devised to allow banking entrepreneurs to serve more customers in a wider range of geographic areas.

Chain Banking

The system known as *chain banking* appeared in the late nineteenth century, almost entirely in states that at that time prohibited branching. It provides for control of two or more banks through stock ownership by one or more individuals. Banks in the chain preserve their identities and have their own boards of directors, although interlocking directorates are common. Chain banking exists today only to a limited extent.[8]

Group Banking

The growth of the group banking system is a direct consequence of the various federal and state laws prohibiting full-scale interstate branch banking and limiting the scope of bank activities. State laws that ban intrastate branching also contributed to the movement. In group banking today, ownership of the involved banks rests with a holding company.

In 1923 the Federal Reserve ruled that state-chartered members could not open branches outside their home office cities and that specific Fed approval was needed for all branches.[9] The McFadden Act (1927) allowed national banks to branch only in those states where state banks could branch. It effectively banned all interstate branching. In 1969 the U.S. Supreme Court, upholding the McFadden Act, stated that any bank facility or location at which "deposits were received, checks paid, or money lent" would be classified as a branch.[10]

Holding companies—corporate entities exercising control over other companies through stock ownership—have traditionally been part of the structure of corporate business in the United States. In many cases banks were included in these, and examples existed of holding companies that, in addition to their bank holdings, controlled securities and investment, real estate, and restaurant companies.[11] Some holding companies were formed as a means of unifying and strengthening smaller and/or failing banks, even when the institutions were located in more than one state.

The Glass-Steagall Act, in addition to its other provisions, addressed the question of those holding companies in which banks were involved. It required all such entities to divest their investment- and securities-related activities and to be subject to periodic examinations by federal regulators. However, it exempted from laws prohibiting interstate banking those holding companies in which banks already operated across state lines. The present First Interstate Bancorp serves as a prototype of the exempted entities. Its steady growth has resulted in a holding company consisting of twenty-three banks in twelve western states, with 950 branches and total assets of almost $50 billion.[12] It has evolved from the original group of banks owned by Transamerica Corporation and was formerly known as Western Bancorp and Firstamerica Corporation.

Throughout the years following passage of the Glass-Steagall Act, the Fed repeatedly pointed out to Congress that numbers of holding companies were being formed as a means of creating networks of banks that circumvented restrictions on intrastate and interstate banking. The Fed also noted that these holding companies were gathering under a single roof many activities outside the "business of banking."[13] In 1956 Congress responded to pressure from the Comptroller of the Currency and the Fed by passing the Bank Holding Company (BHC) Act. This legislation defined all such entities as

> [O]rganizations that directly or indirectly controlled 25 percent or more of the voting stock of two or more banks, or in any way controlled the election of a majority of the directors of two or more banks.[14]

Therefore, existing chain banks that came under the second heading automatically became classified as BHCs.

All BHCs, as defined in the Act, were required to register with the Fed and to divest themselves of all nonbanking activities. The Fed was given authority to regulate the formation of BHCs and all mergers or acquisitions in which BHCs were involved. The individual states, however, were allowed to prohibit and/or restrict BHCs within their borders.[15]

The Douglas Amendment to Section 3(d) of the BHC Act has often been cited as exemplifying those regulations that were seen as necessary in the past but that are unduly restrictive today. The Amendment specifically prohibits BHC acquisitions across state lines, unless the state in which the bank to be acquired is located gives its approval. Those BHCs that were operating on a multistate basis at the time the Act was passed (e.g., the then-Western Bancorp) were grandfathered and allowed to continue in operation.

With the passage of time, the words *two or more banks* in the language of the BHC Act assumed increasing importance. Given the banks' desires to offset the effects of disintermediation, diversify and expand their range of services, and seek greater profits, it became apparent that a BHC in which only one bank was involved would not be affected by the Act and therefore would be free to engage in other activities.

Forming a one-bank BHC was simple. A holding company was formed; all outstanding stock in the bank was surrendered and replaced by stock in the new corporation; and the latter could, through subsidiaries, become involved in leasing, factoring, mortgage servicing, or data processing. These operations would generate profits but were not, strictly speaking, parts of the business of banking.

In 1965 the Meadow Brook National Bank (New York), which later became National Bank of North America, was purchased by CIT Corporation. Bankers deeply resented this acquisition of a commercial bank by a nonbank company, even though it was perfectly legal, since the reverse type of transaction was strictly prohibited. The loophole in the 1985 BHC Act offered the solution. During a fifteen-year period, as shown in table 11–2, tremendous growth took place in the one-bank BHC movement. The ability of these new entities to diversify into many nonbank activities created new fears of concentrations of economic power. In addition, it raised questions about the interrelationship of the bank component in the BHC and the nonbank entities. Would, for example, the bank ignore normal credit criteria to lend to its affiliate in the holding company? Would it lend to an affiliate at preferential rates? Would tie-in contracts become common, with banking services extended on a quid pro quo basis to the exclusion of outside bidders? Would the one-bank BHC eventually become the owner of a steel mill, a fast-food chain, or some other unrelated business?

The 1970 Bank Holding Company Act

Public Law 91-607 (December 31, 1970), incorporated into Regulation Y of the Fed, brought all BHCs, regardless of their nature, under the jurisdiction of the Federal Reserve. The 1970 Act gave the Fed complete and exclusive

Table 11–2
One-Bank Holding Companies, Selected Years from 1955 to 1971

	1955	*1965*	*1967*	*1969*	*1971*
Number of one-bank BHCs	117	550	810	894	1,414
Deposits ($ billions)	11	15	108	181	207
Deposits as a percentage of all bank deposits	6	5	27	42	38

Source: Association of Registered Bank Holding Companies, and Board of Governors of the Federal Reserve System, *Annual Reports.*

authority to determine exactly what activities all BHCs could perform. Through a grandfather clause, it excluded nonbank activities if the BHC in question had continuously engaged in them since June 30, 1968. The new Regulation Y, as noted earlier, also redefined the term *commercial bank*.

Under the terms of the 1970 Amendments, the Fed must decide whether a proposed type of activity is (1) closely related to banking and (2) of such a nature that public benefits will result. The Fed, if an activity is to be approved, must rule that the benefits more than offset any adverse effects. Some nonbank activities are automatically permitted for BHCs by Fed regulation; that is, they appear on the Fed's approved list, and a BHC need not submit a specific request to engage in them. Others may be allowed in response to an application filed with the Fed by a BHC. Table 11–3 contains a list of selected examples of approved and denied activities.

At year-end 1984 there were 6,146 registered BHCs; a survey by the Fed of the 345 largest indicated that they alone controlled about 70 percent of all commercial bank assets.[16] By year-end 1985 the number of BHCs had risen to 6,453, and these controlled some 92 percent of total bank assets.[17] At that time, every one of the nation's 100 largest commercial banks was a BHC member.

By law, the Fed is equired to conduct periodic examinations of BHCs and

Table 11–3
Permitted and Denied Activities for BHCs as of 1986

Permitted Activities	*Denied Activities*
Extensions of credit	Underwriting general life insurance or combining sales of mutual funds and insurance
Industrial banks and loan companies	Real estate brokerage and land investment and development
Loan servicing	Real estate syndication
Trust operations including financial or investment advising	General management consulting and property management
Bookkeeping, data processing, and leasing services	General management consulting and property management
Underwriting credit life, accident, and health insurance or acting as insurance agent or broker in connection with extensions of credit	Underwriting property and casualty, home loan life, and mortgage guaranty insurance or selling credit life insurance
Courier services, management consulting to depository banks, discount brokerage, sale of money orders, travelers checks, and savings bonds	Operating a travel agency
Underwriting and dealing in certain federal, state, and municipal securities	

their nonbank subsidiaries; the appropriate federal regulatory agency examines the bank components. In 1985 the Fed, "inspired by what has happened in the banking industry over the last few years," announced that it would increase the frequency of its examinations and would strengthen the rules for disclosing examination results to bank managers and board members. Fed spokesman Joseph Coyne, in announcing this step, alluded to the banks' losses from agricultural, energy, real estate, and Third World loans and the increase in the number of bank failures.[18]

Multibank BHCs have served as effective substitutes for full-scale branching in some states in which branch banking is not allowed. Texas, for example, remains among the relatively few unit bank states; six of the nation's fifty largest BHCs are located in that state, and they control a total of 355 banks with no branches.

The Garn–St Germain Act of 1982 took cognizance of the troubled state of many banks and included a provision allowing BHCs of satisfactory capital strength to acquire failing institutions in other states. By 1984 the Fed had liberalized its policies so BHCs could, with specific Fed approval, operate a distressed S&L in the same state or acquire a distressed S&L in another state.[19] Chapter 12 discusses these policies under the heading of interstate banking. As of mid-1986, Congress had not taken definitive action to indicate the extent to which it would allow interstate expansion of BHCs.

In addition to the permitted BHC activities listed in table 11–3, the Fed has authorized seven that, in its judgment, have met the requirement of being closely related to banking. These are:

1. Financial feasibility studies and credit ratings,
2. Tax preparation services for individuals,
3. Real estate consulting services,
4. Services relating to credit card processing,
5. Employee benefits consulting,
6. Acting as a broker for municipal securities brokers,
7. Servicing student loans.[20]

The Fed, in interpreting the restrictive provisions of the Garn–St Germain Act, has also grandfathered insurance subsidiaries of BHCs to continue operations provided they were engaged in that business prior to 1971 and has authorized BHCs to clear and execute futures contracts on stock indexes through major exchanges.[21]

Figure 11–1 is an example of a Federal Reserve announcement amending Regulation Y so that BHCs are authorized to conduct an activity closely related to banking. More specifically, the Board, in approving an application, must determine that the activity in question is "so closely related to banking or managing or controlling banks as to be a proper incident

FEDERAL RESERVE BANK OF NEW YORK

Circular No. 9537
August 17, 1983

REGULATION Y

Amendment Adding Discount Securities Brokerage and Related Margin Lending to Permissible Activities for Bank Holding Companies

The Federal Reserve Board has amended its Regulation Y—Bank Holding Companies—to add securities brokerage and related margin lending to the list of activities generally permissible for bank holding companies. . . . The action codifies a previous position taken by the Board in approving the acquisition by BankAmerica Corporation of Charles Schwab Corporation, a retail discount securities broker. . . .

The Board specified that the brokerage activities are to be restricted to buying and selling securities solely as agent for the account of customers . . . securities underwriting or the provision of investment advice is not included, and margin lending on securities is to be conducted by a nonbank subsidiary of the bank holding company.

ANTHONY M. SOLOMON,
President

Figure 11–1. Federal Reserve Bank of New York, Regulation Y

thereto."[22] Conversely, an application must be denied if, in the board's judgment,

> [T]he transaction would result in a monopoly . . . or the effect of the transaction may be substantially to lessen competition in any section of the country . . . or in any other manner be in restraint of trade, unless the Board finds that the transaction's anticompetitive effects are clearly outweighed by its probable effect in meeting the convenience and needs of the community.[23]

The Fed's favorable decisions in permitting expansion, whether geographic or in terms of services, can have the effect of reinforcing the traditional concerns of smaller institutions regarding excessive concentrations of economic power in the hands of the money-center giants.[24]

Citicorp

Since 1965, the term *BHC* almost immediately conjures up in the banking industry the Citicorp name, and whenever a spokesperson for the industry is quoted, the chances are excellent that it is Walter Wriston. During his tenure as Chairman, Citicorp pioneered the one-bank holding company, and by 1980 it had created a financial empire embracing some 400 consumer finance, Edge Act, loan production, and mortgage banking offices in thirty-eight states and the District of Columbia.[25] Its growth has continued unabated since 1980 and reflects Wriston's earlier statements:

> Good companies have a defined set of goals which are understandable, clear, and endlessly repeated. We decided a long time ago that what we were . . . [was] a bank, and a very good one—and our goal is to deliver a financial service in every market in the world in every segment where we are legally permitted to do so at a profit.[26]

That growth has made Citicorp the largest BHC (and bank) in the United States in terms of assets ($174 billion at year-end 1985) and deposits ($95 billion),[27] far outstripping Bank of America and Chase Manhattan, which the then National City Bank of New York had trailed for many years.

The overall approach of Citicorp to the total marketplace for financial services is one of innovative aggressiveness. It has been on the leading edge of efforts to relax or eliminate federal laws that geographically and functionally restrict BHCs. While awaiting the outcome of those efforts, it has consistently identified and used legal loopholes to circumvent the restrictions. It has established a reputation as a pioneer in many areas, willing to assume substantial risk, moving at a rapid pace to grow in today's environment and build a base for tomorrow's.

In addition to introducing the large-denomination negotiable CD and being the first money-center giant to implement the one-bank BHC concept, Citibank positioned itself in the New York City metropolitan area by making a huge investment to install 400 ATMs. By 1980 these ATMs were processing 68 percent of the bank's daily cash withdrawals, at greatly reduced per-transaction costs.[28]

Citicorp's legally permitted acquisitions of troubled thrifts in Florida, California, and Texas have made it a force to be reckoned with in those states.[29] These acquisitions, often seen as a prelude to full-scale interstate branching, are discussed in chapter 12.

Through intensive nationwide solicitation, Citibank has become the leading issuer of bank cards. With nine million accounts, it outstrips the second-largest bank issuer by two million and has more than double the number of accounts of the third-largest bank.[30] Citibank's approach to the card problem exemplifies innovation. In 1973 it had launched the nation's first major debit card program by issuing almost two million cards and installing the necessary POS terminals to handle them.[31] Usury laws in New York State, however, prevented it from charging more than 12 percent on card outstandings, even when the prime lending rate exceeded 20 percent. When the South Dakota legislature, anxious to attract business and create job opportunities, voted to abolish rate ceilings and to facilitate entry into the state by BHCs, Citibank transferred its entire card-processing facility to a bank it established in Sioux Falls. All loans made from that location, and all card outstandings handled there, have no restrictions on interest rates.[32] In July 1986, Citibank and Mobil Oil Corporation announced an electronic debit program, allowing over one million Citicard holders to purchase up to $500 per day at Mobil stations and have the purchases charged directly to their accounts.[33]

Walter Wriston's long-range strategic plan envisioned a world of thirty-five million Citicorp customers, each of whom would generate average earnings of $30 for the BHC:

> [We intend eventually] to become a preeminent distributor of financial database services nationwide and worldwide. We will integrate banking, electronic publishing, and telecommunications services . . . through a global system having 20,000 electronic connections.[34]

John Reed, successor to Walter Wriston as Citicorp's Chairman, is implementing this plan through the 400 consumer-finance, loan-production, mortgage-lending, and Edge Act offices and the network of almost 300 New York metropolitan area branches. The bank was a pioneer in establishing a Controlled Disbursement facility and chose Delaware as its site because of that state's highly favorable tax structure on bank earnings. Citicorp's industrial banks (which do not accept demand deposits) in Kentucky and Tennessee are also part of the BHC structure.[35] The emphasis that Citicorp has placed on consumer business, added to its traditional loan-and-deposit relationships with the one hundred largest U.S. corporations, has created a loan portfolio that is almost equally divided between commercial and retail lending, with some $58 billion in each category.[36]

No approach to today's financial services industry can omit insurance; Walter Wriston believed that all forms of insurance might represent 40 percent of the total package of services. Citicorp's Arizona subsidiary offers homeowner insurance, and other forms of coverage (including about $2 billion in credit insurance) are available through other BHC affiliates.[37]

In 1986 Citicorp also completed its acquisition (for $680 million) of Quotron Systems, Inc., a Los Angeles-based provider of stock quotations and other financial information.[38]

The respect achieved by Citicorp because of its tremendous growth in deposits and assets, and its diversification (both functional and geographic), is tempered to some extent by the fears of bankers in smaller communities, who wonder if they may eventually be swallowed up by the New York–based giant. Their apprehension may reflect a statement by Walter Wriston to the effect that changes in interstate banking laws would simply allow the Citicorp offices throughout the country to replace their signs with new ones, indicating that they were now full-scale Citibank branches.[39]

J.P. Morgan & Co., Inc.

In the post–World War II period, the then Citibank embarked on a program of expansion of its branch network and aggressive marketing, much of which was aimed at the consumer and featured additional retail services. Conversely, the Morgan Guaranty Trust Company (formed in 1950 through the merger of the Guaranty Trust Company with the original J.P. Morgan & Co., Inc.) never deviated from its traditional philosophy of providing the highest quality, most in-depth service only to those market segments with which it wished to deal. Morgan Guaranty has always been the prototype wholesale bank, and today's J.P. Morgan & Co., Inc., the holding company owning all its outstanding stock, is the antithesis of Citicorp in many respects.

Morgan Guaranty operates approximately one-fiftieth the number of Citibank branches in the New York metropolitan area. It has never attempted to attract the retail market through low-balance checking accounts or installment loans. Aside from Morgan Guaranty Trust Company (which generates 95 percent of the BHC's earnings), the holding company owns only one other bank, a Delaware facility used for Controlled Disbursement accounts and a limited range of other services. The following discussion cites its track record to indicate courses of action a BHC can take in today's financial services industry, unlike those adopted by Citicorp.

From 1971 through 1980 Morgan Guaranty outperformed sixteen of the nation's largest banks in growth in earnings per share (EPS),[40] averaging 13.4 percent per year over that decade. Some analysts and observers speculated on whether Morgan could maintain such growth, given the pressures of the industry and the Morgan tradition of concentrating on wholesale business. The more recent figures answer their questions. At year-end 1985 Morgan's total assets of $69.4 billion were 40 percent of Citicorp's; yet its earnings of $705 million were 70 percent of Citicorp's.[41] Those earnings represented an increase of 31.2 percent over the record figure reported by the BHC in 1984 and were double those of 1981. During the same five-year period stockholders' equity grew from $2.3 billion to $4.4 billion.[42] Morgan's Return on Equity (ROE) of $18.06 for 1985 and its Return on Assets (ROA) of $1.06 ranked first among the nation's fourteen largest banks.

The deregulation that many other large BHCs may be seeking is of less importance to Morgan. It is not actively attempting to position itself on a nationwide basis; domestically, the only other bank owned by the BHC is Morgan Bank (Delaware), which handles domestic and international business and is the site of the bank's Controlled Disbursement facility. Indeed, whatever changes eventual deregulation may bring about will have little impact on Morgan. This fact is implicit in the most recent statement of senior management's philosophy:

> We continue to find growth opportunities in serving corporations, institutions, governments, and a select private clientele around the world, but growth of assets has no attraction if the additions cannot meet our expectations for return on equity and our standards of credit quality. We are also cautious about embarking on new activities . . . . We seek to provide financial services that our clients value highly and that command a price reflective of that value. . . . We believe the best course for us . . . is to stay with the kind of client we have always served.[43]

Under the BHC umbrella, thirty-seven direct or indirect subsidiaries of Morgan conduct trust, real estate, investment, international, and merchant banking business in every corner of the world. In this respect, Morgan has resemblances to Citicorp's global banking network; however, the essential difference remains. While Citicorp will use the BHC as the vehicle for serving thirty-five million consumers with the widest possible range of services, Morgan will employ the same vehicle to focus on those segments of a highly select market that it can serve best.

Mergers and Acquisitions

During the 1950s, many of the largest mergers in U.S. banking history took place, especially in New York City, where six of the nation's ten largest banks had been part of a merger that was intended to enable one institution to expand into an area of specialized services and/or to acquire an existing network of branches. The size of the institutions involved in these transactions created concerns over the traditional issues of "bigness" and concentrations of economic power. The Bank Merger Act of 1960 was accordingly passed by Congress as a means of establishing specific authorities to evaluate the factors involved in each proposed merger and to approve or disapprove.

In each case, the designated authority—the Comptroller of the Currency, the Fed, the FDIC, or the appropriate state banking department, depending on the type of bank involved—was instructed to disapprove a proposal unless the potential gains to the community and depositors outweighed any anticompetitive effects.[44] The Act defined the factors to be considered in each merger application and was intended to avoid any conflicts among authorities regarding approvals.[45]

In its 1963 landmark decision (*U.S.* v. *Philadelphia National Bank,* 374 U.S. 321), however, the Supreme Court brought commercial banking, for the first time, under the provisions of Sherman and Clayton antitrust legislation. As noted earlier, the Court held that the cluster of commercial bank products was the relevant product market for antitrust purposes.[46] The Court assumed that commercial banks compete only with other banks and excluded all other providers of financial services from anticompetitive analysis. It held that mergers were illegal if they

> produced a firm controlling an undue percentage share of the relevant market, and resulted in a significant increase in the concentration of firms in that market.

In *U.S.* v. *Phillipsburg National Bank and Trust Company* [300 U.S. 350 (1970)] the Court reaffirmed the 1963 ruling, and in *U.S.* v. *The Connecticut National Bank* (418 U.S. 656) it did so again. In the latter case, it stated that while savings banks had expanded their range of services to include checking accounts and commercial loans (as permitted by Connecticut law), they still could not be considered competitors of the commercial banks.

Through these decisions, the Supreme Court made antitrust considerations the key factor in mergers and acquisitions. Therefore, the Bank Merger Act of 1960 was, in effect, contravened, and the U.S. Justice Department was empowered to determine the anticompetitive effects of any merger and to oppose it in federal court. In 1982, the Justice Department issued its merger guidelines, indicating that any proposal in which the acquired bank's market share was 20 percent or more would most probably be opposed.[47]

If commercial banks would like to see a single element in the current regulatory maze eliminated, it is this totally outdated set of rulings on acquisitions and mergers. Any uniqueness that commercial banks once enjoyed has long since disappeared. Many nonbank providers now offer substitutes for nearly all the traditional banking products that the Supreme Court included in the cluster.

There is some evidence of at least partial relief for the banks. During 1985 the Federal Reserve Board approved several requests by out-of-state banking organizations to acquire distressed thrift institutions and upheld several interstate BHC applications that reflected new state laws.[48] The Supreme Court upheld the Board's approvals and rulings and found that they satisfied the Douglas Amendment requirements; throughout 1985, the Justice Department left these approvals unchallenged.[49]

Types of Deregulation

Because the question of deregulation of banks and BHCs is so critical, timely, and controversial, the first basic point in any discussion of it must focus on the proposed type of deregulation. The terms *geographic* and *functional* have frequently been used in this context, and both are relevant to any discussion.

Geographic deregulation goes to the question of possible repeal or relaxation of the Douglas Amendment, the McFadden Act, and/or state laws so that banks and BHCs would be allowed to expand by branching or to make acquisitions across state lines. This remains the prime concern of the smaller community banks, whose representatives are both resentful of increased competition and fearful of the money-center giants who might push them out of local markets. Citicorp is again an example of the BHC responsible for these local concerns. If Congress and the States repealed existing statutes and permitted full-scale interstate branching, Citicorp could immediately convert each of its 170 consumer finance offices in twenty-seven states, adding tellers' facilities and installing new signs.[50] The Independent Bankers Association is still the leading opponent of this form of deregulation.

Nevertheless, as is discussed more fully in chapter 12, the community bankers who oppose such deregulation appear to be neglecting the fact that the nonbanks have, in so many cases, already positioned themselves throughout the country to offer financial services. It serves little purpose to fight to keep other banks out of an area when Sears, Merrill Lynch, and others have already invaded the same territory and are aggressively competing with local banks wherever possible.

In a statement before a Congressional Subcommittee on June 11, 1986, Paul Volcker addressed this question:

> A transition to interstate banking should help assure that banks are able to compete with other firms, operating nationwide, that can bring the most advanced technology to bear in serving customer needs.[51]

At the same time, he made a salient point regarding the failure of Congress to act on functional deregulation:

> The Congress has been debating the issues for several years, but every attempt to address them has been stymied because, at least in part, of the efforts to block legislative change by those who perceive a strong particular interest in one part or another of the status quo or in exploiting an existing loophole.[52]

He noted further that

> There is nothing static about the bank holding company concept; the Congress intended to allow it to be adapted over time. We and others came to the conclusion . . . that this could be done by broadening somewhat the scope of permissible nonbanking activities of bank holding companies . . . within a framework that assures that the public interest in safe and sound banking is maintained. We have urged that bank holding companies, through their affiliates, be able to engage in . . . underwriting commercial paper, . . . real estate and insurance brokerage, and travel services.[53]

The banks' desire to expand their range of financial services immediately arouses strong opposition from those large industries that would be affected, such as the insurance companies and brokerage firms. At the same time, it has become evident that the banks have not presented a unified front to Congress in seeking relief. Whatever criticisms are imputed to legislators for their failure to enact enabling legislation must be shared with those banks that have not joined in urging the same legislators to act.

This lack of a strong consensus is directly traceable to the fragmentation of commercial banking that is both traditional and endemic in the United States. The desires, and the strategies, of a large money-center bank may have nothing common with those of a small community institution; yet it is doubtful that any legislative repeal will take place as long as so many banks—even if they have no individual interest in diversifying—remain on the sidelines and do nothing to help the entire industry move ahead.[54]

In 1970 Henry Wallich, member of the Federal Reserve Board of Governors, commented that "Banking, with its three federal and fifty state supervisory authorities and bodies of law to match, is the most overregulated industry in the country."[55] Despite the implementation of the Monetary Control and Garn–St Germain Acts, little has happened to invalidate his opinion. Some deregulation has certainly taken place, but from the commercial banks' standpoint it has been confined chiefly to the liability side of the balance sheet and, on an overall basis, has done relatively little to make them more efficient as competitors for other providers of financial services.

For example, deregulation specifically allowed the banks to offer money-market deposit accounts in 1982 to offset the funds that had attracted $240 billion from the public. Within one year, the banks had succeeded in building up $400 billion in the new accounts. Interest-bearing deposits are clearly better than no deposits at all; in that respect, deregulation was helpful.[56] Whatever expansion of banks into diversified activities has taken place, however, is the result in most instances of various new interpretations of existing laws rather than specific new laws. The banks usually circumvent the statutory restraints; they have not been abolished.[57]

Functional deregulation, then, refers to the *powers* granted to commercial banks as contrasted with those assumed by their many competitors. The discrepancies are sufficiently great to prompt J.P. Morgan, Inc. to consider resigning its banking charter so that it can capitalize on the profit opportunities in securities underwriting—an activity specifically prohibited under its existing structure.[58]

Deregulation has enabled thrift institutions to move onto the banks' turf, allowing them to invest up to 30 percent of their assets in consumer, and 10 percent in commercial, loans; state-chartered thrifts may invest an additional 10 percent in loan participations.[59] Merrill Lynch, GMAC, and Sears never required statutory permission to invade the banks' territory, and the extent of their invasion is not legally circumscribed. Similarly, Anthony Solomon, then President of the Federal Reserve Bank of New York, described the nonbank banks in 1984 as "the most offensive examples" of bank competitors, given their ability to exploit legislative loopholes and the manner in which they can be used by any firm to offer any financial service anywhere in the country.[60]

Arguments against Deregulation

Opponents of functional deregulation can be found within, as well as outside, the banking industry. Their objections often fall under any of the following headings:

the need to separate banking from commerce,

the present troubled state of the banking industry,

the risks inherent in bank diversification,

the correlation between government protection of banks and regulation of banking.

Banking and Commerce

This history of legislation on the subject of bank holding companies (1933, 1956, 1970) indicates that Congress was well aware of the traditional legislative separation of banking from commerce. The BHC Acts and their subsequent Amendments showed Congressional concern over the role that banks play in the U.S. economy and over the possibility of discrimination by the bank component of a BHC in extending credit to an affiliate. In 1969 the White House transmitted this message regarding pending consideration of BHC legislation:

> Legislation in this area is important because there has been a disturbing trend in the past year toward erosion of the traditional separation of powers between the suppliers of money—the banks—and the users of money—commerce and industry.
>
> Left unchecked, the trend toward the combining of banking and business could lead to the formation of a relatively small number of power centers dominating the American economy. This must not be permitted to happen. . . . Banking must not dominate commerce or be dominated by it.[61]

In response, Congress limited BHC activities to those that are "so closely related to banking as to be a proper incident thereto," and the Fed, weighing the potential adverse effects of any application, must apply the test of public benefits. These restrictions have led the Fed, at various times, to deny applications for, or to prohibit specifically, BHC operation of travel agencies; underwriting property, casualty, mortgage guaranty, and non-credit-related life insurance; real estate brokerage and syndication; and property management and general management consulting services.[62]

It would seem, therefore, that there is a valid question about whether a real separation of banking from commerce now exists, given the synergy that links the bank component of a BHC to the other subsidiaries. Paul Volcker has identified the fact that the financial fortunes of the bank in a BHC are necessarily tied to those of the other entities:

> The practical realities of the marketplace and the internal dynamics of a business organization under central direction drives [*sic*] bank holding companies to act . . . as one business entity, with the component parts drawing on each other for marketing and financial strength.[63]

One BHC bought $14.8 million in troublesome loans from its own Real Estate Investment Trust (REIT). In doing so, it admitted potential losses but justified the action as a means of protecting the BHC's stockholders.[64] Andrew Brimmer, of the Federal Reserve Board, stated categorically that "Banks have got a mother-hen complex. Every bank holding company will do whatever it can, at considerable cost, to avoid failure of an affiliate.[65]

Walter Wriston's viewpoint summarizes the case. Those who oppose further functional deregulation on the grounds of the need for separating banking from commerce ignore the fact that BHCs have already integrated the two:

> It is inconceivable that any major bank would walk away from any subsidiary of its holding company. If your name is on the door, all your capital funds are going to be behind it in the real world. Lawyers can say you have separation, but the marketplace is persuasive, and it would not see it that way.[66]

Banking Industry Problems

Opponents of deregulation also point to many of the difficulties banks have encountered in recent years, and use these as an argument against giving the banks added powers that might serve to exacerbate the situation. The validity of this opposition rests on the question of exactly how serious the current problems are.

Those problems cannot be dismissed lightly or ignored. Bank failures in 1985 and 1986 were more numerous than in any year since 1934. From 1980 to mid-1986, 282 commercial banks failed; with 118 failing during a twelve-month period ending in mid-1986, there is obvious cause for concern. However, Frederick H. Schultz, former Vice-Chairman of the Fed, notes that those 118 banks represent 0.1 percent of all bank assets and less than 1 percent of all banks, while for the industry as a whole, nonperforming loans have decreased and loan-loss reserves have doubled since 1981.[67]

The failures of the Penn Square National Bank and Continental Illinois, the banks' problems with global debt, and the weak conditions of many banks involved in agricultural and energy lending in the United States are often cited as evidence of an overall industry weakness. Indeed, during a single week in July 1986, BankAmerica Corporation reported a quarterly loss of $640 million; five bank failures occurred in Kansas, Missouri, Nebraska, Wyoming, and New Mexico; and a billion-dollar bank in Oklahoma City failed and was sold.[68] Increases in problem areas such as real estate loans and card outstandings have also been noted.[69]

Gerald Corrigan, President of the New York Fed, points out, however, that from 1982 to 1985 the primary capital of the twenty-five largest banking organizations in the United States grew by $26.5 billion, or 57 percent.[70] Since 1981, earnings of the fifty largest BHCs have grown by almost 50 percent, and in 1985 the industry as a whole showed an increase in earnings of some 17 percent.[71]

The prophets of doom appear to ignore the fact that the bank failures are largely localized in the farm and energy-reliant areas, that bank management is placing increasingly greater emphasis on asset quality, that the Federal Reserve has shown its willingness to act as a lender of last resort, that the

FDIC is providing substantial assistance wherever necessary, and that Continental Illinois has repaid the loans which were necessary to prevent its liquidation.

Risks in Diversification

In his book *Risk and Other Four-Letter Words,* Walter Wriston stated the following:

> The fact is that bankers are in the business of managing risk. Pure and simple, that is the business of banking. As long as a bank keeps its risks within its risk-taking capabilities, it survives; and if it doesn't, it dies.[72]

Opponents of deregulation express concerns over the ability of banks to assume any additional risks, such as those they might encounter if they were allowed to engage in additional activities in which they have had no prior experience.

There are two rebuttals to this opposition. The first and most important of these reflects the degree of supervision the Federal Reserve exercises over BHCs. If Congress approved the entry of BHCs into the securities or brokerage business, the Fed would still have the right of individual jurisdiction in each case. Under Regulation Y, the Fed is required to assess the financial condition, management competence and character, and future prospects of every BHC applicant. It can readily deny any request if approval would substantially lessen competition or tend to create a monopoly.[73]

Congress has already expressed its faith in the Fed's ability to make these judgments. A BHC applicant without a track record of successful operations and capable management would find its application rejected; its past failure to manage risks successfully would be per se cause for denial. Likewise, the question of monopolistic trends is not germane to discussion of possible bank entry into the brokerage or securities business, where firms such as Merrill Lynch and Prudential-Bache, Sears and Metropolitan Life, Travelers and American Express have already obtained large market shares.

The second rebuttal reflects the actions already taken by the banks' competitors, including those previously mentioned. The degree to which they have already diversified is a reflection of their willingness to make huge commitments and enter new lines of business. The universal banks of Europe have already achieved a high diversification into various bank-related activities and services. It is reasonable to suggest that their U.S. counterparts be given comparable latitude to serve the public.

The risks entailed in possible functional deregulation carry with them opportunities for the banks to compete more effectively in the open market. However, there is an important caveat: The risks must be properly managed, and there must be supervision of every BHC that wishes to incur them. Many banks and BHCs may not do so. For those that do, it is in the common interest that they be subject to examination and a degree of control.

For this reason, even without any further deregulation, all BHCs have been subjected in 1986 to more frequent, thorough examination and more detailed monitoring than before by the Fed.[74] Paul Volcker's message to Congress, urging that BHCs be given more powers, contained a limitation: a clearly stated stipulation that the extent of Federal Reserve supervision would be increased.[75]

Protection and Regulation

The foregoing paragraph indicates that there is an accepted and necessary correlation between the protection extended by the federal government to banks and the degree of regulation it imposes on them. It is entirely unreasonable to suggest that banking be allowed to operate without regulation. All historical evidence shows that unregulated banking leads to crises; the colonists' belief in free banking led to near disaster. A system that is so vital to every segment of the entire economy, that handles over $1 trillion in transactions each day, that serves as the major source of credit, and that accepts the liquid funds of every category of customer cannot be left unregulated.

The liabilities of banks and the stability of depositories have been protected for many years by a so-called safety net, in which the Federal Reserve and the two federal insurers provide a support apparatus. This protection is in exchange for the privileges and powers extended to the banks. In recent years, however, a basic question has surfaced: under that safety net, should big banks be allowed to fail? Is our society willing to have them fail so that federal regulators can exert proper discipline on the system as a whole?

The posture of federal agencies, as witnessed in the Continental Illinois case and later enunciated by regulators, is that major institutions will not be permitted to fail. Some form of government intervention will prevent their liquidation to avoid a dangerous chain reaction in the industry at all costs. The counterpart to that protection, again, lies in regulation.

Two of the nation's top banking regulators, although they expressly favored further deregulation of banking, held an identical viewpoint regarding the necessary interrelationship of protection and regulation. Former Chairman William M. Isaac of the FDIC stated, "I believe very much in deregulation, but we also need substantial improvement in the supervision of banks."[76] C. Todd Conover, then Comptroller of the Currency, was more succinct: "Deregulation does not mean no regulation."[77] Isaac has further noted that

> There's always going to be a fair amount of government involvement in banking. . . . We've had periods when banking was relatively free of regulation. Those periods were characterized by one crisis after another. It's not realistic to think that government will ignore banking; what we're talking about is balance.[78]

In short, the banks do not seek total deregulation; rather, the key issue is the extent to which the regulation over the activities of banks and BHCs must be retained.

Summary

The President of Bankers Trust Company (New York) has spoken on the question of balanced deregulation in these terms:

> The business enterprise that diversifies is more likely to be a profitable—and safe—enterprise. . . . The degree of [regulatory] restrictions will be directly related to the potential for risk reduction. If the restrictions are few and trivial, most of the benefits of diversification can still be realized.
>
> Limitations on diversification say to banks, "We will keep you out of trouble by keeping you out of these businesses." As a matter of fact, they are increasing the likelihood of trouble by refusing to allow banks the opportunity to reduce risk through diversification. At the same time, they are denying consumers the opportunity to pay less for the services they are purchasing. In these circumstances, there is simply no benefit to anyone.[79]

Nineteen eighty-six was an especially difficult year for banks to seek deregulation. During the first eight months of the year, ninety-four banks, insured by the FDIC, failed.[80] Those who would grant no additional powers to the banks point to these failures as proof of the need for continued strict regulation. The fact remains, however, that not one of these failures can be attributed to any deregulation that has already taken place in the banking system. Indeed, the failures support Charles Sanford's thesis; forty-six of them took place among agricultural banks (i.e., those banks whose agricultural loans comprised 25 percent or more of their total portfolios), and a measure of deregulation conceivably could have enabled them to diversify and thereby improve their income.

The debate in Congress cannot be confined to a discussion of a handful of additional activities that might become permissible for banks and BHCs. It must address also the question of the type and degree of regulation that will shape the course of those institutions for the future.

Notes

1. "30th Annual Survey of the World's Top 500 Banks," *American Banker,* July 29, 1986, p. 53.

2. Carol S. Greenwald, "Who's Regulating the Regulators?," *The Bankers Magazine,* March–April 1981, p. 41.

3. In "Banking in Transition," *The Bankers Magazine,* September–October 1978, p. 22.

4. In Ibid., p. 29.

5. Monica Langley, "Rival Bank Regulators Agree Only to Disagree on Most Major Issues," *The Wall Street Journal,* January 23, 1985, p. 1.

6. Blanca Riemer, "The Two Trailblazers Leading Banking to the Promised Land," *Business Week,* December 17, 1984, pp. 99–100.

7. F. Daniel Prickett, "Banking on a Segmented Market," *The Bankers Magazine,* March–April 1985, p. 44.

8. Edward W. Reed; Richard V. Cotter; Edward K. Gill; and Richard K. Smith, *Commercial Banking,* 3rd ed. (Englewood Cliffs, N.J.: Prentice-Hall, Inc., 1984), p. 49.

9. A history of the opposition to branch banking can be found in Mary L. King, *The Great American Banking Snafu* (Lexington, Mass.: Lexington Books, 1985), pp. 61–64.

10. 12 U.S.C. 36; and 396 U.S. 135.

11. Michael A. Jessee and Steven A. Seelig, *Bank Holding Companies and the Public Interest* (Lexington, Mass.: Lexington Books, 1977), p. 10.

12. Michael Reese and Eric Gelman, "California Dreamin'," *Newsweek,* August 4, 1986, pp. 36–37.

13. Board of Governors of the Federal Reserve System, *Annual Report 1943,* p. 9.

14. 12 C.F.R. § 225.22.

15. Donald T. Savage, "Depository Financial Institutions," in Richard C. Aspinwall and Robert A. Eisenbeis, eds., *Handbook for Banking Strategy* (New York: John Wiley & Sons, Inc., 1985), pp. 187–189.

16. Martin H. Wolfson, "Financial Developments of Bank Holding Companies in 1984," *Federal Reserve Bulletin,* December 1985, p. 924.

17. Board of Governors of the Federal Reserve System, *72nd Annual Report* (1985), p. 169.

18. In Robert D. Hershey Jr., "Fed Plans to Bolster Bank Examinations," *The New York Times,* October 8, 1985, p. D1.

19. Savage, op. cit., p. 191.

20. Richard M. Whiting, "New Nonbanking Activities: A Look Back and Ahead," *American Banker,* January 8, 1986, p. 54.

21. Ibid.

22. This topic is treated in detail in Reed et al., op. cit., pp. 50–52.

23. 12 C.F.R. § 225.13 (a), as amended February 3, 1984.

24. Lynne Curry, "Citicorp Growth Spreads Fear Among Competitors," *International Herald Tribune,* June 11, 1984, p. 8.

25. Eric N. Compton, *Inside Commercial Banking,* 2nd ed. (New York: John Wiley & Sons, Inc., 1983), p. 223.

26. In Jonathan Hakim, "A New Awakening," *The Economist,* March 24, 1984, p. 10.

27. "1985 Performance of Top U.S. Banking Companies," *American Banker,* June 20, 1986, pp. 22–24.

28. Alan J. Weber, "Bankers Must Change Technology," *American Banker,* September 15, 1980, p. 9.

29. Peter Field, "California, Here They Come," *Euromoney,* May 1984, p. 122.

30. Michael Weinstein, "Credit Card Business Mushrooms at Large Banks," *American Banker,* August 14, 1986, p. 1.

31. King, op. cit., pp. 170–171.

32. "Retail Banking: It's Terrible, It's Wonderful," *ABA Banking Journal,* June 1980, p. 90.

33. Jeffrey Kutler, "Mobil's Point-of-Sale Network Signs up Citibank's Debit Card," *American Banker,* July 30, 1986, p. 11.

34. In Robert E. Norton, "Citicorp Plans Push into Insurance and Data Services," *American Banker,* March 9, 1984, p. 1.

35. Alan Gart, *Banks, Thrifts, and Insurance Companies* (Lexington, Mass.: Lexington Books, 1985), pp. 64–69.

36. Martin Mayer, *The Bankers* (New York: David McKay Co., 1974), p. 259; and Robert M. Garsson, " 'Hybrid' Citicorp Makes Gains on Many Fronts," *American Banker,* June 24, 1986, p. 3.

37. Norton, op. cit.; and Gart, op. cit., p. 66.

38. Garsson, op. cit.

39. Laura Gross, "Citicorp Interstate Plans Rely on Office Conversions," *American Banker,* January 22, 1981, p. 1.

40. John Carson-Parker, "Why the Blue Chips Bank on Morgan," *Fortune,* July 13, 1981, p. 38.

41. "1985 Performance of Top U.S. Banking Companies," p. 22.

42. J.P. Morgan, *Annual Report* (1985), p. 3.

43. Ibid., p. 5.

44. See Howard D. Crosse and George H. Hempel, *Management Policies for Commercial Banks,* 2nd ed. (Englewood Cliffs, N.J.: Prentice-Hall Inc., 1973), pp. 27–30.

45. "Federal Laws Regulating Bank Mergers," *Economic Review* (Federal Reserve Bank of Cleveland), January 1971, p. 18.

46. Detailed analysis of this and subsequent Court decisions regarding bank mergers may be found in Harvey Rosenblum; John Di Clemente; and Kit O'Brien, "The Product Market in Commercial Banking: Cluster's Last Stand," *Economic Perspectives* (Federal Reserve Bank of Chicago), January–February 1985, pp. 24–25.

47. Anthony S. Winer, "Applying the Theory of Probable Future Competition," *Federal Reserve Bulletin,* September 1982, pp. 531–532.

48. Board of Governors of the Federal Reserve System, *72nd Annual Report 1985,* p. 181. These developments in interstate banking are discussed in chapter 12.

49. Ibid., p. 162.

50. Alan Gart, *The Insider's Guide to the Financial Services Revolution* (New York: McGraw-Hill Book Company, 1984), p. 28.

51. In *Federal Reserve Bulletin,* August 1986, p. 549.

52. Ibid., p. 541.

53. Ibid., p. 554.

54. William W. Streeter, "Why the Reluctance to Push for New Services?," *ABA Banking Journal,* June 1986, p. 19.

55. "Banks Need More Freedom to Compete," *Fortune,* March 1970, p. 114.

56. Paul S. Nadler, "Don't Blame Deregulation," *Bankers Monthly Magazine,* January 15, 1985, p. 11.

57. Ibid., pp. 12–13.

58. Raoul D. Edwards, "The Management of Risk," *United States Banker,* June 1986, p. 34.

59. Robert Luke, "Interstate Banking in California: A Gold Rush?," *American Banker,* August 21, 1986, p. 1.

60. Anthony M. Solomon, "Bank Deregulation—What Next?," *Bankers Monthly Magazine,* October 15, 1984, p. 16.

61. In *Federal Reserve Bulletin,* August 1986, p. 544.

62. David D. Whitehead and Pamela Frisbee, "Positioning for Interstate Banking," *Economic Review* (Federal Reserve Bank of Atlanta), September 1982, p. 17.

63. In *Federal Reserve Bulletin,* August 1986, p. 545.

64. Jack M. Guttenberg and Bernard Shull, "Bank Holding Companies and Abuse of the Power to Grant Credit," in Federal Reserve Bank of Chicago, *Conference on Bank Structure and Competition* (April 1977), p. 129.

65. In "An Early Warning System to Spot Sick Banks," *Business Week,* October 26, 1974, p. 92.

66. In *Federal Reserve Bulletin,* August 1986, p. 545.

67. "Why the Banking System Is Getting Stronger," *Fortune,* July 7, 1986, p. 37.

68. Robert E. Norton, "Banks Are Safer than You Think," *Fortune,* August 18, 1986, p. 53.

69. John P. Forde, "Bank Credit Woes Continue into 3rd Quarter," *American Banker,* August 14, 1986, p. 3.

70. In Schultz, op. cit., p. 40.

71. Ibid.

72. In Edwards, op. cit., p. 30.

73. 12 C.F.R. § 225.13 (a)(1, 2) and (b)(1, 2).

74. Board of Governors of the Federal Reserve System, *72nd Annual Report* (1985), pp. 172–175.

75. In *Federal Reserve Bulletin,* August 1986, p. 554.

76. In Riemer, op. cit., p. 98.

77. In ibid., p. 100.

78. In Robert A. Bennett, "A Banking Puzzle: Mixing Freedom and Protection," *The New York Times,* February 19, 1984, p. D1.

79. Charles S. Sanford, "Tradeoff for Banking System: Playing It Safe or Competitive?," *American Banker,* November 7, 1984, p. 12.

80. Jay Rosenstein, "Four More Banks Close; Total of FDIC-Insured Failures at 94 for Year," *American Banker,* August 25, 1986, p. 7.

12
The New World of Interstate Banking

This discussion of interstate banking necessarily begins with a semantic clarification and continues with an outline of the realities of the system as of mid-1986. If *interstate banking* is construed in its traditional sense to mean full-scale, unrestricted branch banking throughout the country, then interstate banking has never existed in the United States as it has in many other major industrial countries. There is no U.S. counterpart to Barclays Bank, Toronto Dominion, Deutsche Bank, or Société Générale. In this context, the McFadden Act and the Douglas Amendment remain in effect and state boundaries restrict bank or BHC expansion.

That interpretation of the term, however, is a narrow one that ignores the developments of the 1980s. Those developments have been so numerous and so dramatic that it has become patently absurd to hold that interstate banking does not exist in the United States. De jure, it is prohibited; de facto, it is very much alive, under a variety of names, and there appears to be little doubt that it represents the banking pattern of the future.

> When major money-center banks establish Edge Act, consumer finance, loan-production, limited-service, equipment-leasing, information-processing, mortgage-servicing, and discount brokerage offices across state lines, interstate banking exists.
>
> When a depositor of a Chicago bank can use his or her bank card to obtain cash from another bank's ATM in Seattle, San Diego, Boston, or Miami, interstate banking, for all practical purposes, exists.
>
> When a bank holding company, acting under the "extraordinary acquisition" provisions of the Garn–St Germain Act, purchases a distressed thrift institution in another state and operates it as one of its subsidiaries, interstate banking exists[1]; when the distressed thrift is subsequently converted into a commercial bank, the reality becomes even more transparent.

When nine banks, headquartered in states from California to New York, announce plans to take advantage of a change in Arizona law by acquiring and operating banks in that state, interstate banking has arrived.[2]

When the legislatures of various states approve regional banking compacts that permit out-of-state entry, interstate banking is a reality. The U.S. Supreme Court, in a unanimous decision on June 10, 1985,[3] upheld the constitutionality of those agreements and the rights of the individual contracting states to specify the states from which entry applications would be considered and those from which acquisitions would be prohibited.[4]

When a survey of chain banking systems discloses that 128 such systems are still in operation across state lines, interstate banking exists.[5]

When a Citicorp spokesperson describes the scope of his BHC's operations in South Dakota, Chicago (Diners Club), St. Louis (mortgage banking), and Nevada, Florida, Illinois, and California (thrift institutions), its 100,000 consumer relationships in the Washington, D.C. area, and its 9 million Visa cards and proprietary cards in ten states, he is clearly describing an interstate banking system.[6]

The overwhelming evidence, then, makes it clear that with the sole exception of actual full-scale branching, interstate banking is a part of the contemporary scene. Complete geographic deregulation is the only missing element. It will become possible when and if Congress comes to a realization that

1. The numerous steps that have already been taken to implement variations of interstate banking make the remaining legal barriers unrealistic and anachronistic;
2. The traditional and theoretical arguments against full-scale interstate branching are no longer valid;
3. Abolishing the remaining obstacles is actually in keeping with the stated objective of the Monetary control Act: to improve competitive equity among financial institutions. S&Ls already operate across state lines,[7] and the unrestricted nationwide activities of nonbank competitors have already been thoroughly documented.

Historical Development

The interstate movement, as outlined, received its first real impetus in August 1981, when Key Banks of Albany, New York, took advantage of Maine's reciprocal banking laws and agreed to acquire Depositors Corporation of Augusta.[8] Since that date, over fifty BHCs have either completed interstate acquisitions or, as authorized under reciprocal agreements among various states (as permitted by the Douglas Amendment), are in the process of doing so. Thirty-one states and the District of Columbia now permit some form of interstate banking.[9]

Since 1982 the trend has increasingly been toward regional pacts, in which state legislatures have allowed the entry of out-of-state entities under specified conditions. In some cases the regional agreements restrict the geographic areas from which acquiring BHCs may come; in others, a state allows those acquisitions regardless of the acquiring BHC's location.

For example, as of mid-1986 Massachusetts allows bank branching and BHC acquisitions on a reciprocal basis with the other New England states.[10] Kentucky, Illinois, Michigan, Indiana, and Ohio have a general agreement allowing acquisitions on a fully reciprocal basis, but in each case the other states from which an acquiring BHC may come are designated.[11] Georgia, Florida, North Carolina, and South Carolina were the pioneers in a Southeast regional agreement (1984), allowing BHC acquisitions on a reciprocal basis among twelve contiguous states and the District of Columbia. Alabama, Maryland, Tennessee, and Virginia subsequently passed similar laws. In every case, an individual state reserved the right to identify the other states from which an acquiring BHC might come.[12] In the Far West, Idaho (with six contiguous states) and Oregon (with eight other states) have entered into reciprocal banking agreements.[13] Alaska and Arizona, as of October 1, 1986, allow BHCs from any other state to acquire their banks.[14]

Many of these regional agreements contain various restrictive clauses that, for example, limit the scope of operations that the entering banks may conduct or stipulate that an acquired bank must have been in business for a specified number of years.[15] Table 12–1 lists some of the major interstate acquisitions and mergers that took place in 1985.

An additional breaching of the wall against interstate branching occurred in August 1986 when First American Bankshares, a BHC headquartered in Washington, D.C. announced that it would allow customers to make deposits through its ATMs in its banks in both Maryland and Virginia. Interstate deposit taking is prohibited by federal law, and it remains to be seen whether First American will be allowed to continue the practice.[16]

It is noteworthy that the regional banking agreements that have been negotiated as of mid-1986 have carefully preserved the rights of individual states to circumscribe the extent of permitted acquisitions. The McFadden Act (1927) superseded the authority of the Comptroller of the Currency by making all national banks subject to state laws on branching; since that time, states' rights have been repeatedly upheld by the courts. In their appeal to the Supreme Court, Citicorp and Northeast Bancorporation posed a challenge

Table 12–1
Major Interstate Acquisitions by BHCs, 1985

Acquirer	*Acquired or Merged Bank or BHC*	*Combined Assets*
Suntrust Banks, Inc., Atlanta	Sun Banks, Inc., Orlando, and Trust Company of Georgia	$15.6 billion
Bank of Boston Corp.	Colonial Bancorp, Inc., Waterbury, Conn., and RIHT Financial Corp., Providence, R.I.	3.8 billion
Bank of New England Corp., Boston	CBT Corporation,[a] Hartford, Conn.	6.9 billion
Norstar Bancorp., Albany, N.Y.	Bank of Maine Corp., Augusta	91 million
First Union Corp., Charlotte, N.C.	Atlantic Bancorp, Jacksonville, Fla.	6.5 billion
First Wachovia Corp., Winston-Salem, N.C.	First Atlanta Corp.	15.7 billion

Source: "1985 Bank Holding Company Acquisitions Made by the Nation's Top 100 Banking Firms," *American Banker,* December 23, 1985, p. 14.
[a]Formerly Connecticut Bank and Trust Company.

to regional agreements that effectively barred them from acquisitions while allowing BHCs from other states to enter an area. By upholding the constitutionality of such agreements, the Court reaffirmed the principle of states' rights. As a result, it is now clear that the states that are parties to an agreement that keeps money-center giants from moving in or that prevents BHCs from certain states from making acquisitions are within their rights. Thus, the legal precedent has been firmly set for future agreements.[17]

John D. Hawke, Jr., former General Counsel to the Federal Reserve Board, has identified the paradox in the current situation: the states have made it far easier for Congress to continue its long-standing policy of avoiding the issue of interstate banking, and nationwide banking (which he considers inevitable) will result from state actions rather than from federal legislation.[18] The states now recognize that their individual rights have been protected, that they can restrict the ability of out-of-state entrants to compete fully with local banks, and that they can exercise various other controls over those entrants.

For example, Delaware, Maryland, Virginia, and Nebraska are among the states that allow limited entry for specific purposes (e.g., to take advantage of liberal usury laws or to provide a desired level of local employment), and as a rule the states seem to have become more comfortable with the notion of out-of-state entry. They recognize that "it's not going to be the end of the world if outsiders come in."[19] They may also be aware of the 1985 survey of 1,004 households in various parts of the country; 57 percent of the respondents in that survey favored interstate banking, and 67 percent felt it would bring them more services.[20]

As of August 1986, there were several additional indications of acceptance by states of the inevitability of interstate banking. California and Texas were among those considering legislation to permit entry by outsiders, and it is interesting to note the contrast between these two: California has always been the prototype of a state that permitted statewide branching, just as Texas has always been cited as the classic example of a unit banking state, fragmented among hundreds of institutions.[21] At the same time, New Jersey's liberalized provisions took effect, allowing reciprocal acquisitions with ten other states but specifically prohibiting entry into New Jersey by New York banks. In advance of the legal starting date, three Pennsylvania banks had entered into merger agreements with New Jersey institutions.[22]

Combinations such as those of North Carolina BHCs with Georgia counterparts or Pennsylvania's with New Jersey's give long-overdue recognition to the fact that barriers to banking across state lines can no longer be supported or accepted. There is no logic in a regulatory system that tries to prevent banks from entering geographic areas that are completely open to both their customers and competitors. Major corporations borrow from banks throughout the country; depositors may live anywhere; and thrift institutions and nonbank banks have no restrictions comparable to those placed on commercial banks.

The theory of a free-market economy is inconsistent with the restrictions that prevent a bank from crossing a state boundary one mile away and operating in a state where many of its clients are located, while at the same time the bank may be establishing branches in countries thousands of miles away. Removal of the existing barriers may help BHCs, through mergers and acquisitions across state lines, become more competitive with the money-center giants that have already established a national presence through subsidiaries, loan-production and Edge Act offices, and huge cardholder bases.[23]

Utah's Commissioner of Financial Institutions is among those who feel that "Interstate banking should strengthen financial institutions as they diversify their markets and increase their efficiency."[24] Indeed, a Presidential Commission on Financial Institutions urged the states to be more progressive in changing their restrictive laws, on the grounds that "Failure to act could encourage the use of inferior organizational and technological means for extending markets."[25]

Fears and Concerns

Any mention of nationwide banking has always prompted spokespersons for banks in smaller communities to reintroduce the cliché of "undue concentrations of economic power" by speculating that the money-center giants would swallow up or force out of business the local banks. For example, a member of the New Hampshire legislature, speaking in opposition to interstate banking, said, "Citicorp or Chase Manhattan would promptly buy BankEast [Manchester, N.H.] and take all . . . [its] deposits and lend those funds to Poland."[26] Although farfetched, this vision of a possible future epitomizes the concerns of many individuals. There are many reasons for believing that these concerns are completely unwarranted.

The most convincing rebuttal comes from the Supreme Court. The individual states clearly have the right to exclude the biggest banks, and/or those from certain geographic areas, from regional agreements or from invading their territories; the decision, as one legal authority has noted, "leaves no room for challenge. It puts the definite imprimatur on the validity of regional statutes."[27] If a state is particularly concerned over the possibilities of takeovers of its banks by institutions from, for example, New York City, it can bar them simply through the language contained in its law. As cited earlier, New Jersey has done this.

A second rebuttal addresses the question of the costs of nationwide acquisitions in contrast to the potential benefits. A 1985 study analyzed the potential expenses in such programs if they were to be conducted by any of the ten largest BHCs and demonstrated that any such plan exceeding a 5 percent expansion in size would be seriously self-limiting.[28] The constraints identified in this study included the costs of capital necessary to pay a premium for each acquisition, a dilution of the stockholders' equity in the acquiring BHC or bank, and the regulatory guidelines on capital/assets ratios applicable to the expanded organization.

Implicit in this rebuttal is the price of a particular interstate acquisition. The President of a New York firm that specializes in analyzing banks' performance studied one purchase and determined that an earnings growth of 19 percent in the acquired BHC would be necessary for the purchaser to recover costs.[29] Some acquirers have been offering more than twice the book value for the shares of those takeover candidates they consider attractive, and in Arizona, banks have sold for an average of two and one-half times book value and more than fifteen times their earnings per share.[30] An offer of this type may have strong appeal to stockholders in the acquired bank, but at the same time the number of potential acquirers becomes extremely small, and a single acquisition by any one of them limits its ability to make further moves. Stockholders in a bank or BHC that is contemplating an interstate acquisition base their vote on what they expect to happen to the earnings. They have no interest in growth for growth's sake or in proposals that will reduce earnings or dilute equity.

The costs of an interstate acquisition are by no means confined to the initial purchase. All the overhead incurred in expansion must be considered, and two studies conducted independently by staff members at the Federal Reserve Banks of Atlanta and Chicago indicate that economies of scale do not necessarily apply to a large-scale acquisition. If the acquirer must install brick-and-mortar facilities and add significantly to the labor force, the expense negates the potential benefits.[31] However, those actions might be inherent in a particular situation.

A national sampling of 3,052 households in 1985 showed that 40 percent of respondents would be comfortable using an out-of-state provider of banking services if a network of branches, high-quality services, ATM availability, and highly competitive pricing of those services were part of the understanding.[32] The BHC or bank that attempted to meet these criteria could find the total costs prohibitive, more so than the purchase price.

In summary, there is strong evidence that the possibility of thousands of nationwide branches of the money-center giants, forcing local community banks out of business, is at least remote. Those institutions certainly may operate to some degree in various parts of the country—Citicorp, for example, may eventually be allowed to convert its existing loan-production offices into full-scale branches—but they cannot possibly afford to expand beyond a certain point, and in any event, state laws could prevent them from doing so.

Table 12–2
BHC Takeovers of Failing Commercial Banks, 1986

Date	*Acquired Bank*	*Deposit Size*	*Acquirer*
January 24	Utah First Bank, Salt Lake City	$33.4 million	Citibank (Utah)[a]
February 14	Park Bank of Florida, St. Petersburg	543.9 million	Chase Manhattan
July 14	First National Bank, Oklahoma City	1.5 billion	First Interstate Bank of Oklahoma City N.A.[b]
July 25	Bank of Park County, Bailey, Colorado	4.8 million	Bank of Mountain Valley, N.A., Conifer, Colorado[c]

Source: "FDIC-Insured Banks That Have Failed or Been Rescued in 1986," *American Banker,* August 20, 1986, p. 12.

[a]Newly chartered subsidiary of Citicorp (New York).

[b]Newly chartered subsidiary of First Interstate Bancorp (Los Angeles).

[c]Newly chartered subsidiary of Mountain Parks Financial Corporation (Minneapolis).

Takeovers of Failing Banks

In four instances during 1986, interstate acquisitions were permitted to allow a financially sound BHC in one area to take over a failing commercial bank in another. These takeovers are listed in table 12–2.

More commonly during the mid-1980s, however, BHCs have availed themselves of the provisions of the Garn–St Germain Act and have expanded geographically through takeovers of failing thrifts. The Act allows a BHC to acquire a federally insured thrift under emergency provisions if the FSLIC and the Federal Reserve Board approve. The worse the financial condition of the thrift, the more quickly the acquisition will be approved.[33]

The Garn–St Germain Act, through this emergency provision, was intended to prevent additional failures. It recognized the fact that the problems of the thrifts, caused in large part by the negative spreads between their long-term, fixed-rate portfolios of mortgage loans and the costs of their deposits, could easily result in a wave of failures. The FDIC and the FSLIC would then face a need for large-scale payouts to depositors, and public confidence would be severely shaken. Both federal insurers, therefore, have become activist organizations, assisting failing thrifts with infusions of funds and playing a part in arranging takeovers by stronger financial institutions. At the same time, this posture on the part of the two agencies has contributed to the controversy over whether any large bank, BHC, or thrift should be allowed to fail; that is, is government intervention always appropriate?

Citicorp

The first of the major interstate acquisitions of failed thrifts occurred in September 1982, when Citicorp received permission to buy Fidelity S&L of Oakland, California. Deposit erosion amounting to $350 million had taken place at that institution over a six-month period. The FSLIC provided $165 million in financial aid to assist in the takeover, and this marked the first time that the Fed had approved a takeover, across state lines, of a thrift by a BHC.[34] The resulting institution, Citicorp Savings, had ninety-two offices as of 1984 in sixty-six California cities, with total assets of $3.3 billion. Its President claimed that it had increased home mortgage lending to $250 million per year, saved 900 jobs and created the possibility of additional employment through statewide expansion, and restored public confidence in the state.[35]

In 1984 the Federal Reserve Board, despite opposition from two of its members, approved two further acquisitions of failing thrifts by Citicorp. In granting permission for the takeover of First Federal S&L (Chicago) and New Biscayne Federal S&L (Miami), the Board imposed a set of restrictive conditions on Citicorp's operation of the two entities and warned that it would weigh competitive factors heavily if Citicorp were to attempt further expansion into the thrift industry.[36]

Early in 1985 the Federal Home Loan Bank Board (FHLBB), which regulates all S&Ls, imposed new capital-reserve requirements on them and liberalized its rules on takeovers. Edwin Gray, Chairman of the Board, expressed fears that excessive risk taking by thrifts and poor management would increase the number of failures and deplete the FSLIC fund, which at that time stood at $6 billion.[37] Only one additional Citicorp acquisition has been made since that FHLBB ruling. In November 1985 Citicorp was allowed to take over All State Thrift, an uninsured S&L in Las Vegas that had failed earlier in the year. In this instance, Citicorp planned to convert the institution into a full-service commercial bank.[38]

Developments in 1985

Problems throughout the thrift industry continued in 1985. In many cases these were considered to be a result of the entry of many institutions into areas of high-risk lending, permitted under the Monetary Control and Garn–St Germain Acts but never attempted by the thrifts. By May 1985, a total of 1,000 thrifts—one-fourth of the total number—had gone out of business over a five-year period, and some analysts began to speculate about whether the industry as such could continue to exist.[39] At year-end 1984, FHLBB statistics indicated that 438 insured thrifts, with $107 billion in assets, had negative net worths and that 856 other thrifts, with $350 billion in assets, had net worths below required minima.[40]

Ohio and Maryland

Two particular crises involved thrift institutions during 1985. In each case, the solution was found in allowing an out-of-state BHC to acquire the failed or failing thrifts and to convert them into full-service commercial banks.

In March of that year Governor Richard Celeste and the Ohio State Legislature ordered the closing of seventy-one thrifts, following a run of massive proportions on these uninsured institutions.[41] Depositors reacted to the failure of Home State Savings Bank (Cincinnati) by making large withdrawals from other thrifts, and original estimates indicated that state funds of at least $200 million would be needed to build up the thrifts' capital and otherwise assist in restoring public confidence.[42]

The State Legislature subsequently approved the application of Chase Manhattan Corporation to take over six of the Ohio thrifts by assuming their liabilities of $457 million and paying $20 million to the thrifts' shareholders and an additional goodwill premium of $25 million. The agreement with Chase specified that the state would be absolved of liabilities and was conditional on legislative approval of conversion of the acquired thrifts into a commercial bank.[43] As a result, Chase Bank of Ohio was formed, with twenty-three branches in the state, and all depositors of the thrifts were fully protected.[44]

A similar crisis took place in Maryland under almost identical conditions. There, the failures of Old Court Savings and Loan Association (the state's second-largest thrift institution) and Merritt Commercial Savings and Loan Association, neither of which was protected by federal insurance, prompted savers at thrifts throughout the state to withdraw $630 million during a two-month period, climaxed by withdrawals of $116 million in a single day. Governor Harry Hughes then invoked emergency powers, ordering the 102 privately insured S&Ls in the state to limit depositors' withdrawals to $1,000 per month.[45]

The Chase Manhattan Corporation, as it had done in Ohio, came forward with a proposal to rescue the thrifts. It received state and Federal Reserve approval to purchase three thrifts, with $500 million in deposits. Again, Chase relieved the state of Maryland from responsibility for them, on the condition that Chase could convert them into commercial banks.[46] As a result, Chase Bank of Maryland, with thirteen offices, opened in November 1985.[47]

The allegations of high-risk lending, unsound management practices, and questionable insiders' activities at Old Court S&L focused attention on the entire thrift industry, many of whose members combined a policy of paying excessively high rates to attract deposits and using the funds in a highly speculative manner with one of relying on private insurance funds rather than on the coverage provided by the FSLIC.[48]

The crises in Ohio and Maryland have had a series impact on Congress, on federal regulatory authorities, and to some extent on the public. As of August 1986 the Senate Banking Committee was to consider, as part of an omnibus banking bill, a possible merger of the FDIC and the FSLIC and a blanket authorization for federal agencies to sell failing thrift institutions across state lines.[49] The proposal to merge the two federal insurers as a means of strengthening the FSLIC reflected serious concerns over the continued adequacy of its insurance fund. Because of its various rescue activities, the FSLIC reserve as of May 1985 had been reduced to $6 billion, or 0.76 percent of the deposits in its insured thrift institutions.[50]

Strong opposition to any such combination of the two insurers surfaced as soon as the idea was advanced by former Chairman William Isaac of the FDIC in 1985. J.G. Cairns, President of the American Bankers Association, immediately voiced the objection of his organization:

> It's absolutely inappropriate to use premiums that banks paid to FDIC to solve the S&L industry's problems. It would be ironic—and improper—to have banks' competitors shored up by the fund that insures banks themselves.[51]

Because 17 percent of the nation's remaining thrifts, governed by the laws of the thirty states in which they are chartered, rely on some form of private insurance coverage, some observers have suggested that federal insurance be made mandatory for all deposit-taking institutions. Such legislation would bolster public confidence in the thrifts and, at the same time, enable the FSLIC to examine their ongoing performance more closely. There is unfortunately a major obstacle to this plan, in that many thrifts do not meet FSLIC requirements for net worth. This problem could be solved by having the thrifts issue net worth certificates, which the FSLIC would buy in exchange for promissory notes.

The public concern resulting from the Ohio and Maryland crises evidences a continuing failure among many individuals to separate commercial banks from thrifts. The failure of a major S&L has a strong spillover effect. Bankers from widely separated parts of the country have expressed their perception that depositors consider the two types of institutions on the same basis. The blurring of distinctions between the two, as thrifts have assumed additional powers comparable in many cases to those of banks, has caused this problem, as noted by one bank Chairman: "The thrifts' exploits are perceived by the media and the public to be bank problems."[52]

As of August 1986, it appears likely that the federal insurers will intensify their efforts to keep troubled banks open through various forms of financial aid. The argument that was used in the Continental Illinois case—that is, that certain banks should never be allowed to fail—may be extended and made more comprehensive, so that very few financial institutions will be allowed to fail. Recapitalization of the FSLIC and an increase in its annual assessments on members also appear probable.

The activist role of the FDIC and the FSLIC in helping to arrange for interstate takeovers of troubled institutions, rather than merely allowing them to fail, continued in 1986. Empire of America, a federally chartered savings bank in Buffalo, New York, acquired two S&Ls in California with $11.2 million in assistance from the FSLIC. Rainier Bancorporation (Seattle) acquired Lincoln S&L (Portland, Oregon) with $21.4 million in FSLIC aid. Empire, with $8.7 billion in assets, already had 136 offices in New York, Michigan, Texas, and Florida, and added 14 in California through the acquisition.[53]

In July 1986 the First National Bank and Trust Company of Oklahoma, with assets of $1.6 billion, failed. This was the second-largest commercial bank failure in U.S. history. Under Oklahoma law, the FDIC was allowed to force a merger, and it arranged for First Interstate Bancorp (Los Angeles) to assume the failed bank's deposit liability of $1.5 billion. The FDIC paid a $72 million premium to the acquirer and took an equity position in the merged bank through preferred (nonvoting) stock. The FDIC also agreed to retain assets of the failed bank with a book value of about $418 million; the realizable value of these assets (chiefly substandard loans), however, is questionable.[54]

Under its authority as the regulator of all activities of BHCs, the Federal Reserve has imposed restrictions on holding companies that acquire thrifts. It prohibits the BHCs from conducting any joint marketing and sales efforts with the thrift units, from linking the thrifts' deposit-taking activities to those of other BHC components, and from advertising BHC products through the thrifts. These restrictions resulted from the Fed's concern that BHCs could circumvent interstate barriers by buying troubled thrift institutions and operating them as commercial banks.

Citicorp and Chemical New York Corporation (the BHC that owns Chemical Bank) joined the FHLBB in 1986 in urging the Fed to lift these restrictions; however, the U.S. League of Savings Associations, BankAmerica Corporation, and many bankers from small communities took the opposite position on the grounds that any relaxation would tend to erode the existing role of the thrift industry.[55]

Proponents of Interstate Banking

Starting in 1984, influential figures in both the banking and political arenas began to announce that they were strongly in favor of deregulation so that interstate banking could become a reality in law as well as in fact. In an address to the Association of Bank Holding Companies in Baltimore, Ms. Martha R. Seger, member of the Federal Reserve Board of Governors, expressed this viewpoint:

> I hope that we will quickly . . . move to full interstate banking. Minimizing the number of potential bidders for existing banks and maximizing the diversity of new entrants into markets should result in a better long-run banking structure. . . .
>
> [However,] interstate banking legislation should be accompanied by some restriction on large interstate bank mergers and acquisitions. . . . The largest banks would face increasingly severe size restrictions on their acquisitions as their share of nationwide banking assets increased.[56]

Ms. Seger's affirmative vote, therefore, contained a cautionary note that may have been intended to allay the fears of many bankers in small communities about concentrations of power in the hands of the money-center institutions.

In 1985 the American Bankers Association dropped its thirty-year support of the Douglas Amendment and endorsed the concept of interstate banking. Again, however, its policy statement, reached by consensus during a leadership conference of 400 bankers, contained a limitation. The Association stated that its support would legitimate regional banking agreements with a trigger that would permit full interstate banking five years after enactment, but only for those states enacting regional interstate legislation.[57] In this way, the Association was careful to preserve the rights of the states to control acquisitions by out-of-state entities.

Also in 1985, Fed Chairman Paul Volcker urged Congress to approve legislation that would permit interstate banking—again, after a three-year period of regional banking. As a safeguard against excessive concentration of banking powers, he recommended that the legislation prohibit acquisitions among the twenty-five largest banks and that no bank be permitted to hold more than 15–20 percent of the banking assets in a single state. On the matters of states' rights, he included a provision allowing any individual state to opt out of interstate banking by refusing to enter a regional agreement.[58] President Gerald Corrigan of the New York Fed has spoken in favor of a similar building-block approach to interstate banking and a specific date when all federal geographic restrictions would be lifted "except for those based on safety and soundness or the need to avoid excessive concentration."[59]

Controversy over the topic reached Congress in June 1985, when Treasury Secretary James Baker, in the face of strong bipartisan opposition from a Senatorial panel, appeared before the Senate Banking Committee to endorse legislation that would permit interstate banking after five years of regional banking. However, Committee Chairman Jake Garn categorically opposed this recommendation, stating that he saw no need for legislation on interstate banking during that year.[60]

In 1986, the Reagan administration renewed its efforts to remove federal barriers to interstate banking. In the annual Economic Report, the President stated flatly that "it is time to move toward true interstate banking." The Report also noted that Congressional approval of interstate banking could bring aid to troubled commercial banks in the agricultural areas of the nation and could be used to prevent additional thrifts from failing:

> The banking and credit system remains rife with regulations and loan guarantees that arbitrarily allocate credit and hamper the system's ability to adapt to changing economic conditions.[61]

As of August 1986, however, Congress had passed no enabling legislation.

The state of the art has been succinctly summarized by the 1986 President of the American Bankers Association:

> The clear fact—which is being ignored in Washington—is that the commercial banking system in America is being required to operate without benefit of any clearly demarcated, rationally developed, and coherently delineated national banking policy, which is adaptable to the realities of today.[62]

Opponents of Interstate Banking

Throughout the debates on interstate banking—even if that topic makes no mention of full-scale branching across state lines—its opponents have presented their case through a series of unchanging arguments. Repetition has unfortunately lent a degree of credence to these arguments, and they have become accepted in many quarters. In each case, the available evidence indicates that most, if not all, of the arguments have little basis in reality; they have acquired the status of myths, in some cases used as scare tactics to thwart any Congressional action.

The most often heard of the arguments addresses the question of an increased concentration of banking power in the hands of a few money-center giants. This concern over potential oligopoly pertains chiefly to retail banking, since the wholesale market (otherwise defined as corporate banking) is already nationwide in scope.

The counterarguments are numerous. In the first place, the number of potential acquirers that could achieve such power is necessarily limited, both by capital constraints that already exist, the costs of widespread acquisitions at a premium, and, in some cases, by the basic operating philosophy of the major banks. If New York, Chicago, and San Francisco or Los Angeles are considered the home bases of the acquirers, then Morgan, Bankers Trust, and United States Trust can be eliminated as acquirers because their stated business plans and their status as wholesale banks preclude nationwide expansion. In Chicago, Continental Illinois is in the process of recovering from its financial debacle; similarly, the recent losses reported by Bank of America limit its ability to consider any acquisitions.

If, among the remaining largest banks, Citicorp is considered the major threat, then a second counterargument involves the antitrust laws that could be invoked to limit its expansion. The Supreme Court, as noted earlier, has brought commercial banking under the Sherman and Clayton Acts. Those statutes can be invoked at any time to prevent anticompetitive activities by the potential acquirers.

A second argument against the liberalization of restrictive banking alleges that such liberalization would threaten the viability of smaller banks and might ultimately lead to a weakening of the financial condition of the acquiring BHCs, thereby having an impact on the banking system as a whole. In rebuttal, note that available data indicate that smaller banks can indeed effectively compete with larger banks. The experiences of New York and California, with their years of statewide banking experience, suggest that liberalized branching and substantial mergers have not adversely affected the smaller banks.[63]

The deregulation that has already taken place is not the cause of the numerous bank failures of 1985 and 1986. The cause is a combination of problems related to oil and farm prices, and in some cases a lack of management expertise and/or integrity, but no recorded failure is a direct result of a relaxation of banking laws. If we examine an earlier period instead, the data show that from 1970 through 1983 45 percent of failed banks were in unit banking states and 74 percent were unit banks. The competitive environment in states permitting statewide or limited branching enabled banks to achieve degrees of diversification that contributed to their survival.[64]

A further refutation of this argument simply restates the power of the Federal Reserve, as the ultimate regulator of all BHCs, to deny any potential acquisition by using its statutory criteria. If, in the Fed's judgment, an interstate takeover would impair the financial condition of the acquiring BHC, the Fed can summarily deny the request. It is unrealistic to believe that the Fed, given its announced policy of increasing its surveillance of BHCs and more thoroughly monitoring their financial performance, would allow acquisitions that might have the effect of weakening them.[65]

A third argument against further deregulation postulates that the interests of consumers—availability of a wide range of services and the pricing of those services—might be adversely affected if larger institutions were to increase their market share. Again, the evidence contradicts this position.

Larger banks find it relatively easy to introduce new services because they use their economies of scale and larger customer base to generate the level of activity necessary for profitability. Smaller banks find it difficult to do so.

Similarly, larger institutions broaden their range of services and offer attractive pricing for competitive reasons. A 1985 study indicates that larger banks provide a wider array of services than smaller banks,[66] and other surveys found cost advantages to consumers resulting from these services.[67]

In summary, therefore, the arguments against relaxation of the remaining barriers to interstate banking lack validity. If the commercial banks are to be allowed to compete effectively with all the competitors who have gained a significant share of the nation's financial assets, the playing field—as so many bankers have described it—must be made more level. Banks do not seek total deregulation, and it would not provide a solution. The need is for liberalization of existing statutes, accompanied by an appropriate degree at all times of the federal and state supervision that will maintain public confidence and contribute to the continued soundness of the overall banking system.

Notes

1. Federal Deposit Insurance Corporation, *1983 Annual Report,* p. 9.
2. Bart Fraust, "Arizona Enters Interstate Era," *American Banker,* August 11, 1986, p. 1.
3. Bartlett Naylor, "Supreme Court Backs Regional Banking Pacts," *American Banker,* June 11, 1985, p. 1.
4. Linda Greenhouse, "High Court Backs Banking Mergers Limited to Regions," *The New York Times,* June 11, 1985, p. A1.
5. Bartlett Naylor, "Study Finds 128 Bank Chains Cross State Lines," *American Banker,* June 10, 1985, p. 3.
6. Robert Trigaux, "Mighty Citicorp Wrestles Washington Bankers," *American Banker,* October 10, 1985, p. 16.
7. A 1984 study identified twenty thrifts that were doing so. See "Interstate Thrifts," *American Banker,* April 4, 1984, p. 14.
8. Dave Phillis and Christine Pavel, "Interstate Banking Game Plans," *Economic Perspectives* (Federal Reserve Bank of Chicago), March–April 1986, p. 23.
9. "Observers Note Fast Growth of Interstate Banking," *American Banker,* June 10, 1986, p. 23.
10. Bart Fraust, "Stoking Hearths," *American Banker,* March 18, 1986, pp. 25–29.
11. Richard Ringer, "Connecting Crossed Wires," *American Banker,* March 18, 1986, pp. 45–48.
12. David Satterfield, "Will Southeast Bubbly Go Flat?," *American Banker,* March 18, 1986, pp. 37–39.
13. Michael Robinson, "How the West Is Being Won," *American Banker,* March 18, 1986, pp. 40–44.
14. Don Munro, "A Rundown of Interstate Banking Laws," *American Banker,* April 22, 1986, p. 24.
15. Individual examples can be found in ibid.
16. Jeffrey Marshall, "Interstate Banking Keeps Rolling Along," *American Banker,* August 25, 1986, p. 9.

17. Philip T. Sudo, "Court Rulings Shape Banking Industry, but Confusion and Controversy Begin," *American Banker,* December 21, 1984, p. 1.

18. John D. Hawke, Jr., "Public Policy Toward Bank Expansion," in Richard C. Aspinwall and Robert A. Eisenbeis, eds., *Handbook for Banking Strategy* (New York: John Wiley & Sons, 1985), pp. 397–399.

19. Ibid., "Interview," *The Bankers Magazine,* November–December 1984, p. 25.

20. David LaGesse, "Public Worries about Adequacy of Federal Insurance Funds," *American Banker,* October 19, 1985, p. 2. The survey was conducted by Reichman Research, Inc.

21. Robert Luke, "Interstate Banking in California: A Gold Rush," *American Banker,* August 21, 1986, p. 1.

22. "Barriers Coming Down for Regional Mergers in 4 Central Atlantic States," *American Banker,* August 21, 1986, p. 2.

23. Marilyn Much, "The Road to Nationwide Banking," *Industry Week,* August 19, 1985, p. 44.

24. In Nina Easton, "The Regulatory Quandary of Interstate Banking," *American Banker,* October 17, 1985, p. 1.

25. In Edward W. Reed; Richard V. Cotter; Edward K. Gill; and Richard K. Smith, *Commercial Banking,* 3rd ed. (Englewood Cliffs, N.J.: Prentice-Hall, Inc., 1984), p. 71.

26. In W.N. DeWitt, "Why Banks Need Interstate Banking," *The Bankers Magazine,* November–December 1984, p. 22.

27. In Robert A. Bennett, "Court Ruling Called Blow to Big Banks," *The New York Times,* June 11, 1985, p. D1.

28. Leon Korobow and George Budzeika, "Financial Limits on Interstate Bank Expansion," *Quarterly Review* (Federal Reserve Bank of New York), Summer 1985, pp. 13–24.

29. David C. Cates, "Banks Are Paying too Much to Merge," *Fortune,* December 23, 1985, p. 15.

30. "Bank Law Seen Near in Texas," *The New York Times,* August 25, 1986, p. D1.

31. In Sung Won Sohn, "The Economic Impact of Interstate Banking," *Bank Administration,* June 1984, pp. 22–25.

32. Donald Shoultz, "Branches Key to Interstate Success, Survey Says," *American Banker,* January 13, 1986, p. 3.

33. Thomas P. Vartanian, "If You're Thinking of Acquiring a Thrift," *ABA Banking Journal,* November 1983, p. 70.

34. Linda W. McCormick and Robert E. Norton, "Fed Lets Citicorp Acquire Fidelity Savings & Loan," *American Banker,* September 29, 1982, p. 1.

35. Betty Sue Peabody, "The Turnaround at Citicorp Savings," *The Bankers Magazine,* September–October 1984, pp. 5–7.

36. "Fed Approves Citicorp Bids for 2 Thrifts," *American Banker,* January 23, 1984, p. 1.

37. In Blanca Riemer, "Regulation May Turn the Thrifts into Raiders' Prey," *Business Week,* February 18, 1985, p. 40.

38. John P. Forde, "Citicorp Gets Full-Service Bank Charter in Nevada with Takeover of Failed Thrift," *American Banker,* November 15, 1985, p. 1.

39. Robert A. Bennett, "Dire Thrift Outlook," *The New York Times,* May 16, 1985, p. D8.

40. Nathaniel C. Nash, "Scramble over Thrift Failures," *The New York Times,* April 26, 1985, p. D1.

41. *Uninsured* refers to the fact that there was no FSLIC coverage. The thrifts belonged to the Ohio Deposit Guarantee Fund, a private insurer permitted by Ohio laws.

42. Mark Russell and Ralph E. Winter, "Rescue of Ohio's Ailing S&Ls Expected to Cost State More than $200 Million," *The Wall Street Journal,* April 22, 1985, p. 8.

43. Robert A. Bennett, "Chase in Pact for 4 Ohio Thrift Units," *The New York Times,* May 8, 1985, p. D20.

44. The Chase Manhattan Corporation, *1985 Annual Report,* pp. 3 and 83.

45. Eric N. Berg, "Maryland Limits All Withdrawals from Thrift Units," *The New York Times,* May 15, 1985, p. A1.

46. "Maryland Adopts Chase Plan," *The New York Times,* October 23, 1985, p. D1.

47. "Interstate Banking Comes to Maryland," *American Banker,* November 5, 1985, p. 13.

48. Christopher S. Eklund, "The Deals Old Court Has Left Undone," *Business Week,* June 3, 1985, p. 39; and Eric N. Berg, "The Thrift Unit Practices Debated," *The New York Times,* May 21, 1985, p. D3.

49. Robert Trigaux, "FDIC-FSLIC Merger—Of Minds," *American Banker,* September 2, 1986, p. 10.

50. Barbara Rudolph, "Another Time Bomb Goes Off," *Time,* May 27, 1985, p. 59.

51. "Bankers Debate Key Thrift Institution Issues," *ABA Banking Journal,* July 1985, p. 42.

52. William H. Bowen, in "Bankers Debate Key Thrift Institution Issues," p. 41.

53. "Regulators Help in Interstate Thrift Takeovers," *American Banker,* July 16, 1986, p. 2.

54. Nina Easton, "FDIC Accepts Costly Deal for Oklahoma's Failed First National," *American Banker,* July 16, 1986, p. 16.

55. Nina Easton, "Restrictions on Thrift Acquisitions Debated," *American Banker,* July 17, 1986, p. 21.

56. In "Given Effective Legislative Controls, Interstate Access Will Help Banking," *American Banker,* January 4, 1985, p. 4.

57. In Robert Trigaux, "ABA Endorses Interstate Banking Plan," *American Banker,* February 11, 1985, p. 1.

58. In Nathaniel C. Nash, "Fed Backs Interstate Banking," *The New York Times,* April 25, 1985, p. D1.

59. In *Quarterly Review* (Federal Reserve Bank of New York), Spring 1985, p. 5.

60. Nathaniel C. Nash, "Administration Backs Interstate Banks Again," *The New York Times,* June 14, 1985, p. D2.

61. Bartlett Naylor, "Reagan Urges Action on Interstate Banking," *American Banker,* February 7, 1986, p. 1.

62. Donald T. Senterfitt, in Michael Weinstein, "Senterfitt Calls for New US Bank Policy," *American Banker,* September 9, 1986, p. 2.

63. Stephen A. Rhoades and Donald T. Savage, "Can Small Banks Compete?," *The Bankers Magazine,* January–February 1981, pp. 59–65.

64. Federal Deposit Insurance Corporation, *Annual Reports* (1970–1983).

65. Board of Governors of the Federal Reserve System, *72nd Annual Report* (1985), pp. 168–169.

66. Pete Rose; James Kolari; and Kenneth W. Riener, "A National Survey Study of Bank Services and Prices Arrayed by Size and Structure," *Journal of Bank Research,* Summer 1985, pp. 72–85.

67. Ibid. See also Donald T. Savage and Stephen A. Rhoades, "The Effects of Branch Banking on Pricing, Profits, and Efficiency of Unit Banks," in *Proceedings of a Conference on Bank Structure and Competition* (Chicago: Federal Reserve Bank of Chicago, 1979), pp. 187–195.

13
The New World Summarized

For I am constant as the Northern Star . . . .
—*Julius Caesar*

Nay, swear not by the moon, th' inconstant moon . . . .
—*Romeo and Juliet*

In the New World of commercial banking, or more particularly the New World of the financial services industry, the inconstant has become the constant, and the unchanging element is change itself. This theme was identified in the opening paragraphs of this text. Each chapter emphasized it as the most noteworthy characteristic of the industry today. As I was writing the manuscript, further dramatic changes continued to take place; given the time frame that necessarily elapses between manuscript preparation and text publication, the reader will no doubt note a continuation of that trend. The only unqualifed prediction that I can safely make regarding the future is that we can expect more of the same.

Banking, an industry long perceived to be relatively static, is now a continuum of evolutionary and revolutionary developments and responses to new crises, new competition, and new regulations. For virtually all commercial banks, the methods of delivery of services, the organizational structure, the techniques of funds management, and the approach to marketing bear little or no resemblance to those that were previously in vogue.

In the early 1980s, several banking textbooks were published. I predicated the validity of the emphasis on change in this text on a synopsis of several of the major changes that have occurred since that time.

> Even the most astute banker, analyst, or observer would have had difficulty in 1980 in predicting that the number of bank failures would exceed 100 in both 1985 and 1986 and that the traditional lines of demarcation between banks and thrifts would largely disappear.
>
> Even the most capable individual in banking could not have foreseen in 1980 that a bank as large and prestigious as Bank of America would suffer bottom-line losses of over $600 million in a three-month period in 1986 and would become a candidate for possible takeover by a domestic BHC or a foreign institution.[1]

An increase in total outstanding consumer debt, over and above home mortgage loans, to the 1986 level of $577 billion would have seemed unrealistic in 1980.

The magnitude of the global debt crisis was largely unpublicized in 1980, and it would have required a rare degree of prescience to state that Mexico in 1986 would require an added $12 billion in credits to prevent its total financial collapse.

In 1980, even the most enthusiastic advocate of EFTS would have felt insecure in predicting that in 1986 General Motors Corporation would announce plans for the electronic payment of 400,000 monthly invoices, with a dollar value of $4 billion.[2]

Community bankers and their counterparts in the money-center giants would not have thought it possible in 1980 that by 1986 Sears, Roebuck would have established over 200 financial centers in its stores, offering a combination of insurance, real estate, brokerage, and bank-related services to consumers.[3]

In 1980, the permanence of the Douglas Amendment and the McFadden Act seemed likely. Interstate regional compacts did not exist, and no one could have prophesized the relaxation of unit banking laws by the legislatures of states such as Texas.[4]

These are but a few of the examples that I could choose in support of the thesis that there is, indeed, a New World of commercial banking—one in which change has become the constant and yesterday's truisms can no longer be accepted. It is a New World in which only those institutions that can successfully anticipate, adjust for, and manage change will maintain their position or, in many cases, survive. Those that choose to ignore the lessons of recent banking history and the overall financial services industry are most likely to fall by the wayside. The application of Darwinian theory to banking may at first seem farfetched, yet there is a certain amount of writing already on the wall for those who can learn from it.

Notes

1. Robert Luke and Nina Easton, "Offer to Acquire BankAmerica May Open Door to More Suitors," *American Banker,* October 8, 1986, p. 1.
2. Tom Ferris, "GM Readies Electronic Bill Paying," *American Banker,* October 1, 1986, p. 1.
3. Laura Gross, "Sears Tops List of Best Known Financial Firms," *American Banker,* September 23, 1986, p. 1; and "Diversified Financial Giants Gaining Consumer Approval," *American Banker,* September 24, 1986, p. 1.
4. David LaGesse and Laura Gross, "Texas Will Open Its Borders to Out-of-State Buyers of Banks," *American Banker,* September 24, 1986, p. 2.

Bibliography

Anderson, Stanley W. *The Banker and EFT.* Washington, D.C.: American Bankers Association, 1982.

Aspinwall, Richard C., and Eisenbeis, Robert A. (Eds.) *Handbook for Banking Strategy.* New York: John Wiley & Sons, 1985.

Beehler, Paul J. *Contemporary Cash Management: Principles, Practices, Perspectives.* New York: John Wiley & Sons, 1983.

Burns, Helen M. *The American Banking Community and New Deal Banking Reforms 1933–1935.* Westport, Conn.: Greenwood Press, 1974.

Carron, Andrew S. *The Plight of the Thrift Institutions.* Washington, D.C.: The Brookings Institution, 1982.

Chorafas, Dimitris N. *Money: The Banks of the 1980s.* New York: Petrocelli Books, 1982.

Clain-Stefanelli, Elvira, and Clain-Stefanelli, Vladimir. *Chartered for Progress: Two Centuries of American Banking.* Washington, D.C.: Acropolis Books, 1975.

Cole, Robert H. *Consumer and Commercial Credit Management* (7th Ed.). Homewood, Ill.: Richard D. Irwin, 1984.

Compton, Eric N. *Inside Commercial Banking* (2nd Ed.). New York: John Wiley & Sons, 1983.

Corson, John J., and Steiner, George A. *Measuring Business's Social Performance: The Corporate Social Audit.* New York: Committee for Economic Development, 1974.

Crosse, Howard D., and Hempel, George H. *Management Policies for Commercial Banks* (2nd Ed.). Englewood Cliffs, N.J.: Prentice-Hall, 1973.

Davis, Steven I. *Excellence in Banking.* New York: St. Martin's Press, 1985.

Donnelly, James H., Jr., Berry, Leonard L., and Thompson, Thomas W. *Marketing Financial Services: A Strategic Vision.* Homewood, Ill.: Richard D. Irwin, 1986.

Driscoll, Mary C. *Cash Management: Corporate Strategies for Profit.* New York: John Wiley & Sons, 1983.

Fisher, David I. *Cash Management.* New York: The Conference Board, 1973.

Fraser, Donald R., and Kolari, James W. *The Future of Small Banks in a Deregulated Environment.* Cambridge, Mass.: Ballinger, 1985.

Friedman, David H. *Deposit Operations.* Washington, D.C.: American Bankers Association, 1982.

Gart, Alan. *Banks, Thrifts, and Insurance Companies: Surviving the 1980s.* Lexington, Mass.: Lexington Books, 1985.

———. *The Insider's Guide to the Financial Services Revolution.* New York: McGraw-Hill, 1984.

Graham, Benjamin, and McGolrick, Charles. *The Interpretation of Financial Statements* (3rd Rev. Ed.). New York: Harper & Row, 1975.

Gup, Benton E. *Management of Financial Institutions.* Boston, Mass.: Houghton Mifflin, 1984.

Hale, Roger H. *Credit Analysis: A Complete Guide.* New York: John Wiley & Sons, 1983.

Heller, Pauline B. *Handbook of Federal Bank Holding Company Law.* New York: Law Journal Press, 1976.

Hendrickson, Robert A. *The Cashless Society.* New York: Dodd, Mead, 1972.

Herrick, Tracy G. *Bank Analyst's Handbook.* New York: John Wiley & Sons, 1978.

Humble, John W. *How to Manage by Objectives.* New York: AMACOM (A Division of American Management Associations), 1972.

Hunt, Alfred L. *Corporate Cash Management and Electronic Funds Transfers.* New York: AMACOM (A Division of American Management Associations), 1978.

Hutchinson, Harry D. *Money, Banking, and the United States Economy* (5th Ed.). Englewood Cliffs, N.J.: Prentice-Hall, 1984.

Jessee, Michael A., and Seelig, Steven A. *Bank Holding Companies and the Public Interest.* Lexington, Mass.: Lexington Books, 1977.

Johnson, Roger T. *Historical Beginnings: The Federal Reserve.* Boston, Mass.: Federal Reserve Bank of Boston, 1977.

Kennedy, Susan Estabrook, *The Banking Crisis of 1933.* Lexington, Ky.: University Press of Kentucky, 1973.

Kettell, Brian, and Magnus, George A. *The International Debt Game: A Study in International Bank Lending.* Cambridge, Mass.: Ballinger, 1986.

Kettl, Donald F. *Leadership at the Fed.* New Haven, Conn.: Yale University Press, 1986.

King, Mary L. *The Great American Banking Snafu.* Lexington, Mass.: Lexington Books, 1985.

Mason, John M. *Financial Management of Commercial Banks.* Boston, Mass.: Warren, Gorham & Lamont, 1979.

Mayer, Martin. *The Bankers.* New York: David McKay, 1974.

McDonald, Jay M., and McKinley, John F. *Corporate Banking.* Washington, D.C.: American Bankers Association, 1981.

McKinney, George W., Brown, William J., and Horvitz, Paul M. *Management of Commercial Bank Funds* (2nd Ed.). Washington, D.C.: American Bankers Association, 1980.

Myers, Margaret G. *A Financial History of the United States.* New York: Columbia University Press, 1970.

Nadler, Paul S. *Commercial Banking in the Economy* (3rd Ed.). New York: Random House, 1979.

Prochnow, Herbert V., and Prochnow, Herbert V., Jr. (Eds.). *The Changing World of Banking.* New York: Harper & Row, 1974.

Reed, Edward W., Cotter, Richard V., Gill, Edward K., and Smith, Richard K. *Commercial Banking* (3rd Ed.) Englewood Cliffs, N.J.: Prentice-Hall, 1984.

Richardson, Linda. *101 Tips for Selling Financial Services.* New York: John Wiley & Sons, 1986.
Ries, Al, and Trout, Jack. *Marketing Warfare.* New York: McGraw-Hill, 1986.
Robinson, Roland I. *The Management of Bank Funds* (2nd Ed.). New York: McGraw-Hill, 1962.
Roussakis, Emmanuel N. (Ed.). *International Banking: Principles and Practices.* New York: Praeger, 1983.
Schellie, Peter D. *Manager's Guide to the 1980 Monetary Control Act.* Washington, D.C.: American Bankers Association, 1980.
Sinkey, Joseph F., Jr. *Problem and Failed Institutions in the Commercial Banking Indusry.* Greenwich, Conn.: JAI, 1979.
Sprague, Irvine H. *Bailout.* New York: Basic Books, 1986.
Staats, William F. *Money and Banking.* Washington, D.C.: American Bankers Association, 1982.
Studenski, Paul, and Krooss, Herman E. *Financial History of the United States* (2nd Ed.). New York: McGraw-Hill, 1963.
Tighe, Rodger. *Structuring Commercial Loan Agreements.* Boston, Mass.: Warren, Gorham & Lamont, 1985.
Trescott, Paul B. *Financing American Enterprise: The Story of Commercial Banking.* New York: Harper & Row, 1963.

Publications of the Board of Governors of the Federal Reserve System (Washington, D.C.)

Burke, Jim. *Antitrust Laws, Justice Department Guidelines, and the Limits of Concentration in Local Banking Markets.* Staff Studies 138, June 1984.
Rhoades, Stephen A. *Mergers and Acquisitions by Commercial Banks, 1960–83.* Staff Studies 142, January 1985.
Simpson, Thomas D., and Parkinson, Patrick M. *Some Implications of Financial Innovations in the United States.* Staff Studies 139, September 1984.
Wolken, John D. *Geographic Market Delineation: A Review of the Literature.* Staff Studies 140, October 1984.

Publications of the District Federal Reserve Banks

Cyrnak, Anthony W. "Chain Banks and Competition: The Effectivenss of Federal Reserve Policy Since 1977." Federal Reserve Bank of San Francisco. *Economic Review,* Spring 1986.
Davis, Richard G. "The Recent Performance of the Commercial Banking Industry." Federal Reserve Bank of New York. *Quarterly Review,* Summer 1986.
Evanoff, Douglas D., and Fortier, Diana. "The Impact of Geographic Expansion in Banking: Some Axioms to Grind." Federal Reserve Bank of Chicago. *Economic Perspectives,* May–June 1986.
Keeley, Michael C., and Furlong, Frederick T. "Bank Regulation and the Public Interest." Federal Reserve Bank of San Francisco. *Economic Review,* Spring 1986.

Keeton, William R. "Deposit Deregulation, Credit Availability, and Monetary Policy." Federal Reserve Bank of Kansas City. *Economic Review,* June 1986.

Volcker, Paul A. "The Rapid Growth of Debt in the United States." Federal Reserve Bank of Kansas City. *Economic Review,* May 1986.

Index

About the Author

Eric N. Compton is a Vice-President with Chase Manhattan Bank in New York. His banking career began in 1950 and includes extensive experience in Branch Banking, Training, Cash Management, and Internal Communications. He has served as a faculty member with the American Institute of Banking in New York since 1961 and is a Past President and Trustee of that organization. He is the author of five textbooks on banking subjects. Mr. Compton received his B.S. in Education from Fordham University, *magna cum laude,* in 1949 and his M.A. from the same university in 1954.